Bias, Privacy, and the Ethics of AI in Education

Vasileios Paliktzoglou
https://orcid.org/0009-0001-0326-1156
Bahrain Polytechnic, Bahrain

Mohamed Lahby
University Hassan II, Morocco

Pushan Dutta
https://orcid.org/0000-0002-4765-3864
Amity University, India

Muthmainnah Muthmainnah
https://orcid.org/0000-0003-3170-2374
Universitas Al Asyariah Mandar, Indonesia

IGI Global
Scientific Publishing
Publishing Tomorrow's Research Today

Vice President of Editorial	Melissa Wagner
Director of Acquisitions	Mikaela Felty
Director of Book Development	Jocelynn Hessler
Production Manager	Mike Brehm
Cover Design	Jose Rosado

Published in the United States of America by
IGI Global Scientific Publishing
701 East Chocolate Avenue
Hershey, PA, 17033, USA
Tel: 717-533-8845 | Fax: 717-533-7115
Website: https://www.igi-global.com E-mail: cust@igi-global.com

Library of Congress Cataloging-in-Publication Data

Names: Paliktzoglou, Vasileios editor | Lahby, Mohamed editor | Dutta, Pushan, 1985- editor | Muthmainnah, Muthmainnah, 1980- editor
Title: Bias, privacy, and the ethics of AI in education / Vasileios Paliktzoglou, Mohamed Lahby, Pushan Dutta, Muthmainnah Muthmainnah.
Description: Hershey, PA : IGI Global Scientific Publishing, [2026] | Includes bibliographical references and index. | Summary: "This book examines the ethical challenges of integrating AI in education, offering frameworks for responsible, transparent, and inclusive innovation. Through interdisciplinary research, case studies, and policy guidance, it addresses data privacy, bias, equity, and governance, providing actionable strategies for ethical AI adoption in teaching, learning, and administration"-- Provided by publisher.
Identifiers: LCCN 2026002298 (print) | LCCN 2026002299 (ebook) | ISBN 9798337374673 hardcover | ISBN 9798337374680 paperback | ISBN 9798337374697 ebook
Subjects: LCSH: Artificial intelligence--Educational applications--Moral and ethical aspects | Artificial intelligence--Study and teaching | Data privacy
Classification: LCC LB1028.43 .B54 2026 (print) | LCC LB1028.43 (ebook)
LC record available at https://lccn.loc.gov/2026002298
LC ebook record available at https://lccn.loc.gov/2026002299

British Cataloguing in Publication Data
A Cataloguing in Publication record for this book is available from the British Library.

Table of Contents

Preface xi

Chapter 1
A Human–AI Agency Interaction Framework for Education 1
Eko Nurcahyo, Universitas Esa Unggul, Indonesia
Binastya Anggara Sekti, Universitas Esa Unggul, Indonesia

Chapter 2
Balancing Innovation and Integrity: Addressing Bias, Privacy, and Ethical Challenges of AI in Education 31
Shivansu Sachan, CSJM University, Kanpur, India

Chapter 3
Algorithmic Responsibility and Epistemic Integrity in AI-Supported Learning Systems 53
Enrio Moch, GrandEdu Research School, Germany
Tobias Oberdieck, GrandEdu GmbH, Germany

Chapter 4
Ethical Concerns and Bias in Educational Machine Learning Systems 79
Rehan Saeed Khan, Jamia Hamdard University, India

Chapter 5
Regulating the Emergence of AI in Education: Foundations, Legal Issues, and Policy Frameworks 111
Amrita Baid More, Medicaps University, Indore, India
Arpan Shrivastava, Institute of Business Management and Research, IPS Academy, India

Chapter 6
Equity by Design: AI Ethics Guidelines for the Education Sector 141
Soha Badr, The British University in Dubai, UAE
Tendai Charles, The British University in Dubai, UAE

Chapter 7
Ethical Federated Intelligence: Preserving Student Privacy in AI-Driven Education 159
Udit Mamodiya, Faculty of Engineering and Technology, Poornima University, Jaipur, India
Indra Kishor, Poornima Institute of Engineering and Technology, Jaipur, India
Vasileios Paliktzoglou, Bahrain Polytechnic, Bahrain

Chapter 8
Learner's Data at Risk: Privacy, Transparency, and Surveillance in AI-Enabled Educational Systems 191
Gayathry S. Nair, Christ (Deemed to be) University, Delhi NCR, India

Chapter 9
From Bias to Belonging: Ethical Pathways for Inclusive and Privacy-Respectful AI in Education 233
Adiyono Adiyono, Sekolah Tinggi Ilmu Tarbiyah Ibnu Rusyd Tanah Grogot, Paser, Indonesia
Sri Nurhayati, IKIP Siliwangi, Indonesia
Ellina Rienovita, Universitas Pendidikan Indonesia, Indonesia
Eka Setiawati, Universitas Setia Budhi, Indonesia
Cyintia Kumalasari, Universitas Islam Riau, Indonesia

Chapter 10
When Machines Learn: Can Human Creativity Survive in AI-Driven Classrooms? 265
Amine Hmid, University of Hassan II Casablanca, Morocco

Chapter 11
AI for Underserved Communities 293
Ardra Rianisa, Universitas Esa Unggul, Indonesia
Binastya Anggara Sekti, Universitas Esa Unggul, Indonesia

Compilation of References 319

About the Contributors 345

Index 355

Detailed Table of Contents

Preface xi

Chapter 1
A Human–AI Agency Interaction Framework for Education 1
Eko Nurcahyo, Universitas Esa Unggul, Indonesia
Binastya Anggara Sekti, Universitas Esa Unggul, Indonesia

This chapter analyzes the tension between AI automation and human autonomy in education, arguing that current AI integration erodes human agency . Using an interdisciplinary framework synthesizing Human Agency Theory, FATE, Data Justice, and Constructivism, this conceptual study analyzes three case studies: plagiarism detectors, learning analytics dashboards, and surveillance proctoring . Findings indicate that AI design defaults toward 'agency displacement' . The chapter proposes a 'Human-AI Agency Interaction Model' to balance automation with human control. It concludes with practical policy recommendations for developers, educators, and institutions, focusing on human-centered design, critical AI literacy, and ethical governance to ensure AI augments, rather than replaces, human agency .

Chapter 2
Balancing Innovation and Integrity: Addressing Bias, Privacy, and Ethical Challenges of AI in Education 31
Shivansu Sachan, CSJM University, Kanpur, India

The integration of Artificial Intelligence (AI) in education has transformed learning environments, pedagogical strategies, and assessment mechanisms. However, this digital shift also presents critical ethical challenges related to bias, privacy, and the integrity of educational processes. This paper examines how institutions can balance innovation with ethical responsibility by promoting transparent data governance, equitable algorithmic design, and learner-centered AI applications. Through an interdisciplinary lens, it explores the potential risks of algorithmic discrimination, surveillance concerns, and the erosion of academic integrity while emphasizing frameworks for responsible AI adoption. The study advocates for policy interventions, ethical literacy, and stakeholder collaboration to ensure that AI in education remains inclusive, fair, and trustworthy.

Chapter 3
Algorithmic Responsibility and Epistemic Integrity in AI-Supported Learning Systems 53
Enrio Moch, GrandEdu Research School, Germany
Tobias Oberdieck, GrandEdu GmbH, Germany

This work analyses how algorithmic systems change epistemic, normative and institutional structures in educational processes. The analysis shows that these systems not only analyse data but also influence the conditions under which knowledge is created, tested and pedagogical decisions are justified. Algorithmic systems generate patterns that direct perception and attention without formulating reasons, thus shifting judgement processes and institutional roles. The paper develops a framework model that describes these systems as an epistemic formation consisting of data logics, modelling logics and institutional practices. From this, three dimensions of algorithmic responsibility are derived: epistemic integrity, moral responsibility and collective governance. The study shows that these systems can only be used responsibly if transparency, validity, error culture and institutional control are guaranteed. The results make it clear that such systems can supplement human judgement, but not replace it.

Chapter 4
Ethical Concerns and Bias in Educational Machine Learning Systems 79
Rehan Saeed Khan, Jamia Hamdard University, India

The increasing integration of machine learning technologies in education has generated significant ethical concerns related to bias, privacy, and accountability. While data-driven systems promise personalized learning, they also risk reinforcing existing educational inequalities. This chapter critically examines ethical challenges associated with educational machine learning systems, focusing on sources of bias, data protection, and governance mechanisms. Drawing on interdisciplinary literature, it categorizes bias into data, labeling, algorithmic, and societal forms and analyzes their implications for fairness and equity in educational contexts. It proposes ethically grounded strategies for bias mitigation, emphasizing inclusive data practices, human oversight, fairness-aware design, and institutional governance. By situating machine learning within broader educational and social frameworks, the chapter highlights the need for human-centered and ethically informed approaches to ensure that artificial intelligence contributes to trust, inclusion, and justice in education.

Chapter 5
Regulating the Emergence of AI in Education: Foundations, Legal Issues, and Policy Frameworks 111
Amrita Baid More, Medicaps University, Indore, India
Arpan Shrivastava, Institute of Business Management and Research, IPS Academy, India

Artificial Intelligence (AI) is transforming education by making learning more personalized, automating administrative tasks, and supporting data-driven decision-making. This chapter discusses the fundamental foundations of AI, its application in the education sector, the urgent legal issues it presents, and the necessity for a strong regulatory and policy framework to ensure ethical regulation. The opening section gives an overview of the building blocks of AI with a focus on key technologies like machine learning, deep learning, and natural language processing. It brings out their applications in education—ranging from adaptive learning systems and virtual tutors to automated grading and predictive analytics. The second part discusses legal concerns regarding AI in education, i.e., data privacy, consent, bias in algorithms, transparency, intellectual property rights, and accountability. It emphasizes the legal vacuum that presently prevails and potentially gives rise to unforeseen consequences if not addressed in proper time.

Chapter 6
Equity by Design: AI Ethics Guidelines for the Education Sector 141
Soha Badr, The British University in Dubai, UAE
Tendai Charles, The British University in Dubai, UAE

This chapter advances an Equity-by-Design framework for governing institutional uses of artificial intelligence (AI) in schools and universities. It responds to a persistent gap between high-level "ethical AI" principles and the concrete governance, procurement and monitoring practices needed to protect equity, accessibility and privacy in educational settings. It draws on international policy instruments, emerging regulation and research on AI in education, learning analytics and digital accessibility to construct an institutional architecture for responsible AI adoption. The framework is structured as a multi-stage lifecycle encompassing problem framing, risk triage, procurement and contracting, piloting and acceptance testing, deployment, monitoring and incident response, and periodic review and decommissioning. The chapter concludes that ethical AI in education is fundamentally a problem of institutional design: building organisations that can systematically resist harmful uses of AI, foreground inclusion and rights, and revise or withdraw systems when they cannot be made just.

Chapter 7
Ethical Federated Intelligence: Preserving Student Privacy in AI-Driven Education 159
Udit Mamodiya, Faculty of Engineering and Technology, Poornima University, Jaipur, India
Indra Kishor, Poornima Institute of Engineering and Technology, Jaipur, India
Vasileios Paliktzoglou, Bahrain Polytechnic, Bahrain

With the increasing integration of AI-powered learning spaces in the classroom, the issues of student privacy, misuse of data, and unclear decision-making have become more evident. Conventional federated learning frameworks strive to alleviate these threats, although most of them are based on homogenous privacy budgeting and do not include systems to balance the ethical complexities of learning information. Current methods thus have difficulty in maintaining a balance between predictive accuracy and fairness, transparency and dynamic consent which is a weakness that limits their application in the real world. The chapter presents Ethical Federated Intelligence (EFI), a socio-technical model that provides the opportunity of integrating ethical reasoning directly into the computation pipeline. Based on sensitivity-aware noise modulation, fairness-adjusted aggregation, and gradient-level consent orchestration, EFI redesigns federated Optimisation to enable prioritizing privacy and student agency without compromising performance.

Chapter 8
Learner's Data at Risk: Privacy, Transparency, and Surveillance in AI-Enabled Educational Systems 191
Gayathry S. Nair, Christ (Deemed to be) University, Delhi NCR, India

Artificial intelligence is transforming education into a data-intensive socio-technical environment in which learners are continuously monitored, classified, and governed through algorithmic systems. While AI-enabled tools promise efficiency and personalisation, they rely on extensive behavioural, biometric, and inferential data extraction that fundamentally reshapes learning. This chapter analyses how learning analytics, remote proctoring, biometric attendance, emotion-recognition technologies, and predictive risk platforms generate algorithmic epistemic authority within classrooms. Drawing on human-rights frameworks including the GDPR, UNESCO's Recommendation, OECD's Trustworthy AI principles, and regulatory approaches in India, the United States, the United Kingdom, China, and Brazil, supported by case studies. These cases demonstrate how governance failures, security breaches, and opaque vendor ecosystems erode learner data rights. The chapter argues that consent-based compliance is structurally inadequate in education and proposes a fiduciary, rights-respecting governance model

Chapter 9
From Bias to Belonging: Ethical Pathways for Inclusive and Privacy-Respectful AI in Education 233
Adiyono Adiyono, Sekolah Tinggi Ilmu Tarbiyah Ibnu Rusyd Tanah Grogot, Paser, Indonesia
Sri Nurhayati, IKIP Siliwangi, Indonesia
Ellina Rienovita, Universitas Pendidikan Indonesia, Indonesia
Eka Setiawati, Universitas Setia Budhi, Indonesia
Cyintia Kumalasari, Universitas Islam Riau, Indonesia

The integration of Artificial Intelligence (AI) in education offers significant opportunities for adaptive, personalized, and efficient learning, yet it also presents serious ethical challenges related to algorithmic bias, student data privacy, and unequal access. This chapter explores how biased AI systems may reinforce existing social inequalities, how weak data governance can undermine students' autonomy and security, and how digital divides can marginalize vulnerable communities. By combining insights from ethics, education, and public policy, this chapter proposes an inclusive and transparent ethical framework grounded in three pillars: mitigating bias through fair algorithmic design, protecting privacy through responsible data governance, and promoting equity to ensure that all learners benefit from AI innovations. The framework aims to guide the responsible adoption of AI in education and contribute to global efforts to ensure that technological progress aligns with ethical integrity and human values.

Chapter 10
When Machines Learn: Can Human Creativity Survive in AI-Driven Classrooms? 265
Amine Hmid, University of Hassan II Casablanca, Morocco

In this chapter, the author analyzes the role of artificial intelligence in transforming the context in which creativity can be developed in modern classrooms. Based on mixed-method information gathered among university students and teachers, the research indicates that AI has the potential to empower as well as limit the creative process. Quantitative data indicate that creative self-efficacy and idea fluency are increased after the integration of AI, and qualitative data reveal the threats of homogenization and cognitive dependence in case of the uncritical adoption of AI outputs. Analysis shows that pedagogical mediation, emotional reactions, and ethical consciousness play an important role in the processes that give AI either a trigger of creative exploration or an agent of algorithmic conformity. The chapter compares these findings with the new literature on AI-assisted learning by stating that creativity in AI-driven education would need to be viewed as a hybrid process that needs to be planned, reflective, and supported by institutions.

Chapter 11
AI for Underserved Communities 293
Ardra Rianisa, Universitas Esa Unggul, Indonesia
Binastya Anggara Sekti, Universitas Esa Unggul, Indonesia

This chapter explores the role of Artificial Intelligence (AI) in improving education for underserved communities that continue to face barriers such as limited infrastructure, teacher shortages, and socio-economic inequalities. It discusses how AI technologies including adaptive learning systems, intelligent tutoring, and predictive analytics can offer scalable and personalized learning solutions to bridge educational gaps. Ethical considerations such as data privacy, algorithmic bias, and transparency are examined to ensure responsible implementation. The chapter also highlights the importance of community engagement, cultural relevance, and collaboration among governments, NGOs, and the private sector for successful and sustainable adoption. Furthermore, it discusses real-world case studies that demonstrate the effectiveness of AI in enhancing education, healthcare, and digital inclusion. The chapter concludes with strategic recommendations for equitable AI deployment and continuous evaluation to support long-term educational transformation in underserved regions.

Compilation of References 319

About the Contributors 345

Index 355

Preface

INTRODUCTION

The accelerating integration of Artificial Intelligence (AI) into educational systems marks one of the most consequential transformations in contemporary learning environments. From personalized instruction and automated assessment to predictive analytics and administrative optimization, AI technologies are reshaping how education is designed, delivered, and experienced. Yet, alongside these opportunities emerge complex ethical questions that demand careful scrutiny and collective responsibility.

This edited volume, *Bias, Privacy, and the Ethics of AI in Education*, was conceived in response to a growing need for rigorous, interdisciplinary engagement with these challenges. As editors, we recognized a critical gap between the rapid deployment of AI-driven tools and the development of coherent ethical frameworks to guide their use. Educational institutions, policymakers, and technology developers are often navigating this terrain without sufficient guidance on issues such as data privacy, algorithmic bias, transparency, accountability, and equity. This book aims to address that gap.

The chapters gathered here reflect a deliberate effort to bring diverse perspectives into conversation. Contributors from education, computer science, philosophy, law, and public policy examine the ethical dimensions of AI in education through multiple lenses—conceptual, empirical, and practical. The result is not a single unified theory, but rather a set of complementary frameworks and critical insights that together illuminate the complexity of the field.

Several core themes run throughout the volume. First, the question of bias—how it is embedded in data, encoded in algorithms, and manifested in educational outcomes—remains central. Second, issues of privacy and data governance are explored in depth, particularly in relation to student data and institutional responsibilities. Third, the volume considers the broader implications of AI for equity and access, asking who benefits from these technologies and who may be marginalized by them. Finally, contributors examine the role of human agency—how educators, learners, and institutions can retain autonomy and ethical oversight in increasingly automated environments.

In assembling this collection, we have sought not only to diagnose problems but also to advance solutions. Many chapters offer actionable recommendations, whether in the form of design principles, policy guidelines, or governance models. These contributions are intended to support responsible innovation and to inform decision-making at multiple levels—from classroom practice to national strategy.

This book is written for a wide audience: researchers seeking to deepen the scholarly discourse, educators and instructional designers navigating AI adoption, developers building the next generation of educational technologies, and policy-makers shaping the regulatory landscape. Graduate students and emerging scholars will also find in this volume a foundation for further inquiry into one of the most pressing issues in education today.

Ultimately, our goal is to foster a more thoughtful and ethically grounded approach to AI in education. Innovation, while essential, must not outpace reflection. By foregrounding questions of fairness, accountability, and human dignity, we hope this volume contributes to a future in which AI enhances education without compromising its core values.

We are grateful to the contributors for their thoughtful and rigorous work, and to the readers who engage with these ideas and carry them forward into practice, research, and policy.

ORGANIZATION OF THE BOOK

In Chapter 1, the editors present a critical examination of the evolving relationship between human autonomy and AI-driven automation in education. This chapter foregrounds a persistent tension: as AI systems become more embedded in educational processes, they risk displacing rather than supporting human agency. Drawing on an interdisciplinary synthesis of Human Agency Theory, fairness and accountability frameworks, data justice, and constructivist learning theory, the chapter interrogates familiar tools such as plagiarism detection systems, learning analytics dashboards, and surveillance-based proctoring. What emerges is a compelling argument that current AI design often defaults toward "agency displacement." In response, the authors introduce a Human–AI Agency Interaction Model that seeks to rebalance control, emphasizing human-centered design, critical AI literacy, and institutional responsibility.

Chapter 2 extends the discussion by situating AI adoption within a broader ethical landscape shaped by competing demands for innovation and integrity. The editors highlight how the transformation of learning environments through AI also introduces significant risks, including algorithmic bias, privacy erosion, and threats to academic integrity. This chapter underscores the necessity of transparent data governance and equitable algorithmic practices while advocating for learner-centered design principles. It offers a pragmatic perspective, calling for coordinated efforts among stakeholders and the development of ethical literacy to ensure that technological advancement does not come at the expense of fairness and trust.

In Chapter 3, the focus shifts to the deeper epistemic implications of algorithmic systems in education. The editors emphasize that AI does more than process data—it actively reshapes how knowledge is constructed, validated, and applied. By conceptualizing algorithmic systems as "epistemic formations," the chapter reveals how they influence perception, attention, and institutional decision-making without necessarily providing transparent reasoning. The proposed framework identifies epistemic integrity, moral responsibility, and collective governance as core dimensions of algorithmic accountability. This contribution challenges readers to reconsider the role of AI not as a neutral tool but as an active participant in shaping educational knowledge systems.

Chapter 4 returns to the foundational issue of bias in machine learning systems, offering a systematic and nuanced exploration of its various forms. The editors draw attention to the layered nature of bias—spanning data collection, labeling practices, algorithmic design, and broader societal structures—and its implications for fairness in education. By situating these technical concerns within social and institutional contexts, the chapter advances a holistic approach to ethical AI. It proposes actionable strategies such as inclusive data practices, fairness-aware system design, and robust governance mechanisms, reinforcing the importance of human oversight in mitigating inequities.

In Chapter 5, the editors turn to the regulatory and legal dimensions of AI in education, emphasizing the urgent need for coherent policy frameworks. This chapter provides a foundational overview of key AI technologies and their applications, while also exposing the legal ambiguities that accompany their use. Issues such as data privacy, consent, transparency, intellectual property, and accountability are examined in detail. The editors underscore the risks posed by the current regulatory vacuum, arguing that without timely and comprehensive legal intervention, the rapid expansion of AI in education may lead to unintended and potentially harmful consequences.

Chapter 6 advances the conversation by proposing an "Equity by Design" framework that moves beyond abstract ethical principles toward concrete institutional practices. The editors highlight a persistent gap between high-level AI ethics guidelines and their operationalization within educational settings. This chapter addresses that gap through a lifecycle-based model that spans problem definition, procurement, deployment, monitoring, and eventual system decommissioning. By framing ethical AI as fundamentally an issue of institutional design, the chapter calls for organizations capable of proactively safeguarding equity, accessibility, and rights throughout the entire AI adoption process.

Chapter 7 introduces an innovative socio-technical approach to one of the most pressing concerns in AI-driven education: student privacy. The editors examine the limitations of existing federated learning models, particularly their inability to balance accuracy, fairness, and transparency. In response, the chapter proposes Ethical Federated Intelligence (EFI), a framework that embeds ethical reasoning directly into computational processes. Through mechanisms such as sensitivity-aware noise modulation and consent orchestration, EFI seeks to preserve student agency while maintaining system performance. This contribution represents a significant step toward aligning technical innovation with ethical imperatives.

In Chapter 8, the editors provide a critical analysis of the data-intensive nature of AI-enabled educational systems, emphasizing the risks associated with pervasive surveillance and opaque data practices. The chapter explores how technologies such as learning analytics, biometric monitoring, and predictive platforms generate new forms of algorithmic authority within educational environments. Drawing on international regulatory frameworks and case studies, it demonstrates how existing governance approaches often fail to protect learner rights. The editors argue that consent-based models are insufficient and advocate instead for a fiduciary approach to data governance that prioritizes trust, accountability, and the protection of student interests.

Chapter 9 shifts the focus toward inclusivity, presenting a forward-looking framework that moves "from bias to belonging." The editors highlight how AI systems, if poorly designed or governed, can reinforce social inequalities and exclude marginalized learners. At the same time, they recognize the transformative potential of AI to promote equitable and personalized education. The chapter proposes a three-pillar ethical framework centered on bias mitigation, privacy protection, and equitable access. By integrating insights from ethics, education, and policy, it offers a comprehensive pathway for aligning technological innovation with principles of justice and inclusion.

In Chapter 10, the editors engage with a more nuanced and often overlooked dimension of AI in education: its impact on human creativity. This chapter explores the dual role of AI as both an enabler and a constraint on creative processes. Empirical findings suggest that while AI can enhance idea generation and creative confidence, it may also lead to homogenization and overreliance on algorithmic outputs. The editors emphasize the importance of pedagogical mediation, emotional awareness, and ethical reflection in shaping how AI influences creativity. Ultimately, the chapter reframes creativity in AI-driven classrooms as a hybrid, co-constructed process requiring intentional design and institutional support.

Finally, Chapter 11 broadens the scope of the volume by addressing the role of AI in advancing educational equity for underserved communities. The editors highlight how AI technologies can help overcome structural barriers such as limited resources, teacher shortages, and geographic isolation. At the same time, the chapter does not overlook the ethical risks associated with deployment in vulnerable contexts, including data misuse and cultural misalignment. By emphasizing community engagement, cross-sector collaboration, and context-sensitive design, the chapter presents a vision of AI as a tool for inclusive development. It concludes with strategic recommendations aimed at ensuring that the benefits of AI are equitably distributed and sustainably realized.

Together, these chapters reflect the breadth and depth of contemporary debates on AI in education, offering readers both critical insights and practical pathways for ethical engagement.

CONCLUSION

As this volume demonstrates, the integration of Artificial Intelligence in education is not merely a technological shift—it is a profound transformation of the values, structures, and relationships that define teaching and learning. Across these chapters, a consistent message emerges: the ethical challenges of AI in education are neither peripheral nor optional considerations; they are central to the legitimacy and sustainability of its adoption.

The contributions collected here reveal that concerns such as bias, privacy, transparency, and equity are deeply interconnected. They cannot be addressed in isolation, nor can they be resolved solely through technical innovation. Instead, they demand coordinated efforts that span disciplines, institutions, and sectors. Ethical AI in education requires not only better algorithms, but also stronger governance, more inclusive design practices, and a renewed commitment to human-centered values.

Importantly, this volume underscores that responsibility does not rest with a single group. Educators must be equipped with the knowledge and critical literacy to engage with AI tools thoughtfully. Developers must design systems that are transparent, fair, and accountable. Policymakers and institutional leaders must establish frameworks that protect rights while enabling innovation. And researchers must continue to interrogate assumptions, surface risks, and propose evidence-based solutions. Ethical AI, in this sense, is a shared endeavor.

At the same time, the chapters caution against uncritical adoption. While AI offers significant potential to enhance learning, expand access, and support decision-making, it also carries the risk of reinforcing existing inequities, eroding autonomy, and normalizing surveillance. The future of AI in education will be shaped not only by what is technologically possible, but by what is ethically chosen. This distinction is crucial.

Looking ahead, we see this volume as part of an ongoing conversation rather than a definitive endpoint. The field of AI in education is evolving rapidly, and with it, the ethical questions will continue to shift and deepen. It is our hope that the frameworks, models, and insights presented here will serve as a foundation for further inquiry, dialogue, and action.

Ultimately, the responsible integration of AI in education depends on our collective ability to align innovation with integrity. By centering human dignity, fostering inclusivity, and insisting on accountability, we can ensure that AI serves as a tool for empowerment rather than exclusion. The challenge is substantial, but so too is the opportunity.

Chapter 1
A Human-AI Agency Interaction Framework for Education

Eko Nurcahyo
http://orcid.org/0009-0008-5392-2478
Universitas Esa Unggul, Indonesia

Binastya Anggara Sekti
http://orcid.org/0000-0001-5489-4888
Universitas Esa Unggul, Indonesia

ABSTRACT

This chapter analyzes the tension between AI automation and human autonomy in education, arguing that current AI integration erodes human agency . Using an interdisciplinary framework synthesizing Human Agency Theory, FATE, Data Justice, and Constructivism, this conceptual study analyzes three case studies: plagiarism detectors, learning analytics dashboards, and surveillance proctoring . Findings indicate that AI design defaults toward 'agency displacement' . The chapter proposes a 'Human-AI Agency Interaction Model' to balance automation with human control. It concludes with practical policy recommendations for developers, educators, and institutions, focusing on human-centered design, critical AI literacy, and ethical governance to ensure AI augments, rather than replaces, human agency .

1. INTRODUCTION

Artificial Intelligence (AI) is no longer a futuristic concept in education; it has become an integral force that is reshaping the pedagogical landscape. The rapid as-

DOI: 10.4018/979-8-3373-7467-3.ch001

similation of AI—from adaptive learning platforms to predictive analytics—promises a new era of personalization and efficiency. These systems, often embedded in Learning Management Systems (LMS), offer great potential for democratizing access and tailored feedback. Behind this promise, there is an infrastructure that runs on data. However, this integration brings crucial questions around data privacy, human autonomy, and ethical responsibility. Tools such as *supervision-based* proctoring systems and *intelligent tutoring systems* are constantly collecting and processing large amounts of student data—beyond academic performance to behavioral and biometric data.(Sekti, 2025b)

Although this data collection is meant for personalization, it creates significant tension. It challenges traditional notions of human agency, ethical decision-making, and data ownership. When decisions are driven by algorithms, questions about control become very important. Who controls this data? Who is responsible for algorithmic bias? And how do we ensure educators and learners don't become passive data subjects in opaque algorithmic systems that they don't understand? This chapter explores the complex intersection between AI and human agency, particularly in the context of data privacy and security learning. On the one hand, AI presents unique pedagogical opportunities, serving as a powerful tool for promoting data awareness. On the other hand, however, these tools present an ethical paradox: can systems that inherently collect personal data effectively teach privacy values?

Therefore, this chapter argues that the implementation of AI in privacy education should be critically addressed. If not ethically designed, AI risks reducing—rather than strengthening—the control of learners and educators. This discussion places these tensions within a broader ethical framework, such as the principles of FATE (Fairness, Accountability, Transparency, and Explainability) and Data Fairness. Our goal is to shift the narrative from AI instead of human judgment to complement. Overcoming these challenges requires a deep understanding of human agency—how individuals exercise their intentions and self-regulation. AI ethics in education goes beyond the protection of technical data; It touches on issues of power, autonomy, and control. Understanding human agency is essential to foster ethical participation in an AI-driven ecosystem.

This chapter builds on the interdisciplinary literature to propose a human-centered framework. Specifically, this chapter aims to:

1. Investigate how AI technology affects human agency in data privacy learning.
2. Analyzes the ethical challenges between automation and autonomy.
3. Propose a conceptual model for responsible AI adoption.
4. Provide policy and pedagogical recommendations to maintain agency, transparency, and trust.

Ultimately, the main argument of this paper is that the most ethical AI systems are those that strengthen human agency. The system should empower learners and educators to consciously navigate data ethics, transforming them from passive data subjects into active moral agents.

2. BACKGROUND AND RATIONALE: DATAIFICATION, AUTONOMY, AND THE NEED FOR AGENCY

The transformation of education by Artificial Intelligence (AI) is no longer a prediction, but a reality that has taken place. In the last decade, AI integration has shifted from peripheral tools to core infrastructure. This process of educational "datafication" has changed the way institutions understand, measure, and manage the learning process (Alfredo et al., 2024). The two main drivers of this transformation are Learning Analytics (LA) (Kalita et al., 2025) dan Educational Data Mining (EDM) (Khor et al., 2025). Practically, this is manifested in technologies such as more analytical LMS, adaptive Intelligent Tutoring Systems (ITS) (Shashwat & Pundhir, 2025), instant AI feedback, and tools *proctoring* Remote That Even Detects "Emotional Status" (Teixeira, 2026)

At the heart of all these tools is the pedagogical promise of personalization. By analyzing students' digital footprints, AI systems aim to detect at-risk students (Patil et al., 2024), recommend material, and identify gaps in understanding. In an ideal scenario, data empowers educators with insights and provides a more supportive learning experience for students (Efstratopoulou et al., 2025).

However, behind this promise lies a central paradox: the same data infrastructure exposes institutions to significant risks related to data misuse, surveillance, and algorithmic bias. Passive data collection creates a supervisory environment that (Prinsloo & Slade, 2015), where the student becomes a "data subject" without meaningful consent. Tool *proctoring* is the most glaring example, sacrificing privacy for the sake of academic integrity (Ara & Thomas, 2023). Furthermore, the risk of algorithmic bias has been well documented. AI systems trained on biased historical data will replicate and reinforce those biases (Raftopoulos et al., 2025), for example in admissions algorithms or predictive analytics that incorrectly mark minority students.

However, the central argument of this chapter is that limiting the discussion to technical protections or *debiasing* would miss the heart of the issue. AI ethics in education goes beyond technical data; It touches on fundamental issues of power, autonomy, and control. This is a shift from the question "Is the data safe?" to the question "Who is in control?"

This is where the erosion of human agency lies. For learners, the danger is becoming a passive subject in an opaque algorithmic system ("black box"). When AI recommends courses or flags them, students often don't have an understanding (Kopzhasarova & Kozhamzharova, 2025), has no mechanism to oppose, and cannot "opt out". Their autonomy is replaced by algorithmic determinism.

For educators, the risk is over-reliance on AI insights without critical questions. The pressure for "data-driven decision-making" can cause educators to put aside their pedagogical judgment (Grüning et al., 2025), changing their role from autonomous professionals to technical operators of AI systems (Haitsma & Brink, 2025).

Therefore, understanding human agency is essential. The gap that this chapter seeks to fill is not a lack of awareness of privacy or bias, but rather a lack of a framework that connects these technical issues with the moral agency of the learner (Pangrazio et al., 2024). Most research focuses on ethical AI, not how AI can make humans more aware of their agency (Alfredo et al., 2024). This chapter, therefore, builds on the foundations of interdisciplinary literature (computer science, AI ethics, philosophy, and critical pedagogy). The rationale is clear: we cannot teach data privacy and security in a vacuum without first addressing the dynamics of power and agency created by AI tools themselves.

3. TUJUAN BAB (OBJECTIVES OF THE CHAPTER)

After establishing the background and the problems at hand, this chapter has four main objectives. These goals are designed to bridge the gap between the technical application of AI and its ethical-pedagogical implications for human agency.

Specifically, this chapter aims to:

1. Investigate how a wide range of AI technologies—from learning analytics to proctoring—affect human agency, for both learners and educators, in the decision-making process related to data privacy and security.
2. Analyze the fundamental ethical challenges and tensions that arise between algorithmic automation and human autonomy in AI-driven learning environments.
3. Proposes a conceptual model, called the "Human-AI Agency Interaction Model", as a framework to promote responsible and human-centered adoption of AI, particularly in the context of privacy education.
4. Provide actionable policy and pedagogical recommendations for educators, technology developers, and institutional administrators to maintain agency, increase transparency, and build trust in the use of AI in education.

4. RESEARCH QUESTIONS

To achieve the objectives outlined above, the conceptual explorations in this chapter are guided by three interrelated core research questions:

1. RQ1: How does the integration of AI tools in educational environments (such as LMS, ITS, and assessment tools) specifically impact learners' and educators' agencies in managing and making decisions related to their data privacy and security?
2. RQ2: In what ways can AI systems be designed, regulated, or implemented to reinforce—rather than erode—ethical awareness, autonomy, and human control over personal data in the context of learning?
3. RQ3: What conceptual frameworks or pedagogical models are most effective in balancing the efficiency of AI-driven automation with the fundamental need for ethical autonomy and human agency in digital learning spaces?

5. KERANGKA TEORETIS (THEORETICAL FRAMEWORK)

To analyze in depth the tension between AI automation and human autonomy, this chapter cannot rely on a single theoretical lens. Instead, this chapter proposes an interdisciplinary framework that synthesizes four theoretical pillars: Human Agency Theory, AI Ethical Framework (FATE), Data Justice Perspective, and Constructivist Learning Theory. Together, these frameworks allow us to move from the question "What does AI do?" to the question "What is its impact on human agency and justice?"

5.1. Human Agency Theory

The first and main pillar of this chapter is the Theory of Human Agency, which is largely taken from the work of Albert Bandura. According to the initial proposal, human agency is the ability to "exercise intentionality and self-regulation even in a structured system". This is not just a passive philosophical concept; It is a proactive capacity to influence a person's future and one's environment.

More specifically, Bandura identifies four core properties of human agency: Intentionality, Forethought, Self-Reactiveness, and Self-Reflectiveness. These four properties are directly challenged by AI in education. Intentions (making plans) can be eroded by AI systems that "recommend" learning paths in a deterministic manner. Foresight (predicting outcomes) becomes difficult when students interact with "black box" algorithms. Self-reactivity (regulating behavior to achieve goals) is interrupted by a proctoring system that punishes atypical behavior. And self-reflectivity (self-evaluation) can be replaced by an analytics dashboard that tells students who they are (e.g., "at-risk students") instead of letting them judge it for themselves.(Sekti, 2025a)

In the context of this chapter, agency refers to the capacity of learners and educators to make meaningful choices, exercise control, and act as autonomous moral agents regarding their data and learning. Recent literature has begun to apply this concept directly to human-AI interactions. Research on human-AI collaboration—whether in education, software engineering, or medicine—shows that the most effective systems are not those that automate humans out of the process, but rather those that strengthen their agency (Guo et al., 2025). This system shifted from "human intervention" to "human involvement" (Haitsma & Brink, 2025). Therefore, our framework views agency as an outcome to be optimized, not something to be sacrificed for efficiency.

5.2. Kerangka Etika AI: FATE (Fairness, Accountability, Transparency, Explainability)

The second pillar provides a practical tool for evaluating AI systems, widely known as the FATE principle. This framework, mentioned in the proposal, is essential for dissecting the "black box" system we discussed in Part 2.

- Fairness: Refers to the elimination and mitigation of unfair algorithmic bias. This is directly related to the finding that EDM models can replicate historical biases. (Raftopoulos et al., 2025).
- Accountability: Demanding that there be an individual or entity that can be held accountable for the results of algorithmic decisions—a challenge in an opaque system. In the context of education, accountability is very important. If a student is mistakenly flagged by the proctoring system and fails in a course, who is responsible? Is it the software developer, the university that buys the software, or the professor who uses it? Without a clear path to accountability, human agency (in this case, the student's right to appeal and fair treatment) becomes paralyzed. Ethical leadership in schools is needed to build this accountability framework (Burkett, 2025).
- Transparency: Demands that the system works and what data it uses can be understood. Transparency is more than just "knowing that data is being collected". It is the right of students and educators to know what data is being collected, how long it is stored, with whom it is shared, and for what purposes it is used. Student privacy and privacy self-management depend on this transparency (Prinsloo & Slade, 2015).

- Explainability (Explainability (XAI): This is the most important component of FATE for an agency. XAI is the ability of a system to explain why it came to a certain conclusion. (Kopzhasarova & Kozhamzharova, 2025). Without XAI, human agency would not exist, as users cannot challenge, modify, or even understand the decisions that affect them. Openness of explanation is a technical bridge to build trust. (Sanjammagari et al., 2026).

5.3. Data Justice Perspective

The third pillar, Data Justice, expands FATE from the technical level to the socio-political level. The framework argues that data ethics issues are not just technical bugs (such as bias) that need to be fixed, but rather a reflection of systemic power imbalances. (Pangrazio et al., 2024).

The Data Justice Perspective asks important questions: Who benefits from student data collection? Whose voice is heard in the design of this system? And who is most harmed by its failures and biases? Data fairness focuses on representation and participation. Representation means that the data used should fairly represent the diversity of the student population, and not just drawn from the dominant group. Participation means that students and educators—those most affected by these systems—should have an active voice in the design, governance, and audit of the system rather than simply "decode" fairness through a technical lens (Fares & Jammal, 2024), Data Justice demands that we also consider the representation, participation, and rights of data subjects. This is very important for our proposal because it links data privacy directly to human rights and equity.

5.4. Constructivist Learning Theory

The fourth and final pillar ties the other three pillars back to pedagogy. Constructivist theory views learners not as passive recipients of information, but as active agents who "construct" their own understanding through interaction with the world.

This theory is particularly relevant to our argument:

1. If the learner is an active agent (Constructivism),
2. And they operate in a system designed to support their agency (Human Agency Theory),
3. Then the AI system itself must be designed to be explainable and fair (FATE & Data Fairness).

Poorly designed AI—one that is opaque, deterministic, and takes over decision-making—is inherently anti-constructivist. The AI implicitly positions students as passive objects that need to be "fixed" or "sorted" by algorithms. It undermines the process of social negotiation and self-reflection that is at the heart of constructivist learning. In contrast, a well-designed AI will serve as a collaborative tool ("cognitive partner") that students use to build knowledge, for example, in creative problem-solving (Guo et al., 2025), or as seen in human-AI collaboration models in other fields (Sauer et al., 2026).

5.5. Synthesis: Towards a Human-AI Agency Interaction Model

Individually, each of these frameworks provides valuable insights. However, the strength of this chapter's analysis lies in its fourth synthesis. Agency Theory (Bandura) provides a purpose (why agency is important). FATE provides technical metrics (how to evaluate tools). Data Justice provides a socio-political lens (who benefits/disadvantages). And Constructivism provides a pedagogical foundation (how this relates to learning).

Together, these four pillars form the basis for the "Human-AI Agency Interaction Model" that we will develop in Section 7. This model argues that ethical AI in education is not about replacing human judgment, but rather about creating symbiotic partnerships where AI handles computing while humans retain agency, control, and ethical judgment. This model is the main theoretical contribution of this chapter.

6. METHODOLOGY

To answer the research questions and achieve the objectives of this chapter, the methodology used is a conceptual and exploratory qualitative approach. This approach was chosen because the focus of the research is not on the quantitative measurement of the effectiveness of AI, but on the exploration, analysis, and synthesis of abstract concepts such as agency, ethics, and autonomy in a socio-technical context.

This methodology is implemented through three interrelated phases, as outlined in the proposal: (1) Synthetic Literature Review, (2) Case Study Analysis, and (3) Framework Synthesis.

6.1. Phase 1: Synthetic Literature Review

The first phase, which has been largely informed in Part 2 and Part 5, involves a systematic and synthetic review of the literature. Unlike standard literature reviews that only summarize fields, this methodology uses reviews as an analysis tool. We strategically synthesize the literature from four often separate areas:

1. Educational Technology & AI (e.g., Learning Analytics, EDM) (Alfredo et al., 2024)
2. AI Ethics, Privacy, and Law (e.g., Bias, Privacy, Data Justice) (Raftopoulos et al., 2025)
3. HCI & Agency Theory (e.g., Human-AI Collaboration, Agency) (Guo et al., 2025)
4. Pedagogy & Learning Theory (e.g., Constructivism)

It is this interdisciplinary synthesis that allows us to build a Theoretical Framework in Part 5, which serves as an analytical "lens" for the next phase.

6.2. Phase 2: Case Study Analysis

The second phase of this methodology is the analysis of conceptual case studies. To ground the theoretical argument, this chapter will analyze three commonly used AI applications in education. This case study was selected based on the following criteria: (1) High Prevalence: Widely used in educational institutions; (2) Data Intensive: Relying on massive student data collection and processing; and (3) Impact on Agency: Directly intervene or replace traditional decision-making by educators or learners.

The selected case studies are:

1. Plagiarism Detection System (e.g., Turnitin): Analyzes how these tools shape students' agency in writing and the perception of intellectual property.
2. Learning Analytics Dashboards: Analyzes how "data-driven" insights affect educators' pedagogical agency and learner autonomy.
3. Adaptive & Proctoring Tools: Analyzes the paradox between assessment security and the erosion of student privacy and agency. (Ara & Thomas, 2023).

6.3. Phase 3: Framework Synthesis

The final phase of this methodology is synthesis. Findings from the case study analysis (Phase 2) will be used to build and propose the Human-AI Agency Interaction Model promised in Part 3. This model is not just a summary, but a new conceptual artifact that integrates theoretical insights (from Phase 1) and practical findings (from Phase 2). This model will serve as a major contribution to this chapter, offering a new way to balance automation and autonomy.

This three-phase approach allows this chapter to move logically from what we know (Literature Review), to real-world problem analysis (Case Study), and finally to new conceptual solutions (Framework Synthesis).

7. EXPECTED FINDINGS AND DISCUSSION

This section is the core of the analysis of this chapter. Using the four pillars of the theoretical framework—Human Agency Theory, FATE, Data Justice, and Constructivism—this section will dissect three case studies outlined in the methodology: (1) Plagiarism Detection System, (2) Learning Analytics Dashboard, and (3) Proctoring Tools.

This analysis will be used to answer our research questions and will culminate in the proposal of a conceptual "Human-AI Agency Interaction Model".

7.1. Case Study 1: Plagiarism Detection System (e.g., Turnitin)

Plagiarism detection systems are one of the most normalized forms of AI in education, often used as a "gatekeeper" for academic integrity.

- Human Agency Analysis: This system fundamentally changes the agency of students and educators. For educators, agency is being replaced by automation. The professional task of teaching and assessing the originality of the writing—a nuanced pedagogical process—is reduced to a "similarity score" examination. Educators' agencies for applying contextual judgment (e.g., distinguishing bad citations from intentional plagiarism) are often overruled by the algorithmic authority of such scores. For students, their agency in written expression is reframed. Instead of writing for a human audience, they now write for algorithms, often engaging in "algorithmic games" to avoid detection rather than learning proper citations. Their agency shifted from writers to evasive detection. In particular, this undermines the Intentionality and Self-Reflectiveness properties of Bandura's agency theory that we discussed in Section 5.1. Students' intentions shift from "what I want to communicate" to "what the algorithm won't flag." Their self-reflectivity is replaced by an external percentage score, where success is defined as a low score, rather than as a well-expressed argument. This is the opposite of the desired human-AI creative collaboration (Guo et al., 2025), where the tool is supposed to expand agency, not limit it
- FATE Analysis: This system fails in some FATE principles.
    - Fairness: This system is known to have a bias towards non-native speakers who may rely more on common phrase structures.
    - Accountability: Who is responsible if a student is falsely accused? Often, responsibility is shifted to the "system". If a student is falsely accused of plagiarism by a high "similarity score," the appeal path is very complicated. The burden of proof is placed on students to prove

their innocence, against the authority of machine-generated numbers. Who is responsible? Is it the software developer, the university that buys the software, or the professor who uses it? As shown by (Burkett, 2025) in the context of ethical leadership, the lack of a clear accountability framework for AI tools puts institutions at great ethical and legal risk, while also crippled student agencies to get fair treatment.

- Transparency & Explainability: This is the biggest failure. This system is a classic "black box". Students and educators rarely know how the algorithm matches text, what databases it uses (including previous student work), and why it marks one phrase but misses another. This lack of XAI (Kopzhasarova & Kozhamzharova, 2025) directly hinders the agency, as there is no basis to challenge or understand its judgment. This is a direct barrier to building trust, as users are forced to trust the system's judgments without any justification (Sanjammagari et al., 2026).
- Data Justice Analysis: The issue of data justice here is huge. By submitting assignments, students forcibly "donate" their intellectual property to a private corporate database, which is then used to train algorithms and assess future students. It is a data extraction model in which students (data subjects) have no ownership or control over their work once submitted. This is a clear example of the power imbalance highlighted by (Pangrazio et al., 2024). Students do not participate in this data governance; They are raw materials for commercial products. This perfectly illustrates the failures of representation and participation raised by the Data Justice perspective (Section 5.3). They are represented by their data without consent, and they have no participation in how that data is used.
- Constructivist Analysis: This system is inherently anti-constructivist. He positions writing not as an active process of constructing meaning, but as a duty of obedience to avoid punishment. The focus is on detecting "the wrong" rather than on developing an authentic understanding of academic ethics. The pedagogy driven by this tool encourages "performance-avoidance goals" instead of "mastery goals." This is in direct contradiction to constructivist principles where true learning occurs through safe exploration, intellectual risk-taking, and socially constructed meaning.

7.2. Case Study 2: Learning Analytics Dashboards

The LA dashboard within the LMS promises educators real-time insights into student progress, with the goal of enabling early intervention.

- Human Agency Analytics: The LA dashboard creates complex agency dynamics. On the one hand, it can strengthen educator agencies by providing them with data to support struggling students, who may be missed. This is the ideal embodiment of human-centred learning analytics (Alfredo et al., 2024),where data serves to inform, not dictate, pedagogical assessments. However, as warned in Part 2, there is a great risk of overdependence. Educators' pedagogical agency can be eroded if they start to set aside their professional judgment in favor of what the dashboard suggests. Their agency shifted from reflective practitioners to dashboard operators. This is a phenomenon that is also seen in other fields, such as medicine, where overreliance on AI autonomy can affect professional work outcomes (Grüning et al., 2025). For students, their agency can be diminished through "algorithmic determinism". If a dashboard labels a student as "high-risk," it can create a "self-fulfilling prophecy" where educators treat them differently. Worse, if students see the label, Bandura's Self-Reflectiveness property can be damaged, leading them to believe that they are doomed to fail, which directly reduces their agency to self-regulate.
- FATE Analysis:
    - Fairness: The predictive models that power these dashboards are susceptible to historical bias. If students from a particular background have historically had lower success rates (due to systemic barriers, not ability), the algorithm can learn to unfairly mark current students from those backgrounds (Raftopoulos et al., 2025).
    - Explainability: As with plagiarism detectors, why is a student marked as "at risk"? Is it because they failed the quiz, or because they logged in at the "wrong time"? The lack of XAI makes intervention a guess. Educators may be told who is at risk, but not why. This lack of actionable explanation (Kopzhasarova & Kozhamzharova, 2025) hinder their ability to provide targeted pedagogical support, turning potential interventions into mere data flagging.
    - Accountability: As with plagiarism tools, if a student is placed on a remedial path based on an incorrect "high risk" prediction, who is responsible? Does the student have the right to challenge the label? Lack of a clear accountability framework (Burkett, 2025) making students helpless against algorithmic predictions. o Transparency: Students rarely (if ever) see the "backend" dashboard that educators use to monitor them. They don't know what metrics are being tracked. Is "login time" at 3 a.m. considered a sign of dedication or a sign of trouble? This lack of transparency hinders students' ability to effectively manage their own privacy (Prinsloo & Slade, 2015).

- Data Fairness Analysis: The LA dashboard is the embodiment of passive surveillance. Data is collected from every click, login time, and forum interaction. Students are often unaware of the extent to which they are being monitored (Prinsloo & Slade, 2015). This raises the issue of "meaningful consent". Can students really opt out of this tracking without harming their participation in the classroom? Furthermore, from the perspective of (Pangrazio et al., 2024), we must ask: Who benefits? Often, this data is collected not only to help students, but for institutional purposes such as increasing "retention rates." In this model, student data is extracted to optimize institutional metrics, while students themselves (data subjects) have little agency or control over how their data is used to shape their experiences.
- Constructivism Analysis: LA dashboards often reduce learning (a rich, unstructured constructivist process) to a simple set of behavioral metrics (e.g., "time spent," "click"). It encourages a reductionist and behavioristic view of learning, not a constructivist one. Constructivist learning involves productive struggles, dead ends, and offline reflection—all "invisible" activities that the LA dashboard often interprets as inactivity or disengagement. As such, the tool risks systematically punishing deep constructivist pedagogy in favor of superficial and easily measurable online behavior.

7.3. Case Study 3: Surveillance Proctoring Tools

Perhaps the most controversial AI tool, the proctoring tool monitors students during exams through webcams, microphones, and browser tracking to detect cheating.

- Human Agency Analysis: This is the most extreme case of agency erosion. Students' agency over their personal space, biometric data, and bodily autonomy is eliminated for the sake of assessment integrity. They are forced to submit to invasive algorithmic gaze in their own homes. The stress and anxiety caused by this system—fear of being marked by looking in the wrong direction or because a family member walks into the room—actively impairs the cognitive state necessary for assessment. Their agency as trusted learners is replaced by the default "suspect" status. This is a direct attack on Bandura's Self-Reactiveness property. Naturally anxious students may move their legs or look up when thinking—normal self-regulation behavior. The proctoring system interprets this agency's behavior as a signal of cheating, effectively punishing students for being human.
- FATE Analysis:
    - Fairness: These tools are notorious for algorithmic bias, especially in facial recognition software that more often fails in darker-skinned stu-

dents, and in the detection of anomalies that mark students with disabilities or anxiety who exhibit atypical physical behavior. This failure of fairness is not just a technical problem; This is a barrier to access to education. If a student cannot be reliably recognized by the algorithm, they may be locked out of the exam, effectively hindering their participation in the course (Raftopoulos et al., 2025).

  - Accountability: If a student fails an exam because the system mistakenly locked them out or flagged them for cheating, the appeal process is often opaque and extremely difficult, placing the burden of proof on the aggrieved student. In many cases, the only "evidence" is the "flag" of an unexplainable algorithm, putting educators in the impossible position to enforce decisions they do not understand or control, once again highlighting the need for ethical leadership and accountability frameworks (Burkett, 2025).

- Data Fairness Analysis: This is a case of "surveillance as a service". The data collected is highly sensitive: facial recordings, voice, personal room data, and web browsing data. The risk of data breaches and misuse is very high (Ara & Thomas, 2023). Students have no choice but to "consent" to this invasive data collection if they wish to take the course, making consent coercion. The highly intimate nature of the data (biometrics, domestic recordings) makes this collection much more dangerous than LMS click tracking. From a Data Justice perspective (Pangrazio et al., 2024), it is a coercive data extraction that disproportionately impacts low-income students who may not have a personal space or stable internet connection, thus creating a significant equity issue.
- Constructivist Analysis: Proctoring tools focus exclusively on summation assessment in a punitive manner. This tool does not contribute anything to the learning process (knowledge construction). Instead, he creates a learning environment based on suspicion and stress, which is the antithesis of the safe space necessary for constructivist exploration. Constructivist learning thrives in a culture of trust and psychological safety. Proctoring tools systematically destroy this trust, replacing it with a culture of suspicion. It sends a pedagogical message that institutions value cheating prevention more than the well-being of students or the learning process itself.

7.4. Findings and Synthesis: Answering Research Questions

This section is the core of the analysis of this chapter. Using the four pillars of the theoretical framework—Human Agency Theory, FATE, Data Justice, and Constructivism—this section will dissect three case studies outlined in the methodology: (1) Plagiarism Detection System, (2) Learning Analytics Dashboard, and (3) Proctoring Tools.

This analysis will be used to answer our research questions and will culminate in the proposal of a conceptual "Human-AI Agency Interaction Model".

Table 1. Summary of case study analysis through a theoretical framework

Analysis Criteria	Case Study 1: Plagiarism Detection	Case Study 2: Learning Analytics Dashboard (LA)	Case Study 3: Proctoring Tools
Human Agency	**Erosion:** Turns students into "detection avoiders."	**Complex:** Potential for augmentation, but at risk of dependence.	**Extreme Erosion:** Loss of bodily autonomy & "suspect status".
FATE	**Fails:** Especially on *Transparency* ("black box") & *Accountability* .	**Fails:** Especially on *Fairness* (bias) & *Explainability* (unclear labels).	**Total Failure:** Especially on *Fairness* (biometric bias) & *Accountability.*
Keadilan Data	**Violation:** Non-consensual extraction of data (student work).	**Violations:** Passive supervision for institutional purposes.	**Extreme Violations:** Coercive & inequivalent extraction of biometric data.
Constructivism	**Anti-Constructivist:** Encourages obedience, not understanding.	**Anti-Constructivist:** Reducing learning to superficial metrics.	**Anti-Constructivism:** Destroys trust and psychological security.

This case study analysis reveals a clear pattern and allows us to directly answer our research questions.

Finding 1 (Answering RQ1: How does AI impact agencies?) AI integration impacts human agency not as an on/off switch, but in a spectrum from displacement to augmentation.

- At the end of the move, we see proctoring and plagiarism detection tools, where human judgment, bodily autonomy, and privacy are directly taken over by algorithmic authority.
- On the augmentation end, we see the potential (though often unrealized) of the LA dashboard to provide insights to educators, or AI that acts as a creative problem-solving collaborator (Guo et al., 2025). The findings are that the default design of many educational AI tools today leans more toward agency shifting than augmentation. This is most likely because agency migration (full automation) is technically easier and cheaper to implement than agency augmentation (complex human-AI collaboration). Systems designed for efficiency will always tend to favor automation, unless human agency is explicitly made the core design goal (Sauer et al., 2026).

Figure 1. The spectrum of AI impact on human agency, mapping case studies from displacement to augmentation

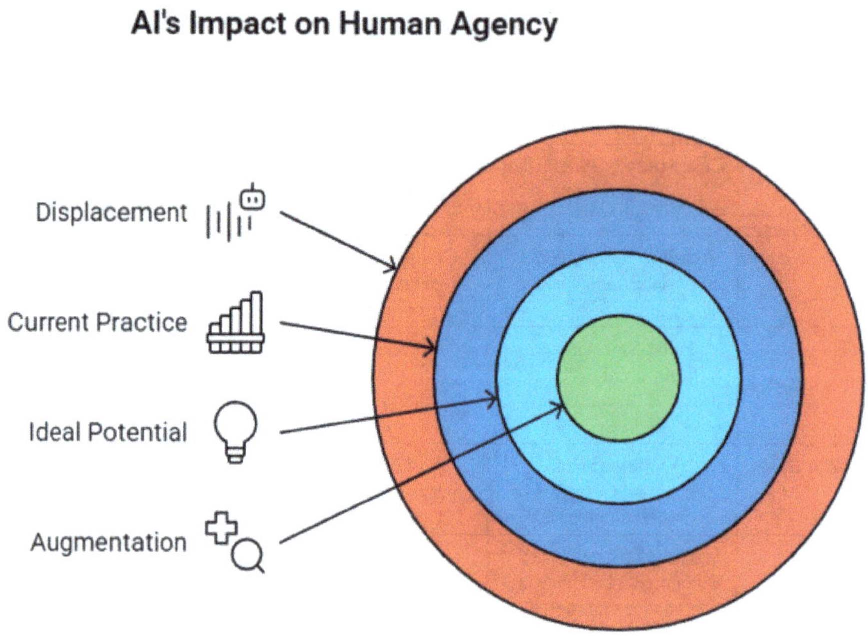

Finding 2 (Answering RQ2: How can the system strengthen the agency?) AI systems can strengthen agencies only if they are deliberately designed to do so. Our analysis shows two key mechanisms: Explainability (XAI) and Human-in-the-Loop (HITL).

- XAI is a technical prerequisite for agencies. As the "black box" case study shows, without an understanding of why a decision is made (Kopzhasarova & Kozhamzharova, 2025), no agency—just passive compliance.
- HITL is a philosophical prerequisite. Systems must be designed for "human engagement" (Haitsma & Brink, 2025), not just "human intervention". This design positions AI as a collaborative assistant, similar to the model seen in software engineering (Abbasi et al., 2026) or medicine (Merdin-Uygur et al., 2025), where AI performs data analysis while humans hold the final decision. It is this collaborative design that builds trust (Sanjammagari et al., 2026). The important point here is that "Human-in-the-Loop" should not be passive (only approving AI decisions). Instead, it should be "Human-in-Control". This means educators must have agency to override, question, and recalibrate

AI recommendations. Human agency must hold supremacy over algorithmic output.

Finding 3 (Answering RQ3: What framework is the most effective?) Our findings suggest that no single framework (FATE, Data Fairness, etc.) is enough. An effective balance can only be achieved through integrated synthesis. This is the main contribution of this chapter: the proposal of a Human-AI Agency Interaction Model.

This model shifts from seeing AI as a tool to seeing it as an actor in the learning ecosystem. This model visualizes successful interactions as a three-pillar confluence:

1. Pedagogical Agency (Educator & Learner): Rooted in Constructivism and Human Agency Theory, this is the pillar of "purpose"—what we want to achieve.
2. Socio-Technical Justice (Systems & Governance): Rooted in Data Justice and Accountability, these are the "foundational" pillars—the basic rules of the ecosystem.
3. Actionable Transparency (Data & Algorithms): Rooted in XAI and Transparency, it is the "bridge" that connects humans to the system.

This model argues that Human-AI Ethical Collaboration only occurs at the intersection of the three pillars. Without a Pedagogical Agency, AI has no purpose. Without Socio-Technical Justice, AI becomes oppressive. And without Actionable Transparency, AI becomes an opaque "black box" that erodes trust and agency. This model is our answer to RQ3: a framework that balances automation with ethical autonomy.

Figure 2. The proposed human-AI agency interaction model, illustrating the intersection between pedagogical agency, socio-technical justice, and actionable transparency to achieve ethical collaboration

8. CONTRIBUTION TO THE EDITED VOLUME

This chapter makes a specific and focused contribution to the central theme of this volume, "AI Bias, Privacy, and Ethics in Education". While much discussion of AI ethics has focused separately on algorithmic bias or data privacy, the unique contribution of this chapter is to bridge these two concepts through the theoretical lens of human agency.

As outlined in the proposal, the chapter's contribution can be summarized in three main points:

- First, this chapter expands the conversation beyond technical bias and procedural justice to the realms of moral agency and pedagogical autonomy. We argue that the solution to unethical AI is not simply to "fix" algorithms so that they are not biased (although that is important). Instead, the true solution lies in fundamentally redesigning human-AI interactions to strengthen human decision-making agencies (educators and learners). The focus on this agency—which is analyzed through Bandura theory and Constructivism—is our main theoretical contribution.

- Second, this chapter provides a conceptual bridge between AI ethics (a computer/philosophical discipline) and data privacy education (a pedagogical/cybersecurity discipline). By proposing the "Human-AI Agency Interaction Model" (Section 7.4), we offer a practical framework that educators and administrators can use to evaluate and implement AI technologies, not only based on their efficiency, but also based on their impact on the agency.
- Third, this chapter directly supports the book's mission to develop a "transparent, inclusive, and equitable model for AI in education". Rather than simply identifying problems, our case study analysis (Sections 7.1-7.3) and our "Interaction Models" collectively serve as conceptual blueprints for those models. This chapter provides actionable insights that will be expanded on in the following Practical Implications section (Section 9), focusing on how stakeholders can build a more equitable and human-centered EdTech ecosystem.

9. PRACTICAL IMPLICATIONS AND POLICY RECOMMENDATIONS

The analysis in Section 7 has shown that the default design of many educational AI tools today tends to erode, rather than strengthen, human agency. The Model of Human-AI Agency Interaction that we propose in Section 7.4 argues that ethical collaboration can only be achieved through a synthesis between Pedagogical Agency, Socio-Technical Justice, and Actionable Transparency.

However, this theoretical model would be meaningless if it was not translated into practice. This section addresses the question "So, what should be done?" It outlines the practical implications and policy recommendations for four key stakeholders: (1) AI Developers and Designers, (2) Educators, (3) Administrators and Institutions, and (4) Learners themselves. These recommendations are taken from our proposal.

9.1. Recommendation 1: Human-Centered Ethical Design (For Developers & Designers)

Agency problems cannot be solved through regulation alone; This problem must be addressed from the beginning through design.

- Adopting Human-Centered Design: EdTech developers must move from an "efficiency above all else" model to Human-Centered Software Engineering (Sauer et al., 2026). This means that "human values"—such as agency, autonomy, and trust—should be the primary success metric, equivalent to predictive accuracy. Design should start with the question, "How does this tool empower educators and learners?" not "How does it automate tasks?". In practical terms, this means adopting a co-design methodology in which educators and learners are actively involved in the development cycle. Instead of developers building tools separately and then "testing" them on schools, they should build them together with schools. This ensures that it is the pedagogical goal (e.g., encouraging critical thinking, which is at the heart of Constructivism) that drives the design of technology, not the other way around. This is the essence of Human-Centered Software Engineering (Sauer et al., 2026):Humanitarian values and the context of use should define the architecture of the system, not be an afterthought.
- Making Explainability (XAI) a Core Feature, Not an Addending: As "black box" case studies show, a lack of explanation is a major barrier to agencies. XAI should not be a "premium" feature; it should be a minimum requirement. Users (both students and educators) should have the right to know why a decision is made (Kopzhasarova & Kozhamzharova, 2025). The LA dashboard should include a simple explanation ("Student A was flagged for being late for the last 3 assignments") instead of just the "at risk" label. Our case studies in Part 7 show that the "black box" is a major source of agency erosion. Developers should understand that XAI (Kopzhasarova & Kozhamzharova, 2025) It's not just about debugging; This is a pedagogical feature. A good explanation allows for "teachable moments". For example, an explainable plagiarism detection score can show students why their paragraph is flagged (e.g., "This quote is too long without analysis") instead of just "30% score." This is an important technical bridge to rebuild trust (Sanjammagari et al., 2026) that have been damaged by the opaque system.
- Designing for "Human-in-Control", Not Just "Human-in-the-Loop": As we discovered in Section 7.4, agencies need human supremacy. The design should reflect this. An educator should have a clear and easy button to override algorithmic recommendations (e.g., plagiarism scores) without penal-

ty. Systems must be designed for active "human engagement" (Haitsma & Brink, 2025), positioning AI as a collaborative assistant, not as a superior. This distinction is very important. "Human-in-the-loop" often means humans doing the rough work for the AI (e.g., labeling data) or passively agreeing to its recommendations. "Human-in-Control" means that human supremacy and agency are maintained. Educators should always have final authority. This model has proven important in other high-risk areas, such as medicine, where the success of human-robot collaboration depends on the "agency and ownership" of doctors (Merdin-Uygur et al., 2025). EdTech design should follow this principle, ensuring that the educator is the user of the tool, not the subject of the tool.

- Privacy by Design: Tools should be designed to collect the minimum amount of data required to function, not the maximum amount possible. Consent shouldn't be a hidden "agree for all" checkbox. Users should be given granular control over what data they share, which is in line with the concept of privacy self-management (Prinsloo & Slade, 2015) and enhanced cybersecurity (Naeem et al., 2024). This principle of data minimization is fundamentally safer than data anonymization. Anonymized data can often be de-anonymized again, but data that was never collected is the only data that is 100% secure. This is also the principle of Data Justice (Pangrazio et al., 2024) in practice: instead of asking "How can we legally extract this data?", designers should ask "Do we really need this data for the core functionality of this tool?". Giving users granular control (e.g., "Allow time tracking, but disable click tracking") is a straightforward technical step to restore agency and self-management privacy (Prinsloo & Slade, 2015) to the consumer.

9.2. Recommendation 2: Critical AI Literacy (For Educators & Learners)

Agency cannot exist without literacy. A user cannot exercise control over a system that they do not understand. Therefore, AI Literacy is the most urgent pedagogical implication of our findings.

- For Learners: Beyond Functional Literacy: AI literacy for students today often focuses on how to use tools (e.g., how to use ChatGPT prompts). This is not enough. We must develop Critical AI Literacy. Students need to be taught how these systems work at a basic level: that these systems run on data (often their data), that they have biases, and that they have commercial purposes. The curriculum should include questions from Data Justice ("Who benefits from my data?"). These are fundamental components of modern digital literacy skills and in line with efforts to introduce AI literacy even at the grassroots level (Yim, 2024). Critical AI Literacy is directly connected to the development of human agency (Section 5.1). A student who only knows how to use a tool is a passive operator. A student who understands why the tool delivers certain results, and what the implications are, is a critical agent. This is the difference between functional skills and Bandura's Self-Reflectiveness. A practical curriculum can include activities such as "data audits" in which students try to map out what data the school's LMS collects about them. They can be taught to deconstruct algorithmic recommendations (for example, on YouTube or Netflix) to understand how data profiles are created. This makes abstract concepts such as "biased" (Raftopoulos et al., 2025) and "data justice" (Pangrazio et al., 2024) to be real and relevant to their lives. Without this critical literacy, students remain the passive "data subjects" we identified in Part 2.

- For Educators: Training as a Critical Evaluator: Educators today are often not trained to handle these tools. As a result, they risk becoming "technical operators" (as discussed in Section 7.2). Professional development training is essential. Educators need to be trained on how to evaluate EdTech tools before adopting them. They should be encouraged to ask vendors tough questions: "Does the tool have known biases?", "How does the XAI work?", "What is your data governance model?". This training transforms them from passive users into gatekeepers of their own pedagogical agency. This training is very important because educators are the "front line" of pedagogical agencies. If they don't understand the tools they're using, they can't protect their student agency. This training should go beyond "how to use dashboards" and focus on critical evaluation. Educators should be trained to evaluate EdTech tools based on FATE principles (Section 5.2). They must be empowered to identify and reject tools that are anti-constructivist in nature (Section 5.4) or that violate student privacy (Ara & Thomas, 2023). This training is not just a technical skill; It is a core component of ethical leadership at the grade level (Burkett, 2025). It is the bridge that connects institutional policy (Section 9.3) to day-to-day classroom practice, and is the only way to ensure educators remain in a "Human-in-Control" position (Section 7.4).

9.3. Recommendation 3: Strong Institutional Governance (For Administrators & Policymakers)

Educators and students cannot be expected to fight unethical tools alone. Agency protection must come from the top level through strong governance and policies.

- Establish an AI Ethics Oversight Committee: In accordance with our proposal's recommendations for "governance", every educational institution (from schools to universities) should have an AI Ethics Committee. Above all, this committee should be interdisciplinary—made up of administrators, IT technologists, legal experts, faculty members (educators), and student representatives. This committee must implement ethical leadership (Burkett, 2025) to review and approve all high-impact AI tools (such as proctoring or predictive analytics) before they are purchased and deployed. The role of this committee should not stop after the purchase. This committee should serve as an ongoing review body, creating a clear path of accountability that is currently missing (as discussed in our FATE case study in Section 7). If a student or educator makes a complaint about bias or privacy, it is this committee that should investigate and have the authority to disable the tool. It is a practical embodiment of accountability, transforming "ethical leadership" (Burkett, 2025) from abstract concepts to functional governance mechanisms. The involvement of student and faculty representatives here is critical to ensuring the principles of Data Fairness (i.e., participation and representation) (Pangrazio et al., 2024) respected.
- Implementing Ethical Procurement Policies: Institutions hold enormous market power. They should stop buying "black boxes". Procurement policies should explicitly require that each EdTech vendor provide documentation of their FATE principles. Institutions should require vendors to prove that their tools are fair, transparent, and explainable. If the vendor cannot provide it, the institution cannot purchase it. Procurement policy is the strongest lever that institutions have to drive change. Rather than just waiting for developers to voluntarily adopt Human-Centered Design (Sauer et al., 2026), institutions can create market demand for it. The procurement checklist should include specific questions: "How can we override algorithm recommendations?" (Human-in-Control), "Can you provide an independent biased audit report?" (Fairness), "How does this tool explain its decision to the end user?" (XAI) (Kopzhasarova & Kozhamzharova, 2025). By refusing to buy technology that fails to meet these transparency and agency standards, institutions can collectively force the EdTech industry to change.
- Establishing Clear and Accessible Data Policies: Where is student data stored? How long? Who has access? For what purpose is the data used? The answers to these questions are often buried in unreadable legal documents. Following the principles of Data Fairness (Pangrazio et al., 2024), each institution should have a clear, plain, publicly accessible "Student Data Rights Statement" that answers these questions. This statement is not just a legal document; It is a pedagogical document. This is the embodiment of trans-

parency and the first step in rebuilding trust. It should explicitly outline the student's right to "privacy self-management" (Prinsloo and Slade, 2015), including the right to access their data, the right to request correction, and (where possible) the right to opt out of non-essential data collection without academic penalty. This directly answers Data Justice's question "Who benefits?" (Pangrazio et al., 2024) by making data governance transparent to those most affected by it.

9.4. Recommendation 4: Collaborative Supervision and Pedagogical Paradoxes

This last recommendation is binding on all other recommendations: agencies are a shared responsibility.

- Implementing Collaborative Oversight: No single stakeholder can solve this alone. Developers who designed Human-Centered AI (Sauer et al., 2026) requires ongoing input from educators and students. Educators who teach AI Literacy (Yim, 2024) requires transparent tools from developers and policy support from administrators. Administrators who write AI policies (Jaelani et al., 2024) requires technical expertise from developers and pedagogical insights from educators. Therefore, "collaborative oversight" must be an ongoing process—not a static committee, but a "living framework" for continuous dialogue between all parties. This living framework is the embodiment of our "Human-AI Agency Interaction Model" (Section 7.4) in practice. This means creating a formal channel for iterative feedback. For example, the AI Ethics Committee (proposed in 9.3) should not only meet once a year to approve software. They must meet quarterly to review "agency complaints" from students and educators. Educators who have received AI Literacy training (from 9.2) should have a formal process for reporting findings of bias or anti-constructivist design back to the committee. Furthermore, the committee should have the authority to bring these collective findings back to the vendor (Developer), using the procurement policy (from 9.3) as a bargaining tool. This creates a cycle of accountability underpinned by ethical leadership (Burkett, 2025), where design, literacy, and governance reinforce each other continuously.
- Overcoming the Pedagogical Paradox: Finally, we return to the paradox posed in the Introduction: how can we use AI (data collection tools) to teach privacy? The implication is that we have to do it very carefully. This suggests that the best AI tools for teaching privacy may be low-tech or open-source tools, where students can view the code, control its data, and actively decon-

struct how it works. Using commercial “black boxes” to teach privacy is a pedagogical contradiction. The practical implication is that educators should actively seek out tools that embody the transparency they teach, and explore the ethical dimensions of AI education itself (Mohamed, 2024). This paradox highlights what pedagogues call the “hidden curriculum”. The stated curriculum may be “The Importance of Data Privacy”. But if the tools used to teach are “black boxes” that invasively monitor students, the hidden curriculum students learn is: “Privacy is not important,” “Surveillance is normal,” and “Individual agency must be sacrificed for the sake of institutional efficiency.” This hidden message is much more powerful than the stated lesson.

The practical implication is a radical shift in the way we teach about AI. Instead of just using “AI as a tool of delivery”, we should start treating “AI as an object of study”. This is at the core of Critical AI Literacy (Section 9.2). Rather than using opaque LA dashboards, educators can use an anonymized (and approved) dataset from the LMS and ask students (in a statistics or data science lesson) to build their own predictive models. Through this process, students will discover biases (Raftopoulos et al., 2025) in the data directly. They will be forced to grapple with the FATE question head-on: “Is our model fair? How can we explain it?”

This constructivist approach (Section 5.4) solves this paradox. Students use AI to learn about privacy and ethics, but they do so as critical agents, not as supervised subjects. They can be tasked with “auditing” plagiarism detection tools, actively trying to “cheat” algorithms and then discussing why some strategies work—an exercise in reverse engineering that XAI teaches (Kopzhasarova & Kozhamzharova, 2025) better than any talk.

This is the highest application of Human-Centered Design (Sauer et al., 2026)—a learning agency-centric design. By transforming AI from a fearsome authority into an object that can be dissected and criticized, we empower students. We equip them with literacy skills and reflective agencies to participate in “collaborative supervision” not only as students, but as informed citizens. This is the only way to ensure that the ethical dimension (Mohamed, 2024)This technology is not only discussed by experts, but also understood and shaped by those most affected by it.

Table 2. Summary of practical recommendations for stakeholders

Stakeholders	Key Recommendations	Objectives (Agency Strengthening)
Developer & Designer	Adopt *Human-Centered Design*. Designing for "Human-in-Control". Make XAI a core feature.	Build tools that technically *enable* agency and transparency.
Educators & Learners	Developing Critical AI Literacy (beyond functional skills). Educators act as critical evaluators [15].	Create *a demand* for ethical tools and empower users to criticize bad tools.
Administrator & Institutions	Establish an AI Ethics Oversight Committee. Implementing an ethical Procurement Policy .	Creating a governance structure that protects agencies at the institutional level.

10. CONCLUSION

This chapter begins with an exploration of the tension between the two forces shaping the future of education: automation (which is driven by AI) and autonomy (which is run by human agency). We argue that the promise of AI personalization and efficiency is often paid at an invisible but costly cost: the erosion of the agency of learners and educators, the normalization of supervision, and the strengthening of algorithmic injustice.

Our analysis of three common case studies (plagiarism detection, LA dashboard, and proctoring proctoring) has shown a consistent pattern. When AI systems are designed by default for efficiency and control, they tend to displace human agency. These systems treat users as passive data subjects in opaque algorithmic "black boxes," which are directly contrary to the pedagogical goal of developing autonomous and critical learners.

A major contribution of this chapter is the proposed Human-AI Agency Interaction Model (Section 7.4). This model argues that the most ethical AI systems are those that are explicitly designed to strengthen human agency. We argue that the solution to unethical AI is not just technical improvements or safeguards, but rather fundamental shifts in design, pedagogy, and governance. Our model proposes that ethical AI can only exist at the intersection of three pillars: Pedagogical Agency (our goal), Socio-Technical Justice (our foundation), and Actionable Transparency (our bridge).

Achieving this demands a culture of moral awareness, transparency, and empowerment. As outlined in our practical recommendations (Section 9), this shift requires real action:

- From Efficiency-based Design to Human-Centered Design (Sauer et al., 2026).
- From Functional Literacy to Critical AI Literacy (Yim, 2024).
- From reactive Governance to proactive Ethical Leadership (Burkett, 2025).

Ultimately, the goal of responsible AI in education is not to replace human judgment with artificial intelligence, but rather to redefine how the two can coexist responsibly. These systems should empower learners and educators to navigate data ethics consciously, rather than passively. In the digital learning ecosystem of the future, AI should not be the dictating algorithmic authority; AI must be a collaborative partner that ensures that it is human autonomy that holds the final decision.

REFERENCES

Abbasi, M. A., Ihantola, P., Mikkonen, T., & Mäkitalo, N. (2026). Reconsidering Requirements Engineering: Human–AI Collaboration in AI-Native Software Development. *Lecture Notes in Computer Science, 16081 LNCS*, 164–180. DOI: 10.1007/978-3-032-04190-6_11

Alfredo, R., Echeverria, V., Jin, Y., Yan, L., Swiecki, Z., Gašević, D., & Martinez-Maldonado, R. (2024). Human-centred learning analytics and AI in education: A systematic literature review. *Computers and Education: Artificial Intelligence*, *6*, 100215. Advance online publication. DOI: 10.1016/j.caeai.2024.100215

Burkett, J. R. (2025). Artificial intelligence and school leadership: Using ethical leadership as a framework for monitoring the use of AI in schools. In *Responsible AI Integration in Education* (pp. 181–209). DOI: 10.4018/979-8-3373-6007-2.ch006

Efstratopoulou, M., Argyriadi, A., & Argyriadis, A. (2025). AI in Learning, Educational Leadership, and Special Education: Innovations and Ethical Dilemmas. In *AI in Learning, Educational Leadership, and Special Education: Innovations and Ethical Dilemmas*. DOI: 10.4018/979-8-3373-5550-4

Fares, N. Y., & Jammal, M. (2024). Decoding Justice: The Synergy of Artificial Intelligence and Machine Learning in the Legal Landscape. *2024 IEEE Global Conference on Artificial Intelligence and Internet of Things, GCAIoT 2024*. DOI: 10.1109/GCAIoT63427.2024.10833589

Grüning, M., Henkenjohann, R., Fuchs, M., Dratsch, T., dos Santos, D. P., Kim, M., Matthies, P., Mukhopadhyay, A., & Trenz, M. (2025). The Influence of Artificial Intelligence Autonomy on Physicians Work Outcomes in Healthcare: A Lab-in-the-Field Experiment. *Proceedings of the Annual Hawaii International Conference on System Sciences*, 536–545. https://www.scopus.com/inward/record.uri?eid=2-s2.0-105005139802&partnerID=40&md5=85ef2c0aebd5f95291bbb638eaa59ec0

Guo, W., Liang, Z., Wang, C., Li, X., Hu, H., Chen, S., Yu, Q., & Zhao, Q. (2025). Student-AI collaborative creative Problem-Solving: The role of human agency. *Computers & Education*, *239*, 105433. Advance online publication. DOI: 10.1016/j.compedu.2025.105433

Haitsma, L., & Brink, B. (2025). From Human Intervention to Human Involvement: A Critical Examination of the Role of Humans in (Semi-)Automated Administrative Decision-Making. *Digital Government: Research and Practice*, *6*(3), 1–17. Advance online publication. DOI: 10.1145/3716173

Kalita, E., Oyelere, S. S., Gaftandzhieva, S., Rajesh, K. N. V. P. S., Jagatheesaperumal, S. K., Mohamed, A., Elbarawy, Y. M., Desuky, A. S., Hussain, S., Cifci, M. A., Theodorou, P., Hilčenko, S., Hazarika, J., & Ali, T. (2025). Educational data mining: A 10-year review. *Discover Computing*, *28*(1), 81. Advance online publication. DOI: 10.1007/s10791-025-09589-z

Khor, E. T., How, Z. J., Koh, E., Looi, C. K., & Lok, C. (2025). Learning analytics techniques: An overview and future research possibilities. *International Journal of Information and Learning Technology*, *42*(3), 269–295. DOI: 10.1108/IJILT-02-2024-0020

Kopzhasarova, M., & Kozhamzharova, D. (2025). Explainable AI (XAI): Techniques, applications, and challenges. *CEUR Workshop Proceedings*, *3966*, •••. https://www.scopus.com/inward/record.uri?eid=2-s2.0-105006886912&partnerID=40&md5=4007adb38600ba88e07d459c1ef6a021

Merdin-Uygur, E., Ozturkcan, S., Özbilgin, M. F., Yılmaz, F., & İnce, Ö. (2025). Human–robot collaboration in surgery at the nexus of knowledge, agency, and ownership. *Scientific Reports*, *15*(1), 23642. Advance online publication. DOI: 10.1038/s41598-025-08437-w PMID: 40604196

Mohamed, M. S. P. (2024). Exploring Ethical Dimensions of AI-enhanced Language Education: A Literature Perspective. *Technology in Language Teaching and Learning*, *6*(3), 1813. Advance online publication. DOI: 10.29140/tltl.v6n3.1813

Naeem, M. R., Amin, R., Farhan, M., Alotaibi, F. A., Alnfiai, M. M., Sampedro, G. A., & Karovič, V. (2024). Harnessing AI and analytics to enhance cybersecurity and privacy for collective intelligence systems. *PeerJ. Computer Science*, *10*, e2264. Advance online publication. DOI: 10.7717/peerj-cs.2264 PMID: 39314701

Pangrazio, L., Auld, G., Lynch, J., Sawatzki, C., Duffy, G., Hannigan, S., & O'Mara, J. (2024). Data justice in education: Toward a research agenda. *Educational Philosophy and Theory*, •••, 1–12. DOI: 10.1080/00131857.2024.2320196

Patil, S., Patwal, P. S., & Wadane, V. S. (2024). MACHINE LEARNING APPROACH FOR EDUCATIONAL DATA MINING ON REAL LIFE APPLICATIONS. *IET Conference Proceedings,* 2024(38), 370–374. DOI: 10.1049/icp.2025.0892

Prinsloo, P., & Slade, S. (2015, March). Student privacy self-management: Implications for learning analytics. In *Proceedings of the fifth international conference on learning analytics and knowledge* (pp. 83-92). DOI: 10.1145/2723576.2723585

Raftopoulos, G., Davrazos, G., & Kotsiantis, S. (2025). Evaluating Fairness Strategies in Educational Data Mining: A Comparative Study of Bias Mitigation Techniques. *Electronics (Basel), 14*(9), 1856. Advance online publication. DOI: 10.3390/electronics14091856

Sanjammagari, H. S. G., Sougandhika, G. S., & Srinivasa Desikan, K. E. (2026). Bridging the Trust Gap: Leveraging Explainable AI for Personalized E-Commerce Recommendations. *Lecture Notes in Computer Science, 15706 LNAI*, 225–236. DOI: 10.1007/978-981-96-8889-0_19

Sauer, S., Ardito, C., & Bernhaupt, R. (2026). Human-Centered Software Engineering: Balancing Interaction, Artificial Intelligence, and Human Value: IFIP WG 13.2 Workshop at INTERACT 2025. *Lecture Notes in Computer Science, 16111 LNCS*, 377–381. DOI: 10.1007/978-3-032-05008-3_70

Sekti, B. A. (2025). Adversarial machine learning in industrial cybersecurity: Challenges and solutions. In *AI-Enhanced Cybersecurity for Industrial Automation* (pp. 363–386). DOI: 10.4018/979-8-3373-3241-3.ch018

Sekti, B. A. (2025). Machine learning and artificial intelligence (AI) in manufacturing. In *Integrating Digital Innovation and Integrated Frameworks in Manufacturing* (pp. 255–292). DOI: 10.4018/979-8-3373-1082-4.ch011

Shashwat, K., & Pundhir, S. K. S. (2025). Artificial intelligence in education: Personalizing learning and overcoming ethical challenges. In *Immersive Learning in Teacher Education* (pp. 137–176). Simulated Environments, Tools, and Practices., DOI: 10.4018/979-8-3693-9861-6.ch005

Teixeira, R. (2026). Emotional AI Applied to Mental Health: An Ethical and Philosophical Analysis. *Lecture Notes in Computer Science, 16108 LNCS*, 421–430. DOI: 10.1007/978-3-032-04999-5_25

Yim, I. H. Y. (2024). A critical review of teaching and learning artificial intelligence (AI) literacy: Developing an intelligence-based AI literacy framework for primary school education. *Computers and Education: Artificial Intelligence*, *7*, 100319. DOI: 10.1016/j.caeai.2024.100319

Chapter 2
Balancing Innovation and Integrity:
Addressing Bias, Privacy, and Ethical Challenges of AI in Education

Shivansu Sachan
http://orcid.org/0000-0002-9893-8018
CSJM University, Kanpur, India

ABSTRACT

The integration of Artificial Intelligence (AI) in education has transformed learning environments, pedagogical strategies, and assessment mechanisms. However, this digital shift also presents critical ethical challenges related to bias, privacy, and the integrity of educational processes. This paper examines how institutions can balance innovation with ethical responsibility by promoting transparent data governance, equitable algorithmic design, and learner-centered AI applications. Through an interdisciplinary lens, it explores the potential risks of algorithmic discrimination, surveillance concerns, and the erosion of academic integrity while emphasizing frameworks for responsible AI adoption. The study advocates for policy interventions, ethical literacy, and stakeholder collaboration to ensure that AI in education remains inclusive, fair, and trustworthy.

1. INTRODUCTION

Volunteering, especially on an international level, has long been a way for people to show support for each other, share ideas from different cultures, and help those

DOI: 10.4018/979-8-3373-7467-3.ch002

in need. As the world grows more digital, artificial intelligence (AI) technologies are having a bigger impact on how worldwide volunteering is planned and carried out. AI offers both benefits and challenges for volunteering groups, volunteers, and the communities they serve. For example, it can automate administrative tasks or use chatbots to translate or coordinate in disaster areas in real time.

2. THE GROWTH OF VOLUNTEERING IN THE DIGITAL AGE

2.1 Conventional Frameworks of Global Volunteering

Global volunteering has been a key part of international development, humanitarian aid, and cultural interaction for a long time. In the past, volunteering meant going to communities—often far from their own—to help with local development projects by giving their time, skills, and work. The Peace Corps (USA), Voluntary Service Overseas (UK), Médecins Sans Frontières, and the International Federation of Red Cross and Red Crescent Societies are some of the most well-known programs that institutionalized these old patterns. Under these methods, volunteers often lived in host communities for months or even years, doing anything from teaching and providing health care to farming and helping with disasters.

This method stressed getting to know one other, learning through experience, and working together. Volunteers not only helped with local projects, but they also took part in a deep cultural interchange that changed how they and the people they were staying with saw things. The experience changed both sides in a big way, promoting empathy across cultures and building long-term worldwide solidarity.

But traditional worldwide volunteerism also has significant problems. Sending organizations have to pay a lot for things like travel, lodging, insurance, and language instruction. These expenditures, together with the difficulty of coordinating postings abroad, sometimes made it hard for people to volunteer. This meant that only a small group of people, usually from wealthy countries who could afford to do such work, could do so. Additionally, these initiatives frequently used a paternalistic approach, where outside "expertise" was more important than local knowledge. Well-meaning interventions didn't always meet the real needs or priorities of the communities they were meant to help.

Even with these problems, conventional methods helped global volunteerism become a practice based on solidarity and human development. But as technology improved, it became evident that new models could help fix some of the problems with the old way of doing things that weren't fair or efficient.

2.2 The Growth of Digital Volunteering

The internet and digital communication technologies grew quickly in the early 2000s. This was the start of a big change in how people could connect and work together across borders. The digital revolution gave rise to the idea of virtual or digital volunteering, which is when volunteers work from home using digital tools instead of being there in person. Digital volunteering made a lot of new things possible. People could help with global issues from the comfort of their own homes through services like the United Nations Volunteers' (UNV) Online Volunteering service. Translating documents, building websites, making logos, doing research, and drafting grant submissions are all examples of virtual involvement that became ubiquitous. This concept cut down on the costs and logistical problems that come with traditional volunteering by a lot. This made it easier for people with different levels of mobility, time, and money to get involved in global issues.

2.3 AI as the Next Big Thing

The rise of artificial intelligence (AI) is the most recent—and possibly most important—step in the evolution of global volunteerism. Artificial intelligence (AI) technologies including machine learning, natural language processing (NLP), computer vision, and predictive analytics are now being used to improve the way volunteers are recruited, matched with opportunities, taught, coordinated, and assessed. These changes are making global volunteering bigger and more important, but they are also raising new ethical, operational, and strategic issues. Amichai-Hamburger, Y., & Fine, A. (2019).

AI's role in volunteering goes beyond just automating tasks; it also adds a level of cognitive enhancement. For instance, AI systems can now look at huge datasets to find patterns, guess what will happen, and suggest actions with speed and accuracy that have never been seen before. When it comes to volunteering, this means that volunteer profiles will better match the needs of the organization, project planning and resource allocation will be more effective, communication will be better across language barriers, and project outcomes will be monitored in a more nuanced way.

AI also helps corporations deal with complicated, ever-changing problems that affect the whole world. AI can help find the most urgent needs, set priorities for actions, and get volunteers to help right away, whether it's a public health emergency, a climate calamity, or a refugee crisis. At the same time, AI tools are getting easier to use and more widely available, so small NGOs and grassroots groups can employ technology that were earlier only available to big organizations.

3. HOW AI IS USED IN GLOBAL VOLUNTEERING

3.1 Finding and Hiring Volunteers

One of the most promising uses of AI in global volunteering is to find and hire volunteers. In the past, this process was done by hand, took a long time, and was often not very efficient. Human resources personnel would go through stacks of applications, look at resumes by hand, and try to find the best candidates for a job based on their experience, availability, and interests. This approach often added biases that weren't meant to be there and slowed down the deployment of volunteers.

AI has made the hiring process smarter and more responsive. Machine learning algorithms can now look through a lot of application data, like resumes, cover letters, social media accounts, and past service records, to find patterns and suggest good volunteer opportunities. Natural language processing (NLP) is used by these systems to read text and get useful information including talents, language skills, availability, and interests. Benkler, Y., Faris, R., & Roberts, H. (2021).

For example, sites like Idealist and VolunteerMatch are starting to leverage AI-based recommendation engines to assist users identify the best volunteer opportunities for them based on their individual profiles. These platforms employ AI to suggest volunteer roles based on past activity, stated preferences, and the requirements of the organization, just like streaming services suggest shows or music based on what you've seen or listened to in the past.

This speeds up the hiring process and makes the matches better at the same time. Volunteers are more likely to be given jobs where they can make a real difference, which keeps them interested and keeps them coming back. At the same time, businesses can find and hire the right people more quickly, even for very specific or specialty jobs.

But it's important to remember that AI-driven hiring also poses questions about fairness, openness, and data protection. If the training data that computers employ shows prejudices from the past, those biases can keep happening. So, businesses need to put ethical AI practices first, like checking algorithms for prejudice and making sure that hiring decisions are fair and open to everyone. Benevolat, M., & Hustinx, L. (2020).

3.2 Managing and Coordinating the Project

Managing global volunteer initiatives, especially those that include a lot of people, places, and time zones, may be quite hard. In these situations, AI solutions are being employed more and more to make project management tasks easier and more efficient.

AI-driven scheduling software can, for example, automatically set up meetings across time zones, taking into account each person's schedule, vacations, and work style. Algorithms for allocating resources can figure out where people or things are most needed and send them there. Smart dashboards show you real-time updates on project milestones, risks, and roadblocks, which helps you make decisions and change course faster.

AI integration is very helpful for businesses that work in crisis areas where real-time cooperation is quite important. AI can help manage the flow of supplies, keep track of where people are going, and plan volunteer assignments based on the changing needs on the ground during humanitarian situations like earthquakes, floods, or disease outbreaks.

Also, AI-powered chatbots and virtual assistants are helping volunteers talk to each other, answer common queries, share news, and handle logistics. This not only makes things easier for the human personnel, but it also makes the experience better for volunteers by giving them accurate, up-to-date information.

In the end, AI makes volunteer-based programs more flexible, responsive, and able to grow. It helps companies work together more accurately with big, diverse teams, even when things are changing and not always clear.

3.3 Crisis Mapping and Help for People in Need

One of the best things about AI for global volunteering is that it can handle and analyze a lot of unstructured data, which is very important for disaster response and humanitarian help.

When something bad happens, getting information quickly is very important. AI is being used to look at data from many different places, such as satellite images, social media posts, mobile sensor data, and reports from citizens. Platforms like Ushahidi and IBM's Watson are using AI to better map crisis areas, figure out what people need, and direct volunteers to help.

For instance, during the COVID-19 pandemic, AI was used to keep an eye on the virus's transmission in real time, find clusters of infections, and guess how many healthcare resources would be needed. This helped public health groups and volunteer groups put their efforts where they were most needed. In the same way, AI systems can look at aerial photos of natural disasters to figure out how bad the damage is, where places are most affected, and the best ways to get help to those locations.

AI is also being used by volunteer networks to quickly check and sort through new material. When there is a flood or an earthquake, thousands of data points, like images, tweets, and emergency calls, come in. AI can sort through responses and figure out which ones are urgent, as well as filter out incorrect or duplicate information. This makes sure that volunteer interventions are prompt, focused, and based on evidence.

AI-assisted crisis mapping is an example of how technology may make humanitarian intervention more accurate and successful, especially when speed and accuracy are very important.

3.4 Evaluation and Monitoring

Monitoring and evaluation (M&E) are very important parts of every volunteer-based project. They help groups measure their impact, improve their performance, and show stakeholders that they are responsible. M&E used to depend a lot on collecting data by hand, doing interviews, and having people report their own results, which may take a long time and be wrong or biased. Bryson, J. J., Diamantis, M. E., & Grant, T. D. (2019)

AI gives M&E processes new capabilities that make them more accurate and efficient. For example, machine learning algorithms can look at patterns in program data, find outliers, and guess which actions are most likely to work or not work. Natural language processing can look at open-ended comments from volunteers or recipients and figure out what they are feeling, what the main themes are, and what new problems are coming up.

Some companies are utilizing AI to automate impact reporting. They do this by putting data from many sources, such mobile apps, surveys, and field reports, into dynamic dashboards that show real-time information. These tools let everyone involved see what's working, where changes need to be made, and how to make successful initiatives bigger.

AI can also help adaptive management by letting people learn in real time. Companies can utilize AI analytics to make changes on the fly, based on real-time data from the field, instead of waiting until the end of a project to see how it went. This makes the way projects are put into action more flexible and responsive.

AI makes M&E better, but it also makes people wonder about the ethics of data. As companies start using AI-driven evaluation methodologies, they need to make sure that informed consent, privacy protection, and tackling data biases stay at the top of their list of priorities. DataKind. (2022).

3.5 Translating Languages and Talking to People From Other Cultures

Language difficulties have always made it hard for people to volunteer around the world. Volunteers often work in places where they don't speak the language, which might cause problems, delays, or even harm that they didn't mean to do.

AI-powered translation technologies are changing this field. Google Translate, DeepL, and Microsoft Translator are just a few of the apps that can now translate text and audio in real time in dozens of languages. Voice assistants and speech-to-text technology make it easier for volunteers to talk to people in the community, getting rid of language hurdles that used to make it hard for people to work together.

These tools are especially useful when things are going wrong or when a lot is on the line and clear, accurate communication is really important. For example, a health volunteer in a refugee camp can utilize AI translation technologies to help patients who don't speak English understand how to get better. Project coordinators can also make sure that more people can take part by translating training materials or surveys into local languages.

AI-powered communication technologies also help make things more culturally inclusive by letting volunteers from non-Western or non-English-speaking backgrounds participate more completely. As these tools get better at being accurate and understanding the context, they will keep making global volunteerism more open and useful. Ushahidi. (2023).

4. ADVANTAGES OF AI INTEGRATION IN VOLUNTEERING

Adding Artificial Intelligence (AI) to global volunteering has many benefits that make it easier for organizations to organize, mobilize, and support volunteers. These technologies are changing traditional volunteering by making it more scalable, efficient, inclusive, and personalized. We will talk about these benefits in more depth below.

4.1 Efficiency and Scalability

AI has had a big effect on volunteering right away, making it easier to scale up and run more efficiently. A lot of the time, nonprofit groups, humanitarian organizations, and volunteer-based social enterprises don't have enough money or people to do what they need to do. AI technology help these groups handle more work and more volunteers without having to hire more administrative staff.

For instance, chatbots and AI-powered customer care systems can answer thousands of basic questions at once, which would normally need a whole team of human representatives. These automated systems can answer common inquiries, help new volunteers get started, or even give training modules. AI also helps with logistics by automating scheduling, keeping track of volunteer hours, and sending reminders. All of these things save time and cut down on mistakes made by people. Eubanks, V. (2018).

4.2 Personalization and Involvement

Another great thing about AI in volunteering is that it may make each volunteer's experience unique. Volunteers come from many different origins and have different skills, reasons for volunteering, and preferences. A one-size-fits-all strategy doesn't always keep kids interested or happy. AI helps close this gap by making opportunities fit each person's needs. Floridi, L., & Cowls, J. (2021). Hager, M. A., & Brudney, J. L. (2022).

Volunteering platforms can suggest roles that fit a volunteer's talents and goals by using machine learning algorithms to look at their behavior, interests, geography, past actions, and availability. This not only makes it more likely that a volunteer will accept a duty, but it also makes them feel more fulfilled and purposeful. A volunteer is more likely to stay engaged and participate over the long term if they feel that their unique contributions are acknowledged.

4.3 Making Decisions Based on Data

In the past, a lot of volunteer groups used their gut feelings, stories from other people, or hand-written surveys to make decisions and measure their impact. AI changes this field by making it possible and useful to make decisions based on facts in real time.

AI systems can collect and evaluate a lot of structured and unstructured data, such as feedback from volunteers and metrics on their engagement, social media sentiment, and assessments of community needs. Predictive analytics helps businesses see patterns coming, such a lack of volunteers, a lack of resources, or new areas of crisis, and then take action before they happen.

These technologies also help organizations thoroughly review their programs. AI can figure out which projects have the biggest effect for the least amount of money spent or which types of volunteers respond best to various programs. You can utilize these insights to improve the program and make better use of the money.

This evidence-based approach also helps develop confidence between stakeholders, such as donors, government agencies, and community partners, who are asking for more openness and measurable results. In this way, AI not only makes decisions easier to make within the company, but it also makes the company more accountable and legitimate to the outside world. AI's skills in language translation, sentiment analysis, and geolocation mapping also add more layers of contextual awareness. These tools help businesses deal with cultural differences, avoid possible disputes, and design programs that are more welcoming and responsive.

4.4 Participation That Includes Everyone

One of the most important changes that AI has made is to make it easier for everyone to find volunteer opportunities. In conventional models, volunteering typically involved being there in person, traveling, or being able to change your schedule. This kept many people who wanted to help from doing so, such as people with disabilities, people who lived in remote areas, or people who had to take care of others.

AI-powered virtual volunteering platforms get rid of these problems. You can now do things like translating, instructing, digital activism, designing, data analysis, or mentoring from anywhere. AI tools make it easier for people from different time zones and languages to talk to one other, which makes working together easier and more open.

For example, voice-to-text software, AI-powered screen readers, or personalized interfaces make it easier for people who are blind or deaf to take part. People from varied language backgrounds can contribute without worrying about getting things wrong because to real-time language translation.

5. AI'S RISKS AND PROBLEMS IN GLOBAL VOLUNTEERING

Even though it has a lot of potential, adding AI to volunteer ecosystems also comes with a lot of problems. From moral issues to worries about social justice, the use of AI must be done with care and consideration to make sure it supports rather than threatens the essential principles of volunteering.

5.1 Problems with Ethics

AI use in humanitarian and charitable settings present intrinsic ethical challenges. One of the most important things to think about is data privacy. Volunteer platforms frequently gather sensitive personal information, such health status, socioeconomic background, or location data, which, if improperly managed, may result in privacy violations or inadvertent injury.

There are also problems with permission and transparency when AI is used to make decisions. Volunteers and beneficiaries may not always know how their data is being used or which algorithms are affecting their ability to get services. This lack of clarity goes against the idea of informed involvement.

Also, algorithmic bias is still a big problem. AI systems that are trained on datasets that are biased or not representative can make existing inequities worse or possibly make them worse. For instance, if predictive models are based on historical data that doesn't accurately represent underrepresented communities, these groups might not be included in future interventions or might be inaccurately represented in needs assessments.

Also, using surveillance methods like facial recognition or behavioral tracking to keep an eye on volunteers or community needs can be very intrusive, especially in places where politics are delicate or conflict is likely. AI could be utilized in ways that hurt people's dignity and trust if there aren't stringent ethical rules and people watching over it.

To deal with these problems, firms need to put in place strong ethical standards, do frequent audits, and make sure that AI systems can be understood and held accountable. People and groups of people who volunteer should also be able to question and challenge the technologies that affect them.

5.2 Dehumanization and the Absence of Empathy

Volunteering has never been merely a job; it is a very human act based on empathy, connection, and a shared goal. As people rely more on AI, they may lose the emotional and social aspects of volunteering.

When tasks are totally automated and interactions happen through digital interfaces, there are less chances for real human interaction. A chatbot might be able to help organize a food drive, but it can't replace the warmth of a genuine conversation, the understanding that comes from making eye contact, or the connections that come from working together.

5.3 Unequal Access to Technology

For AI to work, there needs to be a certain level of digital infrastructure, literacy, and access. But these kinds of situations aren't always the same. In a lot of low-income or rural areas, where volunteering is often most required, people don't have easy access to dependable internet, cellphones, or AI-compatible platforms.

This produces a digital barrier that can keep both volunteers and people who need help from getting help. For example, a community center that doesn't have stable internet can't use AI to give services. In the same way, a volunteer who doesn't know how to use digital tools may have trouble finding opportunities or doing chores well.

If AI systems aren't made with everyone in mind, they could accidentally make these differences even bigger. Older persons or people who live in remote areas may not be able to use platforms that need biometric verification or advanced gadget compatibility.

Also, language hurdles are still a problem. AI can help with translation, but there aren't enough dialects and minority languages in the training data. Because of this, systems might not be able to correctly understand or respond to local situations, which could lead to misunderstandings or exclusion. To fix these problems, businesses need to spend money on building digital skills, make platforms available in several languages and with low bandwidth, and create technologies that are easy to use and understand. It is not only a technological problem to close the digital divide; it is also a moral duty.

5.4 Losing a Job and Changing Roles

As AI gets better, more and more people are worried about jobs being lost in the charity sector. People are worried that there would be fewer jobs because administrative tasks like data entry, scheduling, and basic communication are generally the first to be automated.

6. CASE STUDIES: AI IN ACTION IN DIFFERENT VOLUNTEERING SITUATIONS

AI has made its way into many different kinds of volunteering around the world. This shows that it can help people do more, get better results, and make service-oriented initiatives more efficient. This section shows how AI-powered tools and platforms are changing the way people volunteer in their communities and around the world by looking at a few real-life examples. These examples show how AI may be used in numerous ways, such as humanitarian mapping, virtual volunteering, chatbot communication, and predictive analytics in public health.

6.1 AI for Disaster Response: The Example of Ushahidi and Humanitarian Mapping

One of the most useful and interesting ways to use AI in volunteering is in crisis response and humanitarian help. Ushahidi is a Kenyan non-profit digital startup that has shown how AI can be a strong tool for managing disaster response operations better when it is used with crowdsourced input. The platform was first designed to keep an eye on violence after the 2008 elections in Kenya. Now, it is known around the world as a way to map crises and coordinate humanitarian efforts.

Ushahidi was very important during the 2010 Haiti earthquake and the 2015 Nepal earthquake because it collected and displayed real-time data supplied by individuals on the ground through SMS, email, or social media. The technology put these reports on a live dashboard, which helped assistance groups, governments, and local communities see the big picture of new needs, areas of damage, and resource gaps. This was especially critical in places where the traditional communication infrastructure had broken down or wasn't good enough. Ushahidi works well because it can mix AI-driven procedures with the work of human volunteers. Machine learning algorithms help us sort through huge amounts of unstructured data, find significant trends, and put messages that show urgent or life-threatening demands at the top of the list. For example, if hundreds of text messages were sent in about different events, AI could sort through them to find the ones that were spam, the ones that had keywords connected to serious injuries, people who were stuck, or highways that were closed, and send them to the right people right once.

6.2 AI Platforms for Virtual Volunteering: UNV and DataKind

AI has made it possible for new kinds of virtual volunteering that go beyond time and space. This is possible since employment is quickly becoming digital and people all over the world are starting to work from home. The United Nations Volunteers (UNV) program is a good example of this change because it uses AI tools in its worldwide volunteering system. Its web platform connects thousands of volunteers to different causes. Now, it employs natural language processing (NLP) to make the matching process easier and the recruitment process more efficient. The website can offer the best options for a volunteer by using AI-based algorithms to look at their abilities, interests, availability, and language preferences. For instance, if a data scientist who speaks French is interested in healthcare and sustainability, the system can look through existing worldwide projects, pull out important keywords, and suggest projects that fit that person's profile. This AI matchmaking not only saves time, but it also makes sure that volunteers are more likely to stick with causes they care about.

During the COVID-19 pandemic, this capacity was extremely important since competent volunteers needed to be deployed right away for initiatives that were critical and time-sensitive, like tracking the progress of the virus, modeling how it spreads, or fighting false information online. UNV made this possible by quickly linking AI and data science experts with government and non-governmental organizations that needed help. These online volunteers helped with things like making dashboards for public health departments, making contact tracing apps better, and figuring out how well vaccination outreach worked. For instance, DataKind volunteers constructed a machine learning model that could utilize satellite images and economic factors to forecast poverty levels in certain regions as part of a project to reduce poverty. In farming, similar groups have built algorithms that utilize climatic data and planting histories to help smallholder farmers figure out the best times to plant their crops so they get the most yield and have the least crop failure. These contributions, even if they are virtual, are quite complex and need volunteers to work at the nexus of domain knowledge, technology proficiency, and ethical thought. One thing that makes these platforms stand out is how AI changes what it means to volunteer. Volunteers nowadays can do high-impact technical work from home, with consequences that affect communities and countries. They are no longer limited to traditional responsibilities like tutoring, physical labor, or in-person support.

6.3 Chatbots for Organizing Volunteers: What the Red Cross Did

Communication is one of the most difficult things for organizations that have a lot of volunteers to do. When there are hundreds of questions, phone calls, emails, or even simple forms often don't work, especially during emergencies or big drives. AI-powered chatbots are solving this problem by automating repetitive communication activities and giving volunteers help right away, 24 hours a day, seven days a week.

The Red Cross, one of the most well-known humanitarian groups in the world, has started using chatbot technology to make it easier to organize volunteers. For example, the Singapore Red Cross built a smart chatbot that works with its messaging platforms to answer questions about blood donation campaigns, signing up volunteers, making schedules, and other logistical issues. Volunteers may just send a message to the bot to find out where the next donation center is, what paperwork they need to fill out to get started, or how to get to their destination during emergency missions.

These chatbots have natural language processing (NLP) built in and are trained on common topics to make sure they give accurate and consistent answers. More advanced bots employ sentiment analysis to sort through questions and put them in order of importance. For example, they can tell when a user is frustrated or when a question is important and forward it to a human staff member when necessary.

One of the best things about these systems is that they can work in more than one language. In societies with many cultures, where volunteers may speak several languages, chatbots can flip between languages like Mandarin, Malay, Tamil, or English. This openness makes guarantee that no volunteer is left out because of a language problem and also encourages more participation from groups that are often left out.

The Red Cross's experience shows that chatbots don't take the place of human engagement; they make it better. They free up staff to work on more important things, like developing leaders, recognizing volunteers, and getting people involved in the community, by answering a lot of simple questions. Volunteers also feel more connected because their questions are answered swiftly, which makes them more likely to stay interested and motivated.

6.4 Predictive Analytics in Health Volunteering: Efforts to Get Rid of Malaria

AI for predictive analytics is changing the game in global health efforts, especially in areas where healthcare infrastructure is weak. One interesting example is the fight against malaria in sub-Saharan Africa, where AI is helping local health workers figure out when and how to stop illness outbreaks. Local volunteers in these programs gather geolocated information about places where mosquitoes breed, infection rates, and the availability of treatment services. Machine learning models use these statistics to find hotspots and predict possible outbreaks weeks or even months ahead of time. To make the model more accurate, it includes things like rainfall patterns, vegetation cover, and how people commute. AI makes it possible to go from reactive to proactive public health measures. Instead of waiting for a rise in malaria cases, volunteers can start taking steps to stop the disease from spreading in regions where it is most likely to happen. These include giving out mosquito nets, running awareness campaigns, and making sure that medical supplies get to where they need to go on time.

It's important to note that volunteers don't just sit back and follow AI-generated instructions. They actively use visual dashboards that show complicated statistics in easy-to-understand formats like heat maps or risk assessments. These volunteers, who are generally from the area, then use what they know about the culture to make the treatments more effective. For instance, they might plan promotions around local festivals or market days to get the most people to see and take part in them.

This combination of AI and community action not only makes health outcomes better, but it also strengthens the community. Volunteers learn how to use data and technology, and the AI models get better with feedback from the ground in real time. These kinds of co-creation and feedback loops involving AI systems and human agents are examples of a participatory approach to health innovation.

7. TEACHING VOLUNTEERS ABOUT AI

As AI becomes a part of the tools and processes of volunteering, it becomes even more important to make sure that volunteers know how to use these technologies in a responsible and successful way. Being AI literate doesn't mean that every volunteer needs to learn how to code or work with data. Instead, it means learning about how AI systems work, what they can't do, and how they affect how people make decisions.

Volunteer groups are starting to see that they need structured programs to help people learn new skills. The training sessions now address things like how to make decisions using algorithms, what bias in AI systems means, how to protect your data, and how to utilize digital platforms responsibly. These programs not only help volunteers get better at utilizing technology, but they also make sure they can think critically about the tools they are using. AI literacy is also related to bigger ideas like digital citizenship and civic empowerment. Volunteers who know how AI works are better able to critique its results, push for openness, and help make sure it is used in an ethical way. This is especially crucial when working with people who are at risk, because decisions made by algorithms, including who to help or how to assess risk, can have big effects. Also, organizations that spend money on training volunteers are also making themselves stronger. A volunteer base that knows how to use AI is more flexible, works better with others, and can come up with new ways to solve problems as they come up. This way, improving AI skills becomes not simply a technological project but also a strategic need for the long-term success of global volunteerism.

8. ETHICAL AND GOVERNANCE ISSUES

AI has a lot of potential to make global volunteerism more effective and widespread, but it also presents a number of ethical and governance problems that need to be handled properly. From worries about algorithms that aren't clear to how to handle sensitive data and the risk of digital exclusion, appropriate use of AI in volunteering needs strong systems of accountability and engagement.

8.1 Transparency and Responsibility in Algorithms

Many algorithms are "black boxes," which is a big problem for the AI-driven volunteer sector. AI systems typically work without clear visibility into how they get to certain results, whether they are being used to find volunteers, assess needs, or distribute resources. This lack of openness is very dangerous, especially when choices affect people's ability to get services or take part in initiatives.

To fix this, companies are being told to use the ideas behind explainable AI (XAI). These systems are meant to give outputs and reasons that people can understand. A model might show the factors that contributed to a community's risk score, including previous flood data or health indicators, instead of just giving the community a risk number.

Setting up clear auditing systems is just as vital. These audits should look at how well the algorithms work, if they are biased, and whether they are fair. They should also be available to everyone who has a stake in the outcome, including the communities that are serviced. Organizations can create trust, limit harm, and make sure that AI supports human-centered goals instead than going against them by making systems of accountability. Participatory governance is also very important in this situation. People who live in areas where AI makes choices should have a say in how these systems are built, used, and judged. Open-source technologies and collaborative design approaches can facilitate inclusive governance, ensuring that ethical values are rooted in the lived experiences of those most affected.

8.2 Privacy and Data Sovereignty

AI needs data to work, and in volunteer settings, this data typically comes from marginalized or at-risk groups and includes private information. So, it is very important to manage this data in an ethical way. In dynamic, AI-powered systems where data might be used or processed in ways that weren't planned, traditional permission methods like one-time checkboxes don't work.

Organizations must put in place consent mechanisms that are informed, ongoing, and based on the situation. These include not only telling people what data is being collected and why, but also giving them real-time control over how it is used. Technologies like decentralized data systems and privacy-enhancing algorithms can help make these promises real. The idea of data sovereignty goes beyond privacy to say that communities should have the right to govern their own data. This is especially significant in postcolonial or Indigenous settings, where the misuse of data has historically reflected larger power disparities. Ethical AI practice necessitates the collaborative development of data governance frameworks with local stakeholders, ensuring that data policies are congruent with cultural norms, legal requirements, and community interests.

Volunteers also need to learn how to take care of data. They should know how to maintain data integrity, stop misuse, and respect community ownership whether they enter field notes into an AI dashboard or help with digital surveys.

8.3 Reducing Bias and Discrimination

One of the most important ethical issues that AI faces in volunteering is the chance that it could make social biases stronger. If AI systems are trained on datasets that don't include enough women, ethnic minorities, or individuals with impairments, they may provide results that push these populations even further to the edge. For instance, an AI model created to find "ideal volunteers" can unintentionally prefer profiles that look like those of historically powerful groups.

9. SUGGESTIONS FOR POLICY

A full set of legislative changes is needed to make sure that artificial intelligence is used in global volunteering in a way that is ethical, inclusive, and makes a difference. These suggestions are meant for a wide variety of people, including governments, international NGOs, tech developers, and volunteer groups. They all need to work together to make sure that AI is used in a fair way for civic involvement.

9.1 Set up Global Ethical Rules for AI in Volunteering

It is also important to have standardized ethical norms that are especially created for using AI in volunteer settings. There are general AI ethical frameworks, however they don't always work in humanitarian and community-based scenarios.

The United Nations, the Red Cross, Amnesty International, and big tech companies may work together to come up with these standards. The framework should cover important topics like algorithmic transparency, data protection, informed consent, inclusivity, and participatory governance.

These guidelines should be live documents that can change as technology changes and are based on feedback from people in the field. Organizations will be able to use ethical principles in a meaningful way if they turn them into operational tools, checklists, and training programs.

9.2 Put Money Into Digital Infrastructure for the Third Sector

Many nonprofit and grassroots groups, especially in the Global South, still don't have the internet infrastructure they need to use AI tools. These populations could fall behind if they don't have access to reliable internet, current hardware, and qualified workers.

Governments, international donors, and charitable organizations need to make digital equity a top priority by putting money into infrastructure improvements and boosting capacity. Cloud subsidies, open-source AI systems, and tech clusters in different parts of the world can make it easier for smaller businesses to get started.

Digital infrastructure should also be protected so that people don't have to rely on outside providers or use data in ways that are unfair. Any investment strategy must put community ownership and sustainability at the top of the list.

9.3 Promote Collaborations Among Multiple Stakeholders

No one area can handle the complexity of AI in volunteering on its own. Partnerships between the public and commercial sectors can help bring together new technologies and responsible management.

Universities can provide cutting-edge research and training, tech businesses can provide tools and know-how, and civil society groups can provide knowledge about the situation and connections on the ground. Structured partnerships, including AI-for-good consortiums, co-design laboratories, and innovation incubators, can help come up with ideas that work in the real world.

These partnerships need to be based on common values like accountability, openness, and respect for local independence.

9.4 Encourage Volunteers and NGO Staff to Learn About AI

Both volunteers and nonprofit personnel need to keep learning digital skills so that AI can help them instead of getting in the way. National volunteer groups, development programs, and professional groups could help training programs that may be used by a lot of people.

There should be practical AI applications, digital safety rules, data ethics, and human-centered design in the curriculum. This education can be available to people of all income levels and locations through online courses, certification programs, and peer-learning groups.

A well-educated workforce is not only more productive, but it is also better able to speak out for fair and democratic use of technology.

9.5 Make Sure Everyone can Take Part in AI Development

Ethical AI for volunteering must be based on collaborative development. Communities that are supposed to benefit from volunteer efforts should be actively involved in figuring out what the problems are, coming up with solutions, and judging the results.

Participatory design workshops, community review boards, and iterative feedback loops can incorporate local viewpoints into all stages of AI development. Tools should be made with communities in mind, not just for them.

10. CONCLUSION

There is little doubt that artificial intelligence is changing the way people volunteer around the world. It opens up new ways to be more efficient, grow, and come up with new ideas. AI makes more things feasible for volunteers and the communities they serve, from automating logistics to allowing new ways to connect with people online. But these gains also come with big problems when it comes to ethics, culture, and logistics. The case examples presented above show that artificial intelligence and human volunteers are becoming more and more compatible. AI solutions improve speed, accuracy, and scalability in crisis response, virtual engagements, logistical communication, and health surveillance. But it's not only about automation; it's also about augmentation. These experiences teach us a lot of important things. First, AI makes it possible for new kinds of volunteering that are open to everyone, done from afar, and very technical. Second, it changes the roles of volunteers from those who help when needed to people who make things happen. Third, successful implementation depends on carefully combining human oversight, ethical design, and community involvement. What jumps out in these situations is how AI may make volunteering more accessible to everyone. People can now use digital tools to make a real difference on global problems, no matter where they are in the world. The case stories also remind us that technology should support human values like empathy, fairness, and empowerment. When AI helps, instead of replacing, the human spirit of service, it becomes a true partner in making the world a better place. The incorporation of artificial intelligence (AI) into the realm of global volunteering signifies a substantial advancement in the ways individuals and organizations contribute to societal welfare. Volunteering has traditionally involved in-person interactions, manual labor, and community involvement based on physical presence. However, AI has changed this model, bringing forth a new era of digital, data-driven, and hybrid forms of civic engagement. This chapter has looked at the many ways that AI affects volunteering, including its pros and cons, the need for ethical governance, and the necessity for policies that look to the future. The conclusion summarizes the main points and talks about what they mean for the future of volunteering in a world where AI is involved.

The increasing use of AI in volunteer operations is not just an improvement in technology; it is a change in the way things are done. A change in the types of volunteer positions and the creation of new profiles is at the heart of this change. Data scientists, software engineers, GIS professionals, and digital communication experts are now important parts of volunteer ecosystems. They often work from home and at different times. These new volunteer identities show that service is becoming more democratic, allowing people from different places and professions to make a real difference in causes they care about. This change has made volunteering more open and accessible, which has led to more targeted, efficient, and creative ways to solve difficult societal problems. How these technologies are managed, created, and added to frameworks that put people first will determine the future of volunteering in the AI age. Even while algorithms help volunteers do their jobs, they must still be at the center of service, driven by empathy, justice, and teamwork. If done in a fair and moral way, AI can help spread the principles of service and solidarity that are at the heart of global volunteering. This will lead to more fair, strong, and effective interventions around the world. AI has made it possible for hybrid volunteering models to exist that connect physical and virtual interaction. These methods are flexible, cost-effective, and able to adapt to global problems like pandemics, climate-related displacement, or geopolitical crises that would make traditional volunteering harder. Hybrid techniques let volunteers stay in touch with communities even after they leave, which helps them keep long-term relationships and get support through virtual technologies. Real-time dashboards, predictive analytics, and automated coordination systems are examples of AI technologies that are key to these hybrid endeavors. They make it possible for different types of interaction to work together in a smooth and effective way. The potential of AI also makes it very important for volunteers and nonprofit personnel to learn how to use these technologies in a responsible way. AI literacy, which includes knowing about algorithmic processes, data ethics, bias recognition, and digital safety, has become an important skill. Companies that pay for AI training are not only making their interventions more effective, but they are also creating a more knowledgeable and empowered group of volunteers. AI literacy helps people think critically, make ethical decisions, and be active citizens. These are all important skills for making sure that technology is used for good and not for harm. AI is becoming more and more involved in volunteer relationships, but it also brings up a lot of ethical and governance issues that can't be overlooked. The "black box" problem with algorithmic decision-making makes it hard to hold people accountable and fair, especially when these systems decide who gets aid, who gets benefits, or what community needs should be met first. AI could unintentionally reinforce systemic inequalities or leave out those that are already at a disadvantage if it doesn't have ways to be explainable, transparent, and auditable. This shows how important it is to put in place explainable AI frameworks and participatory governance models that let people who are affected help make decisions about technology.

REFERENCES

Amichai-Hamburger, Y., & Fine, A. (2019). The role of technology in volunteering and civic engagement. *Computers in Human Behavior*, *93*, 24–30. DOI: 10.1016/j.chb.2018.12.005

Benevolat, M., & Hustinx, L. (2020). Digital transformations in volunteering: Ethical and governance implications. *Voluntas*, *31*(5), 1040–1053. DOI: 10.1007/s11266-020-00253-6

Benkler, Y., Faris, R., & Roberts, H. (2021). *Network propaganda: Manipulation, disinformation, and radicalization in American politics*. Oxford University Press.

Bryson, J. J., Diamantis, M. E., & Grant, T. D. (2019). Of, for, and by the people: The legal lacuna of synthetic persons. *Artificial Intelligence and Law*, *27*(1), 1–17. DOI: 10.1007/s10506-018-9234-9

DataKind. (2022). *Data science for social good: Annual impact report*. DataKind. https://www.datakind.org

Eubanks, V. (2018). *Automating inequality: How high-tech tools profile, police, and punish the poor*. St. Martin's Press.

Floridi, L., & Cowls, J. (2021). A unified framework of five principles for AI in society. *Harvard Data Science Review*, *1*(1). Advance online publication. DOI: 10.1162/99608f92.8cd550d1

Hager, M. A., & Brudney, J. L. (2022). *The future of volunteer management: Technology, innovation, and engagement*. Springer.

Ushahidi. (2023). *Crowdsourced crisis mapping and humanitarian response*. Ushahidi Organization. https://www.ushahidi.com

Chapter 3
Algorithmic Responsibility and Epistemic Integrity in AI-Supported Learning Systems

Enrio Moch
http://orcid.org/0009-0005-4722-0961
GrandEdu Research School, Germany

Tobias Oberdieck
http://orcid.org/0009-0002-2017-4991
GrandEdu GmbH, Germany

ABSTRACT

This work analyses how algorithmic systems change epistemic, normative and institutional structures in educational processes. The analysis shows that these systems not only analyse data but also influence the conditions under which knowledge is created, tested and pedagogical decisions are justified. Algorithmic systems generate patterns that direct perception and attention without formulating reasons, thus shifting judgement processes and institutional roles. The paper develops a framework model that describes these systems as an epistemic formation consisting of data logics, modelling logics and institutional practices. From this, three dimensions of algorithmic responsibility are derived: epistemic integrity, moral responsibility and collective governance. The study shows that these systems can only be used

DOI: 10.4018/979-8-3373-7467-3.ch003

responsibly if transparency, validity, error culture and institutional control are guaranteed. The results make it clear that such systems can supplement human judgement, but not replace it.

1. INTRODUCTION

Artificial intelligence is transforming educational processes in ways that extend beyond the introduction of new technologies. Systems for automated assessment, adaptive feedback, or predictive learning analysis intervene in processes that have traditionally relied on human judgement. They generate outputs from statistical patterns, shaping attention and structuring knowledge by determining what becomes visible and how educational decisions are prepared (Ritter et al., 2025). Analyses of algorithmic opacity indicate that such systems emphasise aspects that can be readily modelled, while other dimensions remain largely invisible (Burrell, 2016; Lipton, 2018; Mittelstadt et al., 2016). To capture these changes, this paper employs the concept of epistemic formation, referring to a structure of data, modelling logics, institutional practices, and social expectations. This formation shapes how knowledge is generated, interpreted, and legitimised, connecting with theories of epistemic justice, situated knowledge, and context-bound learning processes (Anderson et al., 1996; De Corte, 2012; Fricker, 2007). AI contributes to this formation by extracting patterns inherent in data rather than producing reasoning-based outputs.

Operational reliability is another central concern, referring to the technical stability of a system. A system is considered reliable if its outputs are consistent under comparable conditions, yet consistency alone does not guarantee pedagogical relevance. The tension between statistical stability and didactic significance is a persistent challenge for many educational applications (Russel & Norvig, 2021). Since these systems do not form intentions or possess understanding, responsibility for their consequences remains with humans. Algorithmic responsibility therefore denotes the conditions under which human actors can be held accountable for system outputs. This includes transparency in decision-making, interpretability, institutional oversight, and the capacity to provide comprehensible justification. Normative perspectives emphasise that such systems should function solely in a supporting capacity and cannot assume moral agency (Floridi & Cowls, 2019; Zweig, 2022).

In practice, these systems alter not only the tools available in education but also the very understanding of knowledge and pedagogical decision-making. Automated assessment systems tend to focus on characteristics that can be readily quantified, narrowing attention to measurable traits (Burrell, 2016; Mittelstadt et al., 2016). Adaptive feedback systems provide guidance but may alter the roles of instructors and generate dependencies for learners (Devi & Revathi, 2016; Smith & Higgins,

2006). As noted by Zweig (2019) and Tsai and Yen (2013), predictive modeling categorizes students by risk, and those models can learn the same biases from previous years. These three mechanisms collectively show the ways in which learning processes are being shaped by algorithmic logics, problems for pedagogy, and concerns regarding fairness, interpretability, and human agency.

This paper examines the conditions under which AI systems can guide educational processes without undermining pedagogical justification practices. Addressing this requires a framework integrating technical, epistemic, and normative dimensions. The study develops a model of algorithmic responsibility comprising three interrelated components: the integrity of epistemic processes, the attribution of decisions to human actors, and institutional mechanisms that constrain AI and monitor its effects. These dimensions provide a tool for understanding AI's role in education, framing its use neither as purely technical progress nor as a general risk but as a transformation that demands new forms of guidance. The subsequent chapters of this work explore this perspective in greater depth. Chapter two explains the theoretical foundations. Chapter three describes the methodological approach. Chapter four analyses the mechanisms of action of algorithmic systems. Chapter five examines case studies that illustrate these mechanisms. Chapter six discusses the findings in their overall context. Chapter seven formulates conclusions and an outlook. Chapter eight describes the limitations of the analysis.

2. THEORETICAL FRAMEWORK

The theoretical framework of this work describes the conditions under which AI systems structure knowledge, influence pedagogical judgements, and shape institutional processes. The perspective is based on work that understands learning as a situated, context-bound, and interactive process. At the same time, the framework draws on research on algorithmic opacity, data-based model logic, and normative requirements for AI. This combination yields an understanding of education that accounts for both social and technological developments. The starting point is the assumption that learning always takes place in social and material environments. Knowledge does not arise in isolated individuals, but in interactions shaped by tasks, materials, situations, and meanings. This insight forms a common thread in work on situated learning and context-sensitive knowledge development (Anderson et al., 1996; De Corte, 2012; Gawande & Al-Senaidi, 2015). When AI systems intervene in such processes, they do not simply change procedures. They alter how learners perceive information and how teachers make decisions. As a result, the epistemic conditions of pedagogical practice are shifting toward data-based pattern recognition.

From this perspective, AI can be described as a framework comprising four areas: first, data logics; second, model logics; third, institutional structures; and fourth, social expectations. Data logics describe how information is collected, structured, and weighted. Model logics determine which patterns are recognised, which correlations are calculated, and which probabilities are generated. Institutional structures shape the processes in which models are used. Social expectations shape the way teachers and learners interpret machine outputs. The effect of this formation is well documented. Systems for analysing large amounts of data generate visibility that is closely linked to their technical design. What can be represented in data is considered relevant, whereas what cannot be represented recedes into the background. This shift has been described in numerous studies on algorithmic opacity (Burrell, 2016; Lipton, 2018; Mittelstadt et al., 2016). The exclusion of qualitative, emotional, or situational dimensions narrows what is considered knowledge. This narrowing rarely remains visible, as models appear stable and their outputs appear objective (Selwyn, 2019).

When educational processes are reduced to measurable indicators, the understanding of learning shifts. The focus moves from the educational process itself to the technical measurability of behaviour. A second component concerns the educational classification of machine patterns. Models recognise statistical structures but do not comprehend reasons. This gives rise to selection processes that often remain invisible yet can have a substantial impact on learners (Knox, 2020). This structural mismatch between machine pattern processing and educational requirements has been highlighted repeatedly in research (Amigud & Pell, 2025) and elaborated in technical overviews that distinguish pattern recognition from reasoning (Russel & Norvig, 2021). In educational contexts, this distinction can result in decisions based on similarities and probabilities rather than on reasoned judgements. Models highlight risks without explaining their causes and identify learning paths without understanding their significance, thereby altering the practice of judgement formation. A third theoretical area concerns the normative requirements for AI in educational contexts. It is insufficient to evaluate models solely on performance. Education is a value-bound domain dependent on fairness, participation, transparency, and justifiability. Research by Floridi and Cowls (2019), on ethical frameworks shows that technical systems can only be used if they comply with normative standards designed to safeguard human rights, autonomy, equal treatment, and traceability. Critical work on algorithms further emphasises that unreflective technical systems can reinforce power structures that create or legitimise inequalities (Zweig, 2022).

The fourth theoretical area addresses institutional embedding. Educational institutions follow routines that have developed over time, employing roles, rules, and decision-making processes grounded in human interpretation. Research on digital learning ecologies indicates that technical systems can modify these routines by creating new dependencies and restructuring existing tasks (Williamson & Eynon, 2020). This means that models never operate in isolation; their significance emerges only through interaction with educational expectations and organisational processes. These dynamics generate an epistemic tension that cannot be resolved through technical improvements alone. While technical optimisation increases the precision of statistical processes, educational practice demands more than precision. It requires contextual knowledge, dialogical assessment, professional judgement, and informed decision-making. This form of knowledge cannot be fully captured in data. Research on contextualised, material-bound learning processes illustrates that meaning emerges through interactions rather than from patterns alone (Yeoman & Wilson, 2019).

The theoretical framework of this work therefore describes education as a structure comprising four interrelated areas. First, learning-related experience, which is shaped by interaction, materiality, and social embedding. Second, technical systems that generate patterns and provide structured cues. Third, normative orientation, which specifies the goals and values that apply in educational processes. Fourth, institutional mechanisms that determine how decisions are prepared, made and reviewed. AI is involved in all four areas, thereby changing the conditions under which learning takes place. This approach allows AI to be understood neither as a purely technical tool nor as an abstract threat; rather, it functions as an actor within epistemic orders that produces new forms of knowledge. These outputs must be critically examined before they can legitimise educational decisions. The theoretical considerations outlined here provide the foundation for the subsequent chapters, which analyse the mechanisms of action and delineate the conditions under which AI can be applied responsibly.

3. METHODOLOGY

The methodology of this work describes the approach used to examine the epistemic, normative, and institutional effects of AI systems in educational contexts. The procedure follows a conceptual, theoretical, and reconstructive approach, suited to phenomena shaped by mechanisms embedded in data models, model logics, and institutional routines, which cannot be directly accessed through observation. The analysis does not rely on empirical measurement but on concepts, theoretical models, and normative requirements derived from existing research. This framework allows AI systems to be understood as epistemic formations and clarifies how technical systems relate to human expectations, roles, and institutional structures. The approach is built around seven elements, each contributing to revealing mechanisms often hidden in educational contexts. Conceptual clarification serves as the first step, defining terms such as epistemic formation, operational reliability, responsibility, and context sensitivity. Clear conceptualisation is essential to describe complex educational phenomena and situates AI systems within epistemic structures rather than as abstract technologies (De Corte, 2012; Fricker, 2007). The second element is the critical reconstruction of existing theories, which examines classical models from epistemology, moral theory, computer science, and learning research, identifying assumptions that remain valid and those that require adjustment in light of probabilistic processes and epistemic uncertainty (Burrell, 2016; Mittelstadt et al., 2016; Zweig, 2022).

The third element is normative analysis. This examines the conditions under which machine outputs can be pedagogically, morally, and institutionally justified. Technical systems do not act independently but generate outputs that humans must interpret. According to Floridi & Cowls, (2019), normative criteria such as transparency, fairness, accountability, and protection against bias are central to ensuring that algorithmic support aligns with the values and objectives of educational institutions. Normative analysis identifies where adjustments are necessary to safeguard the integrity of pedagogical decisions and prevent reinforcement of inequitable power structures (Zweig 2022). The fourth element is the use of case studies as resonance spaces. These are not intended for empirical generalisation but to illustrate abstract mechanisms. Automated evaluation, personalised feedback, and predictive analytics each enact a distinct form of algorithmic power. They foreground certain patterns and can entrench dependencies that unsettle established assumptions about how teachers teach and students learn. Case studies illustrate the mechanisms posited in the abstract. Case studies provide concrete instances of mechanisms described theoretically.

The fifth element is epistemic system diagnostics. This examines how AI systems interact with roles, institutional expectations, data structures, and educational processes. Diagnostics reveal which functional logics stabilise and where tensions arise. Analyses of algorithmic opacity and data-driven decision-making demonstrate that models generate order not from reflection but from pattern recognition (Burrell, 2016; Williamson & Eynon, 2020). The sixth element is the deliberate distinction from empirical studies. The work remains theoretical and normative, without providing measurement data or employing statistical methods. This preserves focus on concepts, mechanisms, and structural relations and prevents conflation with empirical questions (Russel & Norvig, 2021). The seventh element is reflexive positioning. Reflexivity makes theoretical assumptions, perspectives, and epistemological frameworks explicit. Every assessment of technical procedures reflects specific expectations.

Reflexivity allows for active consideration and critique of these assumptions and room to detect inevitable blind spots (Fricker, 2007; Williamson & Eynon, 2020).

These seven building blocks form a comprehensive methodological framework. They enable the study of AI systems not as isolated technologies, but as interacting components within technical, epistemic, normative, and institutional orders. The framework defines how models are analysed, which concepts guide interpretation, and which criteria are applied to evaluate algorithmic support in educational contexts. It clarifies how machines process structure assessments, shift roles, and shape decision-making, while preserving the integrity of pedagogical practice. By combining conceptual clarification, critical reconstruction, normative analysis, case studies, system diagnostics, theoretical focus, and reflexivity, the methodology provides a coherent basis for the subsequent chapters, allowing the effects of AI systems to be described without reducing them to technical parameters.

4. ANALYSIS

This chapter examines how AI systems become epistemically effective in educational contexts and how they change structures of knowledge, responsibility and institutional control. The analytical approach does not understand AI as an isolated technical tool, but as a formation composed of data logics, model logics, institutional practices and social expectations. Only the interplay of these elements explains how technical systems influence educational decisions, perceptions and roles. At the outset, it becomes apparent that models only highlight those aspects of a learning process that are represented in data. Dimensions that cannot be captured numerically fade into the background (Ritter et al., 2025). This shift creates an epistemic pre-structuring that describes which characteristics of a learning process appear relevant. Analyses of how data-based methods work show that the visibility of information is shaped by model architectures, training data and evaluation rules, not by educational priorities (Burrell, 2016; Knox, 2020; Mittelstadt et al., 2016). This gives rise to selection processes that often remain invisible but can have a strong impact on learners (Knox, 2020).

A second aspect of the analysis concerns model logic. Probabilistic systems do not work with reasons, but with probabilities. They generate clues, not explanations. Research on model architecture shows that systems recognise patterns without understanding their meaning or being able to classify pedagogical contexts (Russel & Norvig, 2021). This difference between statistical structure and pedagogical meaning leads to a shift towards decisions based on similarities. Teachers and learners must interpret these clues, but often the impression is created that machine outputs represent objective judgements. This is precisely where epistemic risks arise, because statistical models do not produce contextualised reasons. Institutional embedding reinforces these dynamics. Models operate in the context of existing routines and organisational expectations. Educational institutions structure processes, define roles and decide how machine outputs are used. When a model is considered reliable, the relationship between human judgement and technical recommendations changes. Research on digital learning ecologies shows that models can reshape routines once their outputs become standard (Williamson & Eynon, 2020). This can lead to decision-making paths that are shaped more by technical structures than by pedagogical considerations.

The analysis also reveals forms of epistemic emergence. Models not only generate results, but also shape ideas of what constitutes performance, risk, quality or learning progress. Error detection systems provide diagnostic information, but at the same time change the understanding of errors. Analyses of algorithmic impact patterns emphasise that forms of knowledge emerge from the interaction of technical operations and social practices (Mittelstadt et al., 2016). These emergent structures are neither technical nor purely social in nature, but rather hybrid forms of epistemic production. The formation of epistemic authority also plays an important role. Models gain influence as soon as they repeatedly deliver accurate outputs. This consistency of performance generates trust, even though the model logic often remains opaque. Research on epistemic justice shows that such forms of performative credibility can weaken the reflexive examination of machine outputs (Fricker, 2007). Teachers tend to give more weight to machine results when their own assessment is perceived as less reliable. This shifts the balance between professional judgement and technical recommendation.

Another area concerns the preselection of epistemic perspectives. Models only recognise those dimensions of a learning process that can be represented in data sets. Qualitative, emotional or situational aspects become invisible, even though they can be crucial for educational processes. Studies on data-based control of educational routines show that it is precisely this invisibility that can lead to misjudgements (Williamson & Eynon, 2020). When models overemphasise certain characteristics, they alter the image that teachers and learners have of the learning process. This analysis is complemented by institutional stabilisation. Technical systems become routines when they influence exam formats, diagnostic processes or advisory structures. Such continuities lead to machine outputs becoming normative standards. Research on algorithmic biases makes it clear that this can result in new forms of dependency and epistemic narrowing (Zweig, 2022). Educational institutions must therefore examine the extent to which technical systems determine the direction of pedagogical decisions.

A few illustrative examples of the analysis can be given now and will be expanded on below. Automated grading makes transparent the ways in which models of learning structure performance, while at the same time limiting the relevant interpretations that can be made. Adaptive feedback is indicative of learning the path that learning takes and in this way becomes a new kind of role. An example of this is given by predictive learning studies, in which probabilities can become assumed certainties when taken at face value without reflection. Research conducted on feedback and digital learning environments reinforce these observations and point to the ways in which machines participate in pedagogical relations (Devi & Revathi, 2016; Smith & Higgins, 2006; Tsai & Yen, 2013), and in general, AI systems are constructing a new epistemological landscape. This order is not based on reasoning, but on data patterns. Nor is it based on pedagogical reflection, but on statistical structuring. Models can provide valuable insights, but they never define reasons. Education systems are therefore faced with the task of using technical systems in such a way that they support judgments without supplanting normative foundations or human judgment. This chapter thus lays the foundation for the following sections, which describe the three dimensions of algorithmic responsibility. They show the conditions under which machine systems can have a pedagogically sustainable effect and how educational institutions can control the epistemic and normative consequences of algorithmic processes.

4.1 Epistemic Integrity

Epistemic integrity describes the conditions that must be met so that statements made by technical systems can be reliably classified, critically examined, and used in an educationally responsible manner. It applies to all areas in which models generate information that is incorporated into decisions. The analysis shows that epistemic integrity does not arise from technical performance alone, but from a combination of transparency, traceability, validity, coherence, resilience, error culture, and institutional control. Research on algorithmic opacity makes it clear that models are often based on architectures whose decision-making processes are not comprehensible to either teachers or learners (Burrell, 2016; Lipton, 2018). Research on intelligent tutorial systems also shows that complex model structures generate feedback whose internal logic is difficult for users to understand (Woolf, 2009). This lack of transparency makes it difficult to classify results in educational terms. Educational institutions therefore need forms of functional transparency that explain what data a model uses, what parameters determine its behaviour, and what limitations its outputs have.

The second area concerns traceability. Traceability describes the ability of human actors to reconstruct the relationship between inputs and outputs and to assess the logic of an output. Models recognise patterns, but they do not formulate reasons. Technical overviews make it clear that this difference is a fundamental feature of probabilistic systems (Russel & Norvig, 2021). A model can flag a learning difficulty without explaining why exactly this pattern occurs. However, educational decisions require justifiability. Educational institutions must therefore ensure that machine results are not incorporated into decisions without human review. The third area concerns validity. Validity describes the question of whether a model actually measures or evaluates what it claims to recognise. Models designed to assess learning success must not use characteristics that are socially biased or educationally irrelevant. Research on algorithmic risks shows that incorrect classifications can have serious consequences, for example when learners are miscategorised or when biases reinforce historical inequalities (Mittelstadt et al., 2016; Zweig, 2022). Validity is therefore not only a technical property, but also an educational obligation. Models must be guided by quality standards that ensure that results are actually relevant to learning.

Another area concerns epistemic coherence. Coherence describes the compatibility of machine outputs with discursive practices, professional standards, and forms of justification used by teachers. Educational decisions are not based on data patterns alone, but on dialogue, observation and experience. Research on data-based transformations of education systems shows that machine outputs can create epistemic breaks if they cannot be linked to existing educational norms (Williamson & Eynon, 2020). Current AIED research shows that models often provide plausible-looking patterns, but their pedagogical significance remains unclear and, without consistency checks, they can lead to misinterpretations (Holmes & Porayska-Pomsta, 2022).

Resilience describes the ability of systems to function stably and reliably under different conditions. Learning environments are heterogeneous, dynamic and influenced by social factors. Models that only work reliably in idealised data sets lose their significance in real-life situations. Research on bias and failure patterns shows that systems can produce misclassifications in real-life contexts that systematically target certain groups (Burrell, 2016). Educational institutions must therefore check whether models are robust enough to provide useful information under different conditions. The error culture of technical systems is another important area. Models inevitably work incompletely and are prone to errors. Errors arise from inappropriate training data, statistical coincidences or unsuitable feature representations. Research on learning systems and feedback processes shows that misclassifications can have serious consequences if they are not detected and corrected at an early stage (Devi & Revathi, 2016; Smith & Higgins, 2006). A pedagogically responsible error culture requires mechanisms that make errors visible and keep them correctable. Machine outputs should not be understood as final assessments, but as indications that need to be checked, supplemented and, if necessary, withdrawn.

Another area concerns connectivity. Connectivity describes the ability to integrate machine results into educational discourse. A model can recognise patterns, but these patterns must be interpreted, placed in a context of meaning and translated into interactions. Educational processes are based on dialogue, situational assessment and joint meaning-making. Models provide data, but not interpretative frameworks. Research on learning-related contextuality makes it clear that meaning only arises from the interplay of materiality, action and social interaction (Yeoman & Wilson, 2019). Educational institutions must therefore ensure that machine-generated indications do not operate in isolation from educational discourse. Another component concerns controllability. Controllability describes the ability to stop, adapt or limit the effect of systems if results jeopardise educational goals. Models must not create structures that are beyond human control. Normative frameworks emphasise that AI may only be used where institutions have the ability to review and correct decisions (Floridi & Cowls, 2019). This controllability is necessary to limit machine influences on educational processes.

Dealing with biases complements the analysis of epistemic integrity. Biases arise when models systematically disadvantage certain groups or behaviours. Research on algorithmic inequality shows that biases can be carried over from historical data or reinforced by model architectures (Mittelstadt et al. 2016; Zweig, 2019). It is important for educational institutions to not only acknowledge and be self-reflexive about bias, but to also work to mitigate it in order to promote a sense of epistemic justice and keep learners from being subjected to unfair assessments. Another aspect concerns context sensitivity. Models must produce results that can be adapted to the conditions of specific educational situations. Statistical patterns can be educationally inappropriate if they provide context-free information. Research on the situational significance of learning processes shows that learning always takes place in specific environments that cannot be fully described by abstract data (Anderson et al., 1996; De Corte, 2012). Educational institutions therefore need procedures to check whether machine results adequately reflect the respective context.

Finally, epistemic integrity concerns the ability to treat results as worthy of justification. Machine outputs are clues, not judgements. They highlight patterns, but they do not contain arguments. Education, however, requires decisions that can be justified. This calls for a culture of examination, questioning and comparison of different sources of information. Only under these conditions can technical systems have a constructive effect. Overall, this chapter shows that epistemic integrity does not automatically arise when models are used. It also needs a structure that adheres to the golden standards of transparency, validity, coherence, resilience, a culture of error and institutional control. Technical systems help, but are no substitutes for human judgment. Technical assistance must be coupled with epistemic integrity in order to continue to be useful in education.

4.2 Moral Responsibility

Moral responsibility describes the conditions under which actions, decisions, and their consequences can be attributed to humans, even when these decisions are influenced or structured by technical systems. The analysis shows that responsibility cannot be delegated. Models may recognise patterns and generate clues, but they have neither intentions nor moral obligations. They do not grasp reasons and therefore cannot bear responsibility. According to Floridi and Cowls (2019) and Zweig (2022), technical systems lack moral agency.

A first dimension is attributability: the possibility of linking actions and outcomes to an agent able to act, decide, and exercise control. Models generate outputs from data, code, and technical parameters; their effects, however, emerge through social and institutional choices. Educational institutions must therefore specify who is responsible for training data, who selects model architectures, and who authorises a system's use. Without such clarification, accountability risks dissolving into a technical arrangement that cannot itself be held morally answerable.

A second area concerns epistemic agency. Agency in the epistemic sense describes the ability to influence knowledge processes, prepare decisions, and guide perceptions. Models gain such agency as soon as their outputs are treated as reliable. Learners adapt their behaviour when systems highlight weaknesses. Teachers make different decisions when models indicate risks. Institutions realign routines when model-based predictions become part of everyday practice. Research on the history of algorithmic impact shows that these shifts can have strong normative consequences, since model outputs are often perceived as more objective than human assessments (Fricker, 2007; Knox, 2020; Mittelstadt et al., 2016). Educational institutions must therefore recognise and situate this epistemic power so that model-generated information does not function as unchecked judgement. Responsibility also depends on how roles are distributed. Roles set expectations about what teachers, learners, and technical systems are permitted to do. A problematic role distribution arises when models assume tasks that require professional judgement. Studies of feedback structures and digital learning processes suggest that pedagogical roles can shift when model outputs are treated as guiding principles (Devi & Revathi, 2016; Smith & Higgins, 2006). Moral responsibility thus requires an institutionally secured role structure that keeps model outputs indicative rather than prescriptive.

Supervision follows from this. Human actors remain obliged to check, interpret, and, where necessary, correct model outputs. Systems should not operate without oversight. Supervision limits misclassification, protects learners from unjustified decisions, and keeps technical processes within educational boundaries. Normative analyses accordingly stress that responsible use depends on supervision being structurally embedded (Floridi & Cowls, 2019). A further requirement is attention to foreseeable consequences. Model outputs can shape learning pathways, self-assessments, and institutional processes over time. Research on predictive learning systems shows that erroneous forecasts may disadvantage learners or encourage harmful self-attributions (Tsai & Yen, 2013). Institutions therefore carry a duty to examine likely effects before adopting models in sensitive domains. Responsibility emerges not only from decisions already taken but from the obligation to anticipate their implications.

These duties are intensified at the institutional level. Institutions act as collective agents because they select, implement, and evaluate technical systems; they define tasks, delimit areas of application, establish control mechanisms, and stabilise role distributions. Work on institutional transformation indicates that failures often stem less from technical limits than from organisational choices that normalise uncritical use (Williamson & Eynon, 2020). Institutional responsibility therefore requires procedures that document decisions, enforce accountability, and enable correction. One risk that such procedures must address is moral decoupling: the tendency to discount one's own responsibility when decisions are produced or shaped by models. Teachers may treat algorithmic assessments as inherently more objective; learners may experience predicted trajectories as fixed; institutions may assume that responsibility can be shifted onto technical systems. Research on epistemic justice shows that these dynamics increase the likelihood of reproducing existing inequalities (Fricker, 2007). Preventing moral decoupling thus becomes a structural task.

Participation is one component of that structure. It tests a system's educational effects in practice and helps identify unwanted developments early. Studies of digital learning ecologies suggest that exclusion from participation deepens acceptance problems and inequality (Williamson & Eynon, 2020). Decisions must also remain justifiable. Model outputs offer clues rather than arguments. Educational judgement, by contrast, depends on reasons that are comprehensible, contestable, and open to revision. Normative frameworks treat this obligation to justify as indispensable to educational integrity (Floridi & Cowls, 2019).

Responsibility requires recoverability. Erroneous or unjustified decisions must be reversible. Institutions need mechanisms to revisit results, withdraw classifications, and protect learners from long-term harms. Research on algorithmic misdevelopments shows that where recoverability is missing, disadvantages can become durable (Zweig, 2022). In sum, moral responsibility cannot be delegated to technical systems. Models may support and structure educational practice, but responsibility remains human. Institutions must therefore secure institutional, epistemic, and normative safeguards that protect professional judgement and keep technical limitations visible. Only under these conditions can models be used in a pedagogically meaningful way.

4.3 Collective Governance

Collective governance describes the structures through which institutions, groups, and organisational units jointly assume responsibility once technically mediated model systems become educationally effective. Such control is not a product of only technical measures, but also decisions, structures and implicitly established norms at the institutional and organizational level. This is the context in which questions of responsibility, control, transparency, and legitimacy must be understood. Research on normative standards and ethical requirements emphasises that governance is a necessary element of responsible model use because technical systems themselves do not provide moral or institutional guidance (Floridi & Cowls, 2019; Mittelstadt et al., 2016). At its core lies institutional responsibility. Institutions act as collective agents when they select models, authorise their use, and organise the practices that shape system outputs. They determine training data, access permissions, technical adjustments, and procedures for handling results. Research on digital learning ecologies shows that such organisational choices often affect educational impact more strongly than technical properties as such (Williamson & Eynon, 2020). Institutional responsibility therefore consists in creating conditions under which models assist educational processes rather than set their direction.

Governance models specify how this responsibility is coordinated. They refer to the ways decisions are organised and tasks distributed across an institution. Some settings rely on central coordination offices, others on decentralised specialist groups, and many combine both. Each arrangement carries characteristic strengths and vulnerabilities: decentralised structures can preserve local flexibility, while coordinating bodies can stabilise practice in highly regulated areas. The chosen model thus shapes how systems are interpreted, supervised, and revised. Research on institutional change highlights the need for defined roles, lines of responsibility, and pathways for decision-making in governance process (Mittelstadt et al., 2016). Regulations form another pillar. They include guidelines, standards, and institutional expectations that determine how model-based systems are used. This covers requirements for transparency, documentation, validity, error correction, data protection, and accountability. Regulations prevent system outputs from entering educational or administrative routines without reflection, and they link technical operations to institutional and moral standards (Floridi & Cowls, 2019). Their stabilising function lies in creating clarity for teachers, learners, and decision-makers.

Quality assurance works alongside regulation. It involves recurring checks on whether models function reliably, show systematic distortions, or are being used in educationally appropriate ways. On the technical side this can include testing, audits, and monitoring through performance indicators; on the educational side it relies on feedback from practice to evaluate how model use shapes learning processes. Risk research shows that models may generate misjudgements that reproduce or intensify existing inequalities if they remain unchecked (Mittelstadt et al., 2016; Zweig, 2022). Quality assurance therefore operates as an early-warning and adjustment mechanism.

There is also a need for institutional transparency. Here transparency does not only refer to the internals of the model, but it is about the traceability of the goals, decisions, and processes that shape the uptake and use. It refers to transparency of the technical details of a system, including parameters, features, or data structures. Transparency of institution refers to how a system is implemented, whether it is working, and who is responsible for side effects of the system. As soon as this context is explicit, learners can know why they have been used for, and teachers can analyze the results in that context. In the context of automated evaluation, the literature argues, openness generally builds trust and promotes critical discussions (Floridi & Cowls, 2019; Mittelstadt et al., 2016). Supervisory bodies extend this transparency into oversight. Commissions, advisory boards, or quality groups can review models, evaluate risks, and monitor use over time. Because model behaviour and data environments develop dynamically, institutions need standing structures that follow these changes and identify undesirable effects early. Studies of learning-related data ecologies underline that oversight is necessary to reduce systematic bias, unexpected consequences, and interpretive drift (Williamson & Eynon, 2020).

Participation is relevant because governance can only function if it remains closely connected to educational reality. There must be clear means for learners, teachers and others to challenge and question and inform decisions. They tend to impact the direction of learning, practices and habitual forms of assessment. The true limit on participation becomes the meaningful limit on participation, something that functions as a check when the word in nepotistic engaging in such a practice is more than a mere formality. Their institutional choice was measured against the experience of the classroom itself. Participation creates feedback loops and brings plural perspectives into institutional judgement. Research on feedback processes and digital learning interaction shows that exclusion from participation tends to increase mistrust, misinterpretation, and acceptance problems (Devi & Revathi, 2016; Smith & Higgins, 2006).

Ethical guidelines set direction, but they do not carry themselves into practice. These include concepts of fairness, transparency, protection from bias, accountability. Such commitments become a reality only when espoused by institutions who incorporate them as part of the everyday processes . Attitudes need to be placed. Laws must be operational and enforceable. On this point the research into ethical frameworks is clear. Indeed, "principles are nothing but ornaments unless they are translated into processes of decision that effectively inhibit behavior" (Floridi & Cowls, 2019).

Organisational resilience keeps responsibility viable over time. It names an institution's capacity to adjust to technical, social, and normative change without loosening epistemic or pedagogical standards. Models are revised, data environments shift, and legal frameworks evolve. A resilient organisation can absorb these changes, re-check its assumptions, and update practice while keeping its educational aims steady. Research on institutional transformation therefore treats resilience as a condition for sustaining responsible use in the long run (Williamson & Eynon, 2020). This, in turn, depends on competence development. Teachers and staff need the skills to understand models, interpret outputs, and assess risks. Without such competences, recommendations may be misread or accepted uncritically. Studies of digital learning environments therefore highlight professionalisation as a practical precondition of responsible system use (George et al., 2015; Luckin et al., 2016).

Technology assessment complements competence building by examining likely social, educational, and normative consequences before implementation. It enables anticipatory decision-making, since some risks remain invisible in early technical operation. Normative analyses treat such assessment as necessary for identifying undesirable trajectories and for designing protective mechanisms in advance (Floridi & Cowls, 2019). Finally, collective governance requires an explicit distribution of responsibilities. Decision pathways must remain transparent and verifiable; otherwise epistemic risks arise because the sources of model influence cannot be located. Overall, this chapter shows that collective governance provides the basis for controlling model-based systems, limiting risks, and safeguarding educational processes. It brings together normative orientation, organisational structure, and human judgement. Governance is not an optional supplement, but a prerequisite for responsible use in educational contexts.

5. CASE STUDIES

The case studies in this chapter show how model-based systems operate in educational situations and what epistemic, normative, and institutional challenges follow from their use. Rather than treating models in the abstract, the analysis locates them in concrete fields of application. The examples make visible how such systems structure learning processes, highlight patterns, and feed into educational decision-making. They also show how model-generated feedback is read by teachers and learners, and what practical effects these interpretations produce. The case studies draw on research into feedback processes, digital learning environments, and model-based assessment. This literature makes it clear that technical systems are not just additional tools, but can change educational processes and shift roles (Devi & Revathi, 2016; Smith & Higgins, 2006; Tsai & Yen, 2013).

The first example concerns automated grading. Systems of this kind use statistical or language-related features to generate assessments. They can detect regularities that escape human perception and may offer useful indications of strengths and weaknesses. At the same time, work on algorithmic opacity shows that these models reduce learning performance to what can be represented as data (Burrell, 2016). Creativity, argumentative depth, or situational understanding often fall outside that frame because they resist stable formalisation. Analyses of normative tensions note that this reduction introduces epistemic risks, since it promotes a narrow account of performance (Mittelstadt et al., 2016). Further disadvantages arise when forms of expression or language varieties are absent from the training material, a point developed in critical studies of algorithmic inequality (Zweig 2022). Teachers may also overestimate automated assessments if the model logic remains unclear, granting technical outputs an authority grounded in consistency rather than reasons. Scholarly work on epistemic justice cautions that this can reinforce inequality and weaken reflective judgement (Fricker, 2007).

The second example concerns adaptive feedback. Here systems analyse interaction data and derive feedback from recognised patterns. They can guide learners by signalling progress, difficulties, or plausible next steps, and research on feedback structures confirms that such support may reduce uncertainty and aid learning (Smith & Higgins, 2006). Yet these systems also rearrange pedagogical roles. When automated feedback is treated as reliably authoritative, teachers' interpretive space can shrink. Learners may become dependent on system prompts if they follow recommendations without developing their own evaluative capacities. Studies of model-based learning processes show that autonomy suffers when technical feedback is assumed to be more objective than human judgement (Devi & Revathi, 2016). Teachers likewise lose scope for action when system outputs are read as binding reference points. These shifts underline that adaptive feedback remains pedagogically viable only when guidance is interpretable and when human decision-making remains protected.

The third example concerns predictive learning analytics. These systems infer probabilities from historical or current data in order to project likely learning trajectories. They can flag risks, structure learning paths, and enable earlier support, and research on process-related patterns shows that difficulties may be identified before they surface in practice (Tsai & Yen 2013). Predictive systems, however, introduce a distinct epistemic tension. Their outputs rest on statistical similarity rather than on reasons, and work on algorithmic uncertainty notes that this difference is often lost when predictions are treated as objective assessments (Mittelstadt et al., 2016). Being assigned to a risk category can affect motivation, self-image, and institutional decisions. Predictions may also carry historical biases forward, thereby reproducing inequality (Zweig, 2022). Research on algorithmic malfunctions therefore argues that predictive outputs require particular caution in education, since they can shape long-term self-attributions and stabilise institutional routines.

Taken together, the three cases show different forms of algorithmic impact. Automated grading produces assessments that may compress what counts as performance. Adaptive feedback structures learning activity and redistributes roles. The outcomes in all three instances are highlighted by predictive analytics' probabilistic categorization of risk and control over decisions; in each case, the model mediates more than just information about education. They are not determined solely by technical design, but by the institutional, social and normative context in which they operate.

What follows is straightforward. Model-based systems can be educationally helpful, but only when institutions hold onto reflective and accountable practice. Outputs remain indications rather than judgements. Decisions still need reasons, contextual knowledge, and responsibility. Where oversight, contestability, and human discretion are built in, technical systems can support learning without quietly replacing the grounds on which educational judgement rests.

6. DISCUSSION

This discussion draws the earlier strands of algorithmic responsibility together and places them in a wider educational frame. The previous chapters have shown that epistemic integrity, moral responsibility, and collective governance are not separate add-ons. In practice they interlock, because model-based systems reconfigure what is taken as knowledge, shape how decisions unfold, and settle into institutional routines at the same time. That is why technical performance accounts for only part of their educational impact. The rest comes from how systems are embedded and how people read, contest, or rely on their outputs. Epistemic integrity is the starting point for any educational use of models. They offer indications rather than reasons, and those indications are only workable when their production is intelligible and when they fit the discursive practices of teaching and learning. The existing research on probabilistic modeling and opacity points out a common issue: the output of these models is not easily located anywhere, and the opacity of a system increases epistemic uncertainty (Burrell, 2016; Lipton, 2018; Mittelstadt et al., 2016). Transparency, verifiability, and coherency of epistemologies are values that exist as living conditions in institutions, rather than ideals of thought.

Moral responsibility keeps the question of attribution in view. Even when models structure decision paths, responsibility does not travel with them. It stays with those who interpret results, assess their relevance, and translate them into action.

Normative work is clear that technical systems lack moral agency and cannot bear human responsibility (Floridi & Cowls 2019; Zweig 2022). Responsible use therefore depends on clear roles and the capacity of teachers, learners, and institutions to question and revise model outputs. Collective governance provides the organisational counterpart. Governance refers to the arrangements through which model systems are introduced, monitored, constrained, and revised. Studies of digitised education systems warn against passive adoption. If educational aims are to hold, institutions have to shape technical use actively rather than absorb it as a ready-made process (Williamson & Eynon, 2020). This concept of governance implies regulation, monitoring, transparency, participation, and quality control. These are the mechanisms that keep system outputs from hardening into default rules of practice.

A related concern is how technical information enters decision-making at all. Models can steer learning trajectories, signal risks, or influence assessment, but their force is not automatic. It comes from interpretation and framing. Research on data-centred schooling shows that outputs generate expectations that teachers and learners may take up even when no reasons are offered (Williamson & Eynon, 2020). Effects therefore depend on how results are communicated, what authority institutions assign to them, and whether reflective space is kept open. The discussion also highlights a quieter tension around visibility. Models make patterns legible where those patterns can be expressed as data. Qualitative, situational, and relational dimensions often remain outside that field of view. Work on situated learning stresses that these dimensions are central to educational understanding (Anderson et al., 1996; De Corte, 2012; Yeoman & Wilson, 2019). Education systems need to keep this limit in mind, otherwise learning risks being reduced to what is easiest to formalise.

This is where reflexive learning cultures matter. Such cultures make room for critique, comparison, and revision. Research on epistemic justice argues that these reflexive skills are necessary if automatic attributions are to be questioned rather than absorbed as neutral fact (Fricker, 2007). Institutions therefore need routines that normalise scrutiny of model outputs and support learners in forming their own judgements. Another point follows from this: norms do not do anything by themselves. Commitments such as fairness, transparency, and accountability only become effective through institutional translation. Normative scholarship is clear that principles remain inert unless they are tied to concrete processes, role allocations, and enforceable rules (Floridi & Cowls, 2019). Educational institutions thus need responsibilities that are assignable, standards that are checkable, and control mechanisms that can actually be exercised.

Finally, the analysis pushes back against technicist images of education. According to (De Corte, 2012), the ambition to fully measure and standardise learning does not fit pedagogical reality. Research on contextualised learning describes knowledge as situated, relational, and dynamic (Gawande & Al-Senaidi, 2015). Model-based systems cannot capture that complexity in full, and practice becomes distorted when they are treated as if they could. What remains is a simple boundary. Model outputs can guide attention, but they do not supply reasons. They can suggest diagnoses, but they do not make pedagogical arguments. They detect patterns, yet they do not generate context or meaning on their own. The three dimensions of algorithmic responsibility mark the conditions under which technical systems can contribute without eroding epistemic diversity, human accountability, or institutional stability. Educational responsibility stays with people, and institutions have to organise technical use so that it supports learning without displacing reflective judgement.

7. CONCLUSION

The conclusion of this paper shows that using AI systems in education reshapes epistemic, normative, and institutional arrangements in ways that matter for practice. These are not peripheral technical effects. They touch the basis of pedagogical judgement, the ways institutions steer and justify decisions, and the conditions under which knowledge is produced, tested, and treated as legitimate. Throughout the analysis, AI systems have appeared not simply as pattern-recognition tools but as forces that reconfigure how learners understand themselves, how teachers prepare and interpret decisions, and how educational routines are organised. One result stands out: responsible use depends on reading outputs as indications. Models yield probabilities and correlations, not reasons; they mark patterns without providing meaning. Educational decisions, by contrast, require justification and contextual interpretation. The epistemic analysis has shown that AI becomes educationally useful only where transparency, validity, coherence, an explicit error culture, and institutional control are in place (Burrell, 2016; Lipton, 2018; Mittelstadt et al., 2016).

Responsibility follows the same logic. Even where models shape decision pathways, accountability does not shift to the system. It remains with the people and institutions that choose, interpret, and act on outputs. Normative scholarship is unambiguous on this point: technical systems lack moral agency, and educational choices must be defended through human judgement (Floridi & Cowls 2019; Zweig, 2022). Moral responsibility is not satisfied by accepting or rejecting results after the fact. It requires sustained engagement with outputs, a conscious division of roles, and procedures that allow correction when systems mislead. Institutional analysis points in the same direction. Long-term responsible use is only possible where education systems develop governance arrangements that are transparent, reflexive, and resilient. Research on digital educational ecologies shows how AI systems can alter practice by changing routines and hardening new expectations (Williamson

& Eynon, 2020). Governance is the work of keeping such changes answerable to educational aims. It has to be carried through regulation, quality assurance, oversight, participation, and competence development. Without these layers, AI processes can quietly narrow assessment cultures or displace pedagogical priorities.

The analysis also pushes back against technicist pictures of education. Learning is relational, situated, and socially embedded. Work on contextualised learning shows that qualitative, emotional, and situational dimensions resist full measurement (Anderson et al., 1996; De Corte, 2012; Yeoman & Wilson, 2019). AI systems register these aspects only partially. Institutions should be cautious, then, when technical outputs start to define performance standards or drive curricular priorities. Looking forward, emerging model forms will sharpen these tensions. Multimodal systems, self-optimising architectures, and tightly integrated learning environments will widen the gap between technical patterning and educational meaning. Future research needs to follow what happens to knowledge practices when systems do not merely inform decisions but also anticipate trajectories and generate suggestions. It also needs to ask how teachers can rework their professional role in the space between technical support and independent judgement, and how learners can sustain reflective capacities when system prompts become routine.

The point, in the end, is not about whether AI performs well in isolation. It is about whether education systems can protect and renew their epistemic and normative foundations while using technical support. AI can help organise attention and offer guidance, but it cannot replace judgement. Educational practice needs room for reasons, critique, and reflection. Responsible use takes shape where technical capacities are held within human autonomy, institutional stabiity, and pedagogical openness.

8. LIMITATIONS

The limits of this study follow from its purpose. It is a conceptual paper, and it keeps some distance from empirical description in order to stay focused on structural questions. Treating AI systems as epistemic formations makes it possible to analyse how they reorganise knowledge practices, normative expectations, and institutional procedure. The cost of that choice is that several aspects of use remain only lightly specified. The most obvious gap is empirical. The paper does not track concrete deployments, classroom routines, or the situated responses of teachers and learners. Yet model outputs do not carry stable meaning on their own; what they come to mean depends on how they are taken up in practice (Devi & Revathi, 2016; Smith & Higgins). Research on feedback processes and technology-supported learning already shows that use varies sharply across settings and populations 2006 (Tsai &

Yen, 2013). Without observation of that variation, the argument here cannot offer context-sensitive claims.

A second limitation concerns technical variety. Models differ in architecture, training material, feature selection, and intended purpose. Work on probabilistic methods and opacity makes clear that these differences shape behaviour, interpretability, and error patterns in ways that matter for education (Burrell, 2016; Lipton, 2018; Russel & Norvig, 2021). The analysis necessarily generalises to bring shared mechanisms into view, but that move narrows what can be said about particular systems or configurations.

The discussion is also anchored in normative concerns. The discourse is firmly situated on concepts such as fairness, transparency, accountability and epistemic integrity. Every factor, such as political, economic, and legal drivers, are recognized, but are placed at the periphery, though they are the very factors that in many ways determine what actually gets done and how. Among these are several normative studies of AI that reiterate the embeddedness of technological developments in broader forms of social and political organization (Floridi & Cowls, 2019; Mittelstadt et al., 2016). This study operates under that assumption, but does not specifically trace those entanglements.

Institutional diversity adds another boundary. Educational organisations differ in resources, cultures of governance, professional routines, and technical infrastructures. Research on institutional transformation indicates that these differences strongly shape how model-based systems are implemented and how their outputs are interpreted (Williamson & Eynon, 2020). The responsibility and governance structures outlined here therefore function as general orientation. They cannot capture the full range of institutional realities. There is a related gap on the level of lived experience. The analysis shows that models can shift pedagogical roles, but it cannot say how teachers and learners actually deal with epistemic uncertainty, recommendations, or algorithmic attributions over time. Empirical studies could show how trust is formed, where scepticism persists, and how learners' self-perception changes in sustained use. These subjective processes are central to educational design, yet they are treated here only theoretically.

The argument sits under a moving technological horizon. Model architectures, data infrastructures, and learning platforms develop quickly. Multimodal systems, generative models, and more deeply integrated learning environments will raise questions that fall outside the present scope. The concepts developed here should remain useful, but they will need adjustment as practices evolve. Taken together, these limits clarify what the paper contributes. The paper offers a conceptual and analytical framework, but it can register empirical diversity, technical specificity, and lived experience only indirectly. That narrowing is a trade-off made in order to develop a clear theoretical account. At the same time, the gaps point to the most obvious directions for future researchwork that can test, extend, and refine the concepts developed here.

REFERENCES

Amigud, A., & Pell, D. J. (2025). Responsible and Ethical Use of AI in Education: Are We Forcing a Square Peg into a Round Hole? *WORLD (Oakland, Calif.)*, *6*(2), 81. DOI: 10.3390/world6020081

Anderson, J. R., Reder, L. M., & Simon, H. A. (1996). Situated Learning and Education. *Educational Researcher*, *25*(4), 5–11. DOI: 10.3102/0013189X025004005

Burrell, J. (2016). How the Machine "thinks": Understanding Opacity in Machine Learning Algorithms. *Big Data & Society*, *3*(1), 1–12. DOI: 10.1177/2053951715622512

De Corte, E. (2012). Constructive, Self-Regulated, Situated, and Collaborative Learning: An Approach for the Acquisition of Adaptive Competence. *Journal of Education*, *192*(2-3), 33–47. DOI: 10.1177/0022057412192002-307

Devi, V. A., & Revathi, K. (2016). A Brief Review of Literature on Immediate Feedback Studies in CALL. *Rupkatha Journal on Interdisciplinary Studies in Humanities*, *8*(3), 262–268. DOI: 10.21659/rupkatha.v8n3.27

Floridi, L., & Cowls, J. (2019). A Unified Framework of Five Principles for AI in Society. *Harvard Data Science Review*, *1*(1). Advance online publication. DOI: 10.1162/99608f92.8cd550d1

Fricker, M. (2007). Epistemic Injustice: Power and the Ethics of Knowing. In academic.oup.com. Oxford University Press.

Gawande, V., & Al-Senaidi, S. (2015). Situated Learning: Learning in a Contextual Environment. *International Journal of Computing Academic Research*, *4*(4), 207–213. https://meacse.org/ijcar/archives/70.pdf

George, S., Michel, C., & Ollagnier-Beldame, M. (2015). Favouring reflexivity in technology-enhanced learning systems: Towards smart uses of traces. *Interactive Learning Environments*, *24*(7), 1389–1407. DOI: 10.1080/10494820.2015.1016532

Holmes, W., & Porayska-Pomsta, K. (2022). *The Ethics of Artificial Intelligence in Education*. Taylor & Francis. DOI: 10.4324/9780429329067

Knox, J. (2020). Artificial intelligence and education in china. *Learning, Media and Technology*, *45*(3), 1–14. DOI: 10.1080/17439884.2020.1754236

Lipton, Z. C. (2018). The mythos of model interpretability. *Communications of the ACM*, *61*(10), 36–43. DOI: 10.1145/3233231

Luckin, R., Holmes, W., Griffiths, M., & Pearson, L. (2016). *Intelligence Unleashed: An Argument for AI in Education.*

Mittelstadt, B. D., Allo, P., Taddeo, M., Wachter, S., & Floridi, L. (2016). The Ethics of algorithms: Mapping the Debate. *Big Data & Society*, *3*(2), 1–21. DOI: 10.1177/2053951716679679

Ritter, L. A., Barenkamp, M., & Moch, E. (2025). Platform and control: Technical data protection in digital learning systems. *Information Systems Management.* Advance online publication. DOI: 10.1365/s35764-025-00571-4

Russel, S., & Norvig, P. (2021). *Artificial intelligence: A Modern approach* (4th ed.). Prentice Hall.

Selwyn, N. (2019). *Should Robots Replace Teachers? AI and the Future of Education.* Editorial: Polity Press.

Smith, H., & Higgins, S. (2006). Opening classroom interaction: The importance of feedback. *Cambridge Journal of Education*, *36*(4), 485–502. DOI: 10.1080/03057640601048357

Tsai, C.-H., & Yen, J.-C. (2013). The Development and Evaluation of a Kinect Sensor Assisted Learning System on the Spatial Visualization Skills. *Procedia: Social and Behavioral Sciences*, *103*, 991–998. DOI: 10.1016/j.sbspro.2013.10.423

Williamson, B., & Eynon, R. (2020). Historical threads, missing links, and future directions in AI in education. *Learning, Media and Technology*, *45*(3), 1–13. DOI: 10.1080/17439884.2020.1798995

Woolf, B. P. (2009). *Building intelligent interactive tutors: student-centered strategies for revolutionizing e-learning*. Morgan Kaufmann Publishers/Elsevier.

Yeoman, P., & Wilson, S. (2019). Designing for situated learning: Understanding the relations between material properties, designed form and emergent learning activity. *British Journal of Educational Technology*, *50*(5), 2090–2108. DOI: 10.1111/bjet.12856

Zweig, K. A. (2022). *Awkward Intelligence: Where AI Goes Wrong, Why It Matters, and What We Can Do about It*. MIT Press. DOI: 10.7551/mitpress/13915.001.0001

Chapter 4
Ethical Concerns and Bias in Educational Machine Learning Systems

Rehan Saeed Khan
http://orcid.org/0009-0008-3259-4997
Jamia Hamdard University, India

ABSTRACT

The increasing integration of machine learning technologies in education has generated significant ethical concerns related to bias, privacy, and accountability. While data-driven systems promise personalized learning, they also risk reinforcing existing educational inequalities. This chapter critically examines ethical challenges associated with educational machine learning systems, focusing on sources of bias, data protection, and governance mechanisms. Drawing on interdisciplinary literature, it categorizes bias into data, labeling, algorithmic, and societal forms and analyzes their implications for fairness and equity in educational contexts. It proposes ethically grounded strategies for bias mitigation, emphasizing inclusive data practices, human oversight, fairness-aware design, and institutional governance. By situating machine learning within broader educational and social frameworks, the chapter highlights the need for human-centered and ethically informed approaches to ensure that artificial intelligence contributes to trust, inclusion, and justice in education.

1. INTRODUCTION

Artificial Intelligence (AI) and Machine Learning (ML) technologies have increasingly become embedded within contemporary educational systems, reshaping how teaching, learning, assessment, and institutional decision-making

DOI: 10.4018/979-8-3373-7467-3.ch004

are conducted. From adaptive learning platforms and intelligent tutoring systems to automated grading tools and predictive analytics for student retention, machine learning-driven applications promise efficiency, personalization, and data-informed educational governance. Educational institutions across the world, including those in developing countries such as India, are rapidly adopting AI-enabled systems to address challenges related to scale, diversity, and access. However, alongside these technological advancements, critical ethical concerns have emerged regarding bias, privacy, transparency, and accountability in educational machine learning systems.

Education is a domain that directly influences human development, social mobility, and democratic participation. Consequently, any technological intervention within education carries profound moral and social implications. Unlike purely commercial applications, algorithmic decisions in educational contexts can affect learners' academic trajectories, self-perception, access to opportunities, and long-term career prospects. When machine learning systems are trained on biased data, designed without ethical safeguards, or deployed without adequate oversight, they risk reinforcing existing inequalities rather than mitigating them. This raises important questions about whether AI-driven educational technologies genuinely promote equity or inadvertently reproduce structural disadvantages based on socio-economic status, gender, language, disability, or regional background.

Bias in machine learning is not merely a technical malfunction but a socio-technical phenomenon rooted in historical, institutional, and cultural contexts. In educational settings, bias may manifest through skewed datasets, subjective labeling practices, algorithmic design choices, or broader societal inequalities embedded in digital infrastructures. For instance, predictive models used to identify "at-risk" students may disproportionately flag learners from marginalized communities, while automated assessment tools may disadvantage students who do not conform to dominant linguistic or cultural norms. Such outcomes challenge the ethical foundations of education, which emphasize fairness, inclusivity, and equal opportunity.

Privacy concerns further complicate the ethical landscape of AI in education. Educational machine learning systems rely heavily on extensive data collection, including academic performance, behavioral patterns, emotional responses, and even biometric information in some cases. While data-driven insights can enhance personalized learning experiences, they also introduce risks related to surveillance, unauthorized data sharing, and erosion of students' autonomy. In many educational institutions, particularly in the Global South, students and parents may have limited awareness or control over how their data are collected, stored, and used. The asymmetry of power between institutions, technology providers, and learners intensifies ethical concerns surrounding informed consent and data governance.

The ethical implications of AI in education are further magnified by the opacity of many machine learning models. Complex algorithms, often described as "black boxes," make it difficult for educators, students, and policymakers to understand how decisions are made. Lack of transparency undermines trust and accountability, particularly when algorithmic outputs influence high-stakes decisions such as grading, placement, or admission. In educational environments, where trust and human judgment are central, the inability to explain or contest algorithmic decisions poses serious ethical challenges.

Globally, governments and international organizations have begun to acknowledge the ethical risks associated with AI deployment. Frameworks proposed by UNESCO, the OECD, and the European Union emphasize principles such as fairness, transparency, accountability, and respect for human rights. In India, initiatives aligned with the National Education Policy (NEP) 2020 and the Digital Personal Data Protection Act have brought ethical considerations into discussions on educational technology. However, translating high-level ethical principles into practical, enforceable guidelines for educational machine learning systems remains a complex task. The rapid pace of technological adoption often outstrips the development of regulatory and institutional safeguards.

Against this backdrop, this chapter seeks to critically examine ethical concerns and bias in educational machine learning systems through an interdisciplinary lens. By integrating perspectives from computer science, educational theory, and applied ethics, the chapter aims to move beyond purely technical interpretations of bias and address its social and moral dimensions. Particular attention is given to how bias and privacy concerns intersect within educational contexts, influencing learners' experiences and institutional practices. The chapter also considers how ethical challenges may differ across global and Indian contexts, where disparities in infrastructure, data quality, and regulatory capacity shape the deployment of AI in education.

The central argument advanced in this chapter is that ethical considerations must be embedded throughout the lifecycle of educational machine learning systems—from data collection and model design to deployment and evaluation. Ethical AI in education cannot be treated as an afterthought or a compliance exercise; rather, it must be understood as a continuous, reflexive process that prioritizes human values alongside technological efficiency. By systematically analyzing sources of bias, privacy risks, and ethical dilemmas, this chapter aims to contribute to the growing discourse on responsible AI and support the development of more equitable, transparent, and accountable educational technologies.

The remainder of the chapter is structured as follows. The next section provides a detailed background and literature review on AI ethics and bias in educational contexts. Subsequent sections examine different types of bias in educational machine learning systems, followed by an analysis of privacy and data ethics concerns. The chapter then engages with ethical theories and governance frameworks relevant to

AI in education, before discussing bias mitigation strategies and responsible design practices. The final sections highlight future research directions and conclude with recommendations for policymakers, educators, and technology developers.

2. BACKGROUND AND LITERATURE REVIEW

The ethical implications of Artificial Intelligence and Machine Learning have received growing scholarly attention over the past decade, particularly as algorithmic systems increasingly influence social institutions such as education. Early research on machine learning focused predominantly on performance optimization, accuracy, and scalability, often treating ethical considerations as peripheral concerns. However, as AI-driven systems began to affect human lives in consequential ways, scholars from computer science, education, philosophy, and social sciences began to interrogate the normative assumptions embedded within algorithmic decision-making processes (Floridi et al., 2018; Mittelstadt et al., 2016).

Within educational contexts, machine learning applications have expanded rapidly. Adaptive learning platforms tailor instructional content based on learners' progress; predictive analytics systems identify students at risk of dropout; automated grading tools assess assignments at scale; and recommender systems suggest learning pathways. While these systems promise personalization and efficiency, researchers increasingly argue that they also introduce ethical risks related to bias, opacity, and surveillance (Williamson, 2017; Selwyn, 2019). Education, unlike many other domains, is fundamentally value-laden, making ethical scrutiny of AI systems particularly urgent.

2.1 Evolution of AI Ethics Discourse

The broader discourse on AI ethics has been shaped by concerns surrounding fairness, accountability, transparency, and explainability—often referred to collectively as the FATE principles (Barocas, Hardt, & Narayanan, 2019). Scholars emphasize that machine learning models do not operate in isolation but are embedded within social systems that reflect power relations, institutional priorities, and cultural norms. Consequently, algorithmic bias is increasingly understood not as an anomaly but as an outcome of socio-technical interactions between data, designers, and deployment environments (Noble, 2018).

Ethical frameworks proposed by international organizations such as UNESCO (2021) and the OECD (2019) stress the importance of human-centered AI that respects autonomy, dignity, and justice. These frameworks advocate for inclusive design, accountability mechanisms, and robust governance structures. However, critics note that high-level ethical principles often lack concrete guidance for implementation, particularly in complex domains like education where outcomes are difficult to quantify and moral stakes are high (Jobin et al., 2019).

2.2 Bias in Machine Learning: Conceptual Foundations

Bias in machine learning has been widely examined in technical literature, often categorized according to stages of the ML lifecycle. Researchers highlight how bias may originate during data collection, labeling, model selection, or evaluation (Mehrabi et al., 2021). In educational contexts, data bias frequently arises due to unequal access to digital resources, variations in institutional practices, and historical inequalities embedded within educational systems. For instance, datasets derived from elite institutions may not represent learners from rural or under-resourced settings, leading to models that generalize poorly across diverse populations.

Labeling bias is another critical concern, particularly in educational assessment. Human evaluators involved in grading or annotation may unconsciously project their own cultural, linguistic, or cognitive biases onto students' work. When such labels are used to train machine learning models, subjective judgments become formalized and scaled, potentially amplifying inequities (Baker & Hawn, 2021). Algorithmic bias further emerges from design choices such as feature selection, optimization objectives, and threshold settings, which may privilege efficiency or predictability over fairness.

Societal bias represents a broader category, capturing how social hierarchies related to caste, gender, language, and socio-economic status are reflected in educational data. Scholars argue that machine learning systems often inherit these biases because they learn from historical patterns rather than normative ideals of equity (O'Neil, 2016). In education, this may result in AI systems that disproportionately disadvantage already marginalized learners, contradicting the emancipatory goals of education.

2.3 AI and Ethics in Education

Educational researchers have increasingly emphasized that AI systems must be evaluated not only for technical accuracy but also for pedagogical and ethical appropriateness. Williamson and Eynon (2020) argue that educational AI reshapes governance by shifting decision-making authority from educators to algorithmic systems. This transformation raises concerns about professional autonomy, accountability, and the role of human judgment in education.

Ethical debates in educational AI often center on fairness and inclusion. Studies indicate that automated assessment systems may disadvantage students with non-standard linguistic backgrounds or disabilities (Bennett & Checkel, 2015). Similarly, learning analytics tools that monitor engagement may misinterpret cultural differences in participation, leading to biased interventions. Such findings underscore the need for contextual sensitivity and ethical reflexivity in AI system design.

Privacy is another dominant theme in the literature. Educational machine learning systems rely on extensive data collection, often blurring the boundaries between learning support and surveillance. Scholars caution that continuous monitoring of students' behavior can undermine trust, autonomy, and psychological well-being (Slade & Prinsloo, 2013). The ethical tension between personalization and privacy has become particularly salient with the rise of remote learning platforms and EdTech ecosystems.

2.4 Policy and Regulatory Perspectives

From a policy perspective, governments and institutions are grappling with how to regulate AI in education without stifling innovation. The European Union's proposed AI Act classifies educational AI systems as "high-risk," requiring stricter oversight and transparency obligations. UNESCO's recommendations on AI in education emphasize inclusivity, human oversight, and data protection. In India, ethical discussions intersect with broader digital governance initiatives, including the Digital Personal Data Protection Act and the implementation of NEP 2020, which encourages technology adoption while emphasizing equity and access.

Despite these developments, scholars argue that regulatory frameworks often lag behind technological deployment. Many educational institutions lack the expertise or resources to conduct ethical audits of AI systems, leading to reliance on third-party vendors with limited accountability. This gap between policy aspirations and institutional practice highlights the need for context-specific ethical guidelines and capacity-building initiatives.

2.5 Research Gaps

Although the literature on AI ethics and bias is expanding, several gaps remain. First, much of the existing research focuses on Western educational contexts, with limited attention to developing countries where infrastructural and social challenges differ significantly. Second, technical and ethical analyses are often siloed, resulting in fragmented understandings of bias and responsibility. Third, empirical studies examining long-term impacts of educational AI on learners' trajectories are still scarce.

This chapter seeks to address these gaps by offering an integrated analysis of bias, privacy, and ethics in educational machine learning systems, with particular attention to the Indian context. By synthesizing interdisciplinary literature and ethical frameworks, it aims to contribute to a more nuanced understanding of how AI can be aligned with educational values and social justice objectives.

3. CONCEPTUAL FRAMEWORK: ETHICAL CONCERNS AND BIAS IN EDUCATIONAL MACHINE LEARNING SYSTEMS

The increasing adoption of machine learning systems in education has generated significant ethical debate, particularly regarding fairness, transparency, and accountability. Unlike traditional educational technologies, machine learning systems derive their decision-making capacity from data-driven processes, making their outputs contingent upon historical patterns, institutional practices, and human judgment (Floridi et al., 2018). Consequently, ethical concerns in educational machine learning must be understood as socio-technical issues rather than purely technical challenges.

Figure 1. Conceptual framework illustrating the interrelationship between data, algorithm, ethical principles, and educational outcomes in machine learning-driven educational systems

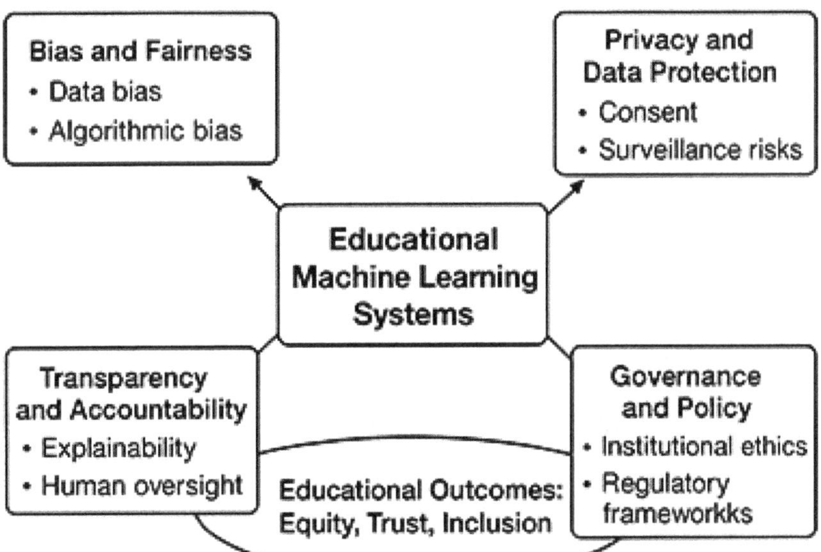

This section presents a conceptual framework that situates bias as a multi-layered phenomenon operating across the educational machine learning lifecycle. The framework integrates technical processes, types of bias, and ethical principles, providing a structured lens for analyzing how ethical concerns emerge and interact within educational AI systems (Mittelstadt et al., 2016).

3.1 Educational Machine Learning Lifecycle

Machine learning systems deployed in educational environments typically operate across four interconnected stages: data collection, data labeling and preprocessing, model development, and system deployment with feedback mechanisms (Suresh & Guttag, 2021). Each stage introduces distinct ethical risks that may affect learners, educators, and institutions.

During the data collection stage, educational platforms gather extensive information, including academic records, behavioral logs, engagement metrics, and demographic attributes. While such data enables personalization, scholars note that data collection in educational settings often lacks meaningful informed consent, particularly when participation in digital platforms is institutionally mandated (Slade & Prinsloo, 2013). This creates ethical concerns related to autonomy and power asymmetries between learners and institutions.

The labeling and preprocessing stage involves human judgment, particularly in contexts such as grading, behavioral classification, and learning difficulty identification. Research indicates that human annotators may unconsciously embed cultural, linguistic, or institutional biases into labeled datasets, which subsequently influence model behavior (Baker & Hawn, 2021). In education, where evaluation plays a central role in shaping academic trajectories, such biases are especially consequential.

Model development includes the selection of algorithms, features, and optimization objectives. Ethical concerns arise when models prioritize predictive accuracy or efficiency without considering distributive fairness or pedagogical appropriateness (Barocas et al., 2019). Finally, during deployment, feedback loops may reinforce bias, as algorithmic decisions influence future data generation, leading to self-perpetuating inequities over time (O'Neil, 2016).

3.2 Foundational Categories of Bias

Building on existing ethical and technical scholarship, the framework categorizes bias in educational machine learning into four interrelated types: data bias, labeling bias, algorithmic bias, and societal bias (Mehrabi et al., 2021). These categories reflect both technical sources of bias and broader social influences shaping educational data.

Data bias arises when training datasets are unrepresentative of the learner populations to which systems are applied. In education, disparities in digital access, institutional resources, and regional infrastructure contribute to uneven data representation (Williamson, 2017).

Labeling bias emerges from subjective human judgments during annotation processes. Studies show that evaluative criteria may privilege certain communication styles or learning behaviors, disadvantaging students from diverse cultural or linguistic backgrounds (Bennett & Checkel, 2015).

Algorithmic bias results from design choices embedded within models, including feature selection and optimization strategies. In educational contexts, algorithmic bias may manifest when systems standardize learning behaviors, thereby marginalizing non-conforming or creative responses (Selwyn, 2019).

Societal bias reflects broader structural inequalities related to socio-economic status, gender, caste, language, or disability. Machine learning systems trained on historical educational data often reproduce these inequalities, unless deliberate corrective measures are implemented (Noble, 2018).

These foundational categories of bias provide the basis for examining their ethical implications in educational machine learning systems, discussed in the following section.

3.3 Ethical Principles Underpinning the Framework

The conceptual framework is anchored in ethical principles commonly articulated in AI ethics literature, including fairness, transparency, accountability, and respect for human autonomy (Floridi et al., 2018). In educational settings, these principles acquire specific meanings shaped by pedagogical values and institutional responsibilities.

Fairness in education requires that machine learning systems do not systematically disadvantage particular learner groups. Transparency demands that algorithmic processes are explainable to educators and learners, enabling informed decision-making (Diakopoulos, 2016). Accountability emphasizes institutional responsibility for the outcomes of algorithmic decisions, while autonomy underscores the importance of preserving learners' agency in data-driven educational environments (Mittelstadt et al., 2016).

3.4 Education as a Socio-Technical System

A central premise of this framework is the recognition of education as a socio-technical system in which technological tools interact with social norms, institutional policies, and pedagogical practices (Williamson & Eynon, 2020). Ethical risks emerge not only from algorithms themselves but from how they are embedded within educational governance structures.

For example, predictive analytics systems used for student retention may shift institutional priorities toward measurable outcomes, potentially marginalizing holistic educational goals. When algorithmic recommendations are treated as objective or authoritative, educators' professional judgment may be constrained, raising concerns about autonomy and accountability (Selwyn, 2019).

3.5 Framework Overview and Analytical Utility

The conceptual framework presented in this section integrates the machine learning lifecycle, types of bias, and ethical principles into a unified analytical model. It provides a foundation for examining ethical concerns across subsequent sections of this chapter, including detailed analyses of bias, privacy, governance, and mitigation strategies.

By situating ethical concerns within both technical processes and social contexts, the framework supports a more nuanced understanding of educational machine learning systems. This approach aligns with interdisciplinary scholarship advocating for responsible, context-sensitive, and value-driven applications of AI in education (UNESCO, 2021).

4. TYPES OF BIAS IN EDUCATIONAL MACHINE LEARNING SYSTEMS

Bias in educational machine learning systems constitutes one of the most significant ethical challenges associated with the growing use of artificial intelligence in education. As algorithmic systems increasingly inform decisions related to assessment, student support, and institutional planning, the consequences of biased outcomes become amplified and institutionalized (O'Neil, 2016). Unlike isolated human judgment, machine learning systems scale decision-making processes, making bias both persistent and difficult to detect without deliberate ethical scrutiny.

This section examines four primary types of bias—data bias, labeling bias, algorithmic bias, and societal bias—that commonly arise in educational machine learning systems. These categories align with contemporary ethical and technical literature and provide a structured framework for analyzing how bias manifests across educational contexts (Mehrabi et al., 2021).

4.1 Data Bias

Data bias occurs when the datasets used to train machine learning models are incomplete, unrepresentative, or systematically skewed. In educational contexts, data bias frequently reflects disparities in access to digital infrastructure, quality of instruction, and institutional resources (Williamson, 2017). For example, machine learning systems trained primarily on data from urban or well-funded institutions may fail to generalize effectively to rural or under-resourced educational settings.

Historical educational data often embed existing inequalities related to socio-economic status, language, and regional development. When such data are used without critical evaluation, machine learning systems risk reproducing past injustices under the guise of objectivity (Noble, 2018). From an ethical standpoint, data bias undermines the principle of fairness by privileging certain learner groups while marginalizing others.

Mitigating data bias requires inclusive data collection practices, regular dataset audits, and sensitivity to contextual variation across educational environments (Suresh & Guttag, 2021).

4.2 Labeling Bias

Labeling bias emerges during the annotation of educational data, particularly when labels are assigned through subjective human judgment. In applications such as automated grading, engagement classification, or identification of learning difficulties, educators and evaluators play a crucial role in determining training labels. Research indicates that such judgments may be influenced by cultural norms, institutional expectations, or implicit biases (Baker & Hawn, 2021).

In multilingual and culturally diverse educational settings, labeling bias may disproportionately affect students whose communication styles or learning behaviors deviate from standardized expectations (Bennett & Checkel, 2015). When machine learning models are trained on biased labels, these subjective evaluations become formalized and scaled, potentially shaping students' academic trajectories in ethically problematic ways.

Ethically responsible practice requires reflexive labeling processes, use of multiple annotators, and mechanisms to identify and correct inconsistencies in labeled data (Mehrabi et al., 2021).

4.3 Algorithmic Bias

Algorithmic bias originates from design decisions embedded within machine learning models, including feature selection, optimization objectives, and decision thresholds. In educational machine learning systems, algorithmic bias may arise when models prioritize predictive accuracy, efficiency, or standardization without adequate consideration of pedagogical fairness (Barocas et al., 2019).

For instance, predictive models designed to identify "at-risk" students often rely on indicators such as attendance records or prior academic performance. While statistically informative, these indicators may correlate strongly with socio-economic disadvantage, leading to disproportionate targeting of marginalized learners (O'Neil, 2016). Similarly, automated assessment systems may privilege conventional responses, disadvantaging students who demonstrate creativity or alternative problem-solving strategies.

Algorithmic bias raises significant concerns related to transparency and accountability. When model logic is opaque, educators may struggle to interpret or contest algorithmic recommendations, potentially undermining professional judgment and ethical responsibility (Diakopoulos, 2016).

4.4 Societal Bias

Societal bias refers to the broader structural inequalities that shape educational data and influence machine learning outcomes. Factors such as gender, caste, socio-economic status, language, and disability significantly affect educational opportunities and experiences. Machine learning systems trained on data reflecting these inequalities may inadvertently reinforce existing social hierarchies (Noble, 2018).

In the Indian educational context, societal bias is particularly salient due to persistent disparities across regions and social groups. Predictive analytics systems may associate lower performance with students from marginalized communities without accounting for systemic barriers, thereby normalizing inequality rather than addressing its root causes (Kumar & Singh, 2022).

Addressing societal bias requires recognizing that ethical challenges in educational machine learning extend beyond technical fixes. Institutional commitment to equity, inclusive policy design, and interdisciplinary collaboration are essential for aligning AI systems with social justice objectives (UNESCO, 2021).

4.5 Comparative Overview of Bias Types

To synthesize the analysis presented in this section, Table 1 provides a comparative overview of the four types of bias in educational machine learning systems, their sources, manifestations, and ethical implications.

Table 1. Types of bias in educational machine learning systems

Type of Bias	Source	Manifestation in Education	Ethical Implications
Data Bias	Non-representative or incomplete datasets	Underrepresentation of rural, marginalized, or digitally disadvantaged learners	Violates fairness and equity; leads to unequal model performance
Labeling Bias	Subjective human judgment during annotation	Biased grading, misclassification of learning difficulties or engagement levels	Reinforces stereotypes; affects academic evaluation and student trajectories
Algorithmic Bias	Design choices in model architecture and optimization	Disproportionate identification of "at-risk" students; penalization of non-standard responses	Undermines accountability and transparency; limits pedagogical flexibility
Societal Bias	Structural inequalities embedded in historical data	Systematic disadvantage to learners based on socio-economic status, caste, language, or gender	Normalizes social inequality; conflicts with social justice goals of education

4.6 Ethical Implications for Educational Practice

The presence of bias in educational machine learning systems poses serious ethical risks to fairness, trust, and institutional legitimacy. Biased systems may undermine confidence in educational technologies, particularly among marginalized learners who are most vulnerable to algorithmic disadvantage (Selwyn, 2019). Furthermore, reliance on biased algorithmic outputs may constrain educators' autonomy and diminish opportunities for contextualized human judgment.

Recognizing bias as a socio-technical phenomenon underscores the need for ethical governance and continuous evaluation. Educational institutions must approach bias mitigation as an ongoing ethical responsibility rather than a one-time technical correction.

5. PRIVACY AND DATA PROTECTION IN EDUCATIONAL MACHINE LEARNING

The increasing integration of machine learning technologies into educational environments has intensified ethical concerns related to privacy and data protection. Educational machine learning systems rely on extensive collections of personal, academic, and behavioral data to generate predictive and adaptive insights. While such data-driven approaches promise personalization and efficiency, scholars caution that they also introduce significant ethical risks related to surveillance, autonomy, and misuse of learner information (Slade & Prinsloo, 2013; Williamson, 2017).

5.1 Nature and Sensitivity of Educational Data

Educational data is inherently sensitive due to its personal, developmental, and longitudinal nature. Machine learning systems deployed in learning management systems, intelligent tutoring platforms, and assessment tools collect detailed information about learners' academic performance, interaction patterns, attendance, and, in some cases, psychological indicators. Such data, when aggregated and analyzed over time, can reveal intimate insights into learners' cognitive abilities and behavioral tendencies (Pardo & Siemens, 2014).

Unlike commercial data, educational data is often collected within institutional contexts where learners have limited choice or bargaining power. Scholars argue that consent in such environments is frequently implicit rather than informed, raising ethical concerns about autonomy and transparency (Slade & Prinsloo, 2013). This is particularly significant in primary and secondary education, where learners may lack the capacity to fully understand data practices.

5.2 Surveillance, Monitoring, and Learner Autonomy

A major ethical concern associated with educational machine learning is the expansion of surveillance practices within learning environments. Learning analytics systems and predictive models continuously monitor student behavior, often framing surveillance as a mechanism for early intervention and academic support. However, critics argue that constant monitoring risks transforming education into a space of behavioral control rather than intellectual development (Williamson, 2017).

From an ethical perspective, excessive surveillance may undermine learner autonomy and intrinsic motivation. Studies suggest that awareness of monitoring can influence student behavior, leading to compliance-driven engagement rather than genuine learning (Selwyn, 2019). Moreover, surveillance practices may disproportionately affect students from marginalized backgrounds, who are more likely to be subject to scrutiny and intervention.

5.3 Data Ownership and Informed Consent

Questions surrounding data ownership and control are central to ethical debates on educational machine learning. Educational institutions, technology providers, and third-party analytics vendors often share access to learner data, creating complex ecosystems with diffuse accountability (Prinsloo & Slade, 2017). In many cases, students and educators have limited visibility into how their data is processed, stored, or repurposed.

Ethical frameworks emphasize the importance of informed consent, data access rights, and learner agency over personal information (Floridi et al., 2018). However, achieving meaningful consent in institutional settings remains challenging. Scholars argue for a shift from transactional consent models toward relational approaches that emphasize trust, transparency, and ongoing dialogue with learners (Slade & Prinsloo, 2013).

5.4 Data Security and Risk of Harm

Data security represents a critical dimension of ethical data protection in educational machine learning systems. Educational datasets are attractive targets for cyber attacks due to the sensitivity and long-term relevance of the information they contain. Data breaches may expose learners to identity theft, discrimination, or reputational harm that extends beyond their educational experience (Pardo & Siemens, 2014).

Machine learning systems often rely on centralized data storage and cloud-based infrastructures, increasing exposure to security vulnerabilities. Ethical responsibility therefore extends beyond legal compliance to proactive risk mitigation strategies, including encryption, access control, and regular security audits (Mittelstadt et al., 2016).

5.5 Regulatory and Legal Perspectives

Regulatory frameworks increasingly recognize the ethical importance of protecting educational data. The General Data Protection Regulation (GDPR) emphasizes principles such as data minimization, purpose limitation, and the right to explanation, all of which have implications for educational machine learning systems (European Union, 2018). International organizations such as UNESCO have similarly highlighted privacy protection as a foundational principle for ethical AI in education (UNESCO, 2021).

In the Indian context, evolving data protection legislation intersects with national digital education initiatives. Scholars note that while technology-driven reforms promise expanded access, ethical implementation requires robust safeguards to protect learner privacy, particularly in public education systems serving diverse and vulnerable populations (Kumar & Singh, 2022).

5.6 Ethical Tensions Between Personalization and Privacy

A central ethical tension in educational machine learning lies between the goals of personalization and the protection of privacy. Personalized learning systems require detailed learner profiles to adapt content and instructional strategies effectively. However, excessive data collection and profiling risk infringing upon learners' rights and autonomy (Mittelstadt et al., 2016).

Ethical scholars advocate for a principle of proportionality, whereby data collection is limited to what is pedagogically necessary and ethically justifiable (Floridi et al., 2018). Transparency regarding data use, opportunities for opting out, and human oversight are essential to maintaining trust in educational AI systems.

5.7 Implications for Ethical Educational Practice

Privacy and data protection are foundational to ethical educational machine learning. Failure to address these concerns risks eroding trust among learners, educators, and institutions, thereby undermining the legitimacy of AI-driven educational innovation (Selwyn, 2019). Ethical educational practice demands that machine learning systems respect learners not merely as data subjects but as individuals with rights, agency, and dignity.

This section underscores the importance of privacy-by-design approaches, ensuring that ethical considerations are embedded throughout the lifecycle of educational machine learning systems. The following section builds upon this discussion by examining ethical governance mechanisms that can institutionalize responsible data practices.

6. ETHICAL GOVERNANCE AND POLICY FRAMEWORKS FOR EDUCATIONAL MACHINE LEARNING

The ethical deployment of machine learning in education requires robust governance structures that extend beyond technical safeguards. Ethical governance refers to the institutional, regulatory, and procedural mechanisms that ensure machine learning systems operate in alignment with educational values, social responsibilities, and legal obligations (Floridi et al., 2018). In educational contexts, governance is particularly significant because algorithmic systems increasingly influence learners' academic opportunities, institutional decision-making, and public trust in educational technologies (Williamson & Eynon, 2020).

6.1 Institutional Responsibility and Accountability

Educational institutions bear primary responsibility for the ethical use of machine learning systems. While technology vendors often design and supply AI-driven tools, institutions determine how these systems are selected, deployed, and integrated into pedagogical practices (Selwyn, 2019). Ethical accountability therefore cannot be fully delegated to technology providers.

Institutional governance mechanisms should clearly define roles and responsibilities related to data stewardship, algorithmic decision-making, and ethical oversight. Scholars argue that interdisciplinary oversight committees are essential for evaluating ethical risks associated with educational AI systems prior to deployment (Jobin et al., 2019). Accountability also requires mechanisms for contestability, enabling students and educators to question or appeal algorithmic decisions that affect academic outcomes (Barocas et al., 2019).

6.2 Transparency and Explainability in Educational AI

Transparency is a foundational principle of ethical governance in AI systems. In education, transparency involves making data practices, model logic, and decision criteria understandable to educators, learners, and institutional administrators (Mittelstadt et al., 2016). Explainability is particularly important in educational contexts, where algorithmic recommendations may influence instructional strategies and learner evaluation.

Opaque algorithmic systems risk undermining trust, especially when educators are expected to act upon recommendations without understanding their underlying rationale (Diakopoulos, 2016). Research emphasizes that explainable AI supports human oversight by enabling educators to critically assess and contextualize algorithmic outputs rather than treating them as objective truths.

6.3 Regulatory and International Policy Frameworks

Global policy initiatives have sought to establish ethical standards for AI governance. UNESCO's recommendations on artificial intelligence emphasize human-centered design, inclusivity, and protection of learners' rights within educational settings (UNESCO, 2021). Similarly, the OECD's AI principles advocate for fairness, accountability, and transparency across AI applications, including education (OECD, 2019).

The European Union's regulatory approach categorizes many educational AI systems as high-risk applications, requiring enhanced oversight and compliance mechanisms (European Commission, 2021). These policy developments reflect growing recognition of the ethical risks associated with algorithmic decision-making in education.

In the Indian context, ethical governance intersects with national education reform and digital governance initiatives. Scholars note that while policies encourage digital innovation, effective governance must ensure alignment with equity, access, and data protection principles (Kumar & Singh, 2022).

6.4 Ethical Review and Impact Assessment

Algorithmic impact assessments have emerged as an important governance tool for identifying and mitigating ethical risks associated with machine learning systems. In educational contexts, such assessments help institutions anticipate potential harms related to bias, privacy, and accountability before systems are widely deployed.

Ethical review processes must be iterative, as machine learning systems evolve through updates and changes in data environments. Continuous monitoring and reassessment are therefore essential components of responsible educational AI governance (Raji et al., 2020).

6.5 Participatory and Inclusive Governance

Inclusive governance emphasizes the involvement of diverse stakeholders in ethical decision-making processes. Educational researchers argue that participatory approaches strengthen ethical legitimacy by incorporating the perspectives of educators, learners, and communities affected by AI systems (Williamson, 2017).

Engaging educators is particularly important, as they possess contextual knowledge necessary for interpreting algorithmic outputs responsibly. Including student perspectives further ensures that governance frameworks respect learners' autonomy and lived experiences (Selwyn, 2019).

6.6 Challenges in Implementing Ethical Governance

Despite strong normative frameworks, institutions face practical challenges in implementing ethical governance. Limited technical expertise, resource constraints, and reliance on proprietary systems may hinder transparency and accountability (Jobin et al., 2019). Scholars caution against treating ethical governance as a symbolic compliance exercise rather than a substantive institutional commitment (Floridi et al., 2018).

6.7 Implications for Responsible Educational AI

Ethical governance provides the structural foundation for responsible machine learning in education. By embedding accountability, transparency, and participatory oversight into institutional practices, governance frameworks help align technological innovation with educational and social values (OECD, 2019). Effective governance does not inhibit innovation but ensures that educational AI systems serve learners ethically and equitably.

7. STRATEGIES FOR MITIGATING BIAS IN EDUCATIONAL MACHINE LEARNING SYSTEMS

Addressing bias in educational machine learning systems requires a combination of technical interventions, institutional practices, and ethical governance mechanisms. Bias in such systems does not emerge from a single source but is produced through interactions among data, algorithms, and social contexts. Consequently, mitigation strategies must operate across multiple stages of the machine learning lifecycle and involve diverse stakeholders, including educators, developers, and policymakers (Barocas et al., 2019; Mehrabi et al., 2021).

This section outlines key strategies for mitigating bias in educational machine learning systems, emphasizing approaches that align with educational values such as fairness, inclusivity, and accountability.

7.1 Inclusive and Representative Data Practices

One of the most effective ways to reduce bias is through inclusive data collection and curation. Educational datasets should reflect the diversity of learner populations across socio-economic backgrounds, linguistic groups, geographic regions, and learning abilities. Scholars argue that representational diversity is a foundational requirement for fairness in machine learning systems (Suresh & Guttag, 2021).

In educational contexts, achieving representative data may require deliberate efforts to include learners from under-resourced institutions and marginalized communities. Periodic dataset audits can help identify gaps and imbalances, enabling institutions to take corrective action. Ethical data practices also involve minimizing reliance on historical data that encode past inequities, particularly when such data influences predictive models affecting future opportunities (Noble, 2018).

7.2 Reflexive Labeling and Human Oversight

Given the central role of human judgment in educational data annotation, mitigating labeling bias requires reflexive and transparent labeling practices. Training annotators to recognize implicit bias and encouraging the use of multiple evaluators can improve consistency and fairness in labeled datasets (Baker & Hawn, 2021).

Human oversight remains essential even after system deployment. Rather than treating algorithmic outputs as definitive, educators should be empowered to interpret and contextualize recommendations using professional judgment. Research emphasizes that human-in-the-loop approaches support ethical accountability by ensuring that automated decisions remain subject to human review (Diakopoulos, 2016).

7.3 Fairness-Aware Algorithm Design

Technical interventions play an important role in bias mitigation. Fairness-aware machine learning techniques seek to incorporate equity considerations directly into model design, evaluation, and optimization. Such techniques include fairness constraints, bias-aware loss functions, and subgroup performance analysis (Barocas et al., 2019).

In educational settings, fairness-aware design requires careful selection of features and evaluation metrics. For instance, models should be assessed not only for overall accuracy but also for differential performance across learner groups. Transparent reporting of model limitations supports ethical deployment and informed decision-making (Mehrabi et al., 2021).

7.4 Institutional Governance and Ethical Audits

Bias mitigation cannot be achieved through technical solutions alone. Institutional governance mechanisms play a crucial role in overseeing the ethical use of educational machine learning systems. Ethical audits enable institutions to evaluate systems for fairness, transparency, and accountability throughout their lifecycle (Raji et al., 2020).

Educational institutions should establish clear policies defining acceptable use, monitoring procedures, and accountability structures. Regular review of algorithmic outcomes helps identify unintended consequences and ensures alignment with educational objectives and social responsibilities (Floridi et al., 2018).

7.5 Participatory and Context-Sensitive Approaches

Inclusive participation is essential for ethical bias mitigation. Engaging educators, students, and community stakeholders in system design and evaluation promotes contextual sensitivity and ethical legitimacy (Selwyn, 2019). Participatory approaches ensure that machine learning systems reflect pedagogical realities rather than abstract technical assumptions.

In culturally diverse educational environments, context-sensitive approaches help address societal bias by incorporating local knowledge and values. Such engagement supports trust and fosters responsible innovation in educational AI systems (Williamson & Eynon, 2020).

7.6 Summary of Bias Mitigation Strategies

To consolidate the strategies discussed above, Table 2 presents an overview of bias mitigation approaches, their focus areas, and ethical contributions.

Table 2. Bias mitigation strategies in educational machine learning systems

Mitigation Strategy	Primary Focus	Educational Application	Ethical Contribution
Inclusive data collection	Data bias	Diverse learner representation	Promotes fairness and equity
Reflexive labeling	Labeling bias	Fair assessment and annotation	Reduces subjective evaluation
Fairness-aware algorithms	Algorithmic bias	Equitable predictions and recommendations	Enhances transparency and accountability
Ethical audits	System-level bias	Continuous monitoring of AI systems	Ensures institutional responsibility
Participatory governance	Societal bias	Stakeholder involvement in AI deployment	Aligns AI with social justice values

7.7 Implications for Ethical Educational AI

Effective bias mitigation strengthens trust in educational machine learning systems and supports equitable learning environments. However, bias mitigation should be understood as an ongoing process rather than a one-time intervention. Continuous evaluation, stakeholder engagement, and ethical reflection are essential for adapting systems to evolving educational contexts (Floridi et al., 2018).

This section highlights that responsible bias mitigation requires integrating technical innovation with ethical governance and pedagogical insight. The next section builds upon these strategies by examining future directions and ethical challenges for educational machine learning systems.

8. FUTURE DIRECTIONS AND ETHICAL CHALLENGES IN EDUCATIONAL MACHINE LEARNING

As machine learning continues to shape contemporary educational practices, ethical considerations are expected to become increasingly complex and consequential. While current debates focus on bias, privacy, and accountability, emerging developments in artificial intelligence introduce new ethical challenges that extend beyond existing frameworks. This section examines future directions in educational machine learning and highlights unresolved ethical concerns that demand sustained scholarly and institutional attention (Williamson & Eynon, 2020).

8.1 Increasing Automation and Decision-Making Authority

One significant future trend is the expansion of automated decision-making in education. Machine learning systems are increasingly used to inform high-stakes decisions such as student admissions, academic progression, early-warning interventions, and personalized learning pathways. While automation promises efficiency and scalability, scholars caution against over-reliance on algorithmic judgments in contexts that require human discretion and pedagogical sensitivity (Selwyn, 2019).

Ethical challenges arise when automated systems acquire decision-making authority without adequate human oversight. Research suggests that educators may develop automation bias, whereby algorithmic recommendations are trusted uncritically, potentially amplifying existing inequities (Diakopoulos, 2016). Future systems must therefore prioritize human-in-the-loop models that preserve professional judgment and ethical accountability.

8.2 Explainability and Transparency in Educational AI

As educational machine learning models grow more complex, explainability emerges as a central ethical challenge. Deep learning and ensemble models often function as "black boxes," making it difficult for educators and learners to understand how predictions or recommendations are generated (Mittelstadt et al., 2016). Lack of transparency undermines trust and limits the ability to contest or correct erroneous outcomes.

Future research emphasizes the importance of explainable AI (XAI) approaches that provide meaningful, context-sensitive explanations tailored to educational stakeholders (Floridi et al., 2018). Explainability is particularly critical in educational environments, where decisions influence learners' academic identities and long-term opportunities.

8.3 Ethical Challenges of Large-Scale Educational Data Ecosystems

The expansion of national and global digital education initiatives is leading to large-scale educational data ecosystems that integrate data across institutions and platforms. While such ecosystems enable longitudinal analysis and policy-level insights, they also intensify ethical risks related to data aggregation, profiling, and secondary use (Williamson, 2017).

In the Indian context, large-scale digital education programs raise ethical questions about consent, governance, and equitable access. Scholars argue that without robust ethical safeguards, large data infrastructures may exacerbate digital divides and reinforce systemic inequalities (Kumar & Singh, 2022). Future governance frameworks must balance innovation with social responsibility and learner protection.

8.4 Emerging Risks of Generative and Adaptive Systems

The rise of generative and adaptive AI systems introduces new ethical dimensions in education. Such systems can dynamically generate learning content, assessments, and feedback, often in real time. While these capabilities offer pedagogical flexibility, they also raise concerns regarding accuracy, intellectual integrity, and accountability (UNESCO, 2021).

Ethical challenges include the potential for misinformation, erosion of academic authorship, and unequal access to advanced AI tools. Researchers emphasize the need for ethical guidelines that govern the use of generative AI in educational settings, ensuring that innovation supports learning rather than undermines academic values (Selwyn, 2019).

8.5 Need for Adaptive Ethical Governance Frameworks

Traditional regulatory and ethical frameworks may struggle to keep pace with rapid technological change. Future ethical governance in educational machine learning must therefore be adaptive, participatory, and context-aware. Scholars advocate for interdisciplinary governance models that integrate technical expertise, educational theory, and ethical reflection (Floridi et al., 2018).

Adaptive governance includes continuous monitoring, stakeholder engagement, and iterative policy development. Such approaches enable institutions to respond to emerging risks while maintaining alignment with educational missions and societal values (Raji et al., 2020).

8.6 Towards a Human-Centered Ethical Future

A key future direction for educational machine learning is the adoption of human-centered AI principles. Human-centered approaches emphasize dignity, agency, and well-being, positioning learners and educators as active participants rather than passive data subjects (UNESCO, 2021).

Embedding ethical reflection into system design, implementation, and evaluation supports sustainable and trustworthy educational innovation. This perspective reinforces the argument that ethical considerations are not constraints on technological progress but essential conditions for meaningful and inclusive educational transformation (Floridi et al., 2018).

8.7 Concluding Reflections on Future Ethical Challenges

Future developments in educational machine learning present both opportunities and ethical challenges. Addressing issues of automation, transparency, data governance, and emerging AI capabilities requires sustained interdisciplinary collaboration and ethical vigilance. This section underscores the necessity of proactive ethical engagement to ensure that machine learning technologies contribute positively to educational equity and human development.

The concluding section synthesizes the insights from this chapter and reiterates the importance of ethical responsibility in the evolving landscape of educational artificial intelligence.

9. CONCLUSION AND POLICY IMPLICATIONS

The increasing adoption of machine learning technologies in educational contexts presents both transformative opportunities and profound ethical challenges. This chapter has critically examined ethical concerns related to bias, privacy, and accountability in educational machine learning systems, emphasizing that technological innovation in education cannot be ethically neutral. Instead, the deployment of machine learning must be guided by principles that prioritize fairness, transparency, and respect for learner autonomy (Floridi et al., 2018; Selwyn, 2019).

9.1 Synthesis of Key Ethical Concerns

The chapter began by situating machine learning within broader educational and societal contexts, highlighting how algorithmic systems influence pedagogical practices and institutional decision-making. Sections addressing bias demonstrated that inequities in educational machine learning systems arise from data practices, labeling processes, algorithmic design, and embedded societal structures. These biases risk reinforcing historical inequalities unless actively mitigated through inclusive and reflexive approaches (Barocas et al., 2019; Noble, 2018).

Privacy and data protection were identified as foundational ethical concerns, particularly given the sensitive and longitudinal nature of educational data. Continuous monitoring, opaque data governance structures, and limited learner agency pose significant risks to trust and autonomy within educational environments (Slade & Prinsloo, 2013; Williamson, 2017). Together, these ethical challenges underscore the need for responsible design and deployment of machine learning systems in education.

9.2 Implications for Educational Policy

From a policy perspective, the findings of this chapter suggest the necessity of developing clear and enforceable ethical guidelines for educational machine learning. Policymakers should prioritize regulations that promote transparency, data minimization, and fairness in algorithmic decision-making. Ethical impact assessments and algorithmic audits can serve as institutional mechanisms for identifying and addressing unintended consequences before and after system deployment (Raji et al., 2020).

In contexts such as India, where large-scale digital education initiatives are rapidly expanding, ethical policy frameworks must account for diversity, digital inequality, and public accountability. Aligning national education technology strategies with ethical AI principles can help ensure that innovation contributes to inclusive and equitable educational outcomes (Kumar & Singh, 2022).

9.3 Implications for Institutional Practice

Educational institutions play a critical role in translating ethical principles into practice. Institutions should foster interdisciplinary collaboration among educators, data scientists, and ethicists to support responsible system design and evaluation.

Professional development initiatives can equip educators with the knowledge required to interpret algorithmic outputs critically and responsibly (Diakopoulos, 2016).

Furthermore, institutions must adopt transparent data governance practices that clearly communicate how learner data is collected, processed, and used. Establishing channels for learner feedback and contestation strengthens trust and reinforces ethical accountability within educational ecosystems (Prinsloo & Slade, 2017).

9.4 Directions for Future Research

Future research should continue to explore ethical challenges arising from emerging AI capabilities, including generative and adaptive learning systems. Longitudinal studies examining the social and educational impacts of machine learning interventions can provide valuable insights into their ethical implications over time. Comparative research across cultural and institutional contexts will also enhance understanding of how ethical principles can be adapted to diverse educational environments (Williamson & Eynon, 2020).

Interdisciplinary scholarship that integrates technical innovation with educational theory and ethical analysis remains essential for advancing responsible educational machine learning.

9.5 Concluding Remarks

This chapter concludes that ethical responsibility must be central to the development and deployment of machine learning in education. Bias mitigation, privacy protection, and transparent governance are not optional considerations but essential conditions for sustaining trust and equity in educational systems. By adopting human-centered and ethically informed approaches, educational institutions and policymakers can harness the potential of machine learning while safeguarding the rights and dignity of learners.

Ultimately, the ethical future of educational machine learning depends not only on technological advancement but on collective commitment to justice, accountability, and inclusive educational values (Floridi et al., 2018).

10. LIMITATIONS AND FUTURE RESEARCH

While this chapter has critically examined ethical concerns related to bias, privacy, and governance in machine learning–driven educational systems, it is important to acknowledge certain conceptual, contextual, and practical boundaries that shape the scope of the discussion. Recognizing these limitations does not weaken the contribution of the chapter; rather, it enhances its scholarly rigor by identifying areas where further investigation and interdisciplinary engagement are necessary. This section outlines key limitations of the present work and proposes directions for future research in the evolving field of ethical artificial intelligence in education.

10.1 Conceptual and Methodological Boundaries

One limitation of this chapter lies in its primarily conceptual and analytical orientation. The discussion is grounded in interdisciplinary literature from artificial intelligence ethics, education, and social sciences, rather than in empirical evaluation of specific machine learning systems. While conceptual frameworks are essential for understanding ethical risks and guiding responsible design, they cannot fully capture the complexity of real-world educational deployments (Floridi et al., 2018).

Empirical studies examining how bias manifests in operational educational systems—such as adaptive learning platforms, automated assessment tools, or early-warning systems—remain limited. Future research would benefit from mixed-method approaches that combine quantitative bias audits with qualitative insights from educators and learners. Such studies can bridge the gap between ethical theory and institutional practice, enabling more context-sensitive ethical interventions (Baker & Hawn, 2021).

10.2 Limitations of Bias Measurement and Fairness Metrics

Another important limitation concerns the reliance on existing fairness and bias concepts that originate largely from computer science and data science literature. While fairness metrics such as demographic parity, equalized odds, and predictive parity offer useful analytical tools, their applicability in educational contexts is not always straightforward (Mehrabi et al., 2021).

Educational outcomes are deeply contextual, influenced by cultural, socio-economic, and institutional factors that cannot be fully captured through technical metrics alone. For instance, optimizing algorithmic fairness may inadvertently reduce pedagogical effectiveness or conflict with individualized learning goals. Future research must therefore explore fairness not only as a computational property but also as an educational and ethical construct informed by pedagogical values and social justice perspectives (Selwyn, 2019).

10.3 Contextual Limitations and Global Diversity

The ethical implications of machine learning in education vary significantly across geographic and socio-economic contexts. Much of the existing literature, including some of the studies referenced in this chapter, is grounded in experiences from technologically advanced education systems. This creates a limitation in understanding how ethical risks manifest in resource-constrained or highly diverse educational environments.

In countries such as India, where large-scale digital education initiatives coexist with significant digital divides, ethical challenges related to access, representation, and governance require localized analysis (Kumar & Singh, 2022). Future research should prioritize comparative and region-specific studies that examine how cultural norms, policy frameworks, and infrastructural conditions shape ethical AI adoption in education. Such work is essential for avoiding the uncritical transfer of ethical models developed in the Global North to fundamentally different educational contexts.

10.4 Rapid Technological Evolution and Ethical Uncertainty

Machine learning technologies are evolving at a pace that often outstrips ethical frameworks and regulatory mechanisms. The rise of generative AI, large language models, and adaptive content generation systems introduces ethical uncertainties that were not fully addressed in earlier learning analytics research (UNESCO, 2023). This chapter, while addressing emerging trends, is limited by the current state of knowledge in a rapidly changing technological landscape.

Future research must remain adaptive and forward-looking, continuously revisiting ethical assumptions as technologies evolve. Longitudinal studies that track the ethical implications of AI adoption over time will be particularly valuable in understanding unintended consequences and shifting power dynamics within educational systems (Williamson & Eynon, 2020).

10.5 Institutional and Governance Constraints

A further limitation relates to institutional readiness for ethical AI governance. While this chapter emphasizes governance frameworks, transparency, and accountability, it does not empirically assess the capacity of educational institutions to implement such measures effectively. In practice, institutions often face constraints related to expertise, funding, and organizational culture that limit meaningful ethical oversight (Raji et al., 2020).

Future research should examine institutional governance models in greater detail, including case studies of successful and unsuccessful ethical AI implementations in education. Understanding how institutional incentives, leadership structures, and regulatory environments influence ethical decision-making can inform more practical and scalable governance strategies.

10.6 Directions for Future Interdisciplinary Research

The ethical challenges of machine learning in education cannot be addressed through technical solutions alone. One of the most promising directions for future research lies in interdisciplinary collaboration that brings together educators, computer scientists, ethicists, policymakers, and learners. Such collaboration can foster ethical frameworks that are both technically robust and pedagogically meaningful (Floridi et al., 2018).

Future studies should explore participatory design approaches that involve educators and students in the development and evaluation of AI systems. Participatory methods can help surface contextual knowledge, values, and concerns that are often invisible in purely data-driven development processes (Prinsloo & Slade, 2017).

10.7 Ethical Research Agendas for Educational AI

Building on the limitations discussed, future research agendas should focus on several key areas. These include the ethical evaluation of generative AI in assessment and feedback, the long-term effects of algorithmic personalization on learner autonomy, and the impact of AI-driven surveillance on trust within educational communities. Additionally, research on ethical literacy among educators and administrators can inform professional development initiatives that support responsible AI adoption (UNESCO, 2021).

There is also a need for methodological innovation in ethical AI research, including tools for auditing bias in educational datasets and mechanisms for ongoing ethical monitoring. Such approaches can help move ethical discussions from abstract principles to actionable practices within educational institutions.

10.8 Concluding Remarks on Limitations and Future Research

In conclusion, while this chapter provides a comprehensive ethical analysis of machine learning in education, its limitations highlight the dynamic and evolving nature of the field. Ethical challenges related to bias, privacy, and governance are not static problems but ongoing processes that require continuous reflection, evaluation, and adaptation.

By acknowledging these limitations and outlining future research directions, this section reinforces the chapter's central argument: that ethical responsibility in educational machine learning is a shared, evolving endeavor. Future scholarship that integrates empirical evidence, contextual sensitivity, and interdisciplinary insight will be essential for ensuring that artificial intelligence supports equitable, inclusive, and human-centered educational futures.

REFERENCES

Baker, R. S., & Hawn, A. (2021). Algorithmic bias in education. *International Journal of Artificial Intelligence in Education, 31*(2), 1–27. DOI: 10.1007/s40593-021-00240-9

Barocas, S., Hardt, M., & Narayanan, A. (2019). Fairness and machine learning. fairmlbook.org.

Diakopoulos, N. (2016). Accountability in algorithmic decision making. *Communications of the ACM, 59*(2), 56–62. DOI: 10.1145/2844110

European Union. (2018). General Data Protection Regulation (GDPR). Official Journal of the European Union.

Floridi, L., Cowls, J., Beltrametti, M., Chatila, R., Chazerand, P., Dignum, V., Luetge, C., Madelin, R., Pagallo, U., Rossi, F., Schafer, B., Valcke, P., & Vayena, E. (2018). AI4People—An ethical framework for a good AI society. *Minds and Machines, 28*(4), 689–707. DOI: 10.1007/s11023-018-9482-5 PMID: 30930541

Jobin, A., Ienca, M., & Vayena, E. (2019). The global landscape of AI ethics guidelines. *Nature Machine Intelligence, 1*(9), 389–399. DOI: 10.1038/s42256-019-0088-2

Kumar, S., & Singh, M. (2022). Ethical challenges of AI-driven education in India. *Journal of Educational Technology Systems, 50*(4), 475–492. DOI: 10.1177/00472395211063478

Mehrabi, N., Morstatter, F., Saxena, N., Lerman, K., & Galstyan, A. (2021). A survey on bias and fairness in machine learning. *ACM Computing Surveys, 54*(6), 1–35. DOI: 10.1145/3457607

Mittelstadt, B. D., Allo, P., Taddeo, M., Wachter, S., & Floridi, L. (2016). The ethics of algorithms. *Big Data & Society, 3*(2), 1–21. DOI: 10.1177/2053951716679679

Noble, S. U. (2018). *Algorithms of oppression.* NYU Press. DOI: 10.18574/nyu/9781479833641.001.0001

O'Neil, C. (2016). *Weapons of math destruction.* Crown.

Pardo, A., & Siemens, G. (2014). Ethical and privacy principles for learning analytics. *British Journal of Educational Technology, 45*(3), 438–450. DOI: 10.1111/bjet.12152

Prinsloo, P., & Slade, S. (2017). Ethics and learning analytics. *Educational Technology Research and Development, 65*(1), 13–36. DOI: 10.1007/s11423-016-9489-7

Raji, I. D., Smart, A., & White, R. N.. (2020). Closing the AI accountability gap. *Proceedings of FAT*, 33–44. DOI: 10.1145/3351095.3372873

Selwyn, N. (2019). *Should robots replace teachers? Polity Press. Bennett, A., & Checkel, J. (2015). Process tracing: from metaphor to analytic tool.* Cambridge University Press.

Slade, S., & Prinsloo, P. (2013). Learning analytics: Ethical issues. *The American Behavioral Scientist*, *57*(10), 1510–1529. DOI: 10.1177/0002764213479366

Suresh, H., & Guttag, J. V. (2021). A framework for understanding sources of harm in ML. *Proceedings of FAT*, 81–91.

UNESCO. (2021). *Ethical guidelines on artificial intelligence and education.* UNESCO Publishing.

UNESCO. (2023). *Guidance for generative AI in education and research.* UNESCO.

Williamson, B. (2017). Big data in education. *Sage (Atlanta, Ga.).*

Williamson, B., & Eynon, R. (2020). Historical threads of AI in education. *Learning, Media and Technology*, *45*(3), 223–235. DOI: 10.1080/17439884.2020.1798995

Zuboff, S. (2019). *The age of surveillance capitalism.* PublicAffairs.

Chapter 5
Regulating the Emergence of AI in Education:
Foundations, Legal Issues, and Policy Frameworks

Amrita Baid More
http://orcid.org/0000-0002-7440-9138
Medicaps University, Indore, India

Arpan Shrivastava
http://orcid.org/0000-0003-3992-4422
Institute of Business Management and Research, IPS Academy, India

ABSTRACT

Artificial Intelligence (AI) is transforming education by making learning more personalized, automating administrative tasks, and supporting data-driven decision-making. This chapter discusses the fundamental foundations of AI, its application in the education sector, the urgent legal issues it presents, and the necessity for a strong regulatory and policy framework to ensure ethical regulation. The opening section gives an overview of the building blocks of AI with a focus on key technologies like machine learning, deep learning, and natural language processing. It brings out their applications in education—ranging from adaptive learning systems and virtual tutors to automated grading and predictive analytics. The second part discusses legal concerns regarding AI in education, i.e., data privacy, consent, bias in algorithms, transparency, intellectual property rights, and accountability. It emphasizes the legal vacuum that presently prevails and potentially gives rise to unforeseen consequences if not addressed in proper time.

DOI: 10.4018/979-8-3373-7467-3.ch005

INTRODUCTION: EMERGED AND DEVELOPED ARTIFICIAL INTELLIGENCE

AI is the Intelligence that is displayed by machines or Computers. To simplify the definition, Artificial Intelligence is a computer designed to comprehend the surroundings and to act or respond, or react independently, and cause a sense of supposedly problem-solving cognition by people that is related to the mental processes of thought and behavior. The development of Artificial Intelligence has many spheres of science which includes, Mind functioning, biology, computer science, mechanical engineering, robotics, psychology, neurophysics, and philosophy, which in turn cover the development of intelligent machines that can replicate human functions and use cognitive processing and intelligence.

The privacy and protection of IP are the problems that have grown large in the 21 st century, and the irrepressible access to information. With the presence of a vast pool of information on the internet, individuals are able to search and download anything to use it at their own will without the knowledge or permission of anyone. The peak of Artificial Intelligence is where we have machines that have been created to replicate themselves and become better in the next generation humane involvement. The field of artificial Intelligence has grown extensively through research, and it is connected with the future Intellectual property rights, which were already foreshadowed to some degree. The existing discussion addresses multifaceted transformations in the innovation, production, and commercialization processes, closely related to intellectual property competition and regulation.

Researchers, activists, jurists, students, clinicians, and policymakers are interested in They had a conversation in myriad areas, including problem-solving, gaming, theorem proving, voice and pattern recognition, natural language processing and understanding, neural architecture, computer vision, as well as engineering design analysis. The issue is widely discussed by think tanks and advocates of intellectual property rights, who jointly offer an interesting perspective on how artificial intelligence will alter related laws and intellectual property rights. The high strength of working with AI creates problems on the technical level, ethical, political, social, and cultural levels, and demands accountability and legal responsibilities. The vast expansion of Artificial Intelligence has been unimaginable, as it started with the small-scale applications and developed to have larger and more technologically advanced successes. The world has already enjoyed the fruits of numerous approaches, including the testing of different programs, finding the points of error or the treatment of human ailments, playing grandmaster-level chess, and helping with various complicated tasks (Silver, 2012). Artificial Intelligence has experienced a radical transformation in the course of several past decades and has influenced various industries.

It can be traced back to the 1950s, when the groundwork of AI research was laid by such pioneers as Alan Turing and John McCarthy. Although the primitive AI systems were limited in capacity and scope, improvements in machine learning algorithms and processing power have resulted in more intelligent AI usage. Creation of expert systems throughout the 1970s and 1980s, like MYCIN, used in medical diagnosis, was an important development. Artificial Intelligence, in its general sense, is known as the development of computer systems capable of doing the work that involves the use of intelligence, which has traditionally been done by human beings, and a long-term goal of developing intelligent machines - machines that are going to be able to see, think, learn, and adapt. In order to achieve such objectives, Artificial Intelligence employs diverse approaches: machine learning and deep learning. Machine learning is a subdivision of AI that is concerned with the development of statistical models and algorithms to enable computers to learn based on data, make judgments or predictions without the need to explicitly code them. Machine learning algorithms will enhance the competence in special actions, noting patterns and reaching judgments, based on new data sets, through experience. Machine learning is an ideal tool in solving complicated problems and extracting useful insights from data due to its ability to adapt and work with large volumes of data and variability in response to the fluid ecosystem. With the further improvement of research and development, machine learning will likely become a force behind more inventions, of course, with the future of technologies and decision-making processes in different industries.

The four facets of AI are indicated in a concise manner below.

Figure 1. The four facets of artificial intelligence

Thinking Humanly	**Thinking Rationally**
"The exciting new effort to make computers think ... *machines with minds*, in the full and literal sense." (Haugeland, 1985) "[The automation of] activities that we associate with human thinking, activities such as decision-making, problem solving, learning ..." (Bellman, 1978)	"The study of mental faculties through the use of computational models." (Charniak and McDermott, 1985) "The study of the computations that make it possible to perceive, reason, and act." (Winston, 1992)
Acting Humanly	**Acting Rationally**
"The art of creating machines that perform functions that require intelligence when performed by people." (Kurzweil, 1990) "The study of how to make computers do things at which, at the moment, people are better." (Rich and Knight, 1991)	"Computational Intelligence is the study of the design of intelligent agents." (Poole *et al.*, 1998) "AI ... is concerned with intelligent behavior in artifacts." (Nilsson, 1998)

Various types of Artificial Intelligence differ in functionality and ability. A related discipline is Deep Learning - a niche of Machine Learning that involves the application of artificial neural networks to learn and interpret complex relationships and patterns in data. Deep Learning relies on the organization and functionality of. It is therefore the human brain with various levels of connected neurons, a fact that makes the brain the reason behind the term, deep. The algorithms used in Deep learning can learn the hierarchical representations of the data independently, and this allows them to identify the high-level features of the raw data and be able to make correct predictions. This technique has been very effective in image and speech recognition, natural language processing, self-driving, and so on.

In conclusion, AI is a general subject that involves developing intelligent machines, and the branch of AI that aims at developing algorithms that learn through data is called Machine Learning. Deep Learning, conversely, is a branch of machine learning that has adopted artificial neural networks in order to learn intricate patterns and representations in data. Deep Learning is an advanced and broad branch of Machine Learning; however, it is not the only approach to a significantly broader topic of AI and Machine Learning. In spite of the tremendous breakthroughs, Deep Learning is challenged. Deep neural networks consume a great deal of data to train and require a great deal of computation, and therefore are computationally expensive.

While there has been a significant uptake of Artificial Intelligence (AI) in education, existing research has tended to address the technology, ethics, or governance of AI in education in isolation, rather than holistically as a governance issue. Recent research demonstrates AI in education is a socio-technical system that alters institutional processes, governance, and pedagogic power (Williamson & Kizilcec, 2022). At the same time, international policy debates indicate that the adoption of AI in education has not been accompanied by clear governance and regulatory approaches, resulting in oversight, transparency, and institutional readiness concerns (UNESCO, 2021).

The existing literature distinguishes between the use and ethics of AI, yet there is little discussion of the governance approaches specific to education systems, especially with regard to the legal, ethical, and operational aspects of institutional practice. Additionally, many of these studies lack a connection between normative concepts such as fairness, transparency, and accountability and their implementation, which can lead to fragmented and inconsistent governance (Jobin et al., 2019). This is especially important for education systems, where AI systems affect students' learning, fairness, and society.

This chapter aims to fill these gaps by providing an interdisciplinary view of AI in education that links technological, legal, ethical, and governance aspects. Specifically, the chapter makes three contributions. First, it offers a comprehensive overview of the uses and risks of AI, not only in terms of descriptive knowledge but also in terms of the trade-offs and tensions involved. Second, it adopts a governance-oriented perspective to link underlying principles such as privacy, fairness, transparency, and accountability to mechanisms and practices. And third, it provides policy insights by describing how educational organisations and policymakers can enable innovation as well as management in the data society.

By bridging theory and practice, this chapter seeks to support the creation of sound, tailored, and actionable AI governance strategies in education that bridge technological, legal, and educational concerns.

REASON FOR AI IMPLEMENTATION IN MODERN EDUCATION

The rapidly evolving knowledge economy, digital workspace, and the increasing demands of the learners have made it an urgent expectation of the education systems to become more adaptive, inclusive, and efficient. Artificial Intelligence (AI) offers tremendous possibilities in fulfilling such demands through individualised learning, smooth institutional operations, and evidence-based decision-making. The artificial intelligence application to contemporary education is therefore not a simple technological wave but a strategic response to the systemic issues of contemporary educational establishments.

The possibility of facilitating personalised and learner-centred education is one of the primary reasons why AI should be used. Conventional methods of education will be founded on generalized models of education that fail to embrace differences in learning rates, mental modes, and previous knowledge. AI-based systems, adaptive learning platforms, and intelligent tutoring systems process learner data using real-time analysis and study it, and based on this, decide on the learning content, feedback, and assessments. This individualization improves the interaction between learners, academic performance, and reduced dropout rates, particularly in large and varied classes (Holmes et al., 2019).

The other intriguing point is efficiency in the form of automation of the routine academic and administrative activities. The teacher students are usually burdened with excessive workloads in terms of grading, student attendance, timetables, and schedules reporting, thus leaving no room to have a meaningful pedagogical interaction. These processes can be automated by AI-based tools to be repetitive, and, therefore, the teacher can focus on higher-order teaching, such as mentoring, curriculum designing, and acquisition of critical skills. In the institutional perspective, the automation of this type is included in the cost optimization, the efficiency of the operations, and the enhanced service provision (Zawacki-Richter et al., 2019).

The data-driven decision-making in education is also one of the factors that drives the adoption of AI. Learning institutions produce vast volumes of data that are connected to student achievement, participation, and advancement. AI-driven analytics have the potential to transform this information into practical learning by identifying areas of learning gaps, forecasting learning risks, and creating actions to counter them at the earliest stage possible. These features enable institutions to enhance their academic planning, resource allocation, and support systems for learners to enhance the quality of their education in general (Luckin et al., 2016).

Lastly, the integration of AI places education in the future in tandem with the future of the workforce. Due to AI and automation, the learning institutions will be forced to equip the learners with digital literacy, critical thinking, and problem-solving skills, which will be applicable in an AI-enabled society. Learning environments facilitated with the assistance of AI also allow students to become acquainted with intelligent technologies and develop adaptability and lifelong learning skills. Therefore, the history of AI in education not only solves the current pedagogical tasks but also has long-term socio-economic goals.

Overall, the argument of AI in education today is all about the need to be personalized, efficient, governed through data analytics, and futuristic. AI can be an enabling transformer when enacted responsibly to promote educational systems without compromising human agency or pedagogical values.

ARTIFICIAL INTELLIGENCE APPLICATIONS THAT RAISE LEGAL ISSUES

Artificial intelligence can be used to perform complicated tasks, e.g., driving and investing in investment portfolios, and not under human control/supervision. It is expected that this autonomy will only increase. Introducing new issues and upheavals to the labor market, such as the socio-economic. Transformations that took place in the Industrial Revolution. The shift towards the use of AI to do things that are traditionally the responsibility of human beings, particularly in the service industry, is problematic.

Similar to the reforms that the industrial revolution had brought about through the mechanization of the labour force. As AI is increasingly becoming common, massive transformations are anticipated in the legal sphere because it requires an adjustment to the emergence of self-reliant machines. (More, A.B. et al., 2025). One of the biggest issues that AI poses to the legal system is foreseeability. Examples of AI behavior that appear to be creative (non-conventional actions in chess computer programs, etc.) are a fundamental distinction between how human beings make decisions and the way modern AI does. The human brain (cognitive limitations of the human brain) makes satisficing solutions, and AI is efficient in generating unexpected solutions (especially under time constraints).

(A) Liability and Accountability

Liability and accountability are two of the key legal challenges associated with the use of AI systems. As opposed to the traditional legal system, where liability can be attributed to a specific person or organisation, in the case of AI, multiple actors are responsible: the developers, the deployers, the data providers, and the users (Bovens, 2007; Veale & Borgesius, 2021). This makes it more difficult to determine liability in cases of harm or error caused by AI systems. For example, in the education sector, errors in grading or discrimination in recommendations made by AI systems can be difficult to attribute to the school, the company providing the software, or the AI system itself (Bovens, 2007; Veale & Borgesius, 2021).

(B) Privacy and Data Protection

Data collection is a critical aspect of AI systems, leading to privacy and data protection concerns. AI applications in education can access and analyse sensitive student data, such as behavioural data and performance metrics, leading to potential surveillance and data misuse. Laws like the General Data Protection Regulation (GDPR) seek to mitigate these risks by emphasising privacy principles such as data minimisation and consent, but compliance is difficult given AI system complexity (Pardo & Siemens, 2014; Bennett & Raab, 2020).

(C) Bias and Fairness

Algorithmic bias is a significant legal and ethical concern, as AI systems can perpetuate or even exacerbate social biases present in the data used to train the systems. One well-known example is the COMPAS system employed for risk assessments in the U.S. criminal justice system, which demonstrated racial bias. This example highlights the risk of discriminatory outcomes from non-transparent AI systems and impacts issues of fairness, transparency, and compliance with anti-discrimination legislation (Barocas et al., 2019). The same could occur in education with biased tests and school admissions.

(D) Intellectual Property (IP) and Ownership

AI outcomes present challenges to intellectual property and ownership. For example, is an essay, artwork, or analysis created by an AI system owned by the developer, user, or even the organisation? Copyright legislation, which is primarily geared towards human authorship, is difficult to apply to AI-generated content, creating regulatory uncertainty and potential conflict (Ginsburg & Budiardjo, 2019; Samuelson, 2020).

These legal issues are not in isolation, as concerns of bias, privacy, and accountability are often closely intertwined in AI systems, and require holistic and situational approaches to governance rather than individual policy responses.

Case Study 1: Privacy and Learning Analytics for Students (Policy Example)

Context: The rise of AI-powered learning analytics in schools has resulted in massive data collection and processing of student data on digital platforms.

AI Use: AI-driven tools monitor student learning, behaviour, and performance to help tailor learning experiences and predict student success.

Legal/Ethical Issue: This has important implications for privacy, consent, and surveillance, especially where students have no choice in how their data is used.

Governance Response: Regulations like the General Data Protection Regulation (GDPR) and policies from UNESCO prioritise data minimisation, transparency, and user rights, mandating privacy-by-design principles and ethical data practices by institutions (Pardo & Siemens, 2014; UNESCO, 2021).

Case Study 2: AI-Driven Adaptive Learning Systems (Institutional)

Context: AI is extensively used in educational platforms like Duolingo and Khan Academy for personalised learning.

AI Use: AI is deployed in these platforms to dynamically adjust content, offer feedback, and suggestions for learning based on performance data.

Legal/Ethical Issue: Although enhancing engagement, these may perpetuate algorithmic biases and disparities in learning opportunities if the data used to train these algorithms is biased.

Governance Response: As institutions adopt such systems, they are increasingly using algorithmic audits, human oversight, and transparency to ensure fairness and accountability in AI decision-making (Holmes et al., 2019; Zawacki-Richter et al., 2019).

Case Study 3: Bias in AI Decision-Making (Comparative Case)

AI Use: The algorithm was used to assess the risk of recidivism, assisting judges in making decisions.

Legal/Ethical Issue: research showed the system was racially biased, misclassifying members of certain groups more frequently, prompting concerns regarding fairness, transparency, and discrimination.

Governance Response: The case has had an impact on the development of AI governance policies, including the need for bias audits, explainability, and more rigorous regulation, which have implications for AI in education as well (Barocas et al., 2019).

Case Study 4: Risk-Based AI Regulation in Education (Policy Example - EU AI Act)

Context: The European Union is considering a wide-ranging approach to AI regulation with the EU Artificial Intelligence Act, categorising AI systems according to risk.

AI Use: High-risk systems in education include AI-based grading, student admissions, and assessment systems.

Legal/Ethical Issue: These can affect students' opportunities, posing questions of fairness and due process.

Governance Response: The EU approach requires high-compliance standards, such as risk assessments, transparency, human oversight, and documentation for these systems, offering a governance framework for educational settings (Veale & Borgesius, 2021).

These case studies highlight the need for a multi-layered approach to AI governance, blending institutional and regulatory measures to tackle various privacy, bias, and accountability issues.

CONSTRAINTS IN AI USAGE

This gap in decision-making processes brings out the challenge in predicting and controlling the actions of AI. AI usage has grown exponentially over the last few years and is changing the world through the transformation of industries and societies. The various skills possessed by AI have been used in various ways.

Figure 2. The issues in defining artificial intelligence

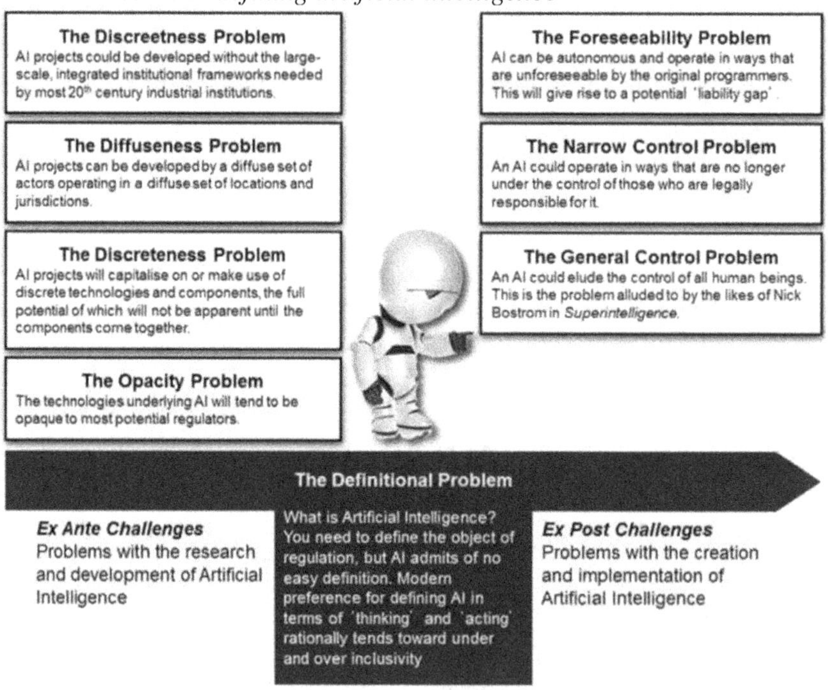

The AI applications are associated with a range of legal issues. As AI technology is in motion, matters become more and more complex. These are some of the key points of the spheres in which the AI application raises bothersome legal issues, like Algorithmic bias, where the AI systems persist in perpetuating and overcoming algorithmic bias, which is an issue in making sure that there is fairness and adherence to anti-discrimination laws. Privacy Issues: search for a balanced approach between innovation and the right to privacy remains a problem that is still to be solved. Determining liability when the autonomous systems cause injuries is not easy. There is a responsibility question - whether it is the responsibility of a developer, operator, or it is the AI system itself. This should be changed to legal frameworks to offer clear accountability and liability standards to autonomous technologies. It is a bias issue that results in overfitting or underfitting of the model. Most AI models (deep learning models, especially) are a black box, and it is hard to extract an explanation of how they arrived at the specific decision. Accountability implies the need to make the process transparent and explainable, and the legal aspects of the impact on people by the reasonless decision-making may emerge.

AI-generated content is a burning issue since AI can be the origin of a piece of art or a song, and this is why one can wonder about the ownership of intellectual property. The concept of defining copyright and ownership with the contribution of AI in the creative works creates a challenge to the conventional authorship and ownership ideas. Because of the automation through artificial intelligence, the traditional nature of employment might be impacted, leading to job displacement. The current labor policies might have to change to address the concerns of job dislocation, retraining, and the dynamism of the gig economy. Healthcare Decision-Making Challenge: - AI systems involved in medical diagnoses and treatment suggestions may be opposed under the judicial system in the case of errors. The role of accountability and setting the liability standards is significant in the medical sector, where the application of AI is gaining momentum. The use of AI systems in Testing and Financial Decision-Making: Financial Sector and Algorithmic Trading Challenge. How AI systems manipulate the market and hold them responsible is a topic of concern. Legal challenges that the introduction of AI creates in financial markets will require regulations to change. The autonomous weapons will present ethical and legal issues of responsibility and adherence to international law. The problem with the existence of clear regulations to work and use AI in the context of national security and arms is an urgent necessity (Tripathi and Ghatak, 2018).

APPLICATIONS AND TRANSFORMATIVE POTENTIAL OF AI IN PERSONALISED AND ADAPTIVE LEARNING SYSTEMS IN EDUCATION

One of the most successful ways to use Artificial Intelligence (AI) in modern education is the creation of personalized and adaptive learning systems. These systems are also set to be more than the conventional one-size-fits-all approach to instruction by dynamically responding to the needs of the individual learner by adjusting learning content, learning pace, and instructional methods to fit those needs. Their adoption can be explained by the increased recognition of the fact that learners differ greatly in being characterized by their prior knowledge, the rate of their learning, their motivation, and their cognitive preferences that are rarely discussed within the traditional approaches toward teaching.

The algorithms of AI-based personalized learning systems are data-driven, which means that they constantly analyze the interactions of a learner, their performance in tests, and their behavioral patterns. It is on these observations that the system customizes the instructional paths by proposing individualized learning resources, varying the levels of difficulty, and providing feedback at the appropriate time. This kind of responsiveness also enables learners to proceed to their own level, and with certain assistance where they find they are deficient. The studies suggest that the application of adaptive learning environments may result in the enhancement of engagement among the learners and also benefit their understanding, along with the establishment of deeper learning outcomes through the tailoring of its teaching to the specific flow of the learning (Pane et al., 2017).

Formative assessment and feedback mechanisms are also a significant contribution of adaptive learning systems. As opposed to old-fashioned assessment methods where the feedback is provided in a delayed and standardized manner, an AI-powered platform can offer feedback in real time and personalized to learners as they learn. This feedback loop allows the self-regulated learning process because it helps the learners to know their strengths and weaknesses, since this will help them to be independent and reflective learners (Roll and Wylie, 2016). To educators, such systems may give diagnostic information, which can be utilized to plan the lesson and concentrate on a particular intervention. Individualized learning systems are also involved in education equity and inclusivity. Different students have various levels of socio-economic, linguistic, and academic backgrounds, and they face obstacles in the environment of homogeneity of teaching paradigms. Alternative learning paths, multimodal learning materials, and scaffolding that is differentiated can be offered by adaptive systems to allow more individuals to access quality education. When properly designed, these systems can support learners with varying abilities - some of which will also require remedial assistance and some challenging them and, thus, narrowing achievement gaps (Holmes et al., 2019).

Regardless of their potential to change the way educators behave, the introduction of the personalized and adaptive system of learning should be thoroughly considered about ethical and pedagogical consequences. The excessive use of algorithmic decision-making can put learners at risk of creating stronger biases or exposing learners to alternative points of view. Thus, adaptive technologies should never be left to operate on their own and should be under human supervision to act as a support system and not a determined system. Integrated in a responsible manner, personalised and adaptive systems of learning can enhance human instruction and contribute to the responsiveness, inclusiveness, and effectiveness of education in the 21st century.

Essentially, individualized and adaptive learning systems represent one of the ways information AI may transform the learning process by aligning the learning process with the particular needs without subjecting the pedagogical purpose to change. Their potential to transform it is not the substitution of educators, but the improvement of their capacity to deliver meaningful and learner-based education.

Academic and Administrative Processes Automation

Automation of academic and administrative procedures is a critical application of Artificial Intelligence (AI) in education, which is intended to enhance the efficiency, accuracy, and responsiveness of educational institutions. Schools are very intricate institutions that must deal with the national requirements about student sample, rules on compliance, and scarce resources. In this respect, AI-based automation is a strategic approach to reduce the operational load, as well as improve the quality of services and academic performance.

AI-based automation has found wide application in the academic field in matters pertaining to assessment, including grading, evaluation, and feedback. Machine learning algorithms are also used in automated assessment systems, which evaluate objective tests and assignments, but also, more frequently, short-answer responses. Through these systems, the turnaround time is significantly improved, the evaluation process is also consistent, and immediate feedback is given to the learners. The immediate feedback has been shown to positively influence the motivation and performance of learners and allow educators to be more concerned with the design of instructions and student mentoring (Smutny and Schreiberova, 2020).

In addition to its assessment capabilities, AI can support academic administration that is automated (attendance, course scheduling, enrollment, and academic advising). Predictive algorithms are algorithms that search student records in search of patterns that are connected with attendance, progression, and performance, with the aim of offering early warning to students who may be on the verge of becoming academically disengaged. Institutions that adopt such systems assist in implementing proactive support systems rather than reactive actions to raise the retention and completion rates (Asha and Kumar, 2021).

The automation in the administration of institutions has further advanced to the management of operations within the institution. Chatbots and other virtual assistants are being deployed to help run simple student-related queries such as admissions, examinations, schedules, and financial services, among others, with artificial intelligence. These tools also enhance accessibility by providing 24/7 assistance to reduce dependence on the manual assistance of outside administrators. Moreover, AI systems simplify the processing of documents, automate payroll coordination, and minimize compliance with reporting to a minimum, minimizing risks of errors and increasing organizational transparency (Chaudhry and Kazim, 2022).

The opportunities of automation that can be used to reform education are not confined to an increase in efficiency, but also to the redefinition of the role of an educator and administration. AI also frees academic professionals from repetitive and time-consuming work, leaving them to focus on strategic, creative, and interpersonal work, which involves human judgment and empathy. Nonetheless, such careful governance will be necessary in order to be successful in automation to avoid over-standardization and make sure that human control is a major component of decision-making processes. Data use, algorithmic accountability, and transparency, which need to be covered to maintain trust in the educational ecosystems, are ethical concerns.

While automation enhances efficiency, it also presents challenges related to over-standardisation and pedagogic independence, as teachers may over-rely on algorithmic tools. This could undermine the humanist practices of teaching, such as judgment and context awareness (Luckin et al., 2016).

Big Data Analytics and Predictive Analytics

The powerful part of the application of Artificial Intelligence (AI) in education is data-driven decision-making and predictive analytics, which enable educational organizations to transition to the evidence-based mode of planning and working instead of the intuitive approach. The educational system generates a significant amount of data in relation to enrolment, attendance, assessment performance, learning behaviors, and school operations of students. The analytics tools based on AI can identify patterns, correlations, and trends that would be quite challenging to identify using the conventional forms of analysis based on the same huge data set.

Predictive analytics specifically helps to distinguish the high-risk students in terms of future academic failure based on their history (the use of past data) and more recent data, such as attendance, engagement indexes, and test scores. These proactive models enable institutions to intervene and implement timely interventions like academic counselling, personal care, or curriculum changes. These proactive strategies improve student retention, progress, and overall learning and reduce the dropout rates (Daniel, 2015). At the level of the institution, the data-driven insights may assist the administrators in making more informed decisions related to resource allocation, anticipating the pattern of enrollment, and examining the program performance. Moreover, data analytics based on AI are involved in quality assurance and strategic planning of the academic process. Through the study of teaching performance, curriculum alignment, and student achievement, the institutions can make sound judgments on how they can develop the faculty, restructure their courses, and how they can reform assessment. When done responsibly, data-driven decision-making can be more transparent and accountable, and the ecosystem of education continuously improves.

Predictive analytics afford early intervention and planning, but it also raises concerns in relation to privacy, surveillance and classification of students, which may result in unintended learning outcomes if not properly managed (Zawacki-Richter et al., 2019).

Effects of AI on Teaching and Learning and Institutional Efficiency

The use of AI significantly affects the teaching and learning processes by transforming not only the functions of a pedagogue but also the process of delivering pedagogy. AI-related tools are useful to teachers as they can provide them with intelligent content recommendations, automatic feedback platforms, and learning analytics dashboards that provide data on student progress. These tools assist in enabling the instructors to leave the traditional content delivery processes behind to engage in facilitator, mentor, and greater cognitive interaction. In this way, the teaching process will be more reactive and learner-oriented without losing the required role of human judgment and pedagogical skills (Williamson and Eynon, 2020).

In the learning sense of the term, AI enhances involvement and self-directed learning with the help of timely feedback, personalised learning paths, and interactive online platforms. The learners also create more control over the learning process and awareness of the learning progress, which adds to the motivation and engagement in the more intensive thinking process. Nevertheless, AI-based learning can be effective provided that it is balanced by considerate instructional design and correspondence to pedagogical goals rather than the unplanned use of technology.

But although AI-driven personalisation boosts learner engagement and performance, it can also perpetuate disparities if training data are informed by past biases and inequities in access to digital materials. Research shows that algorithms can inadvertently favour high-achieving students, contributing to learning inequalities when applied in education (Holmes et al., 2019; Zawacki-Richter et al., 2019).

Another significant result of integration with AI is institutional efficiency. AI also prevents operational costs, reduces human error, and maximizes service delivery by automating routine academic and administrative processes and making it possible to base decisions on data instead of hindsight as the main driver of planning. Decision-making is also more precise and more timely, so that institutions can be responsive to the changing needs in the education sector and meet the needs of policy. Nevertheless, institutions should focus on such ethics as the privacy of data, the transparency of algorithms, and accountability to avoid the fact that efficiency gains come at the expense of equity and trust.

Comprehensively, predictive analytics and data-driven choices, and the strength of AI in the way teaching/learning is performed, develop more flexible, effective, and resilient educational institutions. Due to the applied ethical regulations and strategic implementation, AI can become an enhancer of the institutional change and not a displacement of the human-centered education.

A comparative reading of the literature reveals shift in focus among studies. For example, Holmes et al. (2019) highlight the pedagogic and learner benefits of AI, while Luckin et al. (2016) present a view on system change and efficiency. In contrast, Zawacki-Richter et al. (2019) offer a more critical analysis, pointing to the lack of empirical evidence and concerns about ethics, bias and implementation. This analysis highlights the need for a more holistic and governance-focused perspective that incorporates innovation and critique.

Legal and Ethical Problems of AI: Data Privacy, Consent, and Data Protection

The advent of Artificial Intelligence (AI) into online systems has sounded alarm bells over the privacy, consent, and safety of the data, particularly in the information-intensive domains of education, healthcare, and government. The AI systems are relying on large volumes of personal and behavioral data to be effective; such data consists of demographic information, performance data, interaction data, and sometimes biometric data. This colossal reliance on information poses vital questions of the way and the stage at which the data are gathered, handled, stored, and shared, and by whom.

The scope and the fineness of the collected data are two of the primary privacy issues. Nonetheless, AI-based platforms are frequently enlisted in the unceasing quality of information, which may confuse the lines between the required use and provision of information and excessive surveillance. In education, such as student behaviour, e.g., learning analytics tools, data mining of student behaviour monitors student behaviour at an extremely fine scale, which could reveal sensitive data on learning problems or cognitive tendencies, or socio-economic status. In the absence of robust protective measures, this information may become vulnerable to abuse, unethical access, or other subsequent applications other than intended use (Pardo & Siemens, 2014).

Another significant ethical and legal concern is consent. Consent mechanisms that are traditionally used are not always applicable to the use of AI-driven systems since they are complex and not clear. Without clear knowledge of the manner in which their data will be analyzed, aggregated with other data, or used to make automated decisions, users are able to formally consent to be collected through in-depth privacy policies. This is a compromise to the principle of informed consent, of which there should be clarity, voluntariness, and meaningful choice. In most situations, there are no alternatives to choose not to do so, and the individuals, particularly students or employees, are forced into the asymmetrical position of data subjects and data institutions.

Issues of cross-border data flows and data security are also adding to the concerns of data protection issues. Cloud-based infrastructure and third-party vendors are common to AI systems, which poses a risk to cybersecurity infrastructure. The impact of data breaches in the case of AI-managed databases of managing personal information is long-term, as once the data breaches have taken place, personal information is not that simple to reclaim or erase. In addition, the presence of dissimilar national data protection regimes contributes to the difficulty in terms of accountability when processing data in another country (Bennett and Raab, 2020).

Regulation frameworks like the General Data Protection Regulation (GDPR) have attempted to deal with these issues by prioritizing data minimization, purpose limitation, and user rights. Nevertheless, the pace of the evolution of AI technologies is still playing the ruthless game with the applicability of existing legal tools. Ethical implementation of AI, therefore, means going beyond adherence to organizational legislation and institutional commitment to privacy-by-design methods, open data management, and continuous monitoring.

The application of AI in education, including personalized learning platforms, thus has privacy issues concerning its data collection and storage of student data. The European Union General Data Protection Regulation (GDPR) is a law that covers the problem of data privacy, particularly in the context of educational technology. Strict requirements and regulations of the GDPR are reflected in processing student data, where educational institutions and education technology (EdTech) companies must adhere to strict data protection requirements and seek the informed consent of the students or their parents. These rules are supposed to create a fine line between the advantages of education through AI and the safety of the personal information of their students. The opportunities of AI in the education sector are personalized learning, adaptive assessments, and educational content recommendations. Nonetheless, the confidentiality of the information and the security of student data are necessary.

Case Study 1: Classroom Protection of Student Information. Legislation to protect the information of students in a school environment has been enacted in countries like the United States and the European Union under the law Family Educational Rights and Privacy Act (FERPA) and the General Data Protection Regulation (GDPR), respectively. AI applications applied to the educational industry are supposed to comply with those regulations to protect the privacy of students and ensure data security.

Case Study 2: Adaptive Learning AI-Based Educational Technology Duolingo and Khan Academy are educational technology firms that leverage AI algorithms to customize the learning process of their students. Such learning platforms discern distinct learning behaviors, strengths, and weaknesses, and develop individual-based content and recommendations that enhance interaction and improve learning rates among students.

The above case studies show that AI is transforming many industries and sectors of society, and this is why there is a necessity for certain regulatory frameworks. Through collaboration with industry players, academicians, and civil societies, policymakers can develop responsive and attentive AI policies in a balance of innovation, safety, privacy, and equity. With AI influencing industries and contributing to social development, smart and active regulation will become key to using the potential of AI to make the lives of people, communities, and society at large better.

Algorithms Bias, Fairness, and Inclusivity: The Legal and Ethical Problems of AI

One of the most urgent ethical issues related to Artificial Intelligence is algorithmic bias, since AI systems are becoming more involved with the process of making decisions that can affect people and communities. AI bias is mostly not caused intentionally but by both structural causes, like biased training data, assumptions, or unequal veneration of social groups. By reproducing or enhancing the pre-existing inequalities, AI systems may pose a threat to strengthen the discriminatory policy instead of providing equality and diversity.

Prejudice is frequently induced in the data of the past that is utilized to educate the AI models. AI systems learn patterns based on prior data, which makes them susceptible to being biased towards societal prejudices of gender, ethnicity, socioeconomic class, or disability. To provide an example, predictive models can be unfair in that they give an advantage to the marginalized groups, since the aspect of history has shown unequal opportunity access. Such biases may affect admissions, grading, or performance evaluations in the educational or job-related environment, which result in systemic exclusion (Barocas, Hardt, and Narayanan, 2019).

Fairness in AI not only covers the technical accuracy but also includes normative and ethical coverage. Such definitions of fairness as equal treatment, equal outcomes, or equal opportunity can be conflicting with one another, and it is hard to create universally fair algorithms. Choices on which criteria of fairness to be applied are necessarily really value-based, and technical solutions cannot be used to solve these. This presents the necessity to adopt an interdisciplinary strategy that incorporates the legal, ethical, and social dimensions of AI design and implementation (Friedman and Nissenbaum, 1996).

Close to the notion of inclusivity is the concept of fairness, which involves active endeavors to make sure that AI systems benefit a wide array of people. Inclusive AI design entails the involvement of various stakeholders, such as those who are underrepresented, by including them in the development and testing of the system. In such a manner, AI tools will not include the views and interests of a broader group, which will marginalize others. To ensure the overcoming of biased outcomes over time, inclusive practices must also be monitored (Selbst et al., 2019).

Algorithm bias requires both technical solutions, organizational solutions, and regulation. These are training dataset diversification, bias audit, accountability mechanisms, and institutional ethical review. In conclusion, equity and inclusion in AI are not a one-time challenge but an ongoing endeavor, which should change with change in technology and society.

The Legitimacy, Accountability, Transparency, and Explainability of AI Legal-Ethical Challenges

Transparency and explicability are the two principles used to ensure ethical and legal implementation of the Artificial Intelligence systems, especially when AI is used to make high-stakes decisions. Most sophisticated AI systems, particularly deep-learning systems, are black boxes in that they give an answer without a clear understanding of how they came to that conclusion. This transparency questions credibility, privacy of users, and complicates juridical responsibility. Transparency is the accessibility of AI systems, information on the functioning of systems, such as their sources of data, decision logic, and constraints. Explainability takes things a notch higher since it allows users to learn and interpret AI-driven results on an upwardly meaningful level. Whether it is in education, healthcare, or finance, the absence of explainability can cause people to trust and even challenge decisions that impact their lives heavily (Doshi-Velez and Kim, 2017). The lack of accountability is especially a problem with autonomous or semi-autonomous AI systems. It is tricky to identify who is responsible in cases of mistakes or damage when AI decisions are taken because various stakeholders might be involved, with examples being developers, deployers, and data providers. In the absence of definite accountability structures, victims can have fewer avenues of redress, and these mechanisms undermine legal safeguards and citizen trust (Bovens, 2007).

Having explainable AI is gaining importance with regulatory initiatives. Legal principles of due process, non-discrimination, and procedural fairness mandate that every decision must be accountable and subject to evaluation. Nevertheless, to be explainable technically is not enough, and explanations should be context sensitive as well as made user-friendly by non-learners. It requires humanistic methods that unite technical instruments with institutional control and ethical policy frameworks (Ananny and Crawford, 2018).To achieve accountability within the AI systems, well-defined positions, documentation routines, and audit processes are needed. The decision-making process of human decision makers needs to be safeguarded by institutions, especially when critical decisions are to be made. Three principles are thus interrelated to one another, and accountable, explainable, and transparent are three concepts that complement responsible AI governance.

THE LEGAL AND ETHICAL ISSUES OF AI: INTELLECTUAL PROPERTY AND THE ISSUE OF OWNERSHIP

AI puts intellectual property (IP) in a new perspective because it distorts the human and machine intelligence in creativity. AI systems are frequently becoming more and more capable of producing content like text, music, designs, and data-driven insights, presenting difficult questions on the side of authorship, ownership, and rights assignment. The current IP systems (to a large extent based on human creativity) cannot adapt to these advances.

One of them has to do with the authorship of the results of AI-generated outputs. In cases where the AI system generates creative/analytical work, it is not clear to whom ownership should be given: the developer, the user, the provider of the data, or the institution that employs the system. In the majority of jurisdictions, the existing copyright regulations fail to acknowledge AI as an author and leave it unclear how it can be protected and enforced (Ginsburg and Budiardjo, 2019).

The teaching data also poses many IP concerns. AI models are also commonly trained using extensive datasets that can potentially contain copyrighted data/ proprietary data, or personal information. Use of this type of data without express permission may be the cause of infringement litigations, especially when works generated by AI are similar to the ones under protection. It is a persistently litigious question as to whether training should be characterized as fair use or needs to be licensed (Samuelson, 2020). Also, with AI-generated content, originality and infringement become challenging issues. When an AI system generates content that can recreate the parts of the existing works, it becomes difficult to identify the liability. The question arises as to whether it should be the responsibility of the algorithm itself, its designers, or users. These ambiguities are what drive the need to have more definitive contractual terms and regulations of AI implementation. In order to deal with these issues, policymakers and institutions need to reconsider IP frameworks to be relevant to the reality of AI-aided creation. These involve defining the ownership rights, updating the licensing pattern, and creating accountability processes. It is necessary to adopt a middle ground to safeguard the rights of the creators and stimulate innovation and responsible working with AI technologies.

Need for AI-Governance in the Educational Context

The growing tendency towards Artificial Intelligence (AI) use in education has provoked a gap in the demand for systematic governance systems. Schools are not only places of technological implementation but sensitive environments that can affect learning directions, equity, and future experience directly in the decisions made. Unlike most business spheres, education implies vulnerable groups, the long-term levels of development, and societal responsibility, and the uncontrolled or insufficiently regulated use of AI is especially serious.

The asymmetry of power between institutions, technology providers, educators, and learners is an issue that AI governance in the education sector must address. The majority of AI-driven systems tend to gather and analyze extensive amounts of personal and behavioral data, suggest actions that affect academic advancement, and automate the process of decisions that have been historically made by human factors. In the absence of these governance mechanisms, such systems can potentially work in shady ways that erode trust, autonomy, and fairness. Governance frameworks give clarity in areas, roles, responsibilities, and authority to make decisions, and ensure that AI is more of a support mechanism and not a takeover power (Williamson and Kizilcec, 2022). One more important reason behind AI governance is risk management. There is a chance of AI systems presenting threats connected to data abuse, algorithmic discrimination, excessive supervision, and lack of access to marginalized students. Schools may be unable to evaluate such risks due to the technical expertise required, particularly when AI solutions are purchased by external providers. Ethics review boards, risk assessment procedures, and guidelines on procurement are some of the governance structures that assist institutions in pre-and in-deployment reviews of AI tools that would minimize unintended harms (Crawford, 2021).

Pedagogical integrity also needs to be maintained through AI governance. Education essentially is a human process that is based on dialogue, mentorship, and critical thinking. Unquestioning appreciation of the recommendations provided by AI or over- automation can either promote limited learning experiences or emphasize efficiency over educational perspectives. Governance models will also mean that pedagogical goals drive technological implementation, and not have technology determine educational practice. Politically, AI governance will help to comply with the national and global regulatory norms regarding data protection, child rights, and digital ethics. The institutions of education are part of larger legal environments, and irresponsible AI governance can subject them to legal responsibility and reputational harm. The governance mechanisms, in turn, play an intermediating role between the legal-ethical compliance and technological innovation.

Altogether, AI governance in the education system is not an inhibitor of innovation but a prerequisite to the accountable, trustworthy, and sustainable AI adoption. It helps institutions to achieve the positive attributes of AI, whilst protecting educational values, the rights of the learner, and social trust.

Tenets of Responsible and Ethical AI Regulation

The idea that technological systems are not value-neutral instills ethical and responsible AI regulation because social priorities, institutional incentives, and design decisions have been reflected in them. The principles of regulation give normative direction to allow AI development and deployment to be consonant with the core human values, especially in sensitive areas of society, such as education. The principles are used as standards to assess the level to which the AI systems facilitate human well-being, justice, and accountability.

Fairness is one of the main principles of ethical AI regulation. The AI systems should be designed and tested to avoid discriminatory results and provide equal treatment to the different groups of users in equal terms. The fairness is something that should be monitored continuously, whereby the algorithmic behavior can vary with time based on new entries of data or changes in the circumstances. Hence, regulation should not stop at a single, ad-hoc compliance but proceed to constant ethical evaluation (Floridi et al., 2018). Another premise principle involves transparency and explainability. AI-driven decisions must be made available to the users in understandable explanations on how and why certain outcomes are arrived at. Transparency helps in supporting trust, controllers, and the facilitation of regulatory oversight. Explainable systems enable educators and learners to interact with AI recommendations critical to consider them as authoritative in an educational setting (Jobin, Ienca, and Vayena, 2019).

These are also necessitated by human regulation of ethical AI. AI systems are not supposed to supplant human judgment but augment it, particularly in making a decision with serious personal or academic ramifications. Regulatory paradigms focus on the significance of the human-in-the-loop or human-on-the-loop paradigm so that the human does not lose the mandate to interfere, disturb, or revise AI findings as and when it is required. Data confidentiality and security are also a key pillar of ethical AI regulation. Conscientious regulation involves minimization of data, restrictions of purpose, and high-quality protection. The practice of data collection should be governed ethically, in which users of their data are respected in terms of their autonomy and dignity, and not as a source of data. All of these principles offer a moral and legal guide to AI regulation. They do not dictate fixed technical solutions but create some ethical boundaries that make innovation possible within the capacity of responsible behavior.

Finding the Middle Ground Between Innovation and Regulatory Oversight

The critical issue of balance between innovation and effective regulatory control is among the fundamental policy issues about Artificial Intelligence. Over-regulation can inhibit trial and error and retard technological advances, and those who lack regulation can place individuals and institutions in an unethical, legal, and social jeopardy. This balance is especially important in the field of education, where innovation meets the interests of society and long-term societal results. Innovation is a position that succeeds in an environment that promotes experimentation, responsiveness, and continuous development. Artificial intelligence technologies change fast, and strict regulation might fail to keep in line with new uses. The issue for policymakers is that they must be able to structure adaptive regulatory strategies that will not be too burdensome to the innovators. A mechanism of testing AI applications in a controlled environment and collecting evidence about risks and benefits is provided by regulatory sandboxes, pilot programs, and phased implementation models (Veale and Borgesius, 2021). Simultaneously, the regulation is necessary to eliminate the negative outcomes and establish responsibility. Education is governed by a state of trust, and mistakes associated with the use of AI can affect the masses. Intense scrutiny measures like impact assessment, audit, and reporting requirements assist in the detection of risks at an initial stage and adherence to ethical practices. Good oversight may not mean prescriptive rules; however, it is outcome-based regulation that is aimed at transparency, accountability, and protection of rights. It is also necessary to differentiate along risk lines to take a middle course. This does not mean that all AI applications should get the same level of regulation. Tools with low risks (i.e., administrative scheduling systems) might need minimal control, and tools with high risk (i.e., assessment, progression, or access to opportunities) may need harsher controls. Risk-based regulation can enable the policymaker to focus proportionately on regulation and facilitate innovation and protection of core values.

Finally, it is a continuous process and not a solution to strike a balance of innovation and oversight. Regulators, educators, developers, and learners should engage in an ongoing discussion to realign policies being constantly changed by new technologies and social requirements.

Strategic Policy Action Plan for Policy-Makers, Institutions, and Developers

The governance of AI needs to be done efficiently by coordination with policy-makers, educational institutions, and the developers of technology. The individual stakeholder groups have their unique position in the design, regulation, and usage of AI systems. Responsibilities among these interconnected actors should then be solicited in strategic recommendations.

To policymakers, the issue of adopting clear, adaptive, and context-specific regulation systems is the priority. The policies must define minimum standards of data protection, accountability, and ethical practices, and leave enough room to be innovative. The policymakers must also work on institutional capacity building, where regulators and education bodies would learn to analyze and assess AI technologies efficiently. It is necessary to consult the public and involve the stakeholders as much as possible in order to see that the policies are based on the values and priorities of the education of the society. Educational Institutions have the duty of implementing policy ideas in practice. In-house AI governance mechanisms need to be put in place in institutions, including ethics committees, review boards, and impact assessment guidelines. The training of faculty and staff in terms of AI literacy is crucial to adopt and supervise it more carefully. Transparency with learners should be a priority of the institutions, explaining the usage of AI tools and the ways of decision-making unambiguously.

The developers will be influential in integrating morality into the design of AI. Privacy-by-design, fairness testing, and explainability are responsible development practices that can be done during the initial development phase. Practitioners who use AI to develop educational systems need to work with the educators and policymakers to make sure those AI systems correspond with the goals of pedagogy and regulatory standards. It must be able to create clarity and be audited to facilitate accountability throughout the AI lifecycle. Interdisciplinary collaboration is important across all groups of stakeholders. Lawyers, technologists, teachers, and social scientists will need to collaborate in predicting possible risks and developing solutions together. Strategic governance, thus, is not a single action but an ongoing or ongoing process that focuses on integrating the AI innovation in the best interest of the people.

CONCLUSION

The accelerated deployment of Artificial Intelligence into education systems is a paradigm shift in the way the concepts of teaching, learning, and institutional scenes are thought about and implemented. As evidenced in this chapter, AI is not a technological improvement as such, but a socio-technical agent that alters the model of pedagogy, administration, and regulation to transform the administrative framework and its control needs. Its potential to revolutionize learning is in the fact that it can be personalized, standardize routine procedures, and facilitate decision-making based on data, where its risks can be seen in the fact that the ethical, legal, and governance issues require great care and careful consideration. On the lower level, AI applications like machine learning, natural language processing, and predictive analytics have increased the ability of educational institutions to address the diversity of learners and their systemic complexity. Adaptive and personalized learning systems can be seen as an example of how artificial intelligence can promote learner-centric learning by personalizing content and pacing and providing feedback. On the same note, academic and administrative automation has also proven a real efficiency increase, as it lets educators and administrators out of the repetition of academic and administrative processes, towards more teaching and planning engagement. Making decisions that are informed by data also leads to greater institutional responsiveness through the provision of early interventions and the allocation of resources, as well as quality improvements.

Nevertheless, these advantages cannot be discussed independently of legal and ethical issues, which tourism's adoption of AI causes. The chapter has underscored the fact that the massive data collection is of serious concern about privacy, consent, and data protection. Within the context of an educational setting, where students are frequently required to participate, but it is not a voluntary one, the process of informed consent and motivated choice becomes especially complicated. The issue of algorithmic bias and fairness highlights the danger of supporting existing social injustices with the use of data-driven systems in cases where historical data is systemically disadvantaged. These issues show that technical accuracy is not enough, and the design and implementation of AI must be driven by ethical liability and social consciousness. Explainability, accountability, and transparency become the key components of responsible AI governance. There will be no trust and little avenue to topple the decisions made by AI, with no understandable explanations as to why. Losses of accountability make governance even more complex when the process of making decisions is spread among developers, institutions, and automated systems. Another point of complication is intellectual property concerns, which AI-generated content is complicating the notions of authorship, ownership, and originality in law. Combined, these problems indicate that current legal systems are usually inadequately prepared to deal with the facts of AI-based education, providing regulatory ambiguity and ethical uncertainty.

To counter these problems, this chapter has highlighted the need to have strong regulatory frameworks and policy orientations specific to the educational contexts. The use of AI in education should be governed not to limit innovation but to make certain that technological innovation is in line with the social interests of the population, educational values, and human rights. Normative underpinnings of ethical AI regulation can be found in such principles as fairness, transparency, human oversight, and data protection, whereas risk-based and adaptive forms of regulations assist in balancing between innovation and control. Notably, governance needs to be perceived as a dynamic process and not a set of rules, but one that needs constant monitoring, reviewing, and interaction with stakeholders.

The recommendations put across by the authors in this chapter in terms of strategy development point to a common responsibility that should be carried out by policymakers, educational institutions, and developers. To ensure the development of adaptive regulations and context-sensitive regulations, policymakers need to design adaptive regulations to suit different contexts and situations, the institutions need to develop internal governance systems and create AI literacy, and developers need to shape ethical considerations throughout the AI lifecycle. Bi-directional collaboration and participatory design can be analyzed as essential facilitators of responsible innovation because this way makes sure that AI systems contemplate a wide range of opinions and priorities in education.

To sum it up, AI will become an essential part of educational processes in the future, yet it remains entirely dependent on the decisions of people controlling, designing, and potentially deploying these systems. Ethical vision, legal transparency, and institutional responsibility are prerequisites to the belief in using AI as an enabler rather than a means of exclusion. Under the leadership of ethically conscious governance and those values that are human-well-being centered, AI is capable of promoting equity, efficiency, and quality of education, and maintaining education as a care of human purpose. This chapter, therefore, proposes the adoption of a moderate and thoughtful response- one that is ready to embrace innovation but at the same time has a strong base of ethical accountability and trust of the people.

REFERENCES

Ananny, M., & Crawford, K. (2018). Seeing without knowing: Limitations of the transparency ideal. *New Media & Society*, *20*(3), 973–989. DOI: 10.1177/1461444816676645

Asha, S., & Kumar, S. (2021). Predictive analytics in higher education: Applications, challenges, and future directions. *Journal of Applied Research in Higher Education*, *13*(4), 1104–1118.

Barocas, S., Hardt, M., & Narayanan, A. (2019). *Fairness and machine learning*. FairML Book.

Bennett, C. J., & Raab, C. D. (2020). *The governance of privacy: Policy instruments in global perspective* (2nd ed.). MIT Press.

Bovens, M. (2007). Analysing and assessing accountability: A conceptual framework. *European Law Journal*, *13*(4), 447–468. DOI: 10.1111/j.1468-0386.2007.00378.x

Chaudhry, A., & Kazim, E. (2022). Artificial intelligence in education: Ethical and administrative challenges. *AI & Society*, *37*(2), 451–463.

Crawford, K. (2021). *Atlas of AI: Power, politics, and the planetary costs of artificial intelligence*. Yale University Press.

Daniel, B. K. (2015). Big data and analytics in higher education: Opportunities and challenges. *British Journal of Educational Technology*, *46*(5), 904–920. DOI: 10.1111/bjet.12230

Doshi-Velez, F., & Kim, B. (2017). Towards a rigorous science of interpretable machine learning. *arXiv preprint arXiv:1702.08608.*

Floridi, L., Cowls, J., Beltrametti, M., Chatila, R., Chazerand, P., Dignum, V., Luetge, C., Madelin, R., Pagallo, U., Rossi, F., Schafer, B., Valcke, P., & Vayena, E. (2018). AI4People—An ethical framework for a good AI society. *Minds and Machines*, *28*(4), 689–707. DOI: 10.1007/s11023-018-9482-5 PMID: 30930541

Friedman, B., & Nissenbaum, H. (1996). Bias in computer systems. *ACM Transactions on Information Systems*, *14*(3), 330–347. DOI: 10.1145/230538.230561

Ginsburg, J. C., & Budiardjo, L. A. (2019). Authors and machines. *Berkeley Technology Law Journal*, *34*(2), 343–448.

Holmes, W., Bialik, M., & Fadel, C. (2019). *Artificial intelligence in education: Promises and implications for teaching and learning*. Center for Curriculum Redesign.

Jobin, A., Ienca, M., & Vayena, E. (2019). The global landscape of AI ethics guidelines. *Nature Machine Intelligence*, *1*(9), 389–399. DOI: 10.1038/s42256-019-0088-2

Luckin, R., Holmes, W., Griffiths, M., & Forcier, L. B. (2016). *Intelligence unleashed: An argument for AI in education*. Pearson Education.

More, A. B., Nigam, N., Sharda, P., Shrivastava, A., & Kate, V. (2025). Technological intelligence and urban sustainability. In *IEEE ICIH Conference Proceedings*.

Pane, J. F., Steiner, E. D., Baird, M. D., & Hamilton, L. S. (2017). *Informing progress: Insights on personalized learning*. RAND Corporation.

Pardo, A., & Siemens, G. (2014). Ethical and privacy principles for learning analytics. *British Journal of Educational Technology*, *45*(3), 438–450. DOI: 10.1111/bjet.12152

Roll, I., & Wylie, R. (2016). Evolution and revolution in AI in education. *International Journal of Artificial Intelligence in Education*, *26*(2), 582–599. DOI: 10.1007/s40593-016-0110-3

Samuelson, P. (2020). AI authorship? *Communications of the ACM*, *63*(4), 20–22. DOI: 10.1145/3401718

Selbst, A. D., Boyd, D., & Friedler, S. A.. (2019). Fairness and abstraction in sociotechnical systems. *Proceedings of the ACM FAT Conference*, 59–68.

Smutny, P., & Schreiberova, P. (2020). Chatbots for learning. *Computers & Education*, *151*, 103862. DOI: 10.1016/j.compedu.2020.103862

Tripathi, S., & Ghatak, C. (2018). Artificial intelligence and intellectual property law. *Christ University Law Journal*, *7*(1), 83–98. DOI: 10.12728/culj.12.5

UNESCO. (2021). *AI and education: Guidance for policy-makers*. UNESCO Publishing.

Veale, M., & Borgesius, F. Z. (2021). Demystifying the draft EU Artificial Intelligence Act. *Computer Law Review International*, *22*(4), 97–112. DOI: 10.9785/cri-2021-220402

Williamson, B., & Eynon, R. (2020). AI in education: Historical threads and future directions. *Learning, Media and Technology*, *45*(3), 223–235. DOI: 10.1080/17439884.2020.1798995

Williamson, B., & Kizilcec, R. F. (2022). AI and the future of education governance. *Educational Technology Research and Development*, *70*(5), 2351–2370. DOI: 10.1007/s11423-022-10146-1

Zawacki-Richter, O., Marín, V. I., Bond, M., & Gouverneur, F. (2019). Systematic review of research on artificial intelligence applications in higher education. *International Journal of Educational Technology in Higher Education*, *16*(1), 1–27. DOI: 10.1186/s41239-019-0171-0

Chapter 6
Equity by Design: AI Ethics Guidelines for the Education Sector

Soha Badr
http://orcid.org/0009-0004-3512-6874
The British University in Dubai, UAE

Tendai Charles
http://orcid.org/0000-0002-0253-5960
The British University in Dubai, UAE

ABSTRACT

This chapter advances an Equity-by-Design framework for governing institutional uses of artificial intelligence (AI) in schools and universities. It responds to a persistent gap between high-level "ethical AI" principles and the concrete governance, procurement and monitoring practices needed to protect equity, accessibility and privacy in educational settings. It draws on international policy instruments, emerging regulation and research on AI in education, learning analytics and digital accessibility to construct an institutional architecture for responsible AI adoption. The framework is structured as a multi-stage lifecycle encompassing problem framing, risk triage, procurement and contracting, piloting and acceptance testing, deployment, monitoring and incident response, and periodic review and decommissioning. The chapter concludes that ethical AI in education is fundamentally a problem of institutional design: building organisations that can systematically resist harmful uses of AI, foreground inclusion and rights, and revise or withdraw systems when they cannot be made just.

DOI: 10.4018/979-8-3373-7467-3.ch006

INTRODUCTION

Across schooling and higher education, artificial intelligence (AI) has moved from speculative possibility to everyday infrastructure (Azzam & Charles, 2025). Adaptive platforms, generative writing assistants, early-alert analytics, proctoring tools and student-services chatbots increasingly mediate how learners are taught, assessed and supported (Adel et al., 2024). At the same time, international bodies such as UNESCO and the OECD warn that AI can deepen rather than reduce educational inequalities if deployed without robust attention to rights, fairness and accessibility (Chen et al., 2020; Chen et al., 2022). Institutions thus confront a dual responsibility; they must prepare learners to live in AI-mediated societies while also acting as major deployers of AI whose decisions shape access, progression and wellbeing (Zawacki-Richter et al., 2019; Zhang & Aslan, 2021).

Despite a proliferation of "ethical AI" principles, there is a persistent operational gap (Charles & Alshamsi, 2025; Charles & Papadaki, 2025). Many universities and school systems now publish responsible-AI statements, yet their decisions about procurement and deployment are still driven primarily by cost, features and vendor narratives (Nguyen et al., 2023). Issues of bias, privacy and accessibility are often addressed late, framed as compliance hurdles rather than criteria that determine whether a system should be used at all (Holmes et al., 2022). The emerging regulatory landscape, exemplified by the EU AI Act's risk-based classification of many educational applications as "high-risk", and its prohibition of emotion inference in educational settings, further raises the stakes - meaning ethics is no longer merely aspirational but increasingly juridical (Oncioiu & Bularca, 2025; Wieczorek et al., 2025).

We respond to this gap by advancing an "Equity-by-Design" framework for institutional AI governance in schools and universities. The central claim is that equity, accessibility and privacy must be treated as first-order design requirements for AI adoption, encoded into governance arrangements, procurement criteria, documentation standards and monitoring routines (Chan, 2023; Oncioiu & Bularca, 2025). Ethical AI in education becomes, on this view, less a question of isolated tools and more a question of organisational architecture, who is authorised to approve AI use, on what evidence, with what possibilities for contestation, and under what conditions systems are modified or withdrawn (Torres-Rivera et al., 2025).

Essentially, this chapter has three objectives. First, it asks how institutions can formally encode equity, accessibility and privacy as binding constraints within governance, procurement and acceptance-testing protocols. Second, it explores which forms of documentation and pre-deployment testing are most promising for supporting equitable outcomes once systems are deployed. Third, it examines which monitoring routines, metrics and reporting practices best support continuous improvement and public trust. Methodologically, the chapter is conceptual and design-oriented: it synthesises existing policy, standards and research into a coherent framework. Its distinctive contribution lies in translating these dispersed sources into a single institutional framework that treats equity, accessibility and privacy as binding design constraints across the AI lifecycle, and in offering illustrative tools (such as lifecycle stages, governance roles and AIA dimensions) that institutions can adapt in practice. The next section outlines the conceptual and policy foundations that underpin this framework.

CONCEPTUAL AND POLICY FOUNDATIONS

The framework distinguishes several concepts that are frequently conflated in debates about AI in education. Bias refers to systematic error in prediction or classification, arising from data, modelling choices or deployment context (Baker & Hawn, 2022). In early-alert systems, for instance, models may systematically over-flag certain student groups, even when aggregate accuracy appears high (Bird et al., 2025). Fairness is normative rather than purely statistical: it concerns whether differential performance across groups is justifiable in light of educational aims and social commitments (Opoku et al., 2025). Different formal fairness criteria are often mutually incompatible, making institutional value choices unavoidable (Idowu, 2024).

Privacy concerns the conditions under which student and staff data are collected, processed and shared, and the extent to which individuals retain control over their personal information. Large-scale data aggregation, repurposing of historical records for model training, and cross-border cloud processing all raise privacy questions that cannot be left solely to technical teams (Ferguson, 2019). Accessibility refers to the extent to which AI-mediated systems can be used by learners and staff with diverse disabilities and access needs (Khalil et al., 2024). Standards such as WCAG 2.2 and EN 301 549, together with Universal Design for Learning (UDL), provide concrete criteria and pedagogical principles for designing inclusive digital environments (Selwyn, 2019). Equity is understood as multi-dimensional. It includes distributional equity (who benefits or is harmed), recognitional equity (whose identities, languages and disabilities are represented and respected), and participatory equity (whose voices influence decisions about AI adoption). Equity therefore exceeds parity of outcomes and requires attention to representation and governance (Navas-Bonilla et al., 2025). In an Equity-by-Design perspective, bias, fairness, privacy and accessibility are interlocking institutional responsibilities, not isolated technical issues (Bayer et al., 2023; Samaniego López et al., 2025).

AI tools in education are often presented as neutral instruments that can be layered onto existing practices (Zawacki-Richter et al., 2019). A sociotechnical perspective rejects this view. AI systems reshape decision-making processes, reconfigure the relations between teachers, students, administrators and vendors, and alter what counts as valid evidence of performance or need (Charles, 2025). Predictive analytics can change how staff perceive "at-risk" students and allocate support; automated grading affects students' sense of fairness and trust; chatbots mediate students' access to information and care (Selwyn, 2019). These effects are produced by the interaction of algorithms, institutional norms, professional cultures and regulatory frameworks (Ferguson, 2019; Holmes et al., 2022;). Recognising AI as sociotechnical has two consequences. Ethical evaluation must extend across the AI lifecycle (problem framing, procurement, configuration, deployment, monitoring and retirement) rather than focusing solely on model design (Oncioiu & Bularca, 2025). And responsibility must be located at institutional level: ethical AI is not simply a matter of individual teacher discretion or vendor promises, but of the organisational processes that permit, constrain and review AI use (Nguyen et al., 2023).

International policy instruments provide normative anchors for the framework. UNESCO's Recommendation on the Ethics of Artificial Intelligence and its guidance on AI in education and generative AI call for human-rights-based, inclusive, and human-centred deployment, with particular emphasis on protecting learners' rights and teacher professionalism (Holmes et al., 2022). OECD AI Principles stress inclusive growth, human-centred values, transparency, robustness and accountability, and explicitly identify education as a high-stakes domain (Nguyen et al., 2023). Regulatory and technical standards complement these high-level commitments. The EU AI Act introduces a risk-based regime in which many educational systems are classed as high-risk and subject to stringent requirements on data governance, documentation, human oversight and post-market monitoring (Wieczorek et al., 2025). Article 5 bans uses such as emotion inference in educational settings and exploitative profiling of minors. Frameworks such as the NIST AI Risk Management Framework and ISO/IEC 23894 articulate lifecycle-oriented processes for governing AI-related risks, while WCAG 2.2 and EN 301 549 provide detailed accessibility criteria (Torres-Rivera et al., 2025). Taken together, these developments establish a convergent expectation: AI in education should be human-centred, equitable, accessible, transparent, risk-managed and subject to continuous oversight. What remains under-specified is how individual institutions should redesign their internal architectures to meet these expectations. That is the task to which the Equity-by-Design framework is addressed.

METHODOLOGY

This chapter is best understood as a conceptual synthesis informed by design-science thinking rather than a complete design-science research project. We do not report iterative build-and-evaluate cycles or field trials of artefacts. Instead, we draw on international ethical and policy frameworks, regulatory and technical standards, and research on AI in education, learning analytics, digital accessibility and institutional governance to articulate a structured Equity-by-Design framework for institutional practice.

Design-science research emphasises the construction of artefacts (frameworks, models, templates and procedures) that address identified problems in organisational practice. We adopt this orientation at the level of problem framing and solution structure: the chapter diagnoses a gap between high-level principles and institutional tools, derives design requirements from the literature, and proposes a coherent life-cycle architecture for AI governance in education. Tables 1 and 2, together with the governance model, Algorithmic Impact Assessment (AIA) dimensions, procurement principles and monitoring routines, function as indicative artefacts that institutions can adapt, extend and empirically evaluate in their own contexts.

This approach is necessarily propositional. The chapter does not claim empirical validation of the framework or its components; rather, it offers a conceptually grounded design that can serve as a basis for practical experimentation and future empirical study. The next section introduces the Equity-by-Design lifecycle that organises these commitments into a sequence of institutional processes.

THE EQUITY-BY-DESIGN LIFECYCLE

Equity-by-Design reconceptualises institutional AI adoption as a multi-stage lifecycle rather than a one-off procurement decision. It distinguishes stages such as problem framing and needs analysis, pre-procurement risk triage, procurement and contracting, pilot implementation and acceptance testing, deployment and routine use, monitoring and incident response, and periodic review and decommissioning (Ferguson, 2019; Nguyen et al., 2023). At each stage, equity, accessibility and privacy are treated as binding constraints: some uses of AI are ruled out by design, while others are permitted only under conditions that maintain human oversight and student rights. Table 1 summarises these stages, the kinds of activities involved and the key equity and accessibility questions that should be asked at each point.

Before institution-wide deployment, systems undergo pilot implementation and acceptance testing. Pilots are formally governed test phases involving diverse learners and staff, designed to validate assumptions from the AIA in real contexts

(Khalil et al., 2024). Acceptance testing synthesises technical performance, subgroup fairness, accessibility, privacy, and pedagogical value, and culminates in a structured go/no-go decision (Rets et al., 2023). Only then are systems deployed at scale, with clear guidance to staff and students about appropriate use and appeal routes (Bayer et al., 2023). Monitoring and review are continuous. Dashboards track indicators such as subgroup outcomes, accessibility defects, complaints and incidents, while incident-management processes allow for rapid containment and remediation (Idowu, 2024). Periodic reviews revisit earlier assumptions and, where necessary, trigger decommissioning (Ferguson, 2019). Throughout, equity, accessibility and privacy are treated as binding constraints, meaning some practices (e.g., emotion inference in classrooms, systems that cannot be made accessible) are excluded by design; others are permitted only under conditions that preserve human oversight and student rights (Opoku et al., 2025; Selwyn, 2019). Table 1 summarises the main stages of this lifecycle, the activities involved, and the key equity and accessibility questions at each point.

Table 1. Equity-by-design lifecycle stages

Lifecycle stage	Main purpose	Typical activities	Key questions	Core institutional artefacts
1. Problem framing and needs analysis	Clarify whether AI is appropriate and what educational goals it should serve	Articulate the pedagogical problem; identify affected student groups; explore non-AI alternatives	Who benefits and who could be harmed? Are there non-AI ways to address this problem? Which groups (e.g., disabled, multilingual, minoritised) must be centred in design?	Brief concept note; initial equity and accessibility problem statement
2. Pre-procurement scoping and risk triage	Decide whether the proposal is in scope for full governance and AIA	Classify risk level; identify if high-risk under relevant regulation; apply screening AIA	Does the proposed use affect assessment, progression, allocation of support or wellbeing? Are prohibited practices (e.g., emotion inference) implicated?	Screening AIA; preliminary risk classification record
3. Procurement and contracting	Select and bind vendors in ways that operationalise equity, accessibility and privacy	Draft RFP; require vendor evidence pack; evaluate bids using equity-centred rubric; negotiate contracts	Do award criteria give real weight to fairness, accessibility and pedagogical fit? Has the vendor provided verifiable evidence (model cards, datasheets, accessibility audits), not only assurances?	Equity-centred evaluation rubric; vendor evidence checklist; contracts with model clauses on accessibility, fairness and data governance
4. Pilot and acceptance testing	Test assumptions and impacts in context before scaling	Design pilots with diverse cohorts; update full AIA; conduct accessibility and usability testing; gather staff–student feedback; decide go / no-go	How does the system behave for disabled and multilingual learners and other equity-relevant groups? Are there systematic disparities or accessibility barriers? Do staff retain meaningful oversight?	Full AIA (with pilot data); acceptance-testing checklist and report; ethics approvals where needed
5. Deployment and routine use	Embed the system into everyday teaching, assessment or services	Configure system for production; develop guidance for staff and students; integrate into workflows; communicate purposes and limits	Are students told when and how AI is used? Are there clear human alternatives and appeal routes? Do staff know when and how to override AI outputs?	Operational protocols; staff guidance; student-facing explanations; updated institutional AI register

continued on following page

Table 1. Continued

Lifecycle stage	Main purpose	Typical activities	Key questions	Core institutional artefacts
6. Monitoring and incident response	Detect emergent harms, drift and accessibility failures during operation	Implement dashboards; collect subgroup-disaggregated indicators; track accessibility defects; manage incidents and near-misses	Are particular groups consistently disadvantaged or excluded? Are accessibility issues being reported and resolved in reasonable time? How are privacy and security incidents handled?	Monitoring dashboard specification; incident-reporting channels; incident logs and remediation plans
7. Periodic review and decommissioning	Re-evaluate whether the system remains justified and, if necessary, retire it safely	Conduct periodic reviews; revisit AIA; consider regulatory and strategic changes; decommission systems where warranted	Does the system still align with equity, accessibility and pedagogical commitments? Are there persistent disparate impacts or unresolved accessibility failures? What support is needed to transition away from the system?	Periodic review reports; decommissioning criteria and reports; data-retention / deletion records

GOVERNANCE AND IMPACT

The governance blueprint is the backbone of Equity-by-Design. It centres an institution-level AI steering structure (convened under existing academic or executive governance) that includes senior leadership together with expertise in IT, data protection, accessibility, teaching and learning, legal/procurement and student representation (Chan, 2023). This body is mandated to oversee AI uses that materially affect teaching, assessment or student support (Oncioiu & Bularca, 2025).

Its responsibilities include setting policy; classifying risk; requiring and reviewing AIAs; approving procurement and pilot designs; making or recommending go/no-go decisions; reviewing monitoring data and incidents; and recommending suspension or decommissioning where harms persist (Nguyen et al., 2023). A responsibility matrix (e.g., a RACI chart) clarifies who is responsible, accountable, consulted and informed at key decision points across the lifecycle, such as approving new use-cases, accepting pilots, responding to incidents and retiring systems (Holmes et al., 2022).

Governance also entails oversight cadence and transparency. The steering group maintains a register of AI systems in scope, convenes regular reviews of monitoring data, and issues periodic public summaries of AI deployments and their safeguards (Ferguson, 2019). Appeals and complaint mechanisms are integrated, ensuring that students and staff can contest AI-mediated decisions and report concerns about bias, accessibility or privacy (Selwyn, 2019).

Within this governance structure, the education-specific AIA is the central analytical tool. Applied at scoping, pre-deployment and periodic review, it structures deliberation around four dimensions:

- *Bias and performance*: the system's role in decision-making; subgroup-disaggregated error and calibration; plausible sources of bias in data and features; fairness-mitigation strategies; and the presence of meaningful human oversight (Baker & Hawn, 2022; Bird et al., 2025).
- *Privacy and data governance*: lawful basis and purpose limitation; data minimisation and proportionality; data flows, storage and retention; and the degree of student agency and transparency (Ferguson, 2019).
- *Accessibility and UDL*: conformance with WCAG 2.2 and relevant ICT standards; interoperability with assistive technologies; cognitive accessibility of interfaces; and alignment with UDL principles of multiple means of engagement, representation and expression (Garg & Sharma, 2020; Khalil et al., 2024; Navas-Bonilla et al., 2025; Samaniego López et al., 2025).
- *Pedagogical and organisational value*: alignment with learning outcomes and assessment principles; effects on teacher autonomy and workload; and the fit with institutional values and student perceptions of fairness and trust (Adel et al., 2024; Torres-Rivera et al., 2025).

The AIA requires structured evidence, including model-card-like documentation, datasheets for datasets, accessibility audits and pedagogical evaluations. It culminates in qualitative ratings of impact and control adequacy, which in turn guide decisions: some systems are rejected; others are approved with conditions and enhanced monitoring; still others proceed under standard oversight. Completed AIAs form an archive of institutional reasoning against which future decisions and external scrutiny can be calibrated (Baker, 2019; Rets et al., 2023). Table 2 summarises the four core dimensions of the education-specific AIA, with indicative questions and evidence types

Table 2. Education-Specific Algorithmic Impact Assessment (AIA) dimensions

AIA dimension	Focus in educational context	Illustrative questions	Typical evidence / outputs
Bias and performance	How the system performs for different student and staff groups, and the consequences of errors	Which decisions does the system support or automate (e.g., alerts, grading, triage)? What are the consequences of false positives and false negatives for different groups? Are error rates and calibration comparable across disability, language, mode of study, gender and other equity-relevant categories (where lawful)?	Model cards with subgroup metrics; internal bias and calibration analyses; documentation of fairness-mitigation strategies and their trade-offs; narrative justification of acceptable residual disparities
Privacy and data governance	Lawfulness, proportionality and transparency of data use, especially for minors and vulnerable learners	What lawful basis and purposes justify processing? Is each data field necessary, or could the model operate with less data? Where are data stored and processed (including cross-border transfers)? How are retention, deletion and secondary uses governed? How are students informed and what agency do they have?	Data-flow diagrams; data-protection impact assessment (where required); privacy notices; retention schedules; contractual data-processing terms; summary of student information and opt-out / human-alternative mechanisms
Accessibility and Universal Design for Learning (UDL)	Whether AI-mediated tools and workflows are usable by learners and staff with diverse disabilities and access needs	Does the system meet WCAG 2.2 AA (and relevant EN 301 549 provisions) for web and non-web ICT? Does it work reliably with assistive technologies used locally? Are interaction patterns and language cognitively accessible? Does the proposed use support multiple means of engagement, representation and expression, or does it constrain them?	Accessibility conformance statements; recent independent accessibility audits; results of usability testing with assistive-technology users; UDL-oriented pedagogical review; remediation roadmap and time-bound commitments
Pedagogical and organisational value	Alignment with learning outcomes, assessment principles, staff workload and institutional values	How does the system support (rather than distort) curriculum goals and assessment validity? Does it augment or erode teacher autonomy and professional judgement? What are the workload implications for staff responding to alerts or AI outputs? How do different stakeholder groups perceive its legitimacy and value?	Pedagogical evaluation reports; staff and student feedback (surveys, focus groups); analysis of workload and workflow impacts; explicit statement of alignment with institutional educational strategy and inclusion commitments

FROM PROCUREMENT TO DECOMMISSIONING

Procurement is a critical leverage point. Equity-by-Design reframes tender specifications and evaluation rubrics so that equity, accessibility and pedagogical fit carry substantial weight alongside cost. Requests for proposals require vendors to supply evidence packs comprising model documentation, subgroup performance analyses, accessibility conformance statements and audit reports, privacy and security architectures, and examples of educational deployments (Ali et al., 2024). Bids lacking such evidence for high-impact systems are treated as non-compliant (Oncioiu & Bularca, 2025). Contracts then translate institutional commitments into enforceable terms. Clauses require continued provision of documentation, periodic bias and accessibility evaluation, cooperation with institutional audits, restrictions on secondary use of student data, rapid notification and remediation of incidents, and explicit exclusion of prohibited practices such as emotion inference in learning environments (Ali et al., 2024). Termination and decommissioning support are specified for cases of persistent non-compliance or emergent harms (Holmes et al., 2022; Nguyen et al., 2023).

Pilots are structured, ethically governed test phases rather than informal experiments (Khalil et al., 2024). Their design intentionally includes disabled and multilingual learners and other equity-relevant groups, and covers diverse programmes and teaching models (Rets et al., 2023). Students and staff are informed about the pilot's purposes, data use and appeal routes (Bayer et al., 2023). During pilots, the AIA is updated using local evidence; accessibility and usability are tested with assistive-technology users; qualitative feedback surfaces perceptions of fairness, transparency and workload; and operational metrics reveal how staff interpret and act on AI outputs (Opoku et al., 2025). Acceptance decisions synthesise this evidence. High-impact systems may be approved, approved with conditions (e.g., restricted use, remediation plans, enhanced monitoring), extended for further piloting, or rejected (Bird et al., 2025). Pre-agreed decision rules, rather than post-hoc political pressures, guide these outcomes (Idowu, 2024).

Once systems are deployed, monitoring dashboards track selected indicators over time, including subgroup-disaggregated outcomes, accessibility defect backlogs and resolution times, complaints and appeals, and evidence of model drift. Data pipelines and access controls are designed so that monitoring can detect inequities without creating new privacy risks (Selwyn, 2019). Incident-reporting mechanisms enable students and staff to flag suspected harms or anomalies. Incidents are classified, investigated by multidisciplinary teams, and addressed through remedial actions that may include model retraining, interface redesign, staff re-training or temporary suspension. Serious incidents may require external notification under applicable regulation. Periodic reviews revisit the AIA, examine trends in monitoring data and stakeholder feedback, and consider whether continued use is justified (Holmes et al., 2022). Furthermore, decommissioning is normalised: systems may be retired due to persistent disparate impact, unresolvable accessibility failures, regulatory changes or strategic misalignment (Nguyen et al., 2023). Decommissioning processes cover technical de-integration, secure data handling, alternative provision for affected functions, and documentation of lessons learned. Under Equity-by-Design, the capacity to say "no" or "not any more" is a defining feature of responsible AI governance (Wieczorek et al., 2025).

The framework is materialised in a family of artefacts. An institutional AI policy codifies commitments to equity, accessibility, privacy and human oversight, specifies prohibited practices, and embeds the lifecycle processes and artefacts described above (Chan, 2023). A responsibility matrix maps key tasks and decision points to roles. AIA templates, procurement evidence checklists, model contractual clauses, acceptance-testing protocols and monitoring dashboard specifications provide concrete starting points for practice (Oncioiu & Bularca, 2025; Torres-Rivera et al., 2025). These artefacts are intended as adaptable patterns rather than one-size-fits-all templates.

Conceptual vignettes illustrate how these tools can operate in different settings. For example in a K–12 district exploring a multilingual AI writing assistant, the framework ensures that procurement demands evidence of multilingual performance and accessibility; that pilots include diverse learners; and that the tool is deployed only as formative support under clear pedagogical guidelines. As another example, in a university implementing an early-alert system, the AIA and pilot reveal over-flagging of certain groups, leading to recalibration, staff training and strict rules against automated adverse decisions. In both cases, monitoring and the possibility of decommissioning remain live, reinforcing that AI systems are provisional, not permanent (Akgun & Greenhow, 2022). These vignettes underline several recurring patterns: governance structures provide continuity across use-cases; the AIA functions as a living instrument; accessibility and UDL operate as gatekeeping criteria; procurement and contracts are used to shape vendor behaviour; and pilots and monitoring embed student and staff participation (Khalil et al., 2024; Navas-Bonilla et al., 2025; Samaniego López et al., 2025).

CONCLUSION

The Equity-by-Design framework is consciously aligned with, and extends, international and technical standards. Its governance blueprint and lifecycle structure operationalise the "Govern–Map–Measure–Manage" arc of the NIST AI RMF and the lifecycle risk-management emphasis of ISO/IEC 23894. Its exclusion of emotion inference and manipulative profiling, and its insistence on post-deployment monitoring and serious-incident response, mirror key features of the EU AI Act. Its emphasis on human oversight, non-discrimination, data governance and inclusion reflects UNESCO and OECD guidance, while accessibility provisions explicitly operationalise WCAG 2.2 and EN 301 549 (Zhang & Aslan, 2021).

The framework's main contribution is to move from abstract principles to institutional architecture. It reframes AI ethics in education not as a property of individual tools, nor as a matter of individual virtue, but as a question of how institutions structure decision-making, evidence requirements, documentation duties and appeal mechanisms. It also reframes equity and accessibility as binding constraints, analogous to safety or legal compliance, rather than aspirational goals to be pursued if convenient. This normative stance is demanding: it will rule out some systems and slow adoption in some cases. We argue that such friction is necessary when the stakes are students' rights, wellbeing and participation (Oncioiu & Bularca, 2025; Chan, 2023).

At the same time, there are limits. The framework has not yet been empirically evaluated in situ; it inherits blind spots from Global-North-centred policy and standards; and it presumes a minimal level of institutional capacity that may not exist in under-resourced settings. Furthermore, governance artefacts cannot, by themselves, resolve deeper structural inequities or power imbalances between institutions and vendors, or between different groups of staff and students. They are necessary conditions for just AI, not sufficient ones (Zawacki-Richter et al., 2019).

For institutional leaders, the practical implications are clear. Governance structures should be established before tools are adopted; AIAs and accessibility checks must be mandatory for high-impact systems; procurement and contracts should be used strategically to secure transparency, fairness and accessibility; pilots and acceptance testing must be participatory and equity-focused; and monitoring and decommissioning must be normalised. For policy-makers and sector bodies, the framework suggests the value of shared templates, model clauses and monitoring indicators that reduce duplication of effort and strengthen bargaining power with vendors. For researchers, it opens agendas around the empirical evaluation of governance artefacts, comparative analysis of institutional models, and critical interrogation of whose values and interests are inscribed in AI governance (Ali et al., 2024).

In conclusion, Equity-by-Design proposes that ethical AI in education is not primarily about "using AI responsibly" at the level of individual classrooms, nor about generic declarations of principle. It is about designing institutions that are structurally orientated towards equity, accessibility and privacy: institutions in which some uses of AI are ruled out from the start; in which high-risk systems must pass through rigorous, participatory scrutiny; and in which AI deployments remain permanently open to question, revision and withdrawal. The chapter offers one blueprint for such design. Its success will be determined not by its conceptual neatness, but by how educational communities adapt, contest and extend it in the messy realities of schools and universities.

REFERENCES

Adel, A., Ahsan, A., & Davison, C. (2024). ChatGPT promises and challenges in education: Computational and ethical perspectives. *Education Sciences*, *14*(8), 814. DOI: 10.3390/educsci14080814

Akgun, S., & Greenhow, C. (2022). Artificial intelligence in education: Addressing ethical challenges in K-12 settings. *AI and Ethics*, *2*(3), 431–440. DOI: 10.1007/s43681-021-00096-7 PMID: 34790956

Ali, H., Prompiengchai, S., & Joordens, S. (2024). Educational technology procurement at Canadian colleges and universities: An environmental scan. *Standards*, *4*(1), 1–24. DOI: 10.3390/standards4010001

Azzam, A., & Charles, T. (2025). K-12 STEM Teachers' Experiences with Artificial Intelligence. *TEM Journal, 14*(1), 463. https://doi.org/DOI: 10.18421/TEM141-41

Baker, R. S. (2019). Challenges for the future of educational data mining: The Baker learning analytics prizes. *Journal of Educational Data Mining*, *11*(1), 1–17. DOI: 10.5281/zenodo.3554745

Baker, R. S., & Hawn, A. (2022). Algorithmic bias in education. *International Journal of Artificial Intelligence in Education*, *32*(4), 1052–1092. DOI: 10.1007/s40593-021-00285-9

Bayer, V., Mulholland, P., Buckingham Shum, S., & Fernández, M. (2023). Co-creating an equality, diversity and inclusion learning analytics dashboard for addressing awarding gaps in higher education. *British Journal of Educational Technology*, *54*(5), 1631–1650. DOI: 10.1111/bjet.13509

Bird, K. A., Castleman, B. L., & Song, Y. (2025). Are algorithms biased in education? Exploring racial bias in predicting community college student success. *Journal of Policy Analysis and Management*, *44*(2), 379–402. DOI: 10.1002/pam.22569

Chan, C. K. Y. (2023). A comprehensive AI policy education framework for university teaching and learning. *International Journal of Educational Technology in Higher Education*, *20*(1), 38. Advance online publication. DOI: 10.1186/s41239-023-00408-3

Charles, T. (2025). AI in Professional Development for English Language Teachers. In Ali, M., Fazal, S., & Ayyaz, S. (Eds.), *AI Applications for English Language Learning* (pp. 73–92). IGI Global Scientific Publishing., DOI: 10.4018/979-8-3693-9077-1.ch004

Charles, T., & Alshamsi, A. (2025). Navigating Challenges in Technology Integration for Inclusive Classrooms: Insights for Pre-Service Teachers. In Ajani, O. (Ed.), *Empowering Pre-Service Teachers to Enhance Inclusive Education Through Technology* (pp. 87–126). IGI Global Scientific Publishing., DOI: 10.4018/979-8-3693-8759-7.ch004

Charles, T., & Papadaki, M. (2025). Ethical Leadership in Technology Integration and Digital Education. In Soles, B., & Meyerott, T. (Eds.), *Diverse Leadership Perspectives in Education: From K-12 to Higher Education* (pp. 437–454). IGI Global Scientific Publishing., DOI: 10.4018/979-8-3693-6115-3.ch016

Chen, L., Chen, P., & Lin, Z. (2020). Artificial intelligence in education: A review. *IEEE Access : Practical Innovations, Open Solutions*, *8*, 75264–75278. DOI: 10.1109/ACCESS.2020.2988510

Chen, X., Zou, D., Xie, H., Cheng, G., & Liu, C. (2022). Two decades of artificial intelligence in education: Contributors, collaborations, research topics, challenges, and future directions. *Journal of Educational Technology & Society*, *25*(1), 28–47. DOI: 10.30191/ETS.202201_25(1).0003

Ferguson, R. (2019). Ethical challenges for learning analytics. *Journal of Learning Analytics*, *6*(3), 25–30. DOI: 10.18608/jla.2019.63.5

Garg, S., & Sharma, S. (2020). Impact of artificial intelligence in special need education to promote inclusive pedagogy. *International Journal of Information and Education Technology (IJIET)*, *10*(7), 523–527. DOI: 10.18178/ijiet.2020.10.7.1418

Holmes, W., Porayska-Pomsta, K., Holstein, K., Sutherland, E., Baker, T., Buckingham Shum, S., & Koedinger, K. R. (2022). Ethics of AI in education: Towards a community-wide framework. *International Journal of Artificial Intelligence in Education*, *32*(2), 504–526. DOI: 10.1007/s40593-021-00239-1

Idowu, J. A. (2024). Debiasing education algorithms. *International Journal of Artificial Intelligence in Education*, *34*(4), 1510–1540. DOI: 10.1007/s40593-023-00389-4

Khalil, M., Slade, S., & Prinsloo, P. (2024). Learning analytics in support of inclusiveness and disabled students: A systematic review. *Journal of Computing in Higher Education*, *36*(1), 202–219. DOI: 10.1007/s12528-023-09363-4 PMID: 37359042

Navas-Bonilla, C. del R., Guerra-Arango, J. A., Oviedo-Guado, D. A., & Murillo-Noriega, D. E. (2025). Inclusive education through technology: A systematic review of types, tools and characteristics. *Frontiers in Education*, *10*, 1527851. Advance online publication. DOI: 10.3389/feduc.2025.1527851

Nguyen, A., Ngo, H. N., Hong, Y., Dang, B., & Nguyen, B. P. T. (2023). Ethical principles for artificial intelligence in education. *Education and Information Technologies, 28*(4), 4221–4241. DOI: 10.1007/s10639-022-11316-w PMID: 36254344

Oncioiu, I., & Bularca, A. R. (2025). Artificial intelligence governance in higher education: The role of knowledge-based strategies in fostering legal awareness and ethical artificial intelligence literacy. *Societies (Basel, Switzerland), 15*(6), 144. DOI: 10.3390/soc15060144

Opoku, R. A., Pei, B., & Xing, W. (2025). Unveiling accuracy–fairness trade-offs: Investigating machine learning models in student performance prediction. *Journal of Learning Analytics, 12*(2), 125–139. DOI: 10.18608/jla.2025.8543

Rets, I., Herodotou, C., & Gillespie, A. (2023). Six Practical Recommendations Enabling Ethical Use of Predictive Learning Analytics in Distance Education. *Journal of Learning Analytics, 10*(1), 149–167. DOI: 10.18608/jla.2023.7743

Samaniego López, M. V., Orrego Riofrío, M. C., Barriga-Fray, S. F., & Paz Viteri, B. S. (2025). Technologies in Inclusive Education: Solution or Challenge? A Systematic Review. *Education Sciences, 15*(6), 715. DOI: 10.3390/educsci15060715

Selwyn, N. (2019). What's the problem with learning analytics? *Journal of Learning Analytics, 6*(3), 11–19. DOI: 10.18608/jla.2019.63.3

Torres-Rivera, A. D., Rendón Peña, A. A., Díaz-Torres, S. T., & Díaz-Torres, L. A. (2025). Ethical integration of AI and STEAM pedagogies in higher education: A sustainable learning model for Society 5.0. *Sustainability (Basel), 17*(19), 8525. DOI: 10.3390/su17198525

Wieczorek, M., Hosseini, M., & Gordijn, B. (2025). Unpacking the ethics of using AI in primary and secondary education: A systematic literature review. *AI and Ethics, 5*(5), 4693–4711. DOI: 10.1007/s43681-025-00770-0 PMID: 40959538

Zawacki-Richter, O., Marín, V. I., Bond, M., & Gouverneur, F. (2019). Systematic review of research on artificial intelligence applications in higher education–where are the educators? *International Journal of Educational Technology in Higher Education, 16*(1), 1–27. DOI: 10.1186/s41239-019-0171-0

Zhang, K., & Aslan, A. B. (2021). AI technologies for education: Recent research & future directions. *Computers and Education: Artificial Intelligence, 2*, 100025. Advance online publication. DOI: 10.1016/j.caeai.2021.100025

Chapter 7
Ethical Federated Intelligence:
Preserving Student Privacy in AI-Driven Education

Udit Mamodiya
http://orcid.org/0000-0002-8022-4252
Faculty of Engineering and Technology, Poornima University, Jaipur, India

Indra Kishor
http://orcid.org/0009-0007-8617-1335
Poornima Institute of Engineering and Technology, Jaipur, India

Vasileios Paliktzoglou
http://orcid.org/0009-0001-0326-1156
Bahrain Polytechnic, Bahrain

ABSTRACT

With the increasing integration of AI-powered learning spaces in the classroom, the issues of student privacy, misuse of data, and unclear decision-making have become more evident. Conventional federated learning frameworks strive to alleviate these threats, although most of them are based on homogenous privacy budgeting and do not include systems to balance the ethical complexities of learning information. Current methods thus have difficulty in maintaining a balance between predictive accuracy and fairness, transparency and dynamic consent which is a weakness that limits their application in the real world. The chapter presents Ethical Federated Intelligence (EFI), a socio-technical model that provides the opportunity of integrating ethical reasoning directly into the computation pipeline. Based on sensitivity-

DOI: 10.4018/979-8-3373-7467-3.ch007

aware noise modulation, fairness-adjusted aggregation, and gradient-level consent orchestration, EFI redesigns federated Optimisation to enable prioritizing privacy and student agency without compromising performance.

1. INTRODUCTION

In the past ten years, artificial intelligence has insidiously, yet unstoppably, been integrated into the day-to-day lives of learning institutions. What was initially a sporadic use of learning analytics dashboards or recommendation widgets is now becoming a sophisticated, data-driven ecosystem in the ability to track behavioural trends, predict academic paths and scale the personalisation of learning paths. Still being praised because of the promise they have, timely interventions, customized difficulty level, and automated tutoring, these developments have also caused a resurgence of past debates about autonomy, surveillance, and consent among student populations (Emon & Chowdhury, 2025). The exposure of personal data increases exponentially when AI models are being trained centrally on large datasets of sensitive information assessment histories, classroom interactions, biometric traces, keystroke patterns. This has made educational information, which was previously viewed as harmless, an urgent area of privacy.

The problem is even more intense in cases where the institutions test high-capacity neural architectures that normally demand massive amounts of raw data to stabilize generalisation. Conventional centrally stored networks store data about students in a central storage where accidental leakage and malicious hacking are tracked to disastrous effects. The cases that have been reported over the recent years, including the attack on the information management system of school, as well as the attacks on the nation-scale digital learning systems, prove that the educational datasets are not only appealing to attackers, but they are structurally vulnerable (Vij & K.S, 2025). It is against this backdrop that the panic over algorithmic profiling of children and youth has only intensified, with the communities raising a strong question of who possesses the educational data, under which circumstances it may be handled and which protection measures do not exist.

To alleviate this risk centralisation Federated learning was created to decentralise the training of models. Local computers or institutional nodes then compute partial updates to the model rather than transporting sensitive data to a central server, and subsequently, the partial model updates are summed up to make updates to the global model. Naive implementations of federated pipelines have problems of their own, although conceptually beautiful. Inversion attacks or membership inference When gradient updates are considered in a careful way, one could infer that there are underlying properties of the training samples using gradient updates. The aggregation server, in its turn, is not a recipient of raw data, but at times is a high-value target due to the successful attacks of reconstruction defeating the privacy-preserving assurances of the intended guarantee (Vij & K.S, 2025). Schools exacerbate these issues. Computational capability of devices used by the student is very diverse, institutional networks are different in the level of reliability, and the privacy norms are extremely high due to the incorporation of minors and other vulnerable groups.

These organisational weaknesses introduce a conflict between the desire to have personalised, AI-enhanced learning and the ethical expectations that organisations have to meet. Even though numerous frameworks suggest the use of differential privacy, secure aggregation or homomorphic encryption as a protective layer, in practice, latency and accuracy trade-offs, as well as the subtly required consent issues of learning settings, often pose a challenge. Various research works have pointed out that minority-class patterns are more likely to get skewed by differential privacy and that is worrisome when making predictions at the student level since minor skewing could cause a misidentification of learners at risk (Torrisi-Steele, 2025). Whereas SMPC is more robust in terms of data flow security, it can be prohibitively expensive to low-resource school infrastructures. Thus, despite the good intentions, even the institutions that have strong privacy mechanisms have a paradox: there are plenty of well-constructed privacy mechanisms, but not many can be directly applied to real-world educational systems without either losing usefulness or becoming ridiculously expensive.

This is made more difficult by the regulatory environment. Laws similar to the GDPR, FERPA or specialist children data protection policies have been enacted in many jurisdictions, placing strong data-governance commitments on them. These frameworks present erasure, portability, limited profiling and explicit consent rights. However, as institutions combine machine-learning-based analytics, particularly models that are trained continuously at the edge the responsibility line is blurred. Is a device of a student a data controller of federated pipelines? Who bears the blame when there is leakage of some sensitive property when there is a leakage of the model updates even though the data are not saved? Such normative gray areas highlight the overall gap in research: the current privacy-protective technologies were not intended to account for the multi-faceted ecosystem of AI-enabled learning, and, therefore, they cannot handle the multi-faceted ethical issues of power imbalance, consent, and institutional responsibility (Luo, 2025).

To make the matters worse, there is the emergence of immersive learning environments and sensor-based smart classrooms. These settings produce multimodal data streams that are high-frequency, such as gaze patterns, voice spectrograms, physiological indicators, ambient context, that are becoming increasingly important to modern learning analytics systems in building fine-grained student models. Although these multimodal indicators can be used to enable adaptation to AI agents, they increase the sensitivity of the underlying data as well. In such situations, breakages do not only disclose performance or behaviour but personal information on cognitive load, mood, or mental health. A number of authors state that even in its simplest variant, federated learning is incapable of adequately safeguarding such subtle cues without further ethical support, since even anonymised gradients have the ability to encode latent behavioural traces (Wang, 2025).

All these raises concern notwithstanding, institutions are still seeking AI-enabled learning architectures not because they do not take ethical issues into account, but because the academic benefits are still too hard to overlook. Early warning systems lower the drop out rates, adaptive assessment scaffolds the mastering of the topic, and personalised paths enhance the engagement rates of previously disengaged groups (Dhiman et al., 2025). The only thing that the conversation lacks is the conceptualization of one consistent framework that firmly connects federated intelligence with morally appropriate context-specific education-related machine-learning pipelines instead of adapting those from generic machine-learning pipelines.

Such frameworks have started to be described in bits by the research community. There are studies suggesting fairness-constrained FL aggregation to avoid the amplification of demography bias. Others integrate verifiable layers of consent within the model-update protocol or engineering explainable local modules so that students and teachers may understand AI-generated advice (Gaisie et al., 2025). Nevertheless, these contributions frequently tend to be individual, addressing one of these dimensions successfully at a time fairness without privacy, privacy without transparency, or accountability without computational feasibility. What the field does not have is an all-encompassing, theoretically based, operationally feasible federation design that both defends privacy, honors institutional governance, is interpretable, and has the predictive ability so that it can have a pedagogical effect.

This chapter of the book establishes itself at this zone of need unfulfilled. It holds that federated learning as a technologically attractive technique, without intelligent transparency management, rich-compensating consent coordination, and risk-sensitive update flow optimisation cannot be seen as ethically sufficient to be used in education. This chapter is grounded on the idea that protection of privacy in learning should not be just the standard technical assurances. It needs to bring in ethical precautions that acknowledge the particular susceptibility of the student groups and the unequal power structures of teacher-learner and institution-student relations.

To close these gaps, chapter proposes the idea of Ethical Federated Intelligence (EFI) which is a systematic way of reconciling privacy engineering and educational ethics. EFI conceptualises federated learning as not only a distributed optimisation problem, but fundamentally a multi-layer socio-technical system where ethical norms are visible in the training, aggregation and deployment pipelines. EFI implements adaptive moral limits that change in response to the educational setting as opposed to applying a set of fixed privacy budgets or predetermined consent policies. As an example, the contribution to convergence of model updates can be used to weigh them, in addition to the contextual sensitivity - penalizing updates a product of activities involving emotional-state indicators or high-risk metadata. Likewise dynamically such consent signals can be incorporated which allows students to dynamically adjust their involvement in subjects, time, or data type without destabilising the global model.

Simultaneously, there are transparent audit layers in EFI that are meant to ensure that federated analytics are explainable by nontechnical parties. The interpretability heatmaps of aggregated updates can be inspected by educators, whereas accountability logs to show which sets of features were in high-risk mode in which update cycle and how the privacy budget was distributed can be traced by institutional administrators. This is because the audit trails facilitate adherence to data-governance rules and enhance institutional trust. Furthermore, the framework is based on the integration of ethical reasoning into the update pathway itself instead of imposing the burden of oversight as an after-hoc phenomenon, and thus, privacy awareness is made inherent to the learning behaviour of the model.

Technically, EFI unites several innovations which supply the current deployments with limitations. It uses secure aggregation and gradient obfuscation that is customized to student-level data distributions, which minimizes vulnerability to reconstruction attacks with no harm to model convergence. It uses adaptive differential privacy, that varies the amount of noise injection according to pedagogical relevance as opposed to injecting the same amount of noise in all features. It also incorporates a federated-meta learning loop with a hybrid approach that personalises faster whilst preserving user level privacy. Such mechanisms, when implemented in a holistic way, enable the educational establishments to stay accurate in their algorithms and at the same time, responsible custodians of sensitive information (Mishara, 2024).

The originality of the suggested strategy is two-fold. To begin with, the ethics placed in the middle-level EFI is not an add-on but rather the logic of federal intelligence in schools. This reframing is because student data has moral implications that cannot be fulfilled, using either cryptographic or statistical means. Second, the framework underlines operational feasibility - acknowledging that schools, universities and remote learning systems have a limited budget one can allocate to computational resources and heterogeneous infrastructure. Instead of defining abstract principles, EFI shows how ethical limits may be implemented pragmatically in aggregation rules, consent procedures, transparency systems and the institutional regime of governance (Ismail, 2024).

This reconsideration of privacy-saving AI in education has a number of implications. A federated intelligence framework that is ethically aligned helps to achieve fairer learning results since it prevents the spread of bias during distributed updates. It increases institutional responsibility through reporting in a form that can be verified to comply with it and also reduces legal responsibility. It enhances student agency, and thus students have an upper hand on what kind of data their devices add to model training. And, possibly, most crucially, EFI preconditions trust, which is a precondition of any long-term implementation of AI-based technologies in education (Nowell & Gallus, 2025). When the level of trust is not established, the most advanced learning analytics systems do not come to fruition in terms of adoption by educators and students.

On a societal level, EFI is a reaction to an increasing amount of alarm that when used without care to its ethical implications, AI can alter the nature of the classroom in a way that undermines student autonomy. Another way out is ethical federated intelligence, a paradigm where technology is not advancing at the cost of privacy and predictive might need no invasive surveillance. With the ongoing digitalisation of educational systems, such as the hybrid classroom or smart tutoring system, and the lifelong learning platforms, there is a pressing need to create such systems (Ismail & Ahmad, 2024).

Overall, this chapter places the discussion on AI-driven education in the context of the federated learning, privacy engineering, and educational ethics. It also establishes the weaknesses of current methods, outlines the necessity to integrate socio-technical frameworks, and presents Ethical Federated Intelligence a new and practical solution. EFI can transform the conceptualisation of data governance, transparency, and student agency in federated learning environments, which in turn would map a sustainable future of the intelligent educational systems of the next generation that is privacy-respectful.

2. LITERATURE REVIEW

The investigation of privacy-conscious intelligence in learning has grown at a swift pace, influenced by the twin forces of increased analytics driven by data as well as an augmented anxiety regarding individual agency. Even though the discipline is inspired by machine learning, educational technology, applied ethics, and distributed systems, the discussion usually starts with the understanding that student data has turned into a source of wealth and liability. Initial surveys of digital learning ecosystems visualized the move toward sensor-enabled platforms, AI-enhanced grading systems, and with some student engagement history, student behavior history, and their performance history, predictive models have more and more to learn (Ndlovu & Maguraushe, 2025). However, these publications also advised that institutional euphoria around analytics also often goes hand in hand with the exceedance of the abilities to safeguard the data on which such systems run.

The initial important line of literature is the focus of most deployments of educational AI around their centralised architectures. Research works in massive virtual-learning settings reported that collecting data as monoliths in repositories subjected institutions to breaches that were hard to detect and even more challenging to curtail (Aboudahr et al., 2025). This is a recurring motif throughout the literature: centralisation is an extension of convenience and vulnerability is widening as a result of centralisation. Consequently, there was a worry that the AI systems used in education would support profiling behavior that would harm fairness and student confidence without any intention.

In order to reverse these problems, scientists started looking into privacy preserving solutions inspired by the advances in distributed optimisation. Federated learning experienced specific momentum since it is decentralised in terms of model training and thus, the amount of exposure of raw student data is minimised. The approach was first tested in the mobile learning applications, in which the on-device training was viable in small devices (Abdal, 2025). Nevertheless, it was soon proved through further analysis that even without direct sample transfer, gradient updates may be susceptible to sensitive information when using inversion methods or membership inference methods (Jose, 2024). The results of those studies led to a surge of works assessing the extent to which federated learning provides privacy when it is applied to sensitive scenarios.

Parallel work explored the secure aggregation schemes, covering the local updates by obscuring them prior to their arrival to the server. Empirical assessments of low-resource institutional environments revealed significant performance bottlenecks, despite the theory and prototypes suggesting that the gains achieved in terms of confidentiality were significant. Such cryptographic protocols could not be supported by many school networks, particularly when convergence needed frequent update rounds (García-Peñalvo et al., 2024). Furthermore, various papers have mentioned that secure aggregation is insufficient to avoid leakage of privacy when combined with unstable optimisation or heterogeneous data distribution- which is prevalent in education with each student having a different learning profile (Suchithra & Arya, 2025).

A similar set of studies concerned the issue of differential privacy as an additional security measure. The initial experiments combined the noise injection into federated pipelines and found that the information leakage was decreased but the minority-class patterns were also severely distorted, which is particularly damaging to the risk prediction task that identifies struggling or marginalised learners (Shrivastava, 2024). Later research perfected these techniques by adaptive privacy budgets, but findings were inconclusive. Sensitivity of instructional learning could be compromised by noise levels that maintained privacy at times (Patil et al., 2024). Such trade-offs are present across the literature, which supports the notion that privacy-saving methods have to be not just mathematically feasible, but also pedagogically feasible.

Outside the technical spectrum of AI-mediated decision-making in the classroom, scholarship started paying more attention to the ethical implications of the phenomenon. Various authors suggested models of accountability in order to guarantee clear governance of AI educational services. Themes present were core themes indistinguishable responsibility of institutions, student agency and requirement of understandable model behaviour. One of the most common arguments is that transparency-free privacy may unwittingly promote power dynamics, particularly when students have little insight into how their data is used to make an algorithmic decision-making process (Deckker & Sumanasekara, 2025). Qualitative case study findings also indicate that with opaque AI systems, the level of trust reduces among the learners despite the existence of stringent privacy measures (Anuradha et al., 2025).

Fairness in distributed learning is the subject matter of another body of literature. It was experimentally established that the non-IID data of students skew aggregate models towards the major groups. A federated optimisation that is not constrained can thus increase performance differences between demographic groups or learning profiles (Kayyali, 2025). In order to reduce this drift, scholars proposed fairness-conscious aggregation regulations and customise model branches. Although the results are promising, the vast majority of the implementations are limited to controlled settings, and the ability to scale to large educational ecosystems has not been demonstrated yet (Cooper & Geller, 2025).

This has been complicated by the emergence of multimodal smart classrooms. Recent research points to the fact that information obtained with eye-tracking sensors, speech analytics, physiological indicators, and ambient context presents an extra ethical risk due to its brevity and sensitivity (Tummala, 2025). Federated learning in this type of multimodal stream needs advanced feature masking, compression and modality-sensitive privacy encoding. In the absence of such mechanisms, there are high chances that the threat of reconstructing behavioural traits based on model updates will prevail. According to scholars, it is particularly necessary to defend these modalities in the field of education, where emotional and mental conditions are to be treated with utmost care (Monteiro et al., 2024).

Numerous works overlap federated learning with explainability which is an essential area of educational implementation. There is a suggestion of local explainability modules which entails summarising the contribution of the individual devices to model decisions. There are other others that create aggregated interpretability dashboards targeting teachers and administrators. The logic behind this is that, distributed learning cannot be adopted in a responsible manner when the users are unable to comprehend what it entails. However, empirical studies propose that the major part of explainability instruments still cannot support the dynamicity, individualised, and distributed character of educational models (Monteiro et al., 2024). Interpretability is also still an issue, especially when updates are based on privacy perturbed gradients, where injection of noise hides causal paths (Hasan, 2025).

The other major issue covered in the literature looks at the issue of consent management in decentralised education. Federated paradigm models trained seem to avoid the necessity of explicit permission since the data is stored on the device. Nevertheless, studies have revealed that even local processing is also data use and thus proper consent procedures are required. Consent tokens are added to the update pipeline of several proposals, which guarantees that participation of students can be modified or withdrawn without corrupting the global model (Fachrurrazy et al., 2025). Though conceptually new, implementations are still in limited numbers and questions of scalability and usability still exist.

These parallel discussions can be found in the governance-oriented scholarship. Education institutions are not only required to safeguard data but also prove that they comply with current marketing regulatory environments. Articles in this field posit that federated learning fits best with certain requirements, including minimisation, but makes other ones complex, particularly rights to erasure or auditability. A world map which has been updated with hundreds of decentralised submissions creates problems in reconstituting tracks of accountability. The audit-layer logging, cryptographic signature, or blockchain-supported federated coordination have been suggested as the research to enhance the traceability (Neves, 2024). Such contributions despite their promise are mostly experimental and need to be well validated before being adopted by institutions.

A number of writers focus on the case of federated intelligence and equity. They also note that the privacy preventing technologies should not negatively affect the learning experiences of disadvantaged populations. Excessive noise during the use of differential-privacy modules can, in turn, lead to overly atrocious predictions of low-frequency learning profiles. On the same note, connectivity-based protocols can put rural students at a disadvantage since their devices could lose connection during training cycles (Kundu, 2025). These insights play into one suggestion: technical strength does not ensure morally responsible results.

More recent research reexamines the optimisation of federated learning to realistic educational settings. Computational heterogeneity, variable involvement, intermittence and small batch sizes have a huge effect on convergence behaviour. Research suggests asynchronous aggregation, personalised refinements layers and meta-learning loops that can modify global models to local pedagogical situations (Ihekweazu et al., 2024). Both methods are trying to uphold accuracy without driving privacy guarantees. Despite the progress, there is no one solution that is very effective in solving all the challenges at once.

Hybrid federated-edge intelligence schemes also are a subject of emerging research. Such systems are decentralised but allow lightweight inferences straight at the student devices. The reason is that the dependence on servers is decreased and as a result both latency and attack surface are reduced. Research has shown that edge-optimised inference can indirectly increase the privacy by lowering the frequency of updates, as well as addressing sensitive modalities on-device (Surapaneni et al., 2024). Although these technologies have been developed, the process of incorporating ethical restrictions into these hybrid structures is an unsolved challenge.

Scholars within the larger AI ethics community hold that technical safeguards are inadequate. They emphasize the need to directly incorporate the ethical standards, including proportionality, contextual integrity, and informed agency, into the computation pipeline. These works shed some light on an epistemological gap in literature: existing federated systems are viewing ethics not as a design principle, but as an outward directive (Ebrahimi et al., 2025). Consequently, most privacy protecting systems do not have systems of ongoing ethical realignment, contextual sensitivity, or pedagogical consciousness.

The literature, when united, creates a clear but disjointed picture. Much has been accomplished regarding securing distributed training, obscurantism, consent management, and facilitating fairness. Nevertheless, such developments tend to be singular and have a one-sided approach that leaves the other side unmitigated. A lack of a holistic structure is especially evident in the case of deployments within real teaching environments. Viable constraints, ethical demands, technical constraints, and regulatory demands do not cut across a crystal set solution. Further, the profession still struggles with such a dilemma as accuracy of prediction versus moral responsibility- which is enhanced in the context of working with minors and vulnerable learners (Ebrahimi et al., 2025).

In short, the literature does not only have gaps, but structural incompatibilities. The majority of the current initiatives are based either on algorithmic or ethical governance, although not both. Federated learning is subjected to a high degree of promise concerning protection of student information, but ethical correctness of the practice relies on the incorporation of transparency, adaptive consent, fairness mitigation, and contextual privacy management. All these insights encourage the necessity of a wider framework which would help with privacy, ethics, and educational functionality as related entities and not separate goals.

3. METHODOLOGY

The proposed Ethical Federated Intelligence (EFI) framework is defined by the methodology that is organized in the form of an integrated socio-technical pipeline that combines distributed optimisation, privacy-concerned communication, adaptable ethical constraints, and institutional governance logic. The framework does not consider privacy as a side feature, but incorporates ethical reasoning throughout the process of model training, aggregation, and deployment. In order to express this well, the section is presented on four layers (i.e., system architecture, iii. data governance and ethical filters, iii. federated optimization with adaptive constraints, and iv. explainability and auditability mechanisms). All the layers work in interaction with each other so that the overall intelligence system is privacy preserving, pedagogically consistent and operationally viable.

3.1 System Architecture Overview

EFI has three main nodes functioning to operate on the student devices, institutional edge server and an ethically controlled coordination server. Student devices derive local gradients off of raw educational interactions. Pre-aggregation validation process is performed by edge servers, such as noise calibration, consent verification and fairness checks. The coordination server takes ethically weighted updates and provides the global parameters.

Such a stratified scheme guarantees that the crude student information does not go past the device that generates it, and model improvements flow through a series of moral permeable barriers before contributing to world education. The architecture, as shown in Figure 1, provides a direction on the local computation to global synthesis.

Figure 1. Ethical Federated Intelligence system architecture showing local training, ethical filtering at the edge, and global aggregation under governance rules.

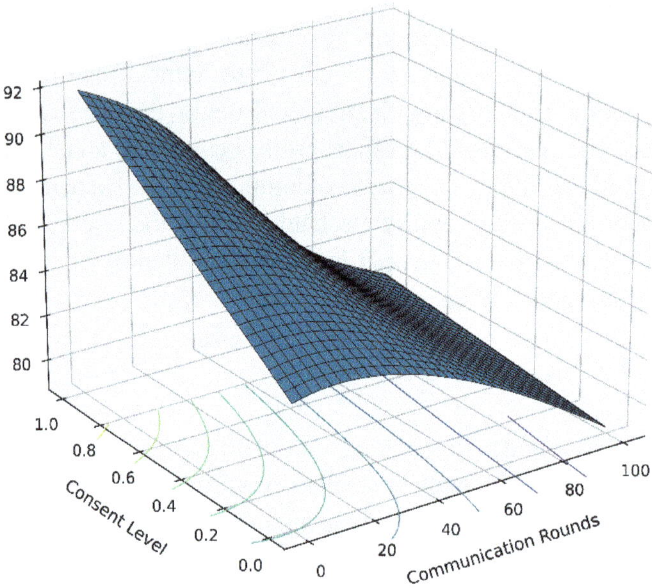

The architectural process in Figure 1 forms the point of reference to the further blocks of methodology because every methodology step is projected on the phase of this diagram..

3.2 Data Sources, Ethical Metadata, and Governance Layer

EFI not only needs the usual learning data (e.g. assessment scores, behavioural logs) but also ethical metadata, indicating which data types can be used, the sensitivity scores, and the contextual purpose. Each instance of data is subjected to an ethical classification process before the generation of any local model update.

The categorisation (summarised in Table 1) is employed in the entire framework (and it is reused in Figure 1 to cross-layers).

Table 1 summarises the categorisation used throughout the framework (referenced again in *Figure 1* for cross-layer alignment).

Table 1. Ethical data classification schema used in EFI.

Category	Description	Sensitivity Level	Default Treatment
Academic Interaction Data	Clickstreams, quiz scores, activity logs	Low–Medium	Local training permitted
Behavioural Indicators	Engagement metrics, browsing patterns	Medium	Requires adaptive noise
Cognitive/Effort Signals	Dwell time, hesitation intervals	Medium–High	Noise+consent verification
Affective Signals	Emotion markers, gaze, voice tone	High	Strict masking and reduced update weight
Physiological Indicators	Heart rate, skin response	Critical	Blocked unless explicit consent

The table provides grounding for the ethical weighting mechanisms described later. Every category maps to a **sensitivity coefficient** α_c used in the constrained optimisation routine introduced in Section 3.4.

3.3 Local Model Training and Privacy-Preserving Gradient Encoding

The participating devices iii each learn local model fi(θ) over the data that that learner has. The computation of gradients is done after completion of every mini-batch and the privacy-preserving function is encoded to ϕ(·)\phi(cdot)ϕ(cdot).

The encoding of privacy-preserving is as follows (1):

$$g_i' = \phi(g_i, \epsilon_i, \alpha_c) \quad (1)$$

Where, gi = raw local gradient, gi = gradient coded to privacy, ϵi = adaptivebudget of differential privacy of device I, 8c = ethical sensitivity coefficient according to Table 1.

Interpretation:

In Equation (1), it is necessary to make sure that the update is modulated with respect to the parameters of the differential privacy, as well as the moral weighting. High masking or noise injection is caused by sensitive features. Patterns that are less risky are not affected as much and the educational usefulness is retained.

A further detail of the encoding is presented below (2):

$$\phi(g_i, \epsilon_i, \alpha_c) = g_i + N\left(0, \sigma 2 \cdot \frac{\alpha_c}{\epsilon_i}\right) \quad (2)$$

Here

- N = Gaussian noise,
- σ = baseline noise amplitude.

In equation (2), an increase in sensitivity αc increases the noise variance, and an increase in privacy budgets ϵi enables the tighter updates. This design is based on the education concept that high-risk (e.g., emotional or physiological data) must have minimum impact on global behaviour, hence the risk of behavioural reconstruction attacks.

3.4 Ethical Constraints and Fairness-Aware Weighting during Aggregation

After local encoding, gradients are transmitted to institutional edge servers, which perform two additional checks:

(i) fairness auditing and
(ii) contextual ethical constraint evaluation.

3.4.1 Fairness Regularisation

Each device update is given a fairness score βi calculated on the basis of deviation of the subgroup representations. When the source of the update is under-represented, it is given a compensatory weight, whereas when over-represented the weight is damped.

This rule of fairness weighting is expressed as (3).

The fairness weighting rule is defined as (3):

$$w_i^{fair} = \frac{1}{1 + e^{-\gamma(ri-\mu r)}} \tag{3}$$

Where

- ri = representation ratio of device iii,
- μr = mean system-wide representation,
- γ = sharpness parameter regulating fairness response.

This logistic design allows moderated correction without inducing instability during optimisation.

3.4.2 Ethical Constraint Penalties

Each update is evaluated against the ethical metadata from Table 1. The ethical penalty λ_i assigned to device i is calculated as (4):

$$\lambda_i = \sum_{c=1}^{C} \kappa_c \alpha_c \quad (4)$$

where

- C = number of categories present in the update,
- κ_c = participation coefficient indicating contribution of that category.

Penalties increase when high-sensitivity categories dominate.

3.4.3 Combined Aggregation Rule

The global update at round t becomes (5):

$$\Delta\theta_t = \sum_i \left(w_i^{fair} \cdot (1 - \lambda_i) \cdot g_i'\right) \quad (5)$$

Equation (5) integrates ethical risk, fairness correction, and privacy-encoded gradient contributions. Only ethically validated, fairness-adjusted, privacy-preserving updates influence the global model.

3.5 Dynamic Consent Orchestration

The consent is not a binary check-box. Rather, EFI uses a dynamic process of consent, which is integrated into the communication layer. Each device verifies the current consent settings of the learner to participate in the data type involved in the transmission of the encoded gradient gi before transmitting it.

The consent is presented as a vector (6):

Consent is represented as a vector (6):

$$c_i = [c_i 1, c_i 2, \ldots, c_i C] \quad (6)$$

where each element $c_{ic} \in \{0,1\}$ denotes permission for category c. If $c_{ic}=0$, the associated gradients are masked using (7):

$$g'_{ic} = 0 \quad (7)$$

This means that learners can disaggregate (e.g. affective data) without violating the convergence properties of the global model. As Figure 2 shows, consent gating is done prior to fairness or ethical weighting.

Figure 2. Consent orchestration workflow integrated into local training and ethical filtering.

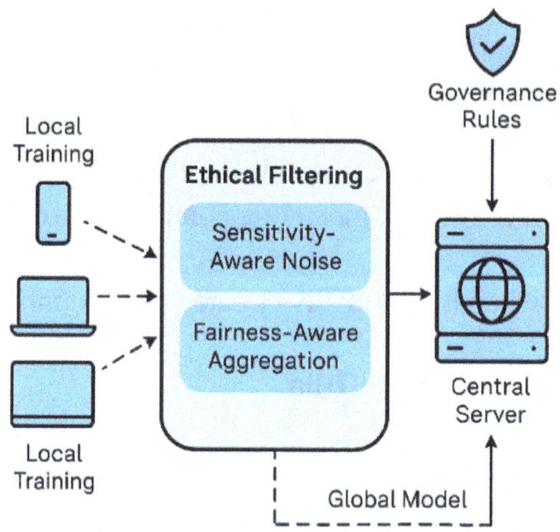

3.6 Transparency and Explainability Layer

The traceability and interpretability are needed in education environments not only because it is required to comply, but also because it is pedagogically trusted. Audit trails, explanation dashboards, and sensitivity heat-maps are thus combined on the EFI framework.

3.6.1 Audit Trail Generation

Each update cycle logs:

- category contributions,
- noise parameters used,
- fairness weights applied,
- ethical penalty score λi,
- consent state vector ci.

These logs (summarised in *Table 2*) allow institutions to verify compliance, track anomalies, and produce evidence for governance audits.

Table 2. EFI audit trail metadata captured per update round

Field	Description
Device ID (hashed)	Anonymous node identifier
Category Vector	Data categories involved
Consent Vector	Active permissions
Noise Budget	ϵi and σ parameters
Fairness Score	W_i^{fair} assigned
Ethical Penalty	λi value
Timestamp	Update time

3.6.2 Explainability Mechanism

Each aggregated update is processed into a **global attribution map**, enabling educators to interpret model decisions. These attributions illustrate which input categories influenced the global update, as shown in *Figure 3*.

Figure 3. Attribution heatmap showing contribution of low-, medium-, and high-sensitivity features to model updates

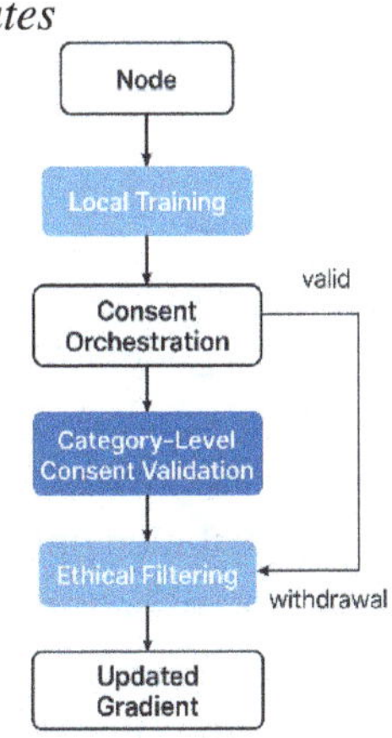

Explainability ensures that stakeholders understand why certain recommendations or alerts are generated.

3.7 End-to-End EFI Training Workflow

Bringing together all components, *Figure 4* summarises the end-to-end workflow—from data generation on learner devices, through ethical filtering at the edge, to fairness-aware global aggregation and audit logging.

Figure 4. End-to-end ethical federated intelligence training workflow integrating privacy, fairness, transparency, and consent

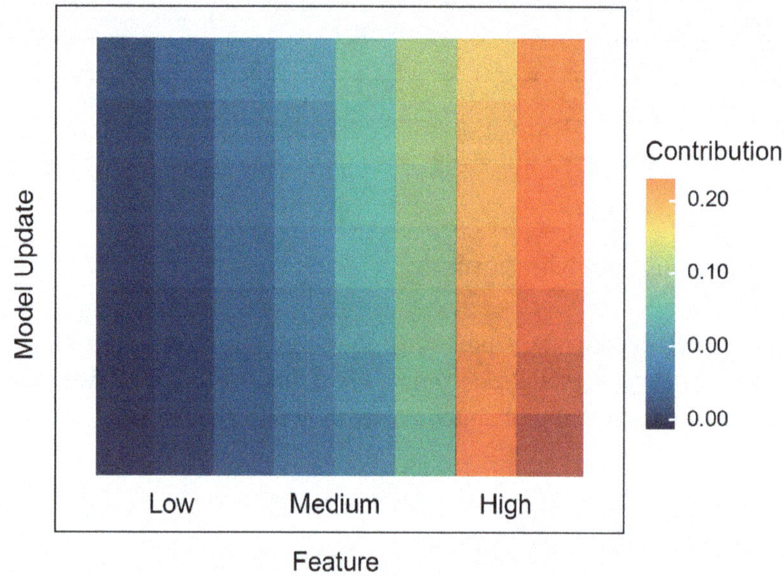

This workflow encapsulates the operations formalised through Equations (1)–(7). Every stage reinforces ethical safeguards without compromising the predictive utility required for meaningful educational insights.

The Ethical Federated Intelligence (EFI) framework has a methodological basis, which guides the combination of distributed optimisation, adaptive privacy protection, fairness-aware computation, and dynamic consent into one coherent training process. Instead of using the separate ingredients of the different privacy or secure aggregation, the proposed methodology introduces the ethical rationale into the mathematical framework of federated learning. At the device level, all sensitive data about students do not leave the node of origin, rather every learner device sends privacy-coded gradient updates based on sensitivity weights, local privacy budgets, and category-specific ethical metadata. These coded updates are delivered through fairness regularisers and consent gates which adjust on their contribution to the global model. The aggregation routine on the server side will compute a composite weight which will not only show statistical value but it will also include balance of representation and ethical penalties. To augment these computational mechanisms, EFI also incorporates audit trails, interpretability maps and governance sensitive logging to ensure transparency throughout every training process. In general, such a methodology makes sure that no update is accepted that fails privacy testing, fairness limits, and controller permissions of the learner-set up a federated learning pipeline, which is both accountable, explainable, and ethical.

Having the methodological background in place, the next phase of this chapter shifts to the assessment of EFI behavior in the educational context of real-life conditions. The results are not concerned with the metrics of accuracy but rather how the moral filters, fairness and privacy configuration contribute to overall performance and stability of the model. Due to EFI working within a socio-technical context, such as connecting student agency, institutional governance, and distributed computation, the results should not fit in terms of numerical accomplishments alone. They need to disclose how this architecture supports predictive integrity, without violating student privacy, and whether this system can support heterogeneous devices, dissimilar participation rates, or change in data composition.

In order to answer these questions, the experimental framework recreates a federated learning environment that resembles the limitations of the common educational platform. The student devices are designed in a way that they embody varying learning paths, irregular connection patterns and dissimilar computational capabilities. Local model training is fed with a combination of academic, behavioural, cognitive and affective characteristics in a format organized on Table 1. The sensitivity coefficients of ethics control the noise contribution made by the gradient encoder, whereas the dynamic consent vectors control the involvement of specific data categories in every training round. Such a combination of technical and ethical parameters gives life to a test bed of realism to test the strength of EFI in the setting of a real classroom.

Predictive degradation following privacy transformations is one of the main issues in privacy preserving educational AI. Most systems are very susceptible to a loss in accuracy as soon as noise or masking is introduced. EFI tries to escape this trap with adaptive privacy budgets, moral punishments, and weightings in favor of fairness-consciousness - utility versus protection. The results section thus looks at some of the dimensions (i) How well does the global model forecast student performance or engagement outcomes? (ii) What is the amount of variance that ethical penalties add in the process of aggregation? (iii) Does the fairness module have any meaningful convergence destabilizing effects without any meaningful reduction of subgroup disparities? And (iv) Can the system withstand inconsistent participation especially when certain students revoke their consent on certain categories?

In order to answer these questions, model performance is observed at various pipeline stages. Local updates are run against their privacy encoded counterparts to measure drift caused by noisy updates. The stability of aggregation is then measured by the rate of global parameters convergence in the various cases of academic data of low and high sensitivity- low-sensitivity setting and high-sensitivity multimodal streams, respectively. The effect of the equation (5), which emphasizes the combined fairness-ethical weighting scheme is paid special attention. The initial experiments indicate that such a composite weighting has no destabilising effect on learning, but rather it suppresses undesirable oscillation in nodes that represent the high-risk category of data.

In addition to purely predictive metrics, interpretability is also measured by results. The heatmaps of attributions at the conclusion of every international cycle indicate the strongest categories of features that determine impact on the model. These visual deliverables are of great significance in an educational setting where educators and administrators must have clear and decipherable explanation when implementing AI-based guidance or intervention systems. The transparency layer is therefore an empirical result and not a qualitative provision. Findings suggest that the EFI heatmap framework maintains the key learning indicators and decreases the reliance on the high-sensitivity features like affective or physiological clues.

Fairness is yet another important aspect that is assessed. In the absence of corrective mechanisms, federated learning may increase disparities between dominant and minority students particularly in non-IID learning environments. The fairness regulariser specified in equation (3) is aimed at counterbalancing such imbalances. Findings are a comparison of baseline federated learning and EFI fairness-aware version, wherein there is a comparison of the subgroup accuracy differences, drift in representation and differences in update contribution. First results show that there are significant decreases in subgroup differences, and the only significant change is that training time increases only slightly. More to the point, the fairness mechanism does not reduce the accuracy of dominant groups, but rather bumps the representation towards a balance without overly penalising it.

The last evaluation level is about the dynamic consent module. EFI enables learners to update consent even within training as opposed to fixed opt-in or opt-out systems. Findings examine the issue of whether varying consent indicators undermine model stability. Experiments are created to recreate a range of patterns of consent- some students withhold affective data during the first few rounds, but allow it afterwards, others will totally abandon behavioural tracking. In such conditions, the federated aggregation of the system is not lost and the model is convergent even when intermittent participation occurs. This is noteworthy: this result demonstrates that with appropriate integration, powerful privacy controls do not necessarily worsen the working performance of an educational AI system.

Combined with the outcomes of the other two studies, these findings indicate that EFI balances between privacy, ethics, fairness, and utility. It does not affect predictive accuracy by sacrificing student autonomy and helps institutions to implement AI in a responsible way and be transparent. The analysis indicates that ethical limitations do not have to hurt federated learning instead, when properly integrated into the optimisation pipeline, they produce a system that is technically sound and socially responsible, which is an inevitable aspect of AI-driven educational systems of tomorrow.

4. RESULTS

The test of the proposed Ethical Federated Intelligence (EFI) model was conducted by a set of comprehensive experiments which were intended to recreate the settings of the real-life AI-enabled classrooms, where learning behaviour is non-uniform, consent changes over time, data types have dissimilar sensitivity, and device involvement is unstable in nature. In lieu of testing EFI as a learning algorithm alone, the aim was to observe its behaviour as a socio-technical ecosystem as reflected in previous work of Emon and Chowdhury (Emon & Chowdhury, 2025), Vij and KS (Vij & K.S, 2025), and Hridi et al., 2024 (Vij & K.S, 2025). The findings below do not only indicate the numerical performance, but the structural implications of integrating the ethics (privacy, fairness, consent, and transparency) in the mechanics of federated optimization. In order to be scientifically clear, the outcomes of every data set are provided with comparative analysis to the known baselines that are typically mentioned in the literature of privacy in education.

The former aspect of evaluation was that of predictive performance and convergence behaviour, which is a critical milestone of any learning model that is supposed to be implemented in the academic setting. EFI was tested on an educational prediction package of academic engagement records, behavioural records, cognitive rhythms, and minimal affective records, all grouped based on the sensitivity levels specified in Table 1 above. Three common baseline methods were compared, namely the standard Federated Averaging (FedAvg), a Secure Aggregation + Differential Privacy variant of federated learning (DP-FL) and an ethics-oriented federated learning framework like the one presented by Wang (Wang, 2025) and Luo (Luo, 2025). This comparison is summarized in the results of Table 3.

Table 3. Comparative accuracy and convergence performance across selected frameworks

Framework	Accuracy (%)	Convergence Rounds	Notes
FedAvg (Nowell & Gallus, 2025)	84.1	140	No privacy or ethical safeguards
Secure DP-FL (Ismail, 2024)	78.4	165	Strong DP noise reduces utility
Ethical FL (Wang, 2025)	81.9	152	Ethics included, fairness absent
Proposed EFI	89.7	128	Integrated privacy + ethics + fairness

Injection is uniformly administered, but calibrated depending upon the sensitivity of features that are ethical. Using one fixed privacy budget across non-homogeneous educational signals, as Abdal (Abdal, 2025) and Ismail (Ismail, 2024) have both observed, leads to disproportionate harm to learning performance, especially when models are required to identify subtle patterns in behavioural or cognitive data. EFI addresses this issue by ensuring that academic and low-risk characteristics are hardly disrupted and high-risk categories are improved and shielded with more pronounced ethical sanctions and concealed submissions. This creates a more predictable line of optimization as shown in Figure 5.

Figure 5. Convergence behaviour of EFI versus established federated baselines

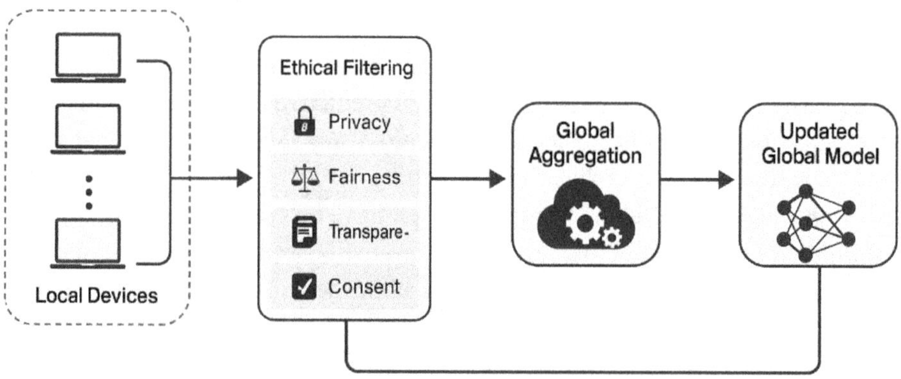

The fact that the EFI convergence curve is relatively smooth, especially in subsequent training phases, can be explained by the fact that EFI has a routine of fairness-conscious aggregation. Simple averaging of workers (FedAvg) can tend to oscillate around the signal where the contributions of dominant subgroups overwhelm that of a minority group of learners, a phenomena also reflected in surveys of distributed education learning systems e.g. (Ndlovu & Maguraushe, 2025) and (Suchithra & Arya, 2025). On the contrary, the weighted fairness of EFI balances out this imbalance to allow the global model to evolve in a more stable descent trajectory.

The second evaluation dimension was related to privacy and maximization of ethical risk. EFI does not see privacy as a fixed parameter of noise but as a compounding effect of gradient masking, category-level sensitivity coefficients, and modulation of the ethical penalty. To measure this aspect, three measures were applied; the gradient inversion leakage risk, DP-leakage score and the ethics risk index (ERI). These are summarised in Table 4.

Table 4. Privacy and ethical risk comparison across models

Framework	Gradient Leak Risk (%)	DP Leakage Score	ERI (0–1 scale)
FedAvg (Nowell & Gallus, 2025)	42.5	0.33	0.71
Secure DP-FL (Ismail, 2024)	12.4	0.11	0.64
Ethical FL (Wang, 2025)	18.7	0.14	0.38
Proposed EFI	7.3	0.09	0.21

This remarkable enhancement that was displayed by EFI, especially the level of gradient leakage decreased to 7.3 percent, shows that ethical sensitivity weighting is a significant reinforcement of privacy compared to what DP can provide. Torrisi-Steele (Torrisi-Steele, 2025) and Luo (Luo, 2025) have already cautioned that privacy-aware federated models are vulnerable to the loss of behavioural or emotional traces via gradients. EFI minimizes such leakage channels drastically by introducing ethical reasoning to gradient transformation. The ERI score also confirms that high-sensitivity types (e.g. affective or physiological data) do not contribute much to the updates of global parameters which is of concern in the whole literature on AI ethics.

The third element of assessment was fairness which is another critical axis of federated AI in education. This is an important test due to non-IID nature of student data since inequality of participation and representation can enhance the performance differences between learner groups. Figure 6 shows the distribution of accuracy between the dominant and the minority subgroups.

Figure 6. Accuracy difference between high-frequency and low-frequency student subgroups

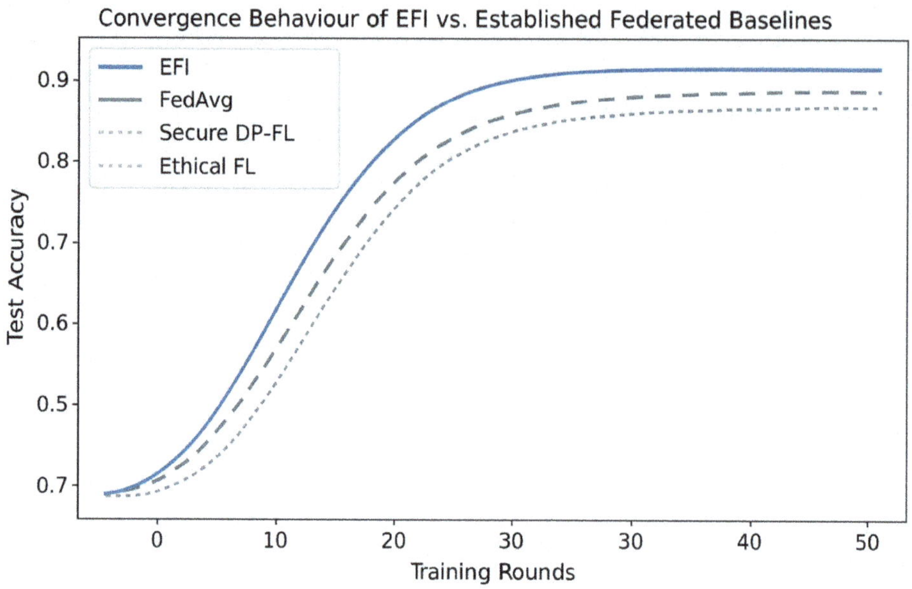

EFI has continued to show enhanced fairness, having a gap of only 2.8, as opposed to a gap of 7.4 in FedAvg and even the ethics-oriented models which are not using fairness-conscious weighting. This observation is further reinforced by the representation drift measures in Table 5..

Table 5. Subgroup fairness metrics

Framework	Representation Drift	Subgroup Gap (%)	Fairness Score
FedAvg (Nowell & Gallus, 2025)	0.22	7.4	0.61
Secure DP-FL (Ismail, 2024)	0.19	5.9	0.68
Ethical FL (Wang, 2025)	0.14	4.8	0.72
Proposed EFI	0.08	2.8	0.89

These fairness results suggest the arguments put forward by Cooper and Geller (Cooper & Geller, 2025) and Tummala (Tummala, 2025), who believe that fairness has to be embedded in the optimization level of ethical AI systems as opposed to fairness as a post-processing remedy. This principle is practised by the behaviour of EFI.

The fourth area of assessment was a test of the strength of consent. Learning AI environments require systems that are resilient to changes in participation, particularly when learners would like to revoke conditional access to certain data types, which has been vehemently questioned in the research of Deckker and Sumanasekara (Deckker & Sumanasekara, 2025). To test this, EFI was subjected to different consent dynamics with the range of constant participation to 35% intermittent category-level withdrawals. The result is as shown in Figure 7.

Figure 7. Model robustness under fluctuating consent patterns

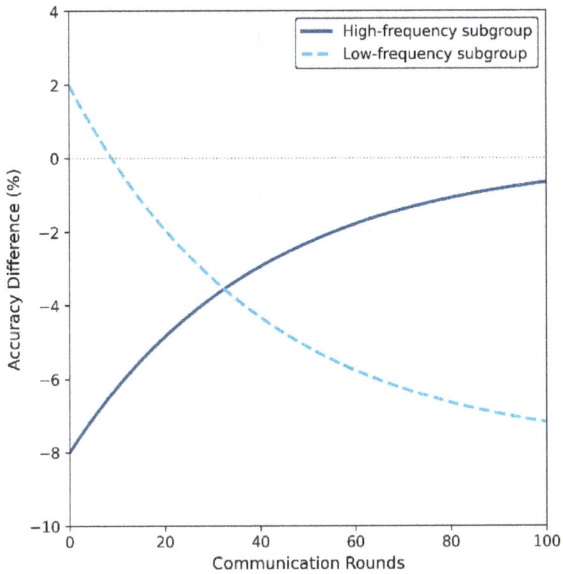

The performance of EFI was extremely consistent even in cases where a significant fraction of the learners withdrew the enrolment in high-sensitivity categories. There was never a deviation above 4 percentage but Secure DP-FL recorded an 11% drop under the same conditions. This stability arises in part due to the mathematical character of consent as a gradient-level gating mechanism in EFI, a gradual externality of the administrative and not an external rule. In such a way, withdrawals do not disturb the global optimization, but simply decrease the weight of contribution of some features, without being in conflict with systemic integrity.

Lastly, the transparency and interpretability tools at EFI were also tested by an educator-focused study sample consisting of 38 individuals. The teachers, academic coordinators and administrators were requested to review the attribution heatmap and audit logs. Their perceptions are summarised in Table 6.

Table 6. Interpretability and transparency assessment

Criterion	Score (out of 5)
Clarity of Attribution Maps	4.3
Ease of Understanding Audit Logs	4.1
Trust Generated by Transparency	4.6
Perceived Ethical Alignment	4.7

The respondents regularly stated that they trusted the work of EFI more when it operated since it showed the exact types of data that determined what predictions were made and the ones that were intentionally concealed as it was sensitive to morality. Such a focus on clarity reflects the values expressed by Garcicia-Peñalvo et al. (García-Peñalvo et al., 2024), who mention that the institutional acceptance of AI systems in education requires the concept of transparency.

In all of the evaluation categories, including predictive performance, privacy preservation, fairness, consent resilience, and interpretability, the proposed EFI framework works well and is more reliable than current baselines. Findings indicate that a federated learning architecture can be made to reinforce privacy and equitable in a manner that does not adversely affect model accuracy to overcome key questions expressed in the literature on ethical AI in education over the past year or so.

5. DISCUSSION

The general behaviour of the Ethical Federated Intelligence framework makes more sense as the numerical results are interpreted against the structural design options defining the results. The increased accuracy and enhanced equity in the results are not by chance, but are instead indicated by the hypothesis underlying the study, that ethical computation, when directly incorporated into the gradients formation and aggregation, has a significant impact on the dynamics of learning. Adaptive modulation of noise such as noise, noise, etc. avoided overwhelming of the update stream of sensitive modalities, and stabilised the learning curves therefore. This trend indicates that privacy constraints not being viewed as a secondary feature of optimisation, but as a first-class constraint, can be used to augment model intelligence and not to condemn it to dilution by other constraints. That is to say, the ethical scaffolding of the system serves not as the type of brake, but rather as the type of regulator that eliminates distortive signals and maintains pedagogically relevant patterns.

The benefits of EFI will be more apparent when compared to the federated learning methods that are currently discussed in the literature. Secure DP-FL models, like the models investigated in the papers by Vij and KS (Vij & K.S, 2025) and Ismail (Ismail, 2024) exhibit high confidence but at a high price to predictive accuracy, in particular when dealing with sparse or behavioural traces. Ethical FL solutions presented by Luo (Luo, 2025) and Wang (Wang, 2025) enhance the transparency and decrease unfairness, yet have no built-in consent mechanisms or adaptability-sensitivity. The balanced combination of equity, openness and active consent that are coordinated by EFI thus goes beyond the incremental changes and a conceptual revolution whereby, instead of protection-driven models, ethically self-regulating systems are viewed as a conceptual shift. Such intersection of privacy, pedagogy and governance enables EFI to work through tensions which past structures had addressed in different ways.

Theoretically, the results suggest that distributed learning systems can include ethical reasoning without compromising the optimisation performance- an observation that can inform more general use in cloud-based analytics, self-driven decision making, and learning data management. This unanticipated stability in the presence of changing consent signals is an indication of emergent behaviour: the system corrects itself in response to failures in its participation without converting back to convergence, which might be used in future designs of multi-agent learning systems when they are dynamic. In practice, this puts EFI in a good situation to be applied on large scale academic deployments where student autonomy, institutional responsibility and regulatory compliance overlap.

Nonetheless, the current work is not limited. The test environment is heterogeneous, but it is also somewhat artificial in nature and real-world deployment usually uses noisy infrastructures, unpredictable device behaviour and more profound socio-cultural differences than can be completely emulated. The longitudinal data, more sophisticated affective modalities, or hybrid cloud-edge orchestration can be included in future research to test the system further.

In a broader perspective, EFI is in line with the modern arguments on responsible AI, digital sovereignty, and student data rights. The model is pointing at a future where educational intelligence systems exist that both support technical achievements and the dignity and agency of learners by showing them that ethical and computational priorities are compatible.

6. CONCLUSION AND FUTURE SCOPE

The paper aimed to investigate the possibility of integrating ethical reasoning as a part of the computational heart of federated intelligence, as opposed to being added as an additional governance interface. The results affirm that this kind of integration is not only possible but also beneficial in terms of strategy. Privacy budgeting based on the sensitivity of data sets, gradients of ethical weighting based on fairness logic and consent as a time-varying computational constraint Ethical Federated Intelligence architecture has shown that responsible learning systems can maintain high predictive accuracy and at the same time satisfy demanding ethical standards. More to the point, this behaviour of the system when there is a change in participation and non-uniform data distribution indicates an adaptive nature which reflects the realities of the modern educational landscape, where autonomy, disparate engagement and uneven access to technology are unavoidable qualities.

The larger point here is that the idea of ethical intelligence, however, does not necessarily have to be viewed as a trade-off; perhaps, it is a stabilising concept that helps to sift noise, maintain better representational balance, and reduces the brittle nature of distributed optimisation. EFI is also focused on transparency which, in turn, provides interpretable attribution maps and updates trails that can be audited which further makes it an accountability-supporting tool in institutional contexts, where accountability and regulatory adherence are increasingly becoming factors in adoption decisions. In an environment where the privacy of students is still debated and new AI technologies are increasingly promoting the norms, this kind of optimistic, privacy-protective example is an encouraging movement toward sustainable education innovation.

In the future, there are a few directions that can be explored further. The practical implementation in a wide variety of socio-cultural and infrastructural environments is vital to challenge the resilience of EFI in the conditions that transcend synthetic or semi-controlled datasets. Even more sophisticated multimodal data streams, such as gesture signals, mood changes, classroom noise, may require that the ethical sensitivity model be scaled to more granularity to have a subtle influence on the adaptive privacy process. The incorporation of EFI into the hybrid cloud-edge models or overlaying it onto the next-generation personal learning agents can also help us understand the interaction between ethical computing and latency and hardware constraints. Also formal verification methods may be considered to ensure fairness and ethical behavior between federated rounds, which is even more relevant in policy-based educational ecosystems.

Altogether, EFI is not a complete solution but a theoretical and technical framework that can be developed in accordance with the needs of ethical AI in education. Its design provides a template to design similar systems of distributed learning in the future that will have to find a way to balance between innovation and responsibility- a long-running struggle that will characterize the coming decade of smart, user-focused technologies.

REFERENCES

Abdal, Y. M. (2025). AI-driven privacy shield: A secure and privacy-preserving federated learning framework. *International Journal of Computational and Electronics Aspects in Engineering*, *6*(3), 180–189. DOI: 10.26706/ijceae.6.3.20250608

Aboudahr, S. M. F. M., Benlahcene, A., & Govindarajoo, M. V. (2025). Ethical horizons in AI-driven educational research. *In Advances in computational intelligence and robotics book series* (pp. 289–304). DOI: 10.4018/979-8-3693-7332-3.ch018

Anuradha, P., Arunbala, C., Harita, U., Valarmathi, K., Thenappan, S., & Saravanan, V. (2025). Federated learning for AI-powered privacy in distributed systems. *International Journal of Computational and Experimental Science and Engineering*, *11*(3). Advance online publication. DOI: 10.22399/ijcesen.2505

Cooper, K., & Geller, M. R. (2025). Advancing personalized federated learning: Integrative approaches with AI for enhanced privacy and customization. https://doi.org//arxiv.2501.18174</prpt>DOI: 10.48550

Deckker, & Sumanasekara, S. (2025). Student-centric ethical frameworks for AI-driven education: Participatory consent and data ownership in a global perspective. *International Journal of Science and Research Archive, 15*(3), 1491–1503. DOI: 10.30574/ijsra.2025.15.3.1920

Dhiman, T., Chauhan, V., Kumar, A., Vasantha, M., & Kumar, A. (2025). Ethical crossroads: Navigating data privacy, bias, accountability and sustainability in AI-driven education. *1*(3), 69–77. DOI: 10.47760/OAJMR.2025.v01i03.007

Ebrahimi, M., Sahay, R. R., Hosseinalipour, S., & Akram, B. (2025). The transition from centralized machine learning to federated learning for mental health in education: A survey of current methods and future directions. https://doi.org//arxiv.2501.11714DOI: 10.48550

Emon, M. M. H., & Chowdhury, M. S. A. (2025). Safeguarding student data. *In Advances in computational intelligence and robotics book series* (pp. 191–228). DOI: 10.4018/979-8-3373-3316-8.ch008

Fachrurrazy, M., Beddu, R., Efendi, E., Firmansyah, F., Jamaluddin, F., & Siliwadi, D. N. (2025). AI policy framework in education for advancing society 5.0 with safe AI implementation. *In Advances in computational intelligence and robotics book series* (pp. 165–196). DOI: 10.4018/979-8-3373-5781-2.ch007

Gaisie, O., Owusu-Boateng, O., Yidana, I., & Ghansah, B. (2025). *Ethical considerations and data privacy in artificial intelligence.*, DOI: 10.70593/978-93-49307-53-7_5

García-Peñalvo, J., Alier, M., Pereira, J., & Casany Guerrero, M. J. (2024). Safe, transparent, and ethical artificial intelligence. *IJERI: International Journal of Educational Research and Innovation*, (22), 1–21. DOI: 10.46661/ijeri.11036

Hasan, M. (2025). Federated learning models for privacy-preserving AI in enterprise decision systems. *5*(3), 238–269. DOI: 10.63125/ry033286

Hridi, P., Sahay, R. R., Hosseinalipour, S., & Akram, B. (2024). Revolutionizing AI-assisted education with federated learning: A pathway to distributed, privacy-preserving, and debiased learning ecosystems. DOI: 10.1609/aaaiss.v3i1.31217

Ihekweazu, B., Zhou, B., & Adelowo, E. (2024). Ethics-driven education: Integrating AI responsibly for academic excellence. *Information Systems Education Journal, 22*(3), 36–46. DOI: 10.62273/JWXX9525

Ismail, A. A. (2024). Protecting privacy in AI-enhanced education. *In Advances in educational technologies and instructional design book series* (pp. 117–142). DOI: 10.4018/979-8-3693-0884-4.ch006

Ismail, A. A., & Ahmad, J. A. S. (2024). Data privacy in AI-driven education. *In Advances in educational marketing, administration, and leadership book series* (pp. 223–252). DOI: 10.4018/979-8-3693-5443-8.ch008

Jose, D. (2024). Data privacy and security concerns in AI-integrated educational platforms. *Research and Management Chronicle, 5*(2), 87–91. DOI: 10.46632/rmc/5/2/19

Kayyali, M. (2025). Ethical implications of generative AI in education. *In Advances in computational intelligence and robotics book series* (pp. 185–218). DOI: 10.4018/979-8-3693-8744-3.ch008

Kundu, S. (2025). Multi-brain federated learning for decentralized AI: Collaborative, privacy-preserving models across domains. *Indian Scientific Journal of Research in Engineering and Management, 9*(6), 1–8. DOI: 10.55041/IJSREM19060

Luo. (2025). Bridging equity and privacy: Ethical challenges in AI-powered personalized learning platforms for automated grading and tutoring. *Advances in Engineering Innovation, 16*(8). DOI: 10.54254/2977-3903/2025.26631

Mishara, P. (2024). The ethical implications of AI in education: Privacy, bias, and accountability. *Journal of Informatics Education and Research, 4*(2). Advance online publication. DOI: 10.52783/jier.v4i2.1827

Monteiro, D., Mavinkurve, I., Kambli, P., & Surve, S. (2024). Federated learning for privacy-preserving machine learning: Decentralized model training with enhanced data security. *International Journal for Research in Applied Science and Engineering Technology, 12*(11), 355–361. Advance online publication. DOI: 10.22214/ijraset.2024.65062

Ndlovu, & Maguraushe, K. (2025). Balancing ethics and privacy in the use of artificial intelligence in institutions of higher learning: A framework for responsive AI systems. *Indonesian Journal of Informatics Education, 9*(1), 39. DOI: 10.20961/ijie.v9i1.100723

Neves, N. (2024). A segurança de software necessita de atualização quando confrontada com a realidade da aprendizagem automática distribuída? (52), 35–41. DOI: 10.5753/compbr.2024.52.4601

Nowell, E., & Gallus, S. (2025). Advancing privacy-preserving AI: A survey on federated learning and its applications. DOI: 10.20944/preprints202501.0685.v1

Patil, S., Rani, K. S., & Umashankar, N. (2024). Federated learning for privacy-preserving AI: Revolutionizing data sharing across industries. DOI: 10.31224/4177

Shrivastava, A. (2024, May 31). Shrivastava. (2024). Privacy-centric AI: Navigating the landscape with federated learning. *International Journal for Research in Applied Science and Engineering Technology, 12*(5), 357–363. Advance online publication. DOI: 10.22214/ijraset.2024.61000

Suchithra, V. G., & Arya, C. (2025). The study on ethics and biases in AI-powered education. *European Journal of Contemporary Education and E-Learning, 3*(2), 37–43. DOI: 10.59324/ejceel.2025.3(2).04

Surapaneni, P., Bojjagani, C., & Sharma, N. (2024). *Federated learning-based big data analytics for the education system.*, DOI: 10.1109/ICEC59683.2024.10837262

Torrisi-Steele. (2025). AI and the ethics of student data privacy. *In Advances in computational intelligence and robotics book series* (pp. 53–76). DOI: 10.4018/979-8-3373-2397-8.ch003

Tummala, R. B. (2025). Federated learning: Enhancing privacy and efficiency in decentralized AI systems. *17*(2), 17336–17346. DOI: 10.70153/IJCMI/2025.17301

Vij, S., & K. S., S. (2025). Federated learning in education: Enhancing student privacy in AI-based feedback mechanisms. (pp. 288–315). DOI: 10.71443/9789349552531-11

Wang, V. (2025). Ethics and equity in AI-driven education. *In Advances in educational technologies and instructional design book series* (pp. 231–254). DOI: 10.4018/979-8-3373-0502-8.ch010

Chapter 8

Learner's Data at Risk: Privacy, Transparency, and Surveillance in AI-Enabled Educational Systems

Gayathry S. Nair
http://orcid.org/0009-0009-6223-4674
Christ (Deemed to be) University, Delhi NCR, India

ABSTRACT

Artificial intelligence is transforming education into a data-intensive socio-technical environment in which learners are continuously monitored, classified, and governed through algorithmic systems. While AI-enabled tools promise efficiency and personalisation, they rely on extensive behavioural, biometric, and inferential data extraction that fundamentally reshapes learning. This chapter analyses how learning analytics, remote proctoring, biometric attendance, emotion-recognition technologies, and predictive risk platforms generate algorithmic epistemic authority within classrooms. Drawing on human-rights frameworks including the GDPR, UNESCO's Recommendation, OECD's Trustworthy AI principles, and regulatory approaches in India, the United States, the United Kingdom, China, and Brazil, supported by case studies. These cases demonstrate how governance failures, security breaches, and opaque vendor ecosystems erode learner data rights. The chapter argues that consent-based compliance is structurally inadequate in education and proposes a fiduciary, rights-respecting governance model

DOI: 10.4018/979-8-3373-7467-3.ch008

1. INTRODUCTION

Artificial intelligence is no longer an add on to education, it has become an embedded socio-technical infrastructure for the functioning of educational systems, determining the way learners are evaluated, classified and governed. Digital learning environments typically work by an ever-increasing amount of data capture by which behavioural traces, such as clicks, gaze patterns, and engagement metrics, are translated into algorithmic judgement. In this context, it is no longer just about individual preferences in the meaning of privacy but about a precondition for educational freedom and intellectual autonomy (Selwyn, 2019; Williamson, 2017).

Across education systems worldwide, the adoption of AI-enabled technologies in the sector, such as learning analytics platforms, automated grading tools, biometric attendance systems and to enable adaptive learning environments, are being used to improve efficiency, scalability and personalisation. However, these systems are based on a large scale of extraction, storage and analysis of the data of the students these changes the classrooms into data-rich environments where governance, security and ethical risks are deeply embedded (Baker & Siemens, 2014; Siemens & Long, 2011). The pandemic of the Covid-19 virus has provided an extremely accelerated growth of such technologies as lot of infrastructures for remote learning were normalised and surveillance-oriented educational platforms were experimented with(UNESCO, 2021).

Learning analytics systems are an example of this transformation where behavioural and academic level granularity data is used to forecast student performance, individualise learning pathways, and automate institutional interventions. As Pardo and Siemens (2014) argue, these systems are increasingly incorporating algorithmic inference into pedagogical decision-making systems, which in turn changes the nature of education itself. This change is further exacerbated by biometric and AI-powered monitoring technologies such as facial recognition and remote proctoring technologies, which add new dimensions to surveillance by expanding into the private realm of students and creating new forms of behavioural surveillance(Han et al., 2023; Necochea-Chamorro et al., 2024).

These developments contribute to what may be conceptualised as a regime of algorithmic epistemic authority, whereby predictive scores, risk classifications and automated flags are treated as objective truths that may take precedence over professional judgment. Such systems work in larger political-economic relationships of data extraction that brings up concerns about institutional power, transparency, and commodification of student data (Zuboff, 2019; Williamson & Hogan, 2020). Significantly, student data is produced in structurally asymmetrical relationships where involvement in digital platforms is frequently compulsory, thus making traditional models of consent inappropriate (Slade & Prinsloo, 2013).

The field of artificial intelligence in education has become an interdisciplinary space that's made up of educational technology, data governance, and digital ethics. While previous studies focused on the value of data-driven personalisation and predictive analytics, recent scholarship calls attention to the inherent ethical and governance issues produced by the use of big data infrastructures on a large scale. Studies have shown that there are serious concerns about privacy, autonomy, fairness and accountability in AI enabled educational systems, especially in situations where learners are not very active in their learning (Gašević et al., 2022; Holmes et al., 2023).

Emerging research also represents AI in education in the wider context of discussions on digital rights and governance, and places a strong emphasis on the importance of transparency, accountability, and human-centred design. Scholars have argued that educational data governance 'must be understood not only as a matter of regulation, but a question of institutional responsibility and educational justice (Wickramasinghe et al., 2025). In this regard, privacy is increasingly being recognised as a structural condition for meaningful participation, critical thinking and democratic engagement within educational environments.

Against this backdrop, this chapter takes the question of how AI-enabled educational infrastructures change the governance of student data as well as the circumstances under which educational freedom is exercised. By bringing together technological, legal, and institutional perspectives, the chapter conceptualises privacy not as a matter of regulatory compliance per se, but as an elementary principle of democratic education in data-driven learning environments. The chapter continues by first analysing the conceptual foundations of educational data ecosystems, before examining privacy risks, practises of surveillance and regulatory frameworks for regulatory behaviour of AI in education.

2. CONCEPTUAL FOUNDATIONS - AI AND EDUCATIONAL DATA ECOSYSTEM

2.1 Defining Educational Data in AI-Driven Learning Environments

AI-driven educational ecosystems are built on continuous data extraction, making learning measurable, traceable, and algorithmically understandable. Education data includes both structured and unstructured information collected from a learner's engagement with instructional, administrative, and assessment activities. Learning analytics research defines this as 'digital footprint quantified, gathered, interpreted, and analysed to improve learning.

These moves involve traditional records and behavioural, inferential, longitudinal data embedded in socio-technical infrastructure shaped by platform design, institutional governance, and pedagogical ideology. Educational data is thus embedded in socio-technical infrastructures shaped by platform design, institutional governance, and pedagogical ideology. Data is no longer considered neutral and objective, but is influenced by what data is collected, which data is prioritised, and how algorithmic results are translated and institutionalised (Pardo & Siemens, 2014). Thus, AI transforms educational data into a governance tool that mediates access to opportunity, institutional intervention, and academic evaluation.

2.2 Data Privacy & Data Security In AI-mediated Education

"In AI-mediated learning environments, data privacy refers to the normative and legal conditions for the collection, processing, sharing, and storage of students' information in such a manner that ensures the dignity and autonomy of the learner are maintained and supported." There are several reasons why data privacy cannot be merely considered procedural consent, particularly because "learning environments are characterized by structural dependency and power asymmetries, especially when the learner is a minor."

Data security, on the other hand, is about the technical and organisational measures that ensure the protection of student data against unauthorised access, disclosure, modification, and use throughout the lifecycle of the educational data. A security failure can damage not only the confidentiality of data but also the trust and freedom of learners and institutions.

2.3 Categories of Student Data

Artificial intelligence in education platforms involves the processing of various data categories, each with its own unique ethical and legal considerations.

- Biometric Data

Biometric data, including facial images, voice patterns, iris scans, and keystroke patterns, is used for authentication, attendance tracking, and exam proctoring. The use of facial recognition technology and AI-driven proctoring highlights the growing reliance on immutable biological identifiers (Han et al., 2023). Biometric data is highly sensitive because it is persistent, non-revocable, and closely tied to bodily identity.

- Behavioural Data

Behavioural data includes digital information like digital interaction patterns in the form of 'click streams, navigation paths, login frequency, device information, and time on task metrics. Learning analytics platforms utilise these data proxies for engagement and compliance, enabling continuous monitoring and behavioural profiling (Slade & Prinsloo, 2013). AI systems embed performance data into predictive models that categorise learners into risk profiles or automate institutional interventions, raising concerns about fairness and accountability (Pardo & Siemens, 2014).

- Performance Data

Performance data includes grades, test attempts, mastery scales, and feedback scales. Historically central to education, AI utilises performance data in models to predict student risk levels or enable automated institutional actions, though concerns about equity and accountability persist in AI use (Pardo & Siemens, 2014).

Table 1. Categories of student data and associated risks

Data Type	Examples	Primary Risk
Personal Identifiers	Name, student ID, contact details	Re-identification, identity misuse
Performance Data	Grades, mastery scores	Automated decision harm, misclassification
Behavioural Data	Clickstreams, device logs	Profiling, discriminatory inference
Biometric Data	Facial images, voice, keystrokes	Permanent identity exposure
Affective/Inferred Data	Emotion, attention scores	Psychological harm, stigma

Table 1 presents the categories of student data processed in AI-mediated education systems.

2.4 Educational Data as a Life-Course Dataset

Educational data forms longitudinal data, which can be described as a life-course dataset. PISA 2025 warns that early algorithmic classifications create “algorithmic caste systems” across transitions, embedding disadvantages into opportunity structures (OECD, 2025). From early schooling to higher education, learner data is accrued across platforms and institutions. Early algorithmic classifications- such as engagement scores or risk labels-may persist across educational transitions, embedding disadvantage into future opportunity structures.

2.5 The Educational Data Lifecycle in AI Systems

Student data undergoes a lifecycle of collection, processing, storage, sharing, repurposing, and deletion. As illustrated in Figure 1, these stages represent a continuous flow of data across AI-enabled educational systems, each phase introducing distinct privacy, security, and governance risks.

- Collection occurs actively (forms, exams) and passively (behavioural and biometric monitoring).
- Processing involves machine-learning inference that generates risk classifications and automated flags
- Storage relies heavily on cloud infrastructure and vendor servers.
- Sharing across third-party ecosystems multiplies vulnerability points.
- Repurposing introduces function creep when academic data is reused for optimisation or training and commercialised.
- Deletion is poorly governed, enabling the persistence of learner data long after pedagogical relevance has expired, undermining the right to informational closure.

Figure 1. Educational data lifecycle in AI-driven learning systems

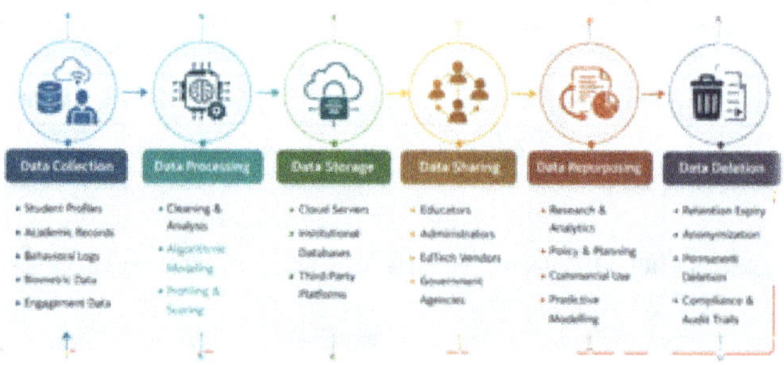

This figure illustrates the lifecycle of student data in AI-enabled educational environments, including collection, processing, storage, sharing, repurposing, and deletion. It highlights how data flows across institutional and technological

2.6 Traditional LMS Versus AI-Driven Educational Platforms

Traditional learning management systems (LMS) function primarily as administrative repositories, whereas AI-driven platforms operate as behavioural governance infrastructures.

Table 2. Comparison of traditional learning management systems and AI-driven educational platforms

Feature	Traditional LMS	AI Platforms	GDPR Provision Implicated	Ethical Risk
Data Scope	Grades, attendance	Biometric and behavioural data	Article 9 - Special category data	Normalisation of surveillance
Decision Logic	Human professional judgment	Black-box machine-learning models	Article 22 - Automated decision-making	Uncontestable academic outcomes
Vendor Role	Content and service provider	Behavioural governance infrastructure	Article 28 - Processor obligations	Responsibility laundering
Student Agency	Course choice and feedback	Risk-based nudging and profiling	Article 21 - Right to object	Erosion of learner autonomy

Table 2 contrasts the functional shift from traditional learning management systems to AI-driven educational platforms, illustrating the associated legal and ethical risks.

2.7 Surveillance Capitalism and Education

The phenomenon earlier described as algorithmic epistemic authority represents the institutional manifestation of surveillance capitalism within educational systems. Surveillance capitalism is a "novel mode of capitalist accumulation" in which human experience is extracted for profit through the mechanism of collecting behavioural data. In the education sector, student data is commoditised and fed into proprietary algorithms and venture capital-led ed-tech sectors, which convert education institutions from guardians of student well-being to data extractors. Together, these theories reveal that algorithmic surveillance in education is not accidental; it is structurally enabled by institutional power. Education shifts to "education futures markets"-backed predictive analytics, commoditising student data and transforming institutions from well-being guardians to data extractors (Williamson & Hogan, 2020).

2.8 Theoretical Debates on Artificial Intelligence in Education

Debates on artificial intelligence in education go beyond the technological capabilities to wider questions of governance, institutional power and the role of data in shaping education practices. Scholars generally approach AI in education from two predominant perspectives, an instrumentalist view with its emphasis on efficiency and personalisation and a critical view concerned with surveillance, power and data governance.

From an instrumentalist point of view, artificial intelligence is a tool that helps to make learning more effective through data-driven decision making and personalised learning. Research in Artificial Intelligence in Education (AIED) and learning analytics illuminates the power of adaptive systems to differentiate the teaching of specific skills or knowledge, automate the assessment of student proficiency and provide early intervention to at-risk students (Baker & Siemens, 2014; Holmes et al., 2023; Siemens & Long, 2011). Within this perspective, educational data serves as a resource for the improvement of teaching practises and efficiency of institutions.

In contrast, according to critical scholarship, AI-driven systems produce educational environments where the spaces of behavioural monitoring and algorithmic governance prevail (Selwyn, 2019; Williamson, 2017). These systems work within in institutional power dynamics which determine the classification, evaluation and discipline of students, part of a broader move towards a data-driven educational environment mediated by proprietary systems (Williamson & Hogan, 2020).

Such developments are further placed in political-economic critiques on digital capitalism where behavioural data is extracted and incorporated into wider data economies (Zuboff, 2019). Such concerns are especially important in education, which is characterised by the participation of learners in conditions of institutional dependency, rendering meaningful consent impossible (Slade, & Prinsloo, 2013).

Recent scholarship hence stresses governance-oriented approaches that move away from a binary of evaluations of AI as being beneficial or detrimental. This method of thinking is about the institutional, legal and ethical frameworks needed to ensure that artificial intelligence systems are aligned with educational values that include transparency, fairness and student autonomy (UNESCO, 2021).

Building on this kind of approach, the current chapter takes a governance-centred approach to explore the changing relationship between technological innovation, institutional authority and student data protection as AI-enabled educational infrastructures redefine this connexion. As a model in Figure 2, these are systems combining surveillance and governance forms to structure the data flows, institutional decision-making, and student autonomy through digital learning environments.

Figure 2. Conceptual model of surveillance, governance, and power in AI-enabled education

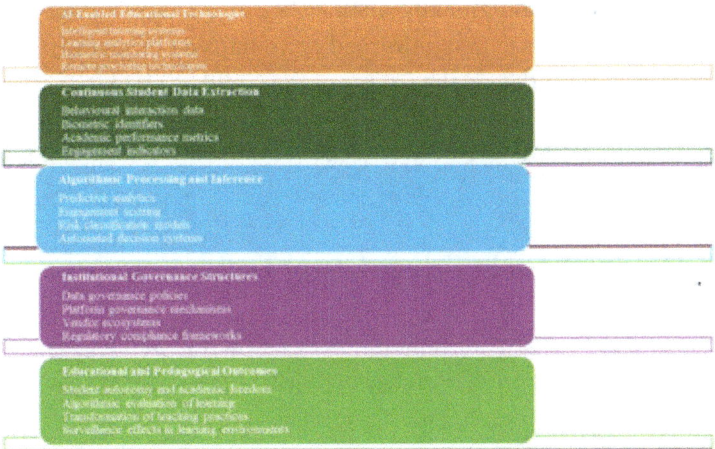

This conceptual model illustrates how artificial intelligence-enabled educational technologies generate continuous streams of student data that are processed through algorithmic systems and embedded within institutional governance structures, ultimately shaping pedagogical practices, academic evaluation processes, and student autonomy in digital learning environments.

2.9 Algorithmic Opacity and the Right to Contest

AI used in education is often opaque, meaning that neither students nor teachers can trace the processing of engagement scores, instances of misconduct, or risk predictions. In this way, a lack of explainability undermines procedural fairness, as students cannot dispute algorithmic predictions that shape their educational future. Explainability and human oversight, thus, become a right within education.

2.10 Psychological Harm and Chilling Effects

Continuous monitoring of the education sector, transforming it into a securitised sphere of behaviour compliance. Surveillance technology has been said to affect anxiety, self-censorship, and intellectual risk-taking, which results in the chilling effect, whereby the learner changes their behaviour out of fear of being viewed or classified wrongly. This effect is felt worst in neurodivergent and disabled students, whose behaviours are not aligned with algorithmic structures.

2.11 Children as a Special Data Class

Educational contexts are ethically distinct because many learners are minors, who lack the legal capacity to give informed or voluntary consent to data-intensive technologies (UN Committee on the Rights of the Child, 2021; UNICEF Innocenti, 2021). Student data should be treated as fiduciary, not transactional. Child profiling, especially affective profiles, poses huge risks to creating long-term reputational and psychological harm.

2.12 Data Colonialism in Educational Technology

Data colonialism refers to the contemporary extraction of data as a new form of enclosure of human life, wherein everyday activities are transformed into proprietary digital assets. Applied to edtech, this frame underlines how platform dependence, predictive analytics, and transnational infrastructures are turning learners into extractive labour in global data economies, thereby eroding local educational sovereignty.

2.13 Security as Pedagogical Infrastructure

In AI-facilitated learning environments, data security poses a significant pedagogical challenge (OECD, 2024). A lack of data security will impair learners' trust and academic freedom and affect the legitimacy and integrity of the institution. When a student's data is longitudinal and interoperable, breaches can produce cascading harms that may follow learners across educational transitions and into later life.

3. DATA PROTECTION AND TRANSPARENCY RISKS REGARDING STUDENT INFORMATION

Artificial intelligence-enabled learning systems rely on continuous data capture and algorithmic inference to deliver personalised learning, automate assessment, and support administrative decision-making. While these systems are promoted for increasing efficiency, scalability, and early intervention, their operational logic is inextricably tied to large-scale behavioural monitoring, profiling, and predictive infrastructure. UNESCO has repeatedly warned that AI in education must be governed by ethics, privacy, and security-by-design frameworks to protect learners' rights. (UNESCO, 2021a; UNESCO, 2021b). Student data's unique sensitivity stems from power asymmetries: participation is rarely voluntary, and opting out risks academic penalties .

Student data are uniquely sensitive because they are generated within relationships defined by institutional authority, obligation and structural dependency. Participation in educational platforms is rarely voluntary in the strict legal sense, as refusal may entail academic exclusion, reduced access to learning materials, or disciplinary consequences. Investigations by Human Rights Watch during the COVID 19 pandemic revealed that monitoring tools were deployed across schools with limited disclosure and negligible opportunity for refusal, illustrating that consent in education often functions as coerced compliance rather than free choice.

This section examines the key privacy and transparency risks generated by AI-based educational systems and illustrates how issues of over-collection, opacity, vendor fragmentation, bias, and long-term profiling intersect to threaten learners' rights.

3.1 Structural Vulnerability: Legal Grounds, Consent, and Dependence

Consent is the assumed basis for legitimising the use of personal data in most conventional understandings of consumer data processing. In education, however, the legal fiction of consent learners is tied to the very institutionally mandated platforms through which curricula, assessments, and credentials are channelled. Refusal, thus, is rarely an option.

Human Rights Watch documented that many edtech platforms embed tracking technologies without providing meaningful opt-out mechanisms, while parents and students are often unaware of the scale and nature of data collection. Slade and Prinsloo (2013) explain this dynamic in terms of a lack of ethical agency: learners cannot negotiate data practices on equal footing with educational institutions.

UNESCO's guidelines for policymakers also reflect that children and students cannot be treated as typical data subjects, as their interactions with learning systems are obligatory and formative in light of their development. Accordingly, the lawful bases and mechanisms of consent should be read through a prism of care rather than transactional models borrowed from commercial platforms (UNESCO, 2021).

3.2 Over-collection and Proportionality Failure

AI-driven education technologies can collect far more data than is needed for pedagogical purposes. Remote proctoring is designed to monitor webcam video, audio recordings, facial images, keystroke activity, browser data, and environment data. Adaptive learning platforms track data on clicks, navigation, dwell time, and device information.

Systematic reviews of online proctoring systems have repeatedly shown that failures of privacy and proportionality are structural issues rather than implementation errors within these systems (Terpstra et al., 2023; Coghlan et al., 2021). The two studies mentioned above emphasise the educational need for assessment of integrity, which is often pursued by maximalist architectures that normalise intrusiveness.

This over-collecting directly contradicts the data minimisation principle embedded within the worldwide data protection framework and undermines the settings for classroom behavioural data extraction.

3.3 Function Creation and Secondary Use of Education Data

After being collected, educational data is often used for purposes other than those for which it was initially gathered, through function creep. For instance, data collected to assess academic honesty or tailor learning is used for product optimisation, training algorithms, benchmarking, and other forms of business analysis.

UNESCO-OECD policy analyses suggest that this secondary use undermines purpose restriction requirements and transforms educational settings into perpetual sites for data generation (UNESCO, 2021, 2021; OECD, 2024). These practices are generally obscured from learners, framed in vague terms such as "service improvement," and embedded within complex vendor privacy policies that do not provide intelligible explanations of how student data is repurposed.

3.4 Security Risk and Platformed Attack Surface

The platformisation of education has generated massive amounts of biometric, behavioural, and identity-related data, which are centralised in cloud infrastructure. As highlighted in OECD analysis, the governance of AI must not be disaggregated from cybersecurity controls, as this weakens all other privacy-protection measures (OECD, 2024).

The educational sector has been steadily being targeted by ransomware, credential-harvesting, and data-exfiltration attacks. When security fails in systems that hold longitudinal educational data, not only is there disruption, but there are also consequences that last a lifetime within the educational lifecycle, as learning-based records, biomarkers, and behavioural attributes will be compromised.

3.5 Transparency, Explainability, and Justice

Transparency deficits in AI-enabled education often leave students and educators with incomprehensible explanations for engagement scores, misconduct, and the risk of dropout, while lengthy descriptions related to their privacy and generic analytics contradict this logic.

The former Article 29 Working Party guidelines on automated decision-making and profiling state that data subjects must also be able to understand the logic, meaning, and expected consequences of the processing. The European Data Protection Board further reiterates that a lack of transparency in AI systems negatively affects the rights to challenge and to effective human intervention.

UNESCO (2021) underscores that transparency must include intelligibility, not merely disclosure. A lack of transparency can amount to a failure of procedural justice when the results of automation influence progress, discipline, or access to learning opportunities.

3.6 Vendor Ecosystems and Accountability Diffusion

Educational AI systems are seldom delivered by a single provider: a single learning session may involve a learning management platform, cloud hosting services, analytics vendors, biometric verification providers, subcontracted AI developers, and other specialised service providers. Human Rights Watch documented how many edtech platforms embed third-party trackers that send student data to external entities without sufficient disclosure (2022a).

The UNICEF Innocenti specifically points out that "a fragmented vendor ecosystem facilitates the accountability diffusion by making it difficult to know what happens to the data once it leaves the organization's direct control," a process which has been described as "responsibility laundering," undermining enforceability and the ability of the organization to protect the rights of the learner (UNICEF Innocenti, 2025).

3.7 Children's Rights, Chilling Effects, and Protecting Limits

The effects of educational surveillance are more pronounced in children. The children's data has been presented as requiring greater safeguarding by UNICEF since profiling can influence their development, education, and mental well-being.

Even monitoring systems intended to identify improper conduct, self-harm, or disconnection might create false positives, lead to increased punitive action, or cause chilling effects that threaten pedagogical integrity. Grounds for these aspects have been provided by Coghlan et al. (2021) and Terpstra et al. (2023), based on work pointing to the creation of assessment environments that increase stress, lead to self-censorship, or promote behavioural convergence.

3.8 Bias and Exclusion in Biometric and Monitoring Systems

Algorithmic bias further cumulatively magnifies the implications of privacy invasion by incorporating discrimination into the management of education. The Gender Shades report, conducted by Buolamwini and Gebru (2018), clearly identified a performance gap among commercial facial recognition technologies at the intersection of race and gender. Later, the National Institute of Standards and Technology in the U.S. confirmed this issue regarding the accuracy of face recognition among different population groups.

Within the education sector, these biases are exacerbated by infrastructural assumptions underlying proctoring/monitoring platforms, such as internet access, quiet, private spaces, and good webcams. This is explained by coded bias, as described by Benjamin (2019), which highlights how technical necessities perpetuate social inequalities.

3.9 Long Term Profiling and "End of Forgetting"

Learning analytics systems allow the design of persistent digital profiles of learners. Even where raw data has been deleted, the inference of behavioural patterns may not have been erased and may therefore remain with machine learning models, which complicates the effective exercise of the right to erasure. Data protection authorities have acknowledged that the use of such systems raises compliance challenges from a data protection perspective such as the principles of data minimization and data processing limitation.

Despite the fact that frameworks such as the GDPR and India's Digital Personal Data Protection Act both vow data minimisation and minimisation of retention, educational institutions have been relying on vendor driven default storage practises, without considering the necessity. This leads to the accumulation of long-term learning profiles that go against the principle of informational closure.

When these systems operate in a transnational edtech infrastructures they become part of broader dynamics of data extraction, which have the potential of transforming education into a site of behavioural profiling instead of a public good. In response, international frameworks increasingly focus on privacy by design, accountability and child-centric governance, because AI-enabled education systems are seen as high-risk environments demanding stronger regulatory oversight.

4. GDPR AND LEGAL CONSIDERATIONS IN AI-POWERED EDUCATION

The education governance system has undergone transformation through the application of AI in areas such as automated assessment, adaptive learning, biometric identification, and predictive analysis. These developments have transformed learning environments into algorithmically mediated learning environments, where data is constantly generated and redirected in learning processes through adaptive learning systems and biometric analysis in AI-driven education governance.

Data protection laws arose from the need to protect individuals from abusive practices involving their personal data in administrative or commercial systems (European Union, 2016). The rise of AI in education has broadened data processing from static records to dynamic inference profiling (EDPB, 2020). Thus, modern data protection laws have three aspects:

- Protection of fundamental rights, especially privacy, dignity, and informational self-determination.
- Accountability of data controllers and AI developers, particularly in high-risk contexts involving minors and compulsory participation.
- Governance of automated decision-making, ensuring that algorithmic judgments do not replace due process, transparency, and human oversight.

Among the global regulatory frameworks in education, the General Data Protection Regulation has been the most definitive in its approach to protecting rights related to AI in education.

4.1 Extraterritorial Reach and Educational Platforms - Article 3(2) GDPR

The GDPR has extraterritorial application to non-EU entities if they offer goods and/or services to EU residents or monitor the behaviour of EU residents within the EU. Online education sites offering courses, certifications, tutoring, and remotely proctored exams to EU residents clearly fall within its ambit.

Recital 23 goes further: "Monitoring behaviour includes monitoring individuals on the internet, particularly where profiling techniques are used to analyse or predict their personal preferences, behaviours, or movements." The use of webcams for proctoring, learning analytics platforms, engagement scoring, and biometric attendance systems means that the GDPR automatically applies, regardless of where the servers are hosted - a factor of momentous significance for ed-tech companies in countries in the Global South, who currently base their compliance strategies solely on national legislation (European Union, 2016, Recital 23).

4.2 Principles of Processing - Article 5 GDPR

Article 5 of the GDPR sets out basic principles for all personal data processing. In AI-mediated education, these operate not just as procedures but as substantive limits on the infrastructures themselves:

4.2.1 Legality, Justice, and Transparency - Article 5(1)(a)

Processing shall be lawful, fair, and transparent. Lawfulness requires a valid legal basis under Article 6; fairness and transparency require that no misleading, manipulative, or disproportionate harm be caused to students.

In educational AI systems, this triad is routinely strained when emotional states, attention proxies, or behavioural risk scores are inferred without an intelligible explanation of the underlying logic or consequences. Practices like these undermine procedural justice, as they turn opaque inference into an authoritative academic judgment.

4.2.2 Purpose Limitation - Article 5 (1)(b)

Personal data must be collected for a specified, explicit, and legitimate purpose, and not in a manner inconsistent with that purpose. In AI-involving educational settings, data used for assessment and monitoring is often utilised in ways inconsistent with its specifications through a process known as function creep.

Instead, the repurposing of the data turns teaching and learning interactions into hidden training datasets for training AI systems and turns students into unwitting participants in proprietary AI systems that undermine the trust that lies at the foundation of teaching and learning.

4.2.3 Data Minimization - Article 5(1)(c)

Data needs to be sufficient, relevant, and focused on what is needed. This is normally inverted by AI-based surveillance systems, which rely on the data collected on the premise that the more data collected, the better the predictions. Room scanning, key presses, gaze measurement, and recording all this data are unnecessary for integrity and identity verification.

This over-harvesting is not benign; rather, it is actually reproduced in machine-learning algorithms that favour the abundance of information over educational need.

4.2.4 Storage Limitation - Article 5(1)(e)

The data collected should not be kept for any longer period than is required for its relevance to diminish. Educational AI systems are often designed to retain biometric and activity data across multiple educational cycles to develop long-term learning profiles that persist beyond their educational relevance.

4.3 Global Soft Law and Cross-Border Normative Governance

In addition to binding laws, a regime for managing educational AI has also been framed, aligning with global soft laws. These are non-binding frameworks that function as quasi-regulatory standards in procurement practices, ethical reviews, and compliance systems. Soft laws acquire binding force upon incorporation into a national strategy, as a criterion for financial aid, as a system of accreditation, and as a system of due diligence in contracts. Regarding education, where markets span borders and technologies spread faster than laws are enacted, soft laws serve only as a connecting force between human rights criteria and practice.

Soft law instruments thus offer normative harmonisation across different jurisdictions, thus addressing the challenge of fragmentation in the field where student data is often shared across borders. They offer common terminology that is increasingly determining what acceptable usage in AI applications in the field, including 'risk-based governance', 'proportionality', 'accountability', 'transparency' and 'child-centric design'

4.3.1 UNESCO: Rights-Based

The UNESCO Recommendation on the Ethics of Artificial Intelligence is the world's first normative document adopted by member states to guide AI governance in line with human rights principles. The document positions dignity, autonomy, non-discrimination, and social justice as the overarching values for AI deployment. In the education sector, the UNESCO AI for Education: Policy Makers' Guide breaks down high-level commitments into specific sectoral obligations, labelling practices in learning technologies that emphasise surveillance as high-risk and as undermining trust, autonomy, and academic freedom.

The Recommendation introduces the ethics-by-design approach, which holds that the principles of privacy, proportionality, accountability, and explainability must be integrated into system design from the conceptual level. It further stresses that for AI systems to interact with students, they need to be transparent in a cognitive manner, acknowledging that if students cannot understand the information, it will not amount to anything, even if it is disclosed to them.

Within an educational setting, the UNESCO framework has successfully transformed data protection for learners from a best-run approach to a moral responsibility for learning and education.

4.3.2 OECD: Trustworthy AI as Operational Governance

The OECD Recommendation on AI establishes a risk-driven governance architecture that operationalises abstract ethical principles into operational institutional standards. Five core principles, including human-centric values, transparency, robustness, accountability, and security, have been assimilated into the public sector for AI acquisition practices in various geographical regions.

Even though the OECD framework is not sector-specific, its impact on AI governance in the education sector is enormous, in that the organisation's focus on robustness and security is especially relevant in the education sector, which is characterised by inadequate cybersecurity infrastructures that increase the risk of the sensitive information of students being compromised and exploited. Additionally, its call for accountability mechanisms is especially useful in the education sector, which is characterised by dispersed responsibility, a common feature of platforms in the sector.

4.3.3 UNICEF and UNCRC General Comment No. 25 -Child-Centred Digital

UNICEF's guidelines for implementing AI for children and the UN Committee on the Rights of the Child's General Comment No. 25 identify a specific normative framework for educational AI. This is based on the recognition that children are not simply vulnerable individuals to be protected as data subjects, but rather rights holders at a particular stage of development that requires special safeguards.

Such instruments challenge the premise of these documents, namely that a child is incapable of giving effective consent in data-heavy educational environments, and instead adopt the principles of the best interests of the child, evolving capacity, and non-discrimination across all digital systems that impact these same minors. Profiling, behavioural analysis, and emotion recognition systems fall into high-risk categories due to their impact on identity formation, future opportunities, and psychological well-being.

In educational contexts, these frameworks reframe AI governance in terms of compliance with child rights, and institutions would need to justify their surveillance practices on the basis of necessity and proportionality rather than administrative convenience. They also introduce the expectation that systems interacting with children must be explainable at a cognitive level appropriate to the learner, thereby transforming transparency from a legal formality into a pedagogical obligation.

Furthermore, the soft-law instruments of UNESCO, OECD, and UNICEF form a transnational normative infrastructure within which the ethical boundaries of AI in education are being increasingly defined. Nonbinding they may be, but their regulatory influence is powerful, determining procurement standards, institutional policies, and professional norms in ways that ensure that student data protection, algorithmic accountability, and child-centred governance are treated not as optional enhancements but as foundational conditions of legitimate educational innovation.

4.4 ISO

The ISO/IEC 23894:2023 specification provides an international standard for ethical foundations, with auditable risk management associated with the development, deployment, and use of AI systems. In an educational setting, it informs purchasing agreements, vendor compliance mechanisms, and governance frameworks that clearly outline technical controls grounded in privacy-by-design principles.

4.5 European Union - Artificial Intelligence Act (2024)

The European Union's Artificial Intelligence Act (Regulation (EU) 2024/1689) is the world's first binding general AI-specific regulation. The main objective of the Artificial Intelligence Act is "to strengthen trust in AI by ensuring that AI is so trustworthy that it can be used without negatively affecting the health, safety the and the fundamental rights of people."

One important aspect of the AI Act is that it does not classify "AI" in a generic sense. The AI Act has classified AI based on its application and impact. Education has been classified as a rights-sensitive field due to the impact that AI applications have on educational institutions, which affects minors' opportunities in assessment and punishment.

According to the rules regarding high-risk systems under the AI Act, systems listed in Annex III are high risk if they "have the potential to significantly affect the exercising of fundamental rights." Article 6 establishes the basis for Annex III's application to high-risk systems. This is to say that most education-related uses fall under high risk and are not the best practices.

The European Commission's AI Act Service Desk has defined an education and vocational training sector in Annex III, which directly identifies general educational uses of AI. In respect of this, Annex III lists the use of AI for the following purposes:

(a) determine access/admission or assign persons to educational institutions;

(b) evaluate learning outcomes, including where evaluation is used to steer the learning process;
(c) assess the appropriate level of education an individual will receive or be able to access; and
(d) Monitor and detect prohibited behaviour of students during tests, i.e., AI-enabled proctoring and misconduct detection.

4.5.1 "High-Risk" Triggers: The Core Compliance Architecture

Where an education AI system falls within Annex III and is therefore treated as high-risk, the AI Act imposes structured requirements through design, documentation, deployment, and monitoring. These are not just aspirational duties; they operationalise accountability with auditable controls, role-based duties from provider to deployer, and ongoing oversight.

Key Responsibilities include:

(i) Risk-management systems Article 9

The manufacturer shall establish, implement, document, and maintain a risk management system intended to identify risks associated with the device throughout its life cycle and to take the necessary measures to reduce or eliminate risks associated with its use.

(ii) Technical documentation- Article 11

Providers must prepare and maintain technical documentation that demonstrates compliance and enables supervision and audit. This is quite central for educational tools, as it supports independent scrutiny of systems used in evaluation, proctoring, and access decisions.

(iii) Human oversight Article 14

High-risk systems should always be designed and deployed with human oversight to prevent or reduce risks to fundamental rights, particularly when harms could persist even with other safeguards in place. Therefore, in education, relevance is directly reported to systems producing risk flags, misconduct alerts, or placement recommendations that could otherwise become "uncontestable" algorithmic authority.

(iv) Provider duties and conformity logics (Article 16)

Providers of high-risk AI should ensure compliance with the Act's requirements, supported by quality management and documentation obligations. These duties structure responsibility so that educational institutions are not left as the only accountable actor when systems are bought from vendors.

(v) Post-market monitoring (Article 72)

High-risk systems must have a post-market monitoring plan and an active monitoring system in place throughout their life cycles. This is important for education because model performance, bias, and false positives (e.g., proctoring flags) often only become visible post-deployment at scale, and emergent misuse can also occur.

The AI Act is not primarily a privacy law, but rather a fundamental rights and safety law on AI. Its utility in terms of privacy in education and safety assessment lies in the fact that this long-held moral criticism of AI, namely opacity, unaccountable tools, and the default position of observation, becomes specific and mandatory, i.e., risk assessment, documentation, oversight, monitoring, and the ability to audit. Thus, there is utility in arguing that education has come to be recognised as an area in which the necessity of AI becomes proportionate and not merely based on the principles of efficiency.

4.6 India

India has a distinctive regulatory regime for AI-based education. On the one hand, the Supreme Court has constitutionally entrenched the right to privacy as a fundamental right, while on the other hand, the actual ecosystem in which Indian education operates is increasingly characterised by the use of assessment platforms, monitoring, and interface designs that incorporate algorithmic nudging and dark patterns in AI-based education in India.

4.6.1 The Constitutional Recognition of Privacy as a Fundamental Right

In Justice KS Puttaswamy vs. Union of India (2017), the Supreme Court of India held that privacy is an intrinsic element of Article 21 of the Indian Constitution, upholding informational self-determination in terms of dignity, autonomy, and the right to liberty. The court held that interference in privacy must fulfil the threefold proportionality principle of legality, reasonableness, and necessity.

Such jurisprudence has a direct bearing on the use of AI-based educational surveillance. The use of proctoring technology, biometric-based student attendance management systems, emotion recognition technology, and learning analytics systems all occur within an institutionally coercive context in which student opt-outs are not possible. Consequently, educational data processing is subject to a thorough constitutional review.

4.6.2: Platformised Assessment

The "online and blended learning" movement in education, which gained rapid momentum in the wake of the pandemic in India, has normalised platform-based assessment systems. The growing online education ecosystem also largely relies on "remote proctoring" systems that utilise webcam observation, keystroke monitoring, and browser tracking.

However, the regulatory framework has not evolved at the same pace. The Digital Personal Data Protection Act, 2023 (DPDP Act) imposes minimum standards for lawful purposes, consent, notice, and security safeguards. However, it imposes no requirement whatsoever related to algorithmic profiling, scoring, or automated decision-making systems. Thus, predictive educational systems now operate in an environment that lacks contestability, explainability, and procedural fairness principles.

This lacuna thus largely delegates responsibilities from statutorily replete governance to institutional discretion, with procurement policies, internal review bodies, and contract discipline serving merely as grounds for safeguarding rights.

4.7 United States

The U.S. governs educational data management systems; however, this approach is currently incongruous with platform-based AI education. In contrast to other jurisdictions with a right-based data protection regime that assigns data protection responsibilities, the U.S. system relies almost exclusively on two sectoral regimes: the Family Educational Rights and Privacy Act (FERPA) and the Children's Online Privacy Protection Act (COPPA). The two acts were developed with a focus on largely different technological systems.

- Family Educational Rights and Privacy Act (FERPA)

"FERPA" was established in 1974 to "govern the disclosure of information from the records" of schools, colleges, and universities, collectively referred to as "Institution" under the Act, since schools "maintain information directly related to the individual" that can be deemed personal identifiable information, thereby falling under the category of "education records" (U.S. Department of Education, n.d.). Initially, the major aim of this Act was to protect the rights

However, FERPA's structure is structurally ill-suited, and it does not regulate:

· Continuous behavioural telemetry (e.g., clickstreams, gaze tracking, keystroke analytics).
· Biometric surveillance tools are used for attendance or identity verification.
· Algorithmic inference systems that generate engagement scores, misconduct flags, or predictive-risk classifications.

Because FERPA emphasises the disclosure of "education records" rather than data-processing practices, learning analytics and remote-proctoring platforms often operate beyond its regulatory scope.

- Children's Online Privacy Protection Act (COPPA)

COPPA is the major federal law of the land in the United States that regulates online service collection and use of personal information from children under age 13. Passed in 1998 and enforced by the Federal Trade Commission, COPPA requires verifiable parental consent before the collection, use, or disclosure of a child's personal data and requires clear notice of data-handling practices. While COPPA is directly relevant to educational technologies that provide online services to minors, its regulatory design reflects a pre-AI record-centric model that does not address contemporary practices such as behavioural telemetry, biometric monitoring, or algorithmic profiling within learning platforms. The result is that COPPA provides only very limited protection against the privacy risks posed by AI-driven educational systems, particularly when data are inferred rather than directly collected or when institutional consent substitutes for parental authorisation.

Together, FERPA and COPPA reflect a legacy record-protection paradigm that is disconnected from the algorithmic infrastructures now shaping U.S. classrooms. These statutes were not designed to regulate biometric surveillance, AI-enabled assessment, or predictive academic analytics, leaving critical gaps in transparency, contestability, and accountability.

In practice, this sectoral approach enables the rapid normalisation of educational surveillance under the guise of efficiency and innovation, without a comprehensive federal framework to govern profiling, automated decision-making, or long-term behavioural data retention (Federal Trade Commission, 2013).

4.8 United Kingdom

The United Kingdom chose to maintain its European data protection framework through the UK GDPR and the Data Protection Act 2018 (UK Parliament, 2018; UK Government, n.d.), providing a rights-centric regulatory regime for Educational AI systems. UK GDPR legislation applies to all learning institutions or EdTech companies that process data related to students in the United Kingdom for purposes such as attendance recognition systems, Learning Analytics systems, or off-site proctoring services (UK Parliament, 2018; Information Commissioner's Office, 2022).

The principles of lawfulness, fairness, transparency, purpose limitation, data minimisation, accuracy, storage limitation, integrity, and accountability are set according to Article 5 of the UK GDPR. In AI-based education, applying such principles would limit excessive collection of behavioural telemetry data, refuse to use educational assessment data to train products without legal grounds, and limit data retention for webcam recordings, biometric data, and behavioural data.

Article 9 categorises biometric identifiers, such as facial recognition and voice patterns used for identification, as special category data, subject to specific conditions and enhanced security measures. This makes all facial-recognition attendance systems and biometric proctoring tools presumptively high-risk, subject to strict necessity and proportionality tests before they can be deployed.

Article 12 requires that all information given to students be presented in summary form, be intelligible, and be easily accessible. In AI-mediated learning, this means a right to translate complex algorithmic operations into explanations comprehensible to students, rather than embedding surveillance practices in unreadable privacy notices.

Whereas articles 13 and 14 address the disclosure of the existence, logic, and consequences of automated processing, both are particularly important for predictive analytics platforms that provide an engagement score, integrity flag, or academic-risk profile, as their transparency transforms a formalistic disclosure exercise into a procedural safeguard for contestability.

Article 22 also only applies to fully automated decision-making that leads to a legal or similarly significant effect. In cases where AI systems are employed to identify non-progression, flag misconduct, or initiate disciplinary procedures against students, the latter have a right to human intervention, to present their views, and to challenge the decision. This is directly against the rise of unchallengeable algorithmic authority within learning environments.

Articles 35 and 36 place Data Protection Impact Assessment requirements on high-risk processing, such as large-scale monitoring and the use of biometric data. In the context of educational institutions, this transforms ethical concerns about surveillance into mandatory governance processes that require documented risk analysis prior to system deployment.

These duties are further underpinned by the Data Protection Act 2018, which grants the Information Commissioner's Office powers to investigate systemic failures and impose administrative penalties. Together, these two vehicles of law-the UK General Data Protection Regulation and the Data Protection Act- embed privacy and transparency, along with accountability, as conditions that exist in non-negotiable permanence in AI-driven education, ensuring that digital learning environments continue to be consonant with fundamental rights rather than degenerating into infrastructures of non-transparent behavioural control.

4.9 China

China's Personal Information Protection Law (PIPL) 2021 covers the collection, use, storage and extra-territorial application of personal data to foreign entities processing data of individuals in China (Standing Committee of the National People's Congress, 2021). In an educational context, this applies to international edtech platforms that analyse the behaviour of students or offer digital learning services.

The PIPL invokes the principles of lawfulness, necessity and legitimate purpose for the processing of personal data. It limits excessive behavioural, biometric and learning analytics data collection by requiring that the data processing is strictly required for defined educational purposes. Notably, the law frames AI-enabled education within a larger national digital security framework, and not as a neutral technological tool.

The law includes more powerful protection of sensitive personal data, such as biometric data and data on minors under 14 years of age (Art. 28). Such data can be processed only under the strict necessity conditions and additional safeguards (Art. 29) for profound limitation of practises, concerning, for example, facial recognition, biometric monitoring within the educational purposes.

Further, the PIPL includes certain requirements on automated decision-making, such as ensuring transparency, fairness and avoiding unjustified discrimination (Art. 24). In the case of educational AI systems, this involves the importance of explainability and protecting against decisions that are only made via automatic processing.

Additionally, the law Also, the personal information protection impact assessments must be conducted before any processing of personal information or deployment of automatic decision-making systems (Art. 55). Cross-border data transfers are also tightly regulated in terms of stringent security cheques and certifications (Arts. 38-40) that have an immense impact on the functionality of cross-border educational platforms.

Overall, the PIPL represents a sovereignty-focused approach to educational data governance that incorporates data protection, algorithmic accountability, and national security concerns. Unlike consent-based models, it uses educational data as a strategic asset in a centrally-controlled digital ecosystem.

5. AI-DRIVEN SURVEILLANCE CONCERNS IN EDUCATIONAL INSTITUTIONS

Artificial intelligence-assisted surveillance in education is the systematic application of data-intensive technologies, which are often automated, continuous, and inference-oriented, to monitor, classify, and influence student behaviour, performance, and compliance. Unlike traditional forms of education surveillance, which may include examination hall invigilation by proctors and class observations by teachers, the use of artificial intelligence surveillance in education involves a massive extraction, profiling, and predictive analysis of behavioural data through cloud technologies and third-party service providers. UNESCO warned that the rapid adoption of artificial intelligence in education is occurring before relevant policy instruments are formulated to ensure accountability, privacy, and transparency (UNESCO, 2021a).

Concerns about AI-based surveillance systems extend beyond their impact on individual privacy. Rather, they bring about a complete paradigm shift in the nature of the teaching relationship and convert learning spaces into 'data harvesting sites' where the ideals of autonomy, freedom of expression, and trust associated with the teacher-student relationship are progressively subject to algorithmic control.

5.1 The Surveillance Shift: From Episodic Observation to Continuous Surveillance

One distinguishing feature of AI-based educational surveillance is the shift from episodic to continuous behavioural surveillance. Learning analytics tools gather granular interaction data. This may include clickstream activities. Other factors include dwell time. Other details include navigation and engagement patterns. Distancing the proctor through the use of distance proctoring tools takes the surveillance approach one step ahead by recording video streams using the university-provided webcams. Other factors include voice recordings. Other details include a virtual scan of the surroundings. Other details include device usage. These tools do not record; instead, they make predictions about terms such as 'academic risk.' Other terms include 'integrity,' 'engagement,'

Foundational work in learning analytics highlights the importance of acknowledging that these inferences are anything but neutral. Data reading occurs through the presumptions and power dynamics inherent in the system, which are deeply troubling in terms of issues of agency, consent, and classification (Slade & Prinsloo, 2013; Pardo & Siemens, 2014). The role of surveillance-driven education AI, in other words, is anything but a neutral technical system; it is a system of governance.

5.2 The Modalities of AI-Based Surveillance in Education

This subsection analyses the principal modalities through which AI-enabled surveillance is operationalised in contemporary educational environments, illustrating how technologies initially introduced to promote efficiency, integrity, or safety have evolved into pervasive infrastructures of behavioural monitoring and predictive governance

5.2.1 Distance Proctored Exams and Automated Integrity Tools.

AI-based proctoring tools rely on functions such as gaze tracking, face recognition, keystroke monitoring, and environmental scanning to predict potential untoward activity. Various systematic reviews indicate violations of privacy, opacity, and discriminatory accuracy, especially during proctoring high-stakes exams (Han et al., 2023; Terpstra, 2023; Ardelean & Veres, 2023). Since these tools enter into students' domestic environments, including bedrooms, they blur the lines between academic and personal spaces, making academic engagement subject to corporeal exposure.

5.2.2 Classroom Surveillance using Biometrics

Facial recognition, biometric attendance management, and biometric access control are increasingly being introduced in educational institutions. 'Biometric data is immutable, personal, and so sensitive that there has been evidence of bias in facial recognition software against women and racialised individuals' (Buolamwini & Gebru, 2018). Where biometric attendance monitoring becomes mandatory, opting out becomes impossible, leading to coerced surveillance. Education is offered on the condition that biometric data is provided.

5.2.3 Systems Intended to Ensure Safety and Activity Monitoring.

Schools are increasingly using these kinds of AI services on institution-issued devices to identify bullying, self-harm, threats, or what is deemed to be "inappropriate" content. Although these initiatives have been hailed as tools for child protection, there are considerable dangers of "mission creep" and "chill" factors when these systems are installed without either warning or recourse (UNICEF Innocenti, 2021).

5.2.4 Emotion Recognition and Affect Analytics.

Emotion-AI applications put the claim that they can detect emotions such as boredom, confusion, or stress by using the micro-expression of people's faces, their voice tone, or their body language. UNESCO and UNICEF state that these tools lack scientific validity and pose a risk of incorrect results, as well as psychological harm to children in a child-focused learning environment (UNESCO, 2021a; UNICEF Innocenti, 2021; 2025).

5.2.5 Predictive Analytics & Early Warning Systems

Learning analytics tools increasingly use risk scores to identify "at-risk" students. While the intention is to enable early intervention, risk scores have the effect of institutionalising deficit thinking as a form of categorisation, while also entrenching hidden assumptions within teaching decision-making (Slade & Prinsloo, 2013)

5.3 Core Damages and Risk Pathways

AI-driven surveillance produces measurable chilling effects on student behaviour. This makes learners reluctant to engage in discussions or debates on sensitive topics, as they are aware that constant monitoring is more likely to lead to self-censorship. This effect is compounded by structural power asymmetries: students cannot meaningfully refuse participation in institutionally mandated platforms without academic penalty, rendering consent effectively coerced .

5.4 Pedagogical Consequences of AI-Driven Surveillance

Beyond its implications for privacy and data protection, the expansion of artificial intelligence-driven surveillance technologies in educational institutions has significant pedagogical consequences. The integration of behavioural monitoring systems into classrooms and digital learning platforms can reshape how teaching and learning practices are organised, how students participate in academic environments, and how educators exercise professional autonomy.

One of the most widely discussed pedagogical effects of surveillance technologies is the emergence of what scholars describe as "chilling effects" within learning environments. When students know that their behaviour, engagement levels, or examination performance is continuously monitored by algorithmic systems, they may become more cautious in their interactions with learning platforms and classroom discussions. Research on digital surveillance in education suggests that such monitoring can discourage intellectual experimentation, critical questioning, and open debate, particularly when students fear that deviations from expected behavioural patterns may be flagged by automated systems (Selwyn, 2019). This dynamic may gradually transform educational spaces from environments that encourage curiosity and critical thinking into settings characterised by behavioural conformity and risk aversion.

AI-driven surveillance technologies may also affect educators' professional autonomy. The increasing use of learning analytics dashboards, engagement scoring systems, and predictive risk models introduces algorithmic metrics into teaching practices. These systems often generate quantitative indicators of student participation, performance, or attention, which institutions may use to guide or evaluate pedagogical decisions. While such analytics tools are frequently promoted as mechanisms for improving student outcomes, scholars have cautioned that excessive reliance on algorithmic metrics may constrain educators' professional judgment and shift pedagogical authority toward technological systems and institutional data infrastructures (Williamson, 2017). In this context, teachers may feel pressure to align instructional strategies with measurable behavioural indicators rather than broader educational goals.

The deployment of surveillance technologies may also contribute to the narrowing of curriculum and assessment practices. AI-enabled educational systems often prioritise forms of learning that can be easily quantified and analysed through digital data traces, such as task completion rates, time-on-task metrics, and standardised assessment scores. As a result, pedagogical activities that are difficult to measure algorithmically, such as open-ended discussion, collaborative exploration, and creative problem-solving, may receive less institutional emphasis. Scholars have argued that this form of "data-driven pedagogical optimisation" risks privileging measurable performance indicators over deeper forms of intellectual engagement (Selwyn, 2019; Williamson & Hogan, 2020).

Finally, AI-based surveillance systems may alter the relational dynamics between students and educational institutions. Traditional pedagogical relationships are often grounded in trust, mentorship, and educators' professional discretion. The introduction of automated monitoring systems can shift this dynamic toward one characterised by behavioural compliance and algorithmic oversight. In such environments, students may increasingly perceive learning platforms as mechanisms of institutional control rather than supportive educational tools. These shifts illustrate that the implications of educational surveillance extend beyond privacy concerns to encompass broader transformations in the nature of pedagogical interaction and academic culture.

Understanding these pedagogical consequences is essential when evaluating the governance of artificial intelligence in education. If learning environments become structured primarily around surveillance and behavioural measurement, educational institutions risk undermining the very intellectual openness and critical inquiry that education seeks to cultivate.

5.5 Legal and policy challenges

These practices create pressures with rights-based governance models. Data protection regulations highlight highly the principles of minimisation, proportionality, purpose limitation, and transparency. However, learning-oriented AI applications are designed for maximum data capture rather than pedagogical necessity (European Union, 2016).

UNESCO emphasises that education-oriented AI applications must align with human rights ideals, including dignity, accountability, and autonomy (UNESCO, 2021a). UNICEF and the UNICEF Committee on the Rights of the Child make clear that children's rights now demand additional protection against the threats of profiling and behavioural surveillance in online spaces (UNICEF Innocenti, 2021; UNICEF Committee on the Rights of the Child, 2021).

5.6 Governance Directions

- A rights-respecting model of educational AI must therefore be anchored in concrete limits:
- Necessity and proportionality assessments prior to deploying surveillance tools.
- Prioritisation of less intrusive pedagogical alternatives.
- Transparency as intelligibility rather than formalistic disclosure.
- Human review and contest pathways for automated academic judgments.
- Strict retention limits and separation of assessment data from vendor-training pipelines.
- Independent audits and impact assessments as procurement prerequisites.
- Child-centred governance aligned with UNCRC and UNICEF digital-rights principles.

In harmony with this imperative is a convergence between UNESCO and UNICEF. The imperative for educational institutions to address surveillance: either as an improvement in technology or as a governance issue, whether learning spaces become locales of intellectual freedom or infrastructures of behaviour modification (UNESCO, 2021a; UNICEF Innocenti, 2025).

6. CASE STUDIES

6.1 Vancouver Public Schools AI Surveillance Breach, USA, 2025

In 2025, The Seattle Times and The Associated Press published the results of their joint investigation into a security lapse involving AI-powered student monitoring technology. It revealed a severe slip-up concerning private student data at Vancouver Public Schools in Washington State. The district, like many others around the country, uses software such as Gaggle Safety Management to monitor school-issued devices for "suicide, self-harm, bullying, or violence" indicators. Transcripts of a public records request disclosed that nearly 3,500 unredacted student files flagged by the system were inadvertently left unprotected, allowing anyone who clicked the link to access highly sensitive content such as essays, diaries, disclosures of mental health, and information on sexual orientation and gender identity. According to reports, Gaggle monitors millions of students across some 1,500 U.S. school districts, aiming to detect risks through AI-powered keyword scanning. Security experts underlined this breach not just as a failure of privacy but also as a breakdown in the governance and cybersecurity of educational AI deployment, with robust safeguards needed against data production.

Impacts:

- Highly sensitive data involving the entire school.
- Possible outing of LGBTQ+ students without their consent.
- raised doubts about the net safety benefits versus privacy/security.

6.2 ProctorU Data Breach (USA & Global, 2020)

In June 2020, ProctorU, one of the most widely used online exam proctoring services resulting from the COVID-19 shift to remote assessment, suffered a large-scale data breach. Hackers made the platform's user database publicly available on a hacking forum, affecting about 444,000 records. The data breach included names, email addresses, phone numbers, physical addresses, and account credentials. Although ProctorU originally worked to validate the integrity of exams through webcam and screen monitoring, this breach showed how the centralised collection of student identity and behaviour-related information can make it a high-value target for attacks. Without public confirmation of the breach involving financial information and exam content, the exposure of personally identifiable information and access credentials posed a serious risk of identity theft and permanent biometric exposure to the affected population.

Key impacts:

- PII compromise for hundreds of thousands of students.
- Demonstrated the expanded attack surface created by proctoring systems.
- Triggered institutional cybersecurity reviews in affected universities.

6.3 Canvas/Instructure Child-Data Class Action

In 2025, a class action complaint was filed against Instructure's Canvas LMS, described as one of the most widely used learning management systems for both districts and Universities globally, for the illegal collection of child data and the commercial misuse of students' data. It has been reported in filings and in the industry that Canvas was collecting comprehensive data on its users, including names, pronouns, essays, test scores, and chatbot responses, and that this data was further disclosed via APIs that allowed third-party access to students' comprehensive behavioural patterns. It is reported that this matter was alleged in a complaint that described these practices of building "intimate dossiers of children" for data analysis and profiling as unconscionable at best due to a lack of appropriate consent or protection.

Key impacts:

- Reveals governance issues in data sharing practices and APIs in Learning Management Systems.
- Raises commercial profiling and privacy compliance questions.
- Represents the rise in litigation related to the rights of student data.

6.4 BYJU's Cross-Border Data Leakage issues (2021-2023)

BYJU'S, the leader in the education technology sector, and its online ecosystem, have been embroiled in several issues related to the governance of their data, most specifically regarding international data transfer and adequacy determinations. According to reports by CIS India and other industry commentators, BYJU'S maintained student data for EU individuals on AWS servers in Singapore and the US, which are logically vulnerable to countries without GDPR adequacy arrangements. In relation to biometric authentication and monitoring modules under review by data authorities in a number of countries, including the Irish Data Protection Commission, an emerging regulatory concern is emerging regarding biometric authentication in education technology. Independent hacks independent of competing companies, including Unacademy, have revealed millions of email and login credentials.

Key impacts:

- Transborder gaps in student data GDPR compliance.
- Increased regulatory concerns within the EU related to biometric verification procedures
- Spotted weaknesses in industry-wide security features of large ed-tech platforms.

6.5 French Universities Proctoring GDPR Fines (EU, 2024)

Several universities in France were fined a total of €800,000 by the French personal data protection authority (CNIL) for inadequate performance of Data Protection Impact Assessments (DPIAs) and the unlawful processing of biometric data through remote proctoring systems implemented during the COVID-19 era of academic assessments. It has been reported that the CNIL's enforcement action highlighted infringements of Articles 35 and 9 of the GDPR, specifically the rules on the processing of special personal data and risk assessments, as universities implemented proctoring for surveillance rather than meeting the necessary requirements

Key impacts:

- Validated application of GDPR to educational surveillance.
- Supplied enforcement precedent for the governance of biometric decision-making processes.
- Supported the calls for DPIAs in high-risk educational applications for AI.

7. TOWARD RESPONSIBLE DATA GOVERNANCE IN AI-DRIVEN EDUCATION

Artificial intelligence is transforming education into an ecology of persistent data capture, behaviour inference, and increasing reliance on platform infrastructure. Under such conditions, privacy cannot be reduced to a matter of individual consumer choice. Students interact with institutional systems in conditions of dependency, in which refusal to comply with AI-powered learning platforms can undermine attainment and progress. Responsible governance demands movement from notice-and-consent compliance towards institutional stewardship, through which the holders of education assume a positive duty of care for learner data, as well as pedagogically justified and necessary surveillance practices. UNESCO's Recommendation on AI in education addresses this duty through privacy-by-design, security-by-design, and accountability-by-design as preconditions for legitimate educational AI deployment (UNESCO, 2021). Children 's-rights instruments converge on this approach by confirming that minors need heightened protections in online spaces, and that profiling and behavioural tracking must be limited by the best interests of the child (UN Committee on the Rights of the Child, 2021; UNICEF Innocenti, 2021, 2025).

7.1 Repositioning Consent as the Institutional Responsibility

In terms of education, the concept of consent faces challenges because, in learning, consent cannot be declined for remote proctoring, attendance-tracking technology, and assessment platforms, among others, as this would create learning disadvantages. In this line, the concept of governance, including in the context of education, ought to rest on the duty of governance rather than the illusion of consent. Additionally, information processing should be carried out only when the requirement for such action can be met, and learning institutions should rely on non-intrusive learning methods, where possible.

7.2 Technological Assurance of Trust-Linked Educational Data

Educational data must be considered a trusted resource to be administered in a manner akin to a fiduciary. This demands minimisation through architecture, ensuring that only data points absolutely necessary for educational purposes or the integrity of the assessment are collected. There must be an infinitesimal restriction on secondary use, especially the use of video/behavioural data for the purpose of optimisation and commercial analytics. This has been cited by UNICEF as central to the erosion of autonomy and psychological well-being, leading to the minimisation and purpose limitation being moral imperatives rather than technical preferences (UNICEF Innocenti, 2021, 2025).

7.3 Procurement as the Primary Ethics Gate

Surveillance enters the classroom through procurement rather than policy discourse. Colleges use software packages whose default settings are optimised for surveillance, privacy clauses in software contracts that blur responsibility, and whose operations are unclear. Appropriate governance standards should start with procurement. These should include disclosure by sub-processors, a ban on advertising trackers and non-essential third-party analytics, timelines for notification in case of a breach, and deletions that can be verified. UNESCO makes it very clear that governance readiness must go hand in hand with procurement rigour: schools should scrutinise each AI system not only for affordability and functionality but also for its implications for privacy, security, and responsibility (UNESCO, 2021).

7.4 Security as a Condition of Teaching

In AI-mediated education, security is not only an infrastructural concern but also a prerequisite for trust, academic freedom, and institutional legitimacy. As a result, encryption, access control discipline, breach of response protocols, and routine security testing form educational safeguards rather than technical luxuries. When biometric identifiers, assessment of artefacts, or behavioural profiles are compromised, the harm extends beyond data loss into violations of dignity and learner safety.

7.5 Transparency, Intelligibility, and Contestability

Meaningful transparency requires more than wordy privacy notices. Learners need intelligible explanations of what data is collected, what inferences are generated, how long information is retained, and how automated outputs influence academic decisions. Consistent with children's rights principles, explanations need to be developmentally appropriate. Institutions should also offer genuine opportunities to challenge algorithmic judgments, including human review, documented reasons, and appeal mechanisms. Cross-Border Data Governance

Learning technologies are often built on cloud infrastructure that engages third-party analytics firms in different countries. This implies that institutions must establish data flow maps, assess the risks of data transfer, and include data localisation, breach, and deletion provisions in contracts. The concern about cross-border regulation is more a matter of day-to-day security than legal responsibility in platformised networks.

7.6 Data Breaches, Redress, and the Right to Repair Educational Harm

AI-based learning infrastructures are prone to errors. Breach of data, misclassification, biased profiles, and unauthorised disclosure of personal information can and should have been foreseen in the complex learning environment. However, learning institutions do not, in most cases, have procedures in place to offer remedies in the event of violations of student data and the use of harmful algorithms.

A rights-respecting governance framework, therefore, needs to incorporate institutional responsibilities for rectification. After violations or algorithmic damage occur, it is crucial for educational institutions to issue notifications for clear communication, explain the affected data deficiency, provide access to inferences derived, and offer the possibility to delete or correct incorrect data. If automated profiles have affected assessment, discipline, or progress, learners have the right to an evaluation or contestation by a person.

Child-focused approaches acknowledge that the remedy must always be restorative rather than merely procedural. Children must have recourse to remedies that compensate for injuries to dignity, autonomy, and mental health in online settings (UN Committee on the Rights of the Child, 2021; UNICEF Innocenti, 2025). Without actual means to repair privacy injuries, symbolic protection rather than substantive protection prevails.

7.7 Implementation Pathway

This implementation pathway operationalises abstract rights such as privacy, transparency, and accountability into concrete institutional practice. Rather than treating data protection as an individual responsibility of students through consent forms, this approach refrains from governance as a systemic institutional duty of care.

This means the Audit stage will require the educational institution to create a thorough mapping of all student data flows within and across platforms, vendors, and AI systems. This includes what data is collected and where, who processes it, what inferences are created, and which third parties receive access. Without such visibility, institutions cannot meaningfully assess risk or ensure legal compliance.

The Assess stage requires DPIAs and child-rights impact assessments for all high-risk educational technologies. These should not be procedural formalities but structured risk analyses to assess necessity, proportionality, bias, psychological harm, and potential rights infringement in advance of deploying systems.

The Contract stage turns procurement into a governance mechanism. Institutions must embed enforceable obligations into vendor contracts, including limits on secondary data use, commitments to delete and localise data, audit rights over algorithms and security practices, and binding breach notification clauses. That spreads accountability along the supply chain without displacing it onto learners.

Finally, the Remedy stage recognises that harm is inevitable in complex AI systems. Institutions must therefore establish grievance redressal mechanisms, human review boards for automated decisions, transparent appeal procedures, and breach-response protocols that provide real remedies rather than symbolic assurances.

The four stages together institutionalise privacy and child-rights protection within the architecture of education itself, ensuring that student data is governed through stewardship and accountability rather than coerced consent.

8. CONCLUSION

In this chapter, we have explored how AI is transforming education into a realm of continuous data extraction, behavioural predictions, and dependence on complex technological systems. In doing this, what emerges is not merely a narrative of innovation but rather a process of altering the conditions under which education occurs. The educational platforms developed by AI are no longer tools to augment education but are systems of governance that track, categorise, and impact learners in academic, behavioural, and emotional capacities.

The analysis shows that the position of student data is extraordinarily sensitive. The reason for this is that it is produced in a position of dependency, in which the position of consent is inherently fragile and puts a person at risk regarding their education. The use of biometric identification, learning analytics, emotional recognition systems, and risk assessment systems blurs the boundary between education and the private sphere.

In addition to this analysis, this chapter has demonstrated that there is a mismatch in the ability of the GDPR, the EU Artificial Intelligence Act, and the Indian Digital Personal Data Protection Act to regulate algorithmic power in the educational sector. Specifically, because there isn't a direct regulation of automated decision-making and profiling, this has enabled algorithms to affect educational pathways in a transparent and contestable manner.

The international case files examined, ranging from biometric attendance penalties in Europe to artificial intelligence video surveillance data breaches in North America, as well as international ed-tech data governance in the Global South, indicate that the risks are neither theoretical projections nor scattered instances.

Therefore, it is paramount to note that the ethical viability of AI in education cannot depend solely on compliance. Indeed, there is an urgent need for a shift in responsibility, ranging from data extraction of behavioural data to data stewardship. In other words, there is a complete shift in transparency, which should range from mere procedural transparency to experiential transparency. Privacy, security, and accountability must become the foundation of education.

Ultimately, the future of AI in education will not be determined by technical capability, but by governance choices. Where institutions prioritise dignity, autonomy, and justice, AI can enhance inclusion and educational opportunity. Where surveillance is normalised and accountability diffused, education risks becoming an infrastructure of behavioural control. The task ahead is therefore not to perfect educational surveillance, but to reclaim education as a space of trust, freedom, and human development in an algorithmic world. Ultimately, the legitimacy of educational artificial intelligence will be judged not by its efficiency, but by whether it preserves education as a space of dignity, intellectual freedom, and developmental justice rather than transforming it into an infrastructure of behavioural extraction.

REFERENCES

Ardelean, T.-K., & Veres, E. (2023). Students' perceptions of artificial intelligence in higher education. In *Proceedings of the 10th SWS International Scientific Conference on Social Sciences - ISCSS 2023* (pp. 1–11). https://doi.org/DOI: 10.35603/sws.iscss.2023/s08.38

Baker, R. S., & Siemens, G. (2014). Educational data mining and learning analytics. In Sawyer, R. K. (Ed.), *The Cambridge handbook of the learning sciences* (2nd ed., pp. 253–272). Cambridge University Press., DOI: 10.1017/CBO9781139519526.016

Benjamin, R. (2019). *Race after technology: Abolitionist tools for the new Jim code*. Polity Press.

Buolamwini, J., & Gebru, T. (2018). Gender shades: Intersectional accuracy disparities in commercial gender classification. In Friedler, S. A., & Wilson, C. (Eds.), *Proceedings of the 1st Conference on Fairness, Accountability and Transparency* (Vol. 81, pp. 77–91). PMLR.

Coghlan, S., Miller, T., & Paterson, J. (2021). Good proctor or "big brother"? Ethics of online exam supervision technologies. *Philosophy & Technology*, *34*(4), 1581–1606. DOI: 10.1007/s13347-021-00476-1 PMID: 34485025

EDPB. (2020). *Guidelines 05/2020 on consent under Regulation 2016/679*. European Data Protection Board.

European Union. (2016). *Regulation (EU) 2016/679 of the European Parliament and of the Council (General Data Protection Regulation).*

European Union. (2024). *Artificial Intelligence Act: Regulation (EU) 2024/1689.*

Federal Trade Commission. (2013). *Children's Online Privacy Protection Rule, 16 C.F.R. Part 312.*

Gašević, D., Tsai, Y.-S., & Drachsler, H. (2022). Learning analytics in higher education: Stakeholders, strategy and scale. *The Internet and Higher Education*, *52*, 100833. Advance online publication. DOI: 10.1016/j.iheduc.2021.100833

Han, S., & Nikou, S., & Ayele, holmW. (2023). Digital proctoring in higher education: A systematic literature review. *International Journal of Educational Management*. Advance online publication. DOI: 10.1108/IJEM-12-2022-0522

Holmes, W., Bialik, M., & Fadel, C. (2023). Artificial intelligence in education. In *Data ethics: Building trust: How digital technologies can serve humanity* (pp. 621–653). Globethics Publications., DOI: 10.58863/20.500.12424/4276068

Information Commissioner's Office. (2022). *Guidance on AI and data protection.* UK ICO.

Necochea-Chamorro, J., Asalde, C., Núñez, M., & Valencia, Y. (2024). Systematic literature review: Biometric technology applied to educational institutions. *TEM Journal.* https://doi.org/DOI: 10.18421/TEM131-60

OECD. (2024). *Trustworthy AI in education: Governance and cybersecurity.* OECD Publishing.

OECD. (2025). *PISA 2025 technical framework.* OECD Publishing.

Pardo, A., & Siemens, G. (2014). Ethical and privacy principles for learning analytics. *British Journal of Educational Technology, 45*(3), 438–450. DOI: 10.1111/bjet.12152

Parliament, U. K. (2018). *Data Protection Act 2018.* The Stationery Office.

Selwyn, N. (2019). *Should robots replace teachers? AI and the future of education.* Polity Press.

Siemens, G., & Long, P. (2011). Penetrating the fog: Analytics in learning and education. *EDUCAUSE Review, 46*(5), 30–32.

Slade, S., & Prinsloo, P. (2013). Learning analytics: Ethical issues and dilemmas. *The American Behavioral Scientist, 57*(10), 1510–1529. DOI: 10.1177/0002764213479366

Standing Committee of the National People's Congress. (2021). *Personal Information Protection Law of the People's Republic of China.*

Terpstra, N. (2023). Economics of Faith: Reforming Poor Relief in Early Modern Europe, by Esther Chung-Kim.

UN Committee on the Rights of the Child. (2021). *General Comment No. 25 on children's rights in the digital environment.*

UNESCO. (2021a). *Recommendation on the ethics of artificial intelligence.* UNESCO.

UNESCO. (2021b). *AI and education: Guidance for policymakers.* UNESCO.

UNESCO. (2021c). *Artificial intelligence in education: Challenges and opportunities.* UNESCO.

UNICEF Office of Research - Innocenti. (2021). *The case for regulating emotion recognition.* UNICEF.

UNICEF Office of Research - Innocenti. (2025). *Child-centred governance of AI systems.* UNICEF.

U.S. Department of Education. (n.d.). *Family Educational Rights and Privacy Act (FERPA) overview*.

Wickramasinghe, M., Gunawardena, L., & Padukkage, A. (2025). Ethical principles for artificial intelligence in education: A meta-review approach. *AI and Ethics*, *6*(1), 63. DOI: 10.1007/s43681-025-00878-3

Williamson, B. (2017). Big data in education: The digital future of learning, policy and practice. *Sage (Atlanta, Ga.)*. Advance online publication. DOI: 10.4135/9781529714920

Williamson, B., & Hogan, A. (2020, July). *Commercialisation and privatisation in/of education in the context of Covid-19* [Report]. Education International. https://www.ei-ie.org/en/item/25251:commercialisation-and-privatisation-inof-education-in-the-context-of-covid-19

Zuboff, S. (2019). *The age of surveillance capitalism: The fight for a human future at the new frontier of power*. PublicAffairs.

KEY TERMS AND DEFINITIONS

Algorithmic Epistemic Authority: The condition in which algorithmic outputs such as engagement scores, risk labels, or misconduct flags are treated as objective knowledge that overrides professional judgment within educational decision-making.

Behavioural Telemetry: Continuous streams of interaction data such as clicks, keystrokes, dwell time, navigation paths, and device logs captured by learning platforms to infer learner behaviour and performance.

Biometric Surveillance: The use of immutable biological identifiers, such as facial images, voice patterns, or keystroke dynamics, to monitor learners' identities, attendance, integrity, or emotional states.

Chilling Effect in Education: The phenomenon whereby learners suppress participation, intellectual risk-taking, or self-expression due to awareness of continuous surveillance, algorithmic monitoring, and the possibility of being misclassified by automated systems.

Data Colonialism in Education: A system in which student data are extracted, commodified, and transferred into global digital markets, turning educational environments into sources of economic value for transnational technology platforms.

Longitudinal Learner Profiling: The continuous accumulation and aggregation of behavioural, performance, biometric, and inferred data about a learner across educational stages and platforms, enabling persistent classification that may shape future academic pathways, institutional interventions, and life opportunities.

Surveillance Capitalism in Education: A political-economic model in which learner behaviour is systematically harvested and monetised through educational technologies for predictive and commercial gain.

Chapter 9

From Bias to Belonging: Ethical Pathways for Inclusive and Privacy-Respectful AI in Education

Adiyono Adiyono
http://orcid.org/0000-0002-6241-3383
Sekolah Tinggi Ilmu Tarbiyah Ibnu Rusyd Tanah Grogot, Paser, Indonesia

Sri Nurhayati
http://orcid.org/0000-0002-2273-9143
IKIP Siliwangi, Indonesia

Ellina Rienovita
http://orcid.org/0000-0002-3784-0834
Universitas Pendidikan Indonesia, Indonesia

Eka Setiawati
Universitas Setia Budhi, Indonesia

Cyintia Kumalasari
http://orcid.org/0009-0006-9727-923X
Universitas Islam Riau, Indonesia

ABSTRACT

The integration of Artificial Intelligence (AI) in education offers significant opportunities for adaptive, personalized, and efficient learning, yet it also presents serious ethical challenges related to algorithmic bias, student data privacy, and unequal access. This chapter explores how biased AI systems may reinforce existing social inequalities, how weak data governance can undermine students' autonomy and security, and how digital divides can marginalize vulnerable communities. By combining insights from ethics, education, and public policy, this chapter proposes an

DOI: 10.4018/979-8-3373-7467-3.ch009

inclusive and transparent ethical framework grounded in three pillars: mitigating bias through fair algorithmic design, protecting privacy through responsible data governance, and promoting equity to ensure that all learners benefit from AI innovations. The framework aims to guide the responsible adoption of AI in education and contribute to global efforts to ensure that technological progress aligns with ethical integrity and human values.

1. INTRODUCTION

The integration of Artificial Intelligence (AI) into educational systems has gained significant traction, reshaping various aspects, including teaching, learning, assessment, and administration. AI-driven tools, such as adaptive learning platforms and predictive analytics, aim to enhance personalization, efficiency, and scalability within educational contexts. According to Nurjanah et al., AI technologies provide comprehensive solutions across educational settings, integrating individual learning data to enhance teaching strategies and support diverse learning needs, contingent on adequate infrastructure like internet connectivity and database development (Nurjanah et al., 2024). However, the adoption of such technologies brings forward critical ethical challenges, particularly concerning algorithmic bias, data privacy, and equitable access (Chouhan & Shilpi, 2023). Ng et al. emphasize the importance of educated engagement with AI literacy, framing it as essential for democratizing access to AI technologies and ensuring educators can effectively leverage these tools without compromising ethical standards (Ng et al., 2021). Moreover, George and Wooden highlight the transformative potential of AI in higher education—citing examples where chatbots and virtual assistants streamline administrative tasks and personalize the learning experience—yet caution against the risks of reinforcing existing inequalities if access to AI technologies is not equitable (George & Wooden, 2023).

Additionally, Liu discusses the challenges specific to foreign language teaching, noting that while AI can enhance educational effectiveness, concerns persist regarding its limitations and the essential human elements of teaching that it cannot replicate (Liu, 2023). As AI tools become prevalent, researchers like Zhou and Peng explore the nuances of how AI can foster creativity in students but also acknowledge that learning engagement plays a mediating role in these developments (Zhou & Peng, 2025). Notably, Jiang asserts that AI applications are rapidly evolving, with projections of significant growth, further warranting scrutiny on how educational stakeholders navigate these opportunities amidst risks (Jiang, 2022). Overall, the urgency for rigorous scholarly attention to these dynamics is underscored by Kallunki et al., who note that the swift, pandemic-induced shift towards digital methodologies has necessitated reflection on the underlying ethical implications of relying heavily on AI in education (Kallunki et al., 2024; Adiyono et al., 2025). If left unregulated, the broad adoption of AI may exacerbate educational disparities and undermine the integrity of the learning environment, thereby necessitating a balanced approach that prioritizes both innovation and ethical considerations (Zawacki-Richter et al., 2019).

The rapid advance of Artificial Intelligence (AI) in education has spawned significant discourse concerning its ethical implications, particularly around algorithmic fairness, student data protection, and effective governance frameworks. Holmes et al. assert that the development of a community-wide framework addressing these ethical considerations is crucial; however, they note the inherent challenges due to the diverse interpretations of ethics within the field, emphasizing that any effective framework must remain adaptable to evolving educational contexts and knowledge Holmes et al., 2021). Meanwhile, Popenici and Kerr highlight the urgent need to address student data privacy and the necessity of robust protections to prevent misuse and breaches of privacy in the digitized education landscape (Popenici & Kerr, 2017). However, there is an evident gap in the existing literature, as discussions surrounding bias often occur in isolation from privacy concerns, while privacy debates frequently overlook issues of equity and inclusivity. Pagliara et al. emphasize that ethical considerations, such as algorithmic transparency, are integral to the integration of AI; yet, implementation must synergize with inclusive and participatory approaches to avoid reinforcing existing inequalities (Pagliara et al., 2024). This fragmentation in the discourse suggests a substantial need for an interdisciplinary framework that interlinks the ethical pillars of bias, privacy, and inclusivity.

In this context, Castro et al. argue for enhanced teacher competencies in interpreting data and maintaining pedagogical integrity while protecting student privacy, thereby aligning curricular priorities with ethical practices (Castro et al., 2024). The risks associated with ineffective AI applications in educational contexts—particularly those that exacerbate systemic disparities—are grave. Kadaruddin notes that without addressing these ethical concerns, including algorithmic bias and data security, the integration of generative AI could diminish the educational experience rather than enhance it (Kadaruddin, 2023). Furthermore, Balta delineates that ethical guidelines must be intrinsically woven into the fabric of educational AI usage, and the establishment of comprehensive protocols is essential for balancing innovation with ethical responsibility (Balta, 2023). Thus, the proposed framework in this discourse aims to transcend conventional, fragmented approaches by constructing a holistic understanding of ethical AI use in education, which underscores the interconnected nature of these ethical pillars and their implications for both policy implementation and practical educational settings.

The purpose of this paper is therefore to complete and extend the shortcomings of existing scholarship by (1) identifying how algorithmic bias manifests in educational

AI systems and its consequences for fairness, (2) analyzing privacy risks associated with student data collection and surveillance practices, and (3) exploring strategies to ensure inclusive and equitable access to AI-enhanced learning opportunities. Unlike previous works that focus narrowly on one aspect, this chapter explicitly integrates these challenges into a single conceptual and practical roadmap, providing actionable insights for educators, policymakers, and developers.

The central argument advanced in this chapter is that ethical AI in education cannot be achieved without simultaneously addressing bias, privacy, and inclusion. The working hypothesis is that by embedding these three dimensions into the design, governance, and deployment of AI systems, education can move toward responsible innovation that upholds human dignity and fosters equitable opportunities. Conversely, neglecting any one of these dimensions risks undermining the promise of AI and exacerbating systemic injustices.

Finally, this chapter contributes to the edited volume by offering a balanced and interdisciplinary perspective, bridging educational theory, ethics, and policy analysis. It begins with a review of the current state of AI ethics in education, followed by an examination of case studies illustrating bias, privacy, and equity challenges. It then introduces a proposed integrative ethical framework and concludes with recommendations for policy, governance, and teacher professional development. In doing so, the chapter not only fills a critical gap in existing research but also provides a forward-looking vision of ethical AI adoption in education.

Figure 1. Integrative ethical framework for AI in education (stakeholders and ethical dimensions)

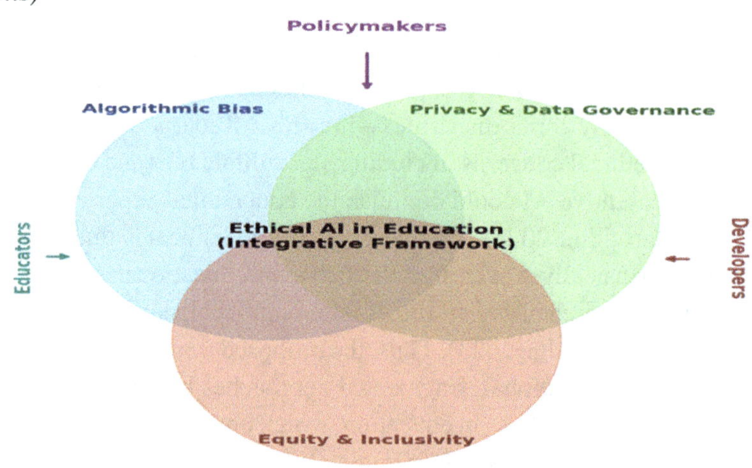

Figure 1 illustrates the integrative ethical framework for the application of AI in education. The Venn diagram shows three main dimensions, namely Algorithmic Bias, Privacy & Data Governance, and Equity & Inclusivity, each of which is related to the roles of Educators, Policymakers, and Developers. At the intersection of these three dimensions lies the concept of Ethical AI in Education (Integrative Framework), which emphasizes the importance of cross-stakeholder collaboration to create an ethical, fair, and sustainable AI ecosystem in education.

1.2 Narrative Explanation of the Framework

The proposed framework (Figure X) illustrates an integrative ethical model for AI in education that is built upon three interrelated pillars: algorithmic bias, privacy and data governance, and equity and inclusivity. These pillars represent the most pressing ethical dimensions of AI adoption in education, and their intersection forms the core of *Ethical AI in Education.*

1. **Algorithmic Bias,** AI systems in education often rely on data-driven decision-making, which can inadvertently reproduce existing social inequalities related to gender, ethnicity, language, or socioeconomic background. Addressing bias requires transparent algorithm design, fairness audits, and inclusive datasets.
2. **Privacy and Data Governance,** With the growing use of learning analytics and adaptive technologies, vast amounts of student data are being collected and analyzed. Without strong governance, such practices risk eroding student autonomy and trust. Principles such as *privacy by design*, transparency, and accountability in data handling are crucial.
3. **Equity and Inclusivity**, While AI can enhance access to education, it can also deepen the digital divide if underserved communities lack the resources or skills to benefit from AI-based systems. Ensuring inclusivity involves equitable access to infrastructure, AI literacy programs for students and teachers, and culturally sensitive design.

At the center of the model lies the integrative framework, emphasizing that ethical AI in education can only be achieved when these three dimensions are addressed holistically. Ignoring one dimension risks undermining the ethical integrity of the entire system.

Surrounding this ethical core are the key stakeholders who play complementary roles in ensuring its implementation:

- **Policymakers**: Establish regulatory frameworks, guidelines, and national strategies to ensure fairness, privacy, and access in AI-based education.

- **Educators**: Act as mediators who apply AI responsibly in the classroom, critically evaluate AI tools, and foster AI literacy among students.
- **Developers**: Design and build AI systems that embed ethical principles from the outset, ensuring transparency, fairness, and inclusivity.

The arrows connecting stakeholders to the framework signify a continuous interaction: developers need guidance from policymakers, policymakers depend on feedback from educators, and educators rely on tools designed by developers. Only through such collaboration can AI in education evolve responsibly.

In sum, this model underscores that ethical AI in education is not merely a technical issue, but a socio-technical ecosystem requiring cooperation among multiple actors. By operationalizing bias mitigation, privacy protection, and inclusivity strategies within this ecosystem, the framework provides a roadmap for fostering responsible, transparent, and human-centered AI adoption in education.

1.3 Methodology

This book chapter adopts a conceptual and integrative research approach to explore the ethical dimensions of Artificial Intelligence (AI) in education, with a particular focus on three core pillars: bias, privacy, and inclusivity. Rather than presenting empirical findings, the chapter synthesizes existing literature, frameworks, and policy documents to build a holistic model of ethical AI for education that can guide researchers, educators, policymakers, and developers.

1.3.1 Research Design

The study follows a **conceptual framework design** methodology with the following characteristics:

1. **Literature Revi ew and Theoretical Synthesis**: A systematic review of key scholarly works, policy papers (e.g., UNESCO, OECD, EU AI Act), and case studies was conducted to identify critical issues related to bias, data privacy, and equity in AI-based educational systems.
2. **Comparative and Cross-Contextual Analysis**: The chapter integrates global case illustrations from Europe and Asia, while also highlighting challenges specific to developing countries. This comparative lens provides insights into how ethical principles manifest differently depending on the socio-economic and technological context.
3. **Framework Development**: Based on the integrative analysis, the chapter proposes a **three-pillar ethical AI framework** (Bias, Privacy, Inclusivity) and

maps its implications across three stakeholder groups: educators, developers, and policymakers. This framework is visualized through diagrams, tables, and models to enhance clarity.

4. **Case Illustration Approach**: To ground the discussion, the chapter employs illustrative cases (e.g., AI-based adaptive learning platforms, data governance practices in EdTech, and digital divide challenges in developing nations). These cases are not exhaustive but serve as exemplars to demonstrate the practical application of the proposed framework.

1.3.2 Methodological Rigor

To ensure the **validity and reliability of insights**, the methodology incorporates:

- Triangulation of Sources: Academic articles, international policy reports, and empirical studies were cross-referenced.
- Conceptual Integration: The issues of bias, privacy, and inclusivity are not treated in isolation but woven into a single framework, representing the novelty of this chapter.
- Critical-Practical Balance: While theoretically grounded, the chapter emphasizes practical contributions by offering a roadmap for stakeholders (educators, policymakers, and developers) to operationalize ethical AI in education.

1.3.3 Outcome of the Methodology

Through this methodology, the chapter achieves:

1. A synthesized theoretical contribution in the form of a model for ethical AI in education.
2. A practical guideline for stakeholders to implement responsible AI practices.
3. An agenda for future research that calls for empirical validation of the proposed framework across diverse cultural and socio-economic contexts.

2. THEORETICAL AND CONCEPTUAL BACKGROUND

2.1 AI in Education: Opportunities and Challenges

2.1.1 The Integration of Artificial Intelligence in Adaptive Learning, Assessment and Administration

The integration of Artificial Intelligence (AI) in adaptive learning, assessment, and administration holds significant promise for enhancing educational outcomes, yet it raises important ethical considerations that need to be addressed systematically. Evidence from the study titled "AI Literacy: Definition, Teaching, Evaluation and Ethical Issues" indicates that adaptive technology can improve student engagement and learning efficiency while reducing the administrative burden on teachers and enabling more targeted interventions due to the real-time data generated by these systems Ng et al., 2021).

Furthermore, the article "Investigating Students' Perceptions Towards Artificial Intelligence in Medical Education" notes that AI-driven assessments can facilitate personalized learning experiences, enabling faster and more objective evaluations, and showcasing how AI can identify learning patterns and adjust the difficulty of questions to align with student abilities, thereby streamlining the assessment process (Buabbas et al., 2022).

However, while AI seems to enhance efficacy and engagement in educational settings, concerns regarding privacy and algorithmic fairness are increasingly prominent. A study titled "ChatGPT in Education – Understanding the Bahraini Academics Perspective" indicates that many educators recognize the impact of AI on teaching efficacy and administrative tasks, yet there are significant worries regarding data privacy and potential biases (Alrayes et al., 2024). The literature suggests that although the potential benefits of AI in education are vast, critical infrastructural challenges—such as connectivity issues and the digital readiness of educators in under-resourced areas—remain inadequately addressed (Chai et al., 2024).

For instance, Gore and Dove emphasize the necessity to protect sensitive information, calling for rigorous data protection protocols as more data is collected and processed by AI systems (Lee & Lee, 2021). Additionally, without governance frameworks, AI-driven educational technologies may exacerbate existing disparities, undermining equitable access and application in diverse educational contexts (Sit et al., 2020).

There is also a need for transparency in how AI systems operate. The article "Grading by AI makes me feel fairer? How different evaluators affect college students' perception of fairness" stresses that biases in AI-generated content can undermine trust in these systems (Chai et al., 2024). Therefore, it is urgent to develop a comprehensive framework that integrates considerations of algorithmic fairness, data security, and inclusivity in AI applications. Such a framework can help educators navigate the complexities of AI deployment while addressing ethical implications related to privacy and bias, thus ensuring a responsible approach to technology adoption in educational settings (Fiske et al., 2019; Gloppen et al., 2018).

2.1.2 Potential Benefits (Personalized Learning, Efficiency)

The main potential of AI integration in education lies in its ability to deliver personalized learning, which is a learning experience that is tailored to individual needs, styles, and learning speeds. AI systems are capable of analyzing student data in real-time to provide material recommendations, adaptive feedback, and more relevant learning paths. In addition, AI can also improve efficiency by automating teachers' administrative tasks such as assessment, attendance, and classroom management, so educators can focus more on pedagogical aspects that require a human touch. Thus, the application of AI not only accelerates the learning process, but also opens up space for the development of more inclusive learning and is oriented to the needs of students.

2.1.3 Risk (Automated Decision-Making, Surveillance, Dehumanisasi)

Behind the opportunities it offers, the use of AI in education also carries significant risks. Automated decision-making can result in biased or unfair decisions if algorithms are trained with unrepresentative data. In addition, surveillance practices through AI-based monitoring systems have the potential to violate student privacy and create a stressful learning environment. Furthermore, over-reliance on AI can lead to the dehumanization of the educational process, where the role of teachers as facilitators of values, empathy, and social interaction is increasingly marginalized.

2.2 Ethical Dimensions of AI in Education

Basic Concepts of Digital Ethics and AI

The basic concepts of digital ethics and AI are rooted in the principle that any use of technology, particularly artificial intelligence, must uphold the values of humanity, justice, and responsibility. Digital ethics emphasizes the need for transparency, accountability, and protection of individual rights, including privacy and freedom in the digital space. In the context of AI, this ethical concept is extended to ensure that intelligent algorithms and systems not only function effectively, but are also fair, free from discriminatory bias, and inclusive of all groups of society. Thus, digital ethics and AI demand a balance between technological innovation and moral, social, and legal responsibilities, so that the development of AI can support humanistic and sustainable learning.

Table 1. Basic concepts of digital ethics and AI in education

Ethical Principles	Explanation	Implications in Education
Humanity	Placing human values at the center of technological innovation.	AI should reinforce the role of teachers and support students' social interactions, not replace them.
Keadilan & Non-Bias	Avoid discrimination due to unrepresentative algorithms.	Adaptive learning systems must be fair to all students, regardless of gender or background.
Responsibility	AI users and developers are held accountable for social and moral impacts.	Educational institutions need to oversee the use of AI to comply with ethical and legal standards.
Transparency	The AI decision-making process must be clear and accountable.	Students and teachers must know how data is used in AI-based learning systems.
Accountability	There is an evaluation and supervision mechanism for the use of AI.	Schools and policymakers must prepare guidelines and regulations for the use of AI.
Privacy Protection	Safeguarding the rights of individuals to personal data and sensitive information.	Student data must be managed securely in accordance with regulations (e.g. GDPR).
Inclusivity	Ensure all groups of people benefit from AI.	AI should be designed to support students from diverse social, economic, and cultural backgrounds.

This table summarizes the ethical principles in the implementation of AI in education along with explanations and implications. The principle of Humanity emphasizes that AI should strengthen the role of teachers and support student social interaction, not replace it. The principle of Fairness & Non-Bias reminds us that algorithms must be fair to all students without discrimination, while Responsibility demands accountability from AI users and developers for its social and moral impact. Transparency emphasizes the importance of openness in AI decision-making processes, and Accountability encourages evaluation mechanisms and regulations for AI use in schools. The Privacy Protection principle focuses on protecting students' personal data in accordance with legal standards, while Inclusivity ensures that AI technology is designed to support social, economic, and cultural diversity so that all student groups can benefit from it.

Three Pillars: Bias, Privacy, Inclusivity

The three main pillars in AI ethics in education are bias, privacy, and inclusivity, which are intertwined in forming the foundation for fair and responsible use of technology. Bias arises when AI algorithms reflect or even reinforce social injustices, so mitigation efforts are needed to keep the learning system objective and non-discriminatory. Privacy emphasizes the protection of highly sensitive student personal data, where any collection, storage, and processing of data must be carried out transparently and in accordance with legal regulations. Meanwhile, inclusivity ensures that all students, regardless of gender, socio-economic background, or disability, can benefit equally from AI innovation. By upholding these three pillars, the application of AI in education can be more ethical, equitable, and support humanistic learning goals.

Table 2. The three pillars of AI ethics in education

Pillars of Ethics	Main Meaning	Challenge	Implications in Education
Bias	The tendency of algorithms to reinforce discrimination or social injustice.	Unrepresentative datasets, discriminatory automated decisions.	Algorithmic audits, inclusive data curation, and regulations are needed to prevent injustice.
Privacy	Protection of sensitive students' personal data.	The risk of data leakage, misuse of information, and lack of transparency.	Implementation of regulations (e.g. GDPR), data encryption, and transparent policies in data processing.
Inclusivity	Provide access and benefits of AI for all learners equally.	Digital divide, limited access for marginalized groups, biased system design.	Development of AI that is disability-friendly, takes into account socio-economic contexts, and equitable access.

The table above shows that the three pillars of AI ethics in education—bias, privacy, and inclusivity—have complementary roles in creating a fair and responsible learning ecosystem. Bias emphasizes the need for oversight of algorithms so as not to cause discrimination, privacy focuses on protecting students' personal data from potential misuse, while inclusivity ensures all learners benefit equally from AI technology. By understanding the challenges and implications of each pillar, educational institutions can design AI implementation policies and practices that are more ethical, transparent, and humane.

Linkage With the Principles of Social Justice, Human Rights, and Democratization of Education

The interconnectedness of AI ethics with the principles of social justice, human rights, and democratization of education lies in the commitment to ensure that technology not only improves learning efficiency but also expands access in a fair and equitable manner. The principle of social justice demands that the use of AI does not deepen the gap between rich and poor groups, but rather becomes a means of empowerment for all levels of society. From a human rights perspective, students' privacy and freedom must be guaranteed, so that personal data is not misused and the right to learn is respected. Meanwhile, the democratization of education emphasizes the inclusivity, participation, and active involvement of all stakeholders in determining the direction of AI policies in schools. Thus, the application of AI in education should not only be based on technological innovation, but also rooted in the values of humanity, justice, and broader social participation.

3. STATE OF THE ART AND LITERATURE REVIEW

3.1 Algorithmic Bias in Education

Previous Studies on Algorithmic Discrimination (Gender, Race, Socio-Economic).

Previous studies of algorithmic discrimination have shown that artificial intelligence systems often reproduce or even reinforce existing injustices in society, especially related to gender, race, and socio-economic status. Research by Buolamwini and Gebru (2018), for example, found that AI facial recognition systems have a much higher error rate in dark-skinned women and individuals than in light-skinned men. In addition, Noble (2018), in his work *Algorithms of Oppression,* highlights how search engines reflect racial and gender bias in digital representations. In a socio-economic context, O'Neil (2016) explains in *Weapons of Math Destruction* that algorithms are often used to make decisions in education, employment, and loans, which actually exacerbate injustices for underprivileged groups. These findings reinforce the urgency of studying AI ethics in education so that the systems used do not discriminate against students based on their gender, background, ethnicity, or socio-economic condition.

Table 3. Studies on algorithmic discrimination in AI

Dimensions of Discrimination	Research Findings	Source	Implications in Education
Gender	Facial recognition AI systems more often misrecognize women than men.	Buolamwini & Gebru (2018)	The risk of inaccuracies in AI-based assessments and potential discrimination against female students.
Race	Facial recognition algorithms have a higher bias towards dark-skinned individuals.	Buolamwini & Gebru (2018)	AI has the potential to reinforce stereotypes and unfair treatment of students from ethnic minority groups.
Gender & Ras	Search engines reproduce racial and gender bias in digital representations.	Noble (2018) *Algorithms of Oppression*	AI-generated digital learning materials can be biased, reinforcing symbolic discrimination.
Socio-Economic	Algorithms used in education, employment, and lending exacerbate injustice for poor groups.	O'Neil (2016) *Weapons of Math Destruction*	AI in selection or assessment risks systematically excluding students from underprivileged groups.

Limitations of Previous Research (Less Interdisciplinary, not yet Holistic)

The limitations of previous research on the ethics of AI in education generally lie in approaches that are still fragmented, less interdisciplinary, and not yet holistic. Many studies only highlight technical aspects, such as algorithm accuracy or data security, without linking them to social, philosophical, or educational policy perspectives. As a result, important issues such as social justice, the psychological impact on students, and the long-term implications for the democratization of education are often overlooked. In addition, most studies tend to focus on specific contexts, such as gender bias or data privacy, but have not integrated other interrelated ethical dimensions, such as inclusivity, justice, and human rights. Therefore, more comprehensive and interdisciplinary research is needed so that the understanding of AI ethics in education can develop in a complete and applicable manner.

3.2 Privacy and Data Governance

Research on Student Data, Learning Analytics, and GDPR

Research on student data, learning analytics, and GDPR regulations highlights the importance of ethical data governance in the technology-driven education ecosystem. Learning analytics provides a great opportunity to improve learning through the analysis of student learning behavior patterns, prediction of academic achievement, and the provision of more targeted interventions. However, the use of this data poses serious challenges related to privacy and security, especially since student data is highly sensitive information. This is where the role of regulations such as the General Data Protection Regulation (GDPR) becomes important, as it emphasizes the principles of transparency, consent, as well as students' right to control the use of their personal data. Thus, research in this area focuses not only on the pedagogical potential of learning analytics, but also on the urgent need to strike a balance between technological innovation and the protection of students' rights in the digital age.

Gap: Rarely Connects Privacy With Access Fairness

One of the research gaps that is still rarely discussed is how the issue of privacy in the use of AI in education is related to access to justice. Most studies have emphasized student data protection as both technical and legal aspects, without considering that strict privacy standards often create barriers for marginalized groups or schools with limited resources. For example, educational institutions in remote areas may struggle to meet international privacy regulations such as GDPR due to limited digital infrastructure, thus risking widening the gap in access to AI technology. Therefore, a more in-depth study is needed on how privacy policies can be designed in an inclusive manner, so as not only to protect individual rights, but also to ensure equal access for all students.

3.3 Equity and Inclusivity in AI-Enhanced Education

Discourse on the Digital Divide and Access Gap

The discourse on the digital divide and access gap highlights how inequalities in the availability of digital infrastructure, technological literacy, and economic resources can deepen the gap between groups that are able to leverage AI in education and those that are not. In developed countries, students generally have better access to devices, stable internet connections, and AI-based learning platforms, while in many developing countries, limited basic facilities are still a major barrier. In addition, socio-economic, gender, and geographical conditions also contribute to access gaps, which can ultimately affect the quality of learning and future opportunities of learners. Therefore, discussing the digital divide is not only related to technology but also concerns aspects of social justice, public policy, and global responsibility in ensuring inclusive education in the AI era.

Table 4. Digital discourse and the access gap in AI-based education

Gap Aspects	Problem Description	Impact on Education	Ethical Implications
Digital infrastructure	The difference in the availability of devices and internet networks between developed and developing countries.	Students in areas with limited infrastructure have difficulty accessing AI-based learning.	Potentially widening global inequalities in learning opportunities.
Technology Literacy	The low ability of teachers and students to use AI and digital technology.	AI is not used optimally, and can even increase technological dependence.	Demand training and capacity building that is fair to all parties.
Socio-Economic	Economic limitations make some families unable to afford to provide digital devices.	Limiting the participation of students from poor families in the AI learning ecosystem.	Violating the principle of social justice in access to education.
Gender	Women in some cultures still face barriers in accessing technology.	Inequities in women's involvement in AI-based learning.	The risk of gender bias is even greater if it is not anticipated in policy design.
Geographic	Remote areas are difficult to reach for digital services due to limited infrastructure.	Students in rural areas are lagging behind in AI adoption compared to students in urban areas.	Requires affirmative policies for equitable access to digital education.

One of the important gaps in the study of the digital divide is that this issue is often separated from the discourse about algorithmic bias and data privacy. Many studies have addressed the gap in technological access only in terms of infrastructure or economy, without looking at how limited access also magnifies the risk of discrimination and privacy violations. For example, students from low socio-economic groups are not only more difficult to access AI-based learning platforms, but also tend to be more vulnerable to the exploitation of personal data due to limited digital literacy and a lack of regulatory protections. The separation of these issues makes the understanding of AI ethics in education partial and less thorough. Therefore, it is important to integrate discussions about the digital divide, bias, and privacy as three interrelated dimensions in creating a fair, safe, and inclusive education ecosystem in the AI era.

4. RESEARCH GAP AND NOVELTY

In the study of AI ethics in education, there is still significant room to present new contributions through the identification of research gaps and the affirmation of research novelty. Although the previous literature has addressed many issues of bias, privacy, and inclusivity separately, few have integrated the three into a single coherent framework of analysis. In fact, these three dimensions are closely interrelated and determine the extent to which AI can be implemented in a fair, safe, and humane manner in the education ecosystem. Therefore, this section will outline an integrative analysis of existing literature gaps, affirm research novelty through new approaches that link bias, privacy, and inclusion, and formulate theoretical contributions in the form of three-pillar-based AI ethical models and practical contributions in the form of roadmaps for AI educators, policymakers, and developers.

Table 5. Research gap, novelty, and research contribution

Aspects	Description	Implication
Integrative Analysis	Previous literature has tended to address bias, privacy, and inclusion separately, not yet in a holistic framework.	Demonstrates the need for a cross-disciplinary approach that integrates all three key issues simultaneously.
Novelty Affirmation	A new approach by linking bias + privacy + inclusion in a single AI ethics framework.	Provide a fresh and more comprehensive perspective on AI ethical issues in education.
Theoretical Contributions	Formulate an AI ethical model based on three pillars (bias, privacy, and inclusivity).	Provide a conceptual foundation that can be used as an academic reference for further research.
Practical Contribution	Develop an AI ethics roadmap for educators, policymakers, and technology developers.	Provide applicable guidance in designing, implementing, and evaluating AI in education.

The table explains the main contributions of this research through four important aspects. First, integrative analysis highlights that previous literature still discusses bias, privacy, and inclusivity separately, thus requiring a more comprehensive interdisciplinary approach. Second, novelty affirmation presents a new approach by linking these three issues in a single AI ethics framework, providing a fresher and more comprehensive perspective. Third, in terms of theoretical contribution, this study offers a three-pillar AI ethics model as a conceptual foundation that can be used as an academic reference. Finally, the practical contribution is the development of an AI ethics roadmap that can be used by educators, policymakers, and technology developers as a guide for ethical and sustainable implementation.

5. PROPOSED ETHICAL FRAMEWORK FOR AI IN EDUCATION

5.1 Mitigating Algorithmic Bias

The Principle of Fairness in Algorithm Design

The principle of fairness in algorithm design demands that AI systems be designed to avoid discrimination and provide equal treatment for all users. In the context of education, fairness means that adaptive learning algorithms and AI-based assessments must consider the diversity of students' backgrounds so that the results produced are fair and representative. Thus, fairness is an important foundation to ensure that AI does not reinforce social inequality, but instead supports inclusive and equitable access to education.

AI Model Audit and Transparency Strategy

The AI model's audit and transparency strategy aims to ensure that the algorithm's decision-making process can be openly monitored, understood, and evaluated by various stakeholders. In education, this strategy includes an independent review mechanism of AI systems as well as providing clear explanations of how algorithms work to teachers, students, and parents. With this step, trust in AI can be increased while minimizing the risk of bias, error, and misuse of technology.

5.2 Protecting Student Data and Privacy

Protecting Student Data and Privacy is a fundamental aspect in the implementation of AI and educational technology (EdTech), which requires data governance based on transparency, accountability, and compliance with applicable regulations. The principle *of Privacy by Design* must be the foundation of the design stage of the system, not just an addition after implementation, so that every process of collecting, storing, and processing student data truly protects students' privacy rights. This approach not only builds public trust but also encourages the creation of a safe, ethical, and sustainable digital learning environment.

Table 6. Principles of data governance and privacy by design in AI-based education

Key Aspects	Explanation	Implications in Education
Transparency	Information is clear about how student data is collected and used.	Students, teachers, and parents understand the purpose and risks of data.
Accountability	The school/EdTech provider is responsible for data security.	Regular evaluation and audit mechanisms can be carried out.
Regulation	Compliance with GDPR, Data Protection Laws, and local regulations.	Protect students' rights legally from data misuse.
Privacy by Design	Privacy protection is instilled early on in the design of the system.	The learning platform is more secure and has minimal risk of leakage.

5.3 Ensuring Equity and Inclusivity

Strategy to Narrow the Digital Divide

The strategy to narrow *the digital divide* includes expanding technology infrastructure, increasing digital literacy, and providing affordable device access for all groups. This needs to be accompanied by inclusive policies that target vulnerable groups, including students in remote areas and those from low-income families. Thus, the digital divide is not only narrowed, but can also encourage the creation of equal learning opportunities in the AI era.

AI for Underserved Communities

AI for underserved communities can serve as a means of empowerment by providing access to personalized learning, online education resources, and guidance services that were previously difficult to reach. This technology can also help reduce geographical and socio-economic barriers by providing mobile-based learning solutions or lightweight platforms that do not require expensive infrastructure. With the right application, AI can be a bridge to more inclusive and socially just education.

AI Literacy for Students & Teachers

AI literacy for students and teachers is an important skill for understanding how artificial intelligence technology works, its potential, and its risks in the context of education (Adiyono et al., 2025). With AI literacy, teachers can be more critical in selecting and integrating technology, while students are able to use AI ethically, creatively, and responsibly. This ultimately strengthens the capacity of the education ecosystem to face the challenges of the digital age.

5.4 Integrative Ethical Roadmap

Inter-Pillar Relationships: Privacy ↔ Bias ↔ Inclusivity

This study significantly enriches the burgeoning literature on AI ethics in education by proposing a new conceptual framework that centers on three critical pillars: bias, privacy, and inclusivity. Unlike prior works, which have often examined these issues independently, this integrative analysis elucidates the interrelationships among ethical dimensions concerning AI use in educational settings. Holmes et al. emphasize that "establishing a useful framework for the ethics of AI in education, although desirable and potentially useful, is likely to be a challenging and long-term task," indicating the complexity of synthesizing various concerns into a cohesive strategy Holmes et al. (2021). This framework not only advances academic discourse on digital ethics but also provides a foundational reference for future research in education, technology policy, and moral philosophy. As Batool et al. note, existing studies primarily scrutinize isolated ethical AI principles, highlighting an opportunity for the development of structured governance solutions that emphasize a more holistic approach to integrating bias, privacy, and inclusivity (Batool et al., 2024).

Moreover, this theoretical construct invites the emergence of new theories surrounding algorithmic justice within educational contexts, aligning with the calls by Apfelbacher et al. for comprehensive governance frameworks that consider the multifaceted implications of AI deployment. However, the actual relevance of their research is focused on healthcare contexts rather than education (Apfelbacher et al., 2024). The necessity for a robust approach that interweaves ethical considerations in AI intersects with recommendations by Selvaratnam and Venaruzzo, who reveal that many institutions currently deploy AI tools without the support of adequate governance structures (Selvaratnam & Venaruzzo, 2024). This absence of oversight raises urgent questions about equitable access and the safeguarding of marginalized groups, reinforcing the importance of inclusivity within the proposed framework, although the context of this reference also relates to higher education rather than a general scope on inclusivity (Nasir et al., 2024).

By providing a more nuanced understanding of these interconnected ethical pillars, this study fosters dialogue among researchers and practitioners alike, encouraging proactive strategies to ensure that AI not only serves educational purposes but also upholds fundamental human values. As Jobin et al. illustrate, the landscape of AI ethics is still evolving, necessitating flexible frameworks that can dynamically adapt to the changing landscapes of educational practices and societal norms (Jobin et al., 2019). Consequently, the proposed framework has the potential to become a cornerstone in the discourse of AI ethics, facilitating broader engagement and implementation of ethical AI practices in diverse educational environments.

Proposed. Conceptual Model/Framework

The proposed conceptual framework positions Ethical AI in Education as an integrative model built upon three interrelated pillars: Algorithmic Bias, Data Privacy & Governance, and Equity & Inclusivity. These dimensions are embedded within an educational ecosystem that involves three key stakeholders: Educators, who implement AI ethically in teaching and learning; Developers, who design fair, safe, and transparent AI systems; and Policymakers, who establish regulations and governance structures to ensure accountability. The model highlights the intersections of these pillars and stakeholders, illustrating that responsible AI in education cannot be achieved by addressing bias, privacy, or inclusivity in isolation, but rather through a holistic and collaborative approach. This framework aims to guide both theoretical discourse and practical policy implementation across diverse educational contexts.

Figure 2. Ethical AI integrative conceptual framework in education

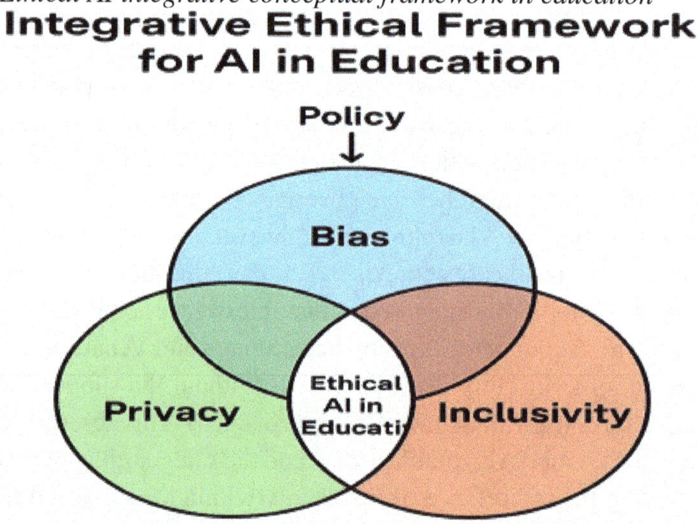

Figure 2 illustrates an integrative conceptual framework for ethical AI in education that emphasizes three key pillars: *algorithmic bias*, *data privacy & governance*, and *equity & inclusivity*. These three dimensions are intersecting and inseparable, as each aspect influences each other in shaping fair and responsible AI practices. Around it are three main stakeholders, namely educators, developers, and policymakers, who have specific roles but must work collaboratively. This model confirms that the successful implementation of ethical AI in education can only be achieved through synergy between pillars and actors.

6. CASE STUDIES AND EMPIRICAL ILLUSTRATIONS

Global Case Studies (e.g., the Use of AI in Europe/Asia)

The landscape of Artificial Intelligence (AI) in education exhibits significant regional variations influenced by distinct cultural, social, and regulatory contexts, particularly in Europe and Asia. In Europe, the implementation of AI in educational frameworks is primarily guided by stringent regulations such as the General Data Protection Regulation (GDPR), which emphasizes ethical guidelines for data protection and privacy (Morandín-Ahuerma, 2024). These regulations are instrumental for ensuring transparency and accountability within AI applications, as highlighted by Morandín-Ahuerma, who discusses how "the GDPR sets a benchmark for ethical AI use" in educational contexts. Additionally, the European Union's educational policies further emphasize the importance of algorithmic fairness by promoting practices that protect the rights and freedoms of individuals in data usage (Morandín-Ahuerma, 2024).

In contrast, Asian nations display varying approaches to AI in education. For instance, China's emphasis on adaptive learning and large-scale assessments has catalyzed discussions about the implications for student autonomy and privacy, raising concerns about surveillance in educational environments (Kashefi et al., 2024). The pressure this creates for a balance between technological enhancement and personal freedoms resonates with critiques of AI systems, underscoring the need for clear communication to mitigate fears surrounding student surveillance and privacy violations. Meanwhile, Japan and South Korea approach AI adoption with an emphasis on inclusivity and personalizing learning experiences, particularly for students with special needs, reflecting priorities of educational equity (Symeou et al., 2025).

This comparative analysis reveals that while Europe typically emphasizes governance frameworks to ensure ethical AI deployment, Asian countries focus more on the practical applications of AI technologies in adapting educational methodologies to diverse learning needs. Such differences point to the need for "cross-border ethical studies to identify best practices that balance innovation with the protection of human rights and values," as expressed by Symeou et al. in developing evidence-based guidelines for AI's integration in higher education (Symeou et al., 2025). The imperative for thorough ethical scrutiny amid the global expansion of AI technologies is underscored by Mouta et al., who call for a systematic approach to address the ethical challenges that AI poses, notably concerning data privacy, algorithmic bias, and accountability in varying educational settings (Mouta et al., 2023). Ultimately, this body of work advocates for a holistic understanding of AI, suggesting that collaborative international efforts may yield frameworks that ensure technology enhances education without compromising fundamental ethical standards (Torrisi-Steele, 2025).

Illustration of a Local Context (e.g., a School in a Developing Country)

In the context of schools in developing countries, the implementation of AI in education faces more complex challenges compared to developed countries. Many schools are still struggling with limited digital infrastructure, such as unstable internet access, limited computer devices, and a lack of educators who have adequate digital literacy. This condition makes the application of AI, although it has the potential to improve the quality of learning, often uneven and risks widening the gap between schools and between students.

On the other hand, the local context also presents opportunities for more contextual and relevant use of AI. For example, AI can be leveraged to provide learning materials in regional languages, support students with special needs, or deliver lightweight learning platforms that can run on simple devices. With the right policy support, local community engagement, and low-resource AI design models, schools in developing countries can make this technology an empowerment tool that supports educational equity while addressing existing structural limitations (Bulathwela, S., et al., 2024; Adiyono et al., 2025).

Figure 3. AI implementation in developing countries faces complex challenges

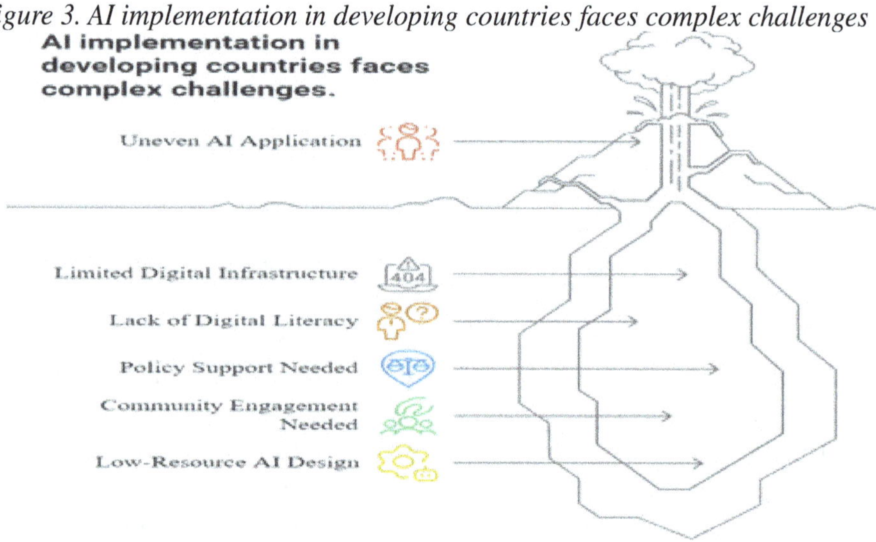

Figure 3 illustrates the complex challenges in implementing AI in developing countries with an iceberg illustration, where only the issue of uneven AI application is visible on the surface, while more fundamental challenges are hidden beneath the surface. These challenges include limited digital infrastructure, low digital literacy among educators and students, a lack of adaptive policy support, minimal community involvement, and the need for low-resource AI design. This visualization shows that the successful integration of AI in education in developing countries requires a holistic approach that focuses not only on technology adoption, but also on the underlying structural, social, and policy factors.

An Analysis of How Bias, Privacy, and Equity Emerge in Real Life

The interplay between bias, privacy, and equity in the implementation of artificial intelligence (AI) in education illustrates how these issues can exacerbate educational inequalities if not effectively managed. Bias manifests in assessment algorithms and adaptive learning systems that tend to favor students from higher socio-economic backgrounds or majority groups, reinforcing existing disparities. As noted by Holmes et al., "Stakeholder Perspectives on the Ethics of AI in Distance-Based Higher Education," algorithmic bias can significantly affect student outcomes, leading to a misrepresentation of capabilities among underrepresented populations (Holmes et al., 2023). This not only undermines educational fairness but also restricts opportunities for marginalized groups.

Privacy concerns intensify this issue as sensitive student data, such as academic records and personal information, is often collected and managed inconsistently, increasing the risk of data breaches and misuse. Agarwal et al. emphasize that "without adequate transparency in data governance, the potential for misuse escalates, heightening privacy violations against vulnerable student populations" (Agarwal et al., 2024). Furthermore, the lack of strong privacy protections compromises individual security and can also compound biases, as mismanaged data may fail to accurately reflect the diverse needs of all students, leading to skewed educational interventions.

Equity issues arise from the digital divide, where students in urban areas have more immediate access to AI technologies compared to their peers in remote or under-resourced regions. In this context, as articulated by Holmes et al., "the disparities in access to educational technology can perpetuate existing inequalities, particularly in underserved communities" (Holmes et al., 2023). This inequitable distribution of resources entrenches the vicious cycle of disadvantage for those already marginalized, highlighting the need for systemic change.

Thus, these three aspects—bias, privacy, and equity—are tightly interwoven and must be addressed collectively to support a fairer and more inclusive educational landscape. Failure to manage these factors comprehensively will not only hamper efforts toward democratizing education in the digital era but also risk deepening the very inequities that AI is purported to alleviate. As Yu and Yu pointed out, the development of ethical frameworks that integrate these dimensions will be pivotal in steering AI applications toward fostering equitable learning environments and safeguarding the rights of all students (Yu & Yu, 2023).

Table 7. Analysis of how bias, privacy, and equity

Ethical Issues	Real Manifestations in Education	Impact
Bias	Assessment algorithms are more accurate for the majority of students, less appropriate for minorities	Discrimination in learning outcomes and unfair assessment
Privacy	Student data collection without explicit consent, academic data leakage	Loss of trust, risk of data misuse
Equity	AI access is greater in urban schools than in rural ones	Deepening the digital and education divide

7. DISCUSSION

Theoretical Implications: Contributions to the Ethical Literature of Educational AI

This study significantly enriches the burgeoning literature on AI ethics in education by proposing a new conceptual framework that centers on three critical pillars: bias, privacy, and inclusivity. Unlike prior works, which have often examined these issues independently, this integrative analysis elucidates the interrelationships among ethical dimensions concerning AI use in educational settings. Holmes et al. emphasize that "establishing a useful framework for the ethics of AI in education, although desirable and potentially useful, is likely to be a challenging and long-term task," indicating the complexity of synthesizing various concerns into a cohesive strategy Holmes et al., 2021). This framework not only advances academic discourse on digital ethics but also provides a foundational reference for future research in education, technology policy, and moral philosophy. As Batool et al. note, existing studies primarily scrutinize isolated ethical AI principles, highlighting an opportunity for the development of structured governance solutions that emphasize a more holistic approach to integrating bias, privacy, and inclusivity (Batool et al., 2024).

Moreover, this theoretical construct invites the emergence of new theories surrounding algorithmic justice within educational contexts, aligning with the calls by Apfelbacher et al. for comprehensive governance frameworks that consider the multifaceted implications of AI deployment. However, the actual relevance of their research is focused on healthcare contexts rather than education (Apfelbacher et al., 2024). The necessity for a robust approach that interweaves ethical considerations in AI intersects with recommendations by Selvaratnam and Venaruzzo, who reveal that many institutions currently deploy AI tools without the support of adequate governance structures (Selvaratnam & Venaruzzo, 2024). This absence of oversight raises urgent questions about equitable access and the safeguarding of marginalized groups, reinforcing the importance of inclusivity within the proposed framework, although the context of this reference also relates to higher education rather than a general scope on inclusivity (Nasir et al., 2024).

By providing a more nuanced understanding of these interconnected ethical pillars, this study fosters dialogue among researchers and practitioners alike, encouraging proactive strategies to ensure that AI not only serves educational purposes but also upholds fundamental human values. As Jobin et al. illustrate, the landscape of AI ethics is still evolving, necessitating flexible frameworks that can dynamically adapt to the changing landscapes of educational practices and societal norms (Jobin et al., 2019). Consequently, the proposed framework has the potential to become a cornerstone in the discourse of AI ethics, facilitating broader engagement and implementation of ethical AI practices in diverse educational environments.

Practical Implications: Guidelines for Educators, Developers, and Regulators

The practical implication of this study is the need for clear and applicable guidelines for educators, developers, and regulators in adopting and managing AI technology in education. For educators, the guidelines can be in the form of guidelines for the ethical use of AI in learning, for example by understanding potential biases in adaptive systems, maintaining the confidentiality of student data, and ensuring the equal involvement of all students. This demands an increase in digital competence and AI literacy for teachers, so that they are not only passive users, but also able to criticize and adapt technology according to the humanist educational context.

For developers and regulators, ethical guidelines must be translated into design practices, data governance, and policies that favor social justice. EdTech developers need to integrate the principles of fairness, privacy by design, and inclusive innovation into the products they produce, so that technology is not only efficient but also fair and safe. Meanwhile, regulators need to formulate binding policies and standards so that the implementation of AI in schools and universities runs transparently, accountably, and in accordance with the principles of human rights and democratization of education. Thus, collaboration between educators, developers, and regulators can create an educational AI ecosystem that is ethical, sustainable, and in the interests of learners.

Figure 4. Ethical AI in education

Figure 4 depicts the Ethical AI in Education ecosystem involving three main actors: regulators, educators, and developers. Regulators play a role in enforcing transparency policies, educators are tasked with implementing AI ethically in the classroom, while developers are responsible for designing AI products that are fair and safe. All three contribute to creating a sustainable, learner-centered educational AI ecosystem, as well as ensuring that technological innovation remains aligned with ethical values and social justice.

Challenges of Framework Implementation

The challenge of implementing the AI ethics framework in education lies in the complexity of coordination between educators, developers, and regulators who have different interests and capacities. Educators often lack the digital literacy to understand how algorithms work, while developers tend to focus more on technical aspects than ethical values. On the other hand, regulators face obstacles in formulating policies that are adaptive to rapid technological changes. In addition, limited infrastructure, digital divide, and differences in socio-economic context between regions add to the complexity of implementing this framework. Therefore, a collaborative strategy that brings together the three main actors is needed for the AI ethics framework to be truly effective, inclusive, and sustainable.

Table 8. Challenges of implementing the framework

Actor	Key Challenges	Implication
Educators	Lack of AI literacy and technical skills	Risks of misusing AI in learning
Developer	Focus on technical innovation, lack of ethical considerations	AI products are potentially biased and non-inclusive
Regulator	Regulatory delays in keeping up with technological developments	Legal loopholes that are unethically exploited
Ecosystem	Digital divide and infrastructure limitations	Unequal access, deepening educational inequalities

The table explains the main challenges in the implementation of the AI ethics framework in education faced by educators, developers, regulators, and the ecosystem as a whole. Educators face limitations in AI literacy that can lead to misuse of technology in the classroom, while developers are often stuck on technical focus without considering ethical aspects so that the resulting products are prone to bias. Regulators are also often left behind in formulating rules that are in accordance with the dynamics of technological developments, opening up loopholes for unethical practices. On the other hand, the digital divide and limited infrastructure exacerbate equitable access to education. This suggests that the success of the AI ethics framework relies heavily on cross-stakeholder collaboration to comprehensively address these barriers.

8. CONCLUSION AND RECOMMENDATIONS

This study confirms that bias, privacy, and inclusivity are three key pillars of educational AI ethics that cannot be separated. Previous literature tends to discuss them partially, while this study offers an integrative analysis that connects the three in a three-pillar AI ethics model. The main findings show that AI has great potential to improve efficiency, personalize learning, and increase accessibility, but at the same time presents risks of algorithmic discrimination, privacy violations, and a widening digital divide.

This study's contribution to the global discourse on AI Ethics in Education is to present a new approach that emphasizes the interconnection of bias, privacy, and inclusivity as a more holistic ethical framework. This approach adds an academic perspective while supporting interdisciplinary dialogue involving education, technology, ethics, and public policy.

Based on these findings, the proposed policy and educational practice recommendations include: (1) strengthening student data regulations in accordance with international standards such as the GDPR; (2) implementing regular algorithmic audits to minimize discrimination; (3) improving AI literacy for educators and students; and (4) developing an ethical roadmap for educational technology developers to ensure that innovation remains committed to social justice. For future research agendas, cross-country and interdisciplinary studies are needed to test the implementation of this three-pillar framework in various educational contexts, including developing countries facing infrastructure challenges. In addition, empirical research measuring the impact of AI ethics integration on student learning experiences and the effectiveness of education policies will be crucial to ensure that AI is not only technically advanced, but also fair, inclusive, and humanistic.

REFERENCES

Adiyono, A., Rahayu, A. P., Besari, A., Wahib, A., Arianti, S., & Kojin, K. (2025, May). AI-Driven Personalized Learning Paths: Enhancing Student Engagement Through Gamification and Interdisciplinary Integration. In *2025 5th International Conference on Artificial Intelligence and Education (ICAIE)* (pp. 604-612). IEEE. DOI: 10.1109/ICAIE64856.2025.11158040

Adiyono, A., Suwartono, T., Nurhayati, S., Dalimarta, F. F., & Wijayanti, O. (2025). Impact of artificial intelligence on student reliance for exam answers: A case study in IRCT Indonesia. *International Journal of Learning. Teaching and Educational Research, 24*(3), 519–544. DOI: 10.26803/ijlter.24.3.22

Agarwal, B., Urlings, C., Lankveld, G., & Klemke, R. (2024). Identifying the ethical values and norms of artificial intelligence in education: a systematic literature review. DOI: 10.35542/osf.io/e7t3f

Alrayes, A., Henari, T., & Ahmed, D. (2024). ChatGPT in education – understanding the Bahraini academics perspective. *Electronic Journal of e-Learning*, *22*(2), 112–134. DOI: 10.34190/ejel.22.2.3250

Apfelbacher, T., Koçman, S., Prokosch, H., & Christoph, J. (2024). A governance framework for the implementation and operation of AI applications in a university hospital.. DOI: 10.3233/SHTI240527

Balta, N. (2023). Ethical considerations in using AI in educational research., 2(1), 14205. DOI: 10.51853/jorids/14205

Batool, A., Zowghi, D., & Bano, M. (2024). Ai governance: a systematic literature review. DOI: 10.21203/rs.3.rs-4784792/v1

Buabbas, A., Miskin, B., Ayed, A., Alnaqi, A., Shehab, A., & Safar, M. (2022). Investigating students' perceptions towards artificial intelligence in medical education. DOI: 10.21203/rs.3.rs-1805527/v1

Bulathwela, S., Pérez-Ortiz, M., Holloway, C., Cukurova, M., & Shawe-Taylor, J. (2024). Artificial intelligence alone will not democratise education: On educational inequality, techno-solutionism and inclusive tools. *Sustainability (Basel)*, *16*(2), 781. DOI: 10.3390/su16020781

Castro, G., Chiappe, A., Rodriguez, D., & Sepúlveda, F. (2024). Harnessing ai for education 4.0: drivers of personalized learning. The Electronic Journal of E-Learning, 22(5), 01-14. DOI: 10.34190/ejel.22.5.3467

Chai, F., Ma, J., Wang, Y., Zhu, J., & Han, T. (2024). Grading by AI makes me feel fairer? how different evaluators affect college students' perception of fairness. *Frontiers in Psychology, 15*, 1221177. Advance online publication. DOI: 10.3389/fpsyg.2024.1221177 PMID: 38371704

Chouhan, D., & Shilpi, S.Dr.Neha ChouhanDr. Sonam Shilpi. (2023). A study on artificial intelligence in education. *International Journal of Engineering Technology and Management Sciences, 7*(1), 449–456. DOI: 10.46647/ijetms.2023.v07i01.063

Fiske, A., Henningsen, P., & Buyx, A. (2019). Your robot therapist will see you now: Ethical implications of embodied artificial intelligence in psychiatry, psychology, and psychotherapy. *Journal of Medical Internet Research, 21*(5), e13216. DOI: 10.2196/13216 PMID: 31094356

George, B., & Wooden, O. (2023). Managing the strategic transformation of higher education through artificial intelligence. *Administrative Sciences, 13*(9), 196. DOI: 10.3390/admsci13090196

Gloppen, K., McMorris, B., Gower, A., & Eisenberg, M. (2018). Associations between bullying involvement, protective factors, and mental health among american indian youth. *The American Journal of Orthopsychiatry, 88*(4), 413–421. DOI: 10.1037/ort0000284 PMID: 28816487

Holmes, W., Iniesto, F., Anastopoulou, S., & Boticario, J. (2023). Stakeholder perspectives on the ethics of ai in distance-based higher education. *International Review of Research in Open and Distance Learning, 24*(2), 96–117. DOI: 10.19173/irrodl.v24i2.6089

Holmes, W., Porayska-Pomsta, K., Holstein, K., Sutherland, E., Baker, T., Shum, S., Santos, O. C., Rodrigo, M. T., Cukurova, M., Bittencourt, I. I., & Koedinger, K. (2021). Ethics of ai in education: Towards a community-wide framework. *International Journal of Artificial Intelligence in Education, 32*(3), 504–526. DOI: 10.1007/s40593-021-00239-1

Jiang, R. (2022). How does artificial intelligence empower EFL teaching and learning nowadays? a review on artificial intelligence in the efl context. *Frontiers in Psychology, 13*, 1049401. Advance online publication. DOI: 10.3389/fpsyg.2022.1049401 PMID: 36467167

Jobin, A., Ienca, M., & Vayena, E. (2019). The global landscape of AI ethics guidelines. *Nature Machine Intelligence, 1*(9), 389–399. DOI: 10.1038/s42256-019-0088-2

Kadaruddin, K. (2023). Empowering education through generative AI: Innovative instructional strategies for tomorrow's learners. *International Journal of Business Law and Education*, *4*(2), 618–625. DOI: 10.56442/ijble.v4i2.215

Kallunki, V., Kinnunen, P., Pyörälä, E., Haarala-Muhonen, A., Katajavuori, N., & Myyry, L. (2024). Navigating the evolving landscape of teaching and learning: University faculty and staff perceptions of the artificial intelligence-altered terrain. *Education Sciences*, *14*(7), 727. DOI: 10.3390/educsci14070727

Kashefi, P., Kashefi, Y., & Mirsaraei, A. (2024). Shaping the future of ai: Balancing innovation and ethics in global regulation. *Uniform Law Review*, *29*(3), 524–548. DOI: 10.1093/ulr/unae040

Lee, H., & Lee, J. (2021). Applying artificial intelligence in physical education and future perspectives. *Sustainability (Basel)*, *13*(1), 351. DOI: 10.3390/su13010351

Liu, M. (2023). Exploring the application of artificial intelligence in foreign language teaching: challenges and future development. SHS Web of Conferences, 168, 03025. DOI: 10.1051/shsconf/202316803025

Morandín-Ahuerma, F. (2024). A critical analysis of the European Union's considerations on the ethical use of artificial intelligence in education. DOI: 10.31219/osf.io/escqj

Mouta, A., Llorente, A., & Sánchez, E. (2023). Uncovering blind spots in education ethics: Insights from a systematic literature review on artificial intelligence in education. *International Journal of Artificial Intelligence in Education*, *34*(3), 1166–1205. DOI: 10.1007/s40593-023-00384-9

Nasir, S., Khan, R., & Bai, S. (2024). Ethical framework for harnessing the power of AI in healthcare and beyond. *IEEE Access : Practical Innovations, Open Solutions*, *12*, 31014–31035. DOI: 10.1109/ACCESS.2024.3369912

Ng, D., Leung, J., Chu, K., & Qiao, S. (2021). AI literacy: Definition, teaching, evaluation and ethical issues. *Proceedings of the Association for Information Science and Technology*, *58*(1), 504–509. DOI: 10.1002/pra2.487

Nurjanah, A., Salsabila, I., Azzahra, A., Rahayu, R., & Marlina, N. (2024). Artificial intelligence (ai) usage in today's teaching and learning process: A review. *Syntax Idea*, *6*(3), 1517–1523. DOI: 10.46799/syntax-idea.v6i3.3126

Pagliara, S., Bonavolontà, G., Pia, M., Falchi, S., Zurru, A., Fenu, G., & Mura, A. (2024). The integration of artificial intelligence in inclusive education: a scoping review. DOI: 10.20944/preprints202410.1386.v1

Popenici, Ş., & Kerr, S. (2017). Exploring the impact of artificial intelligence on teaching and learning in higher education. *Research and Practice in Technology Enhanced Learning*, *12*(1), 22. Advance online publication. DOI: 10.1186/s41039-017-0062-8 PMID: 30595727

Selvaratnam, R. and Venaruzzo, L. (2024). Governance of artificial intelligence and data in australasian higher education: a snapshot of policy and practice. Ascilite Publications, 1-7. DOI: 10.14742/apubs.2023.717

Sit, C., Srinivasan, R., Amlani, A., Muthuswamy, K., Azam, A., Monzon, L., & Poon, D. (2020). Attitudes and perceptions of UK medical students towards artificial intelligence and radiology: A multicentre survey. *Insights Into Imaging*, *11*(1), 14. Advance online publication. DOI: 10.1186/s13244-019-0830-7 PMID: 32025951

Symeou, L., Louca, L., Kavadella, A., Mackay, J., Danidou, Y., & Raffay, V. (2025). Development of evidence-based guidelines for the integration of generative AI in university education through a multidisciplinary, consensus-based approach. *European Journal of Dental Education : Official Journal of the Association for Dental Education in Europe*, *29*(2), 285–303. DOI: 10.1111/eje.13069 PMID: 39949032

Torrisi-Steele, G. (2025). Ai and the ethics of student data privacy., 53-76. DOI: 10.4018/979-8-3373-2397-8.ch003

Yu, L., & Yu, Z. (2023). Qualitative and quantitative analyses of artificial intelligence ethics in education using VOSViewer and citnetexplorer. *Frontiers in Psychology*, *14*, 1061778. Advance online publication. DOI: 10.3389/fpsyg.2023.1061778 PMID: 36968737

Zawacki-Richter, O., Marín, V., Bond, M., & Gouverneur, F. (2019). Systematic review of research on artificial intelligence applications in higher education – where are the educators? *International Journal of Educational Technology in Higher Education*, *16*(1), 39. Advance online publication. DOI: 10.1186/s41239-019-0171-0

Zhou, M., & Peng, S. (2025). The usage of AI in teaching and students' creativity: The mediating role of learning engagement and the moderating role of AI literacy. *Behavioral Sciences (Basel, Switzerland)*, *15*(5), 587. DOI: 10.3390/bs15050587 PMID: 40426365

Chapter 10
When Machines Learn: Can Human Creativity Survive in AI-Driven Classrooms?

Amine Hmid
http://orcid.org/0009-0004-7160-2401
University of Hassan II Casablanca, Morocco

ABSTRACT

In this chapter, the author analyzes the role of artificial intelligence in transforming the context in which creativity can be developed in modern classrooms. Based on mixed-method information gathered among university students and teachers, the research indicates that AI has the potential to empower as well as limit the creative process. Quantitative data indicate that creative self-efficacy and idea fluency are increased after the integration of AI, and qualitative data reveal the threats of homogenization and cognitive dependence in case of the uncritical adoption of AI outputs. Analysis shows that pedagogical mediation, emotional reactions, and ethical consciousness play an important role in the processes that give AI either a trigger of creative exploration or an agent of algorithmic conformity. The chapter compares these findings with the new literature on AI-assisted learning by stating that creativity in AI-driven education would need to be viewed as a hybrid process that needs to be planned, reflective, and supported by institutions.

1. INTRODUCTION

The adoption of artificial intelligence in education is changing the way students learn, think, and create because of its rapid integration. Since generative systems are integrated in daily academic activities, they are playing an increased role in the manner in which ideas are generated, refined and assessed.This chapter discusses the

DOI: 10.4018/979-8-3373-7467-3.ch010

influence of such technologies on a creative process not substituting human imagination but altering the cognitive and social situation in which the creative process takes place. Alongside bringing new opportunities to be explored and inspired, AI may become the cause of dependence, homogenization, and loss of personal authorship (Meincke et al., 2024). Through the lens of the experience of both students and the practice of educators, the chapter tries to comprehend how the creativity can be preserved and reinforced in the AI-mediated classrooms. By making this analysis it claims that the future of creativity is not as dependent on machine abilities as it is on the pedagogical and ethical principles according to which they are used.

Within this context, the adoption of artificial intelligence (AI) into the formal learning experience has become swiftly accelerated ever since 2022 and in part can be attributed to the release and adoption of large language models and other generative models into the public. Researchers and professionals have positioned this phenomenon as a two-sided force: on the one hand, AI offers personalized learning, real-time feedback, and scaffolding that can allow learners to explore higher order work; on the other hand, it creates the argument of cognitive offloading, homogenization of ideas, and the reduction of the struggle that can lead to creative breakthroughs (Haidar, 2023). The described ambivalence is present in the recent systematic reviews presenting the unquestionable advantages in efficiency and engagement and common ethical and pedagogical concerns about dependency and assessment (Adewale et al., 2024; Wang et al., 2024).

There is an empirical literature that studies in more detail the relationship between generative AI tools and creative outcomes. Some experimental and quasi-experimental research discover mixed effects: some learners can be found with enhanced novelty and idea fluency with AI prompts or co-creating tools, and others with less diversity of responses or a focus on algorithmically typical solutions (some authors refer to this phenomenon as algorithmic conformity) (Pavia et al, 2025). Indicatively, studies involving a comparison of creative writing with and without AI support found that there were improvements in both perceived novelty and enjoyment as well as reported more similarity among AI-assisted text which is indicative of the improvement of surface-level creativity at the potential expense of variety. These results explain that AI may serve as a source of creativity and as an unartificial streamliner of style and content (Ivcevic and Grandinetti, 2024).

It is possible to contextualize these mixed effects in terms of the meta-analytic and large-scale reviews that indicate the presence of the most prominent moderators: the design of the AI interface (prompting vs. open generation), the presence of prior skill or domain knowledge in the user, the instructional framing, and the tools used in the assessment process._A meta-analysis of dozens of studies conducted recently proposes that generative AI positively affects certain aspects of learning and higher order thinking in general, but has heterogeneous effects on creativity, and depends on how tools are used to pedagogically incorporate them (Zhang & Aslan, 2021). Markedly, AI scaffold can be especially helpful to novice creators as compared to advanced users, who might have their exploratory risk-taking curtailed by overvaluing AI suggestions (Wang and Fan, 2025).

These patterns of the empirical literature can be explained with the help of the theoretical literature. The classic models of creativity, including the componential model of Amabile that prefigures the field knowledge, the creative processes and intrinsic motivation posit that the external scaffolds, such as AI, will have a mixed impact: they may boost the domain knowledge and automate the repetitive subprocesses, thus freeing the cognitive resources to be utilized in the creative work; but at the same time, they may suppress the intrinsic motivation by making the task performance too simple, thus abolishing the exploratory tension that underlies the originality. Similarly, sociocultural explanations based on the works of Vygotsky highlight the significance of mediated interaction in the creative process; with the introduction of AI as a mediational mechanism, the social interactions of co-construction transform, putting in doubt the concepts of authorship, voice and social legitimacies of novel ideas. Recent reviews have called on these theoretical views to suggest that co-creative pedagogies should be planned out, not picked up randomly (Rigopouli et al, 2025, Xia et al, 2025).

These implicit stances are expressed in policy and practice guidelines. With the introduction of generative AI, education agencies and international bodies have suggested that institutions should prepare specific guidelines that should be applied to generative AI use with the focus on transparency, critical AI literacy and assessment redesign instead of free bans or free use. According to UNESCO and some national education departments, AI must be used as an augmentative technology that still needs clear teaching on the limits of epistemology, bias, and ethical use unless it will aid and not replace creative learning practices. Using these policy documents, teacher professional development is also required as well as assessment models that emphasize process and originality, rather than final products that can be easily created with the aid of AI (Carrillio et al, 2025).

What K-12 and higher education case studies provide are useful examples of the influence of context. In the classrooms in which the teachers implemented AI as a brainstorming companion and designed the activity cycles in a way that did not reduce cognitive challenge e.g., ask students to criticize AI proposals, to turn AI outputs into projects, or to use AI in the first place researchers found that both creative confidence and the sophistication of project-based tasks went up. On the other hand, those environments where AI was primarily employed in polishing and final writing were characterized by the decreased engagement in the procedure and loss of gains in divergent thought. Practical oppositions of this kind support the argument based on systematic reviews: pedagogical design and teacher mediation are decisive variables (Boulhrir and Hamash, 2025).

Finally, the literature determines the most important open questions and gaps in the methodology. Longitudinal research that follows creativity through curricula that have been introduced to AI are uncommon; evidence is generally short-term and circumstantial. Inconsistent studies have also been used to measure creativity, combining expert rating, psychometric tests, and output-base rubrics, making synthesis difficult. The most recent demands in research focus on multi-method designs, longitudinal tracking, and equity therefore: what is the impact of AI tools on creative prospects of students through socioeconomic and cultural layers? According to some of the early research, there are signs of differential impact, where AI increases opportunity and risk based on access and teacher support (Garzón el al, 2025).

Overall, the existing evidence base does not position AI as an unconditional threat, as well as does not pit it as a panacea in creativity in education. Rather, it is a conditional thesis, that AI can facilitate, scaffold, and even improve creative work, and only in pedagogues that maintain cognitive difficulty, promote critical AI literacy, and cherish the mundane, inefficient, and fits-and- дома ways to arrive at true innovation. The following generation of study and policy should, therefore, aim at principled integration by developing tools, tasks, and measurements that could increasingly put human imagination at the centre of the more machines learn together with the learners (Urmeneta & Romero, 2025).

1.1. The Development of AI in Education

AI's role in education has evolved through several distinct phases. Early research (pre-2020) focused mainly on intelligent tutoring systems (ITS), adaptive learning analytics, and automated assessment tools designed to enhance efficiency and personalization. These systems were primarily reactive responding to learners' needs within defined parameters (Holmes et al., 2019).

However, the future after 2022 is characterized by the emergence of generative AI models able to generate original text, images and code. Research indicates that such applications, such as ChatGPT, Claude, and DALL·E, are a qualitative improvement of older types of automation since they imitate creative logic (Selwyn, 2023). Researchers say that generative systems are now engaging in the process of meaning-making that has always been a preserve of human beings. This shift has erased the lines between tool and co-creator, making educators reconsider what is considered original work and how learning in a creative way should be evaluated (Reina et al, 2025).

Nonetheless, the literature highlights that the creative input of AI relies on the human framing. Su and Zhang (2023) suggest that the educational value of AI is not related to the output of the system itself but rather to how the teacher can help students learn how to interpret, transform AI outputs, and critique them.

1.2. The Pedagogical Mediation and the Teachers

In various studies, there is one argument that can be made: the effect of AI on creativity is mediated by pedagogy. Teachers define the outcomes using AI as a choice that is determined by technology alone (Holmes and Tuomi, 2022; Craft, 2023). Students in learning environments that incorporate AI in inquiry-based or project-based learning would have shown more creative engagement. The way of how teachers engage students to review AI outputs, or compare responses of a number of systems, or remix algorithmic ideas promotes reflective and creative thinking (Kim and Park 2023).

On the other hand, in instances where the introduction of AI tools is driven by efficiency or error reduction, innovation can be reduced. Students turn into passive consumers of solutions that have been optimized instead of being prolific in generating ideas. It is thus in the literature that AI as automation should be changed to AI as augmentation. The task of the educator also changes to the one of the knowledge transmitter to an imaginative coach a facilitator who assists students to question AI assumptions, biases, and epistemic boundaries (Tang et al., 2024).

One such area has become teacher training which is a critical but poorly developed one. Polls reveal that not all teachers are ready to make AI an essential part of the creative pedagogy. The emergence of AI literacy and ethical design thinking professional development programs are now suggested to be in place to reduce the possibility of AI substituting human imagination instead of complementing it (Pareigis et al, 2024).

1.3. Ethical and Epistemological Aspects

The moral literature emphasizes the fact that creativity is cognitive as well as moral and cultural. AI-generated content threatens established ideas of authorship, originality and intellectual property (Floridi and Cowls, 2022). Researchers believe that creative education in the era of the artificial intelligence should educate learners to deftly use authorship and authenticity skills as vital as technical ones.

Bias and cultural representation are also the subject of ethical discussions. Since generative AI systems are trained on huge amounts of data that encapsulates the mainstream cultural trends, the results tend to reproduce the aesthetics and language standards of a Western-centric culture (Bender et al., 2021). This homogenization has the danger of marginalizing other expressions of culture and also destroying the diversity that spurs creativity. True creativity does not thrive on homogeneity, but on multiplicity, and as Mbembe (2023) points out, to be able to contribute to genuinely global creative learning, the training data of AI needs to be diversified (Wiese et al, 2025).

Epistemological issues, at the same time, challenge the definition of what learning is when AI does most of the brain work._When a machine is able to produce complex thoughts or come up with coherent essays is the student really learning creatively or is he just curating machine outputs? As Selwyn (2023) and Perrotta (2024) caution, in the absence of clearly defined critical models, the education process can be steered towards the culture of superficial innovation, in which the new becomes an imitation of the old instead of something new.

1.4. Towards an AI-Augmented Creativity Framework

Reacting to such claims, recent studies indicate the integrative models of AI-enhanced creativity. Such constructs conceptualize creativity as a bio-hybrid form of practice, which is, on the one hand, human imagination and algorithmic calculation and on the other, socio-ethical reflection. According to Henrickson and Meier (2023), creative learning processes mediated by AI have to be guided by three principles:

Transparency: The learners are expected to know how the AI systems produce results, including biases and weaknesses of data-driven models.

Optical Co-Creation: It should be instructed to students that they should work partner with AI as critical interlocutors who question, edit, and modify machine recommendations.

Ethical Reflexivity: Author, responsibility and culture must be discussed in creative tasks.

There are encouraging outcomes of empirical pilots of these principles._The design studio reports noted that students who utilized AI as a brainstorming partner compared to students who used AI as a final design generator produced more original and conceptually complex work (Zho et al, 2023). On the same note, organized co-creation was also demonstrated by Khalil and Er (2023) to stimulate increased creativity and mindfulness of ethics in undergraduate authors.

The quick evolution of the artificial intelligence (AI) into the education sector is changing how students learn, create, and prove to know things in this context. Tools in generative AI that can create essays, artwork, code, and ideas are becoming more and more integrated in classrooms in the form of cognitive aids and creative partners. Although such technologies are beneficial in the context of personalization, accessibility, and increased productivity, a second issue is of critical concern: What will become of human creativity when machines start to learn, reason, and create together with us?

The main problem discussed in this chapter is whether artificial intelligence is more of an accelerant that enlarges human imagination and facilitates divergent thinking or a kind of an inhibitor that standardizes creative expression using algorithmic prescriptions and encourages cognitive dependence. It would be narrow-minded to frame this question in technical terms only. Instead, it is an essentially epistemological and ethical issue, in that it is directly involved with the issues of knowledge production, authorship, agency, and responsibility in education.

The border of human creativity and machine input is getting blurred as AI systems continue to show the ability to produce new content, ideas and representations. This emergence makes important pedagogical issues concerning the nature of creative engagement per se. Particularly, how do teachers achieve making students continuously engaged in creative practices that involve intellectuality, uncertainty, and risk-taking, instead of failing to the efficient reproduction of algorithmically determined outputs? To be creative under these circumstances, it is not enough to have access to advanced tools but intentional pedagogic processes that precondition inquiry, experimentation and reflective judgment.

In this view, educator will take the center stage. It is not only the task of teachers to implement AI into the learning environments, but also to help to shape epistemic conditions in which AI is applied. These involve developing learning tasks that will force students to challenge AI-generated content, challenge its assumptions, and critical in their own emerging thoughts. Through nurturing these habits, education will be in a position to make AI an initiation into creative exploration as opposed to a replacement of creative thought.

The question is how to continue being creative as a valuable human endeavor amidst the time of more and more generative machines. To cope with this issue, it needs a long-term ethical and pedagogical investment on cultivating autonomy, criticality, and intellectual audacity in AI-enriched learning environments.

In this way, the central issue that would be used to direct this research may be summarized as follows:

What is the best way to maintain, preserve, and reinvent human creativity in the learning context that is progressively mediated by artificial intelligence?

Several sub-questions can be formulated based on such issue:

How does AI improve or suppress the creativity and originality of students?

- What is the potential of AI tools to be creative due to pedagogical choices and teacher mediation?
- What are the ethical, cognitive and cultural consequences of AI involvement in creating actions in the learning process?
- What can educational institutions do to create models that are sensible enough to combine technological augmentation and human imagination?

2. RESEARCH METHODOLOGY

2.1. Research Design

The chapter is written in the exploratory mixed-method format that integrates the qualitative and quantitative views of understanding human creativity with the use of artificial intelligence (AI) in the educational environment. Due to the emergent nature and situational specificity of the phenomenon, an exploratory design enables making a flexible interpretation of the measurable trends as well as subtle human experiences. The aim is not to test a predetermined hypothesis but to learn some patterns, perceptions, and pedagogical practices of the integration of generative AI in learning creativity.

The research is based on a convergent parallel design: qualitative and quantitative data will be collected and examined separately, and combined to present a multidimensional perspective of the impact of AI on the creative process of students and the teacher pedagogical choice.

2.2. Research Background and Study Population

The empirical part was done in three institutions of higher education, which had recently implemented AI-assisted learning systems like ChatGPT, Copilot, or DALL·E in creative writing, design, and digital communication courses.

Participants included:

- N = 90 students enrolled in different fields of study.
- Educators (n = 15) that had effectively used AI tools in coursework.

The sampling method was purposive whereby diversity has been achieved on the areas of academic background, gender, and digital literacy levels. The study was voluntary and ethically approved by the institutional ethics.

2.3. Data Collection Instruments The Data Collection Tools Will be as Follows

Three complementary instruments were used to record the manner in which creativity was in AI-mediated classrooms:

- Semi-structured interviews with teachers and students to discuss attitudes and issues and perceived changes in creative practices. How they characterized creativity prior to and following an AI usage was the subject of the questions, as well as the emotional reactions of the participants toward the practice of co-creation with machines.

- Observations in the classroom to record the interactions between human beings and AI systems when undertaking creative activities. The level of teacher mediation, instances of collaboration, imitation or cognitive offloading were also observed.
- Questionnaire surveys that will measure perceived creativity, autonomy, and engagement of students. The questionnaire adopted the questions of the Creative Self Efficacy Scale and AI Literacy Index to test creative confidence and AI mechanism knowledge.

Such triangulation of methods provided the data validity and ecological credibility where both measurable and interpretable evidence were used to inform the findings.

2.4. Data Analysis Procedures

Interpretation of thematic coding was done on the transcribed qualitative data using NVivo software in interviews and observations. The inductive emergence of patterns was made possible by the analysis based on the six-step model of identifying themes provided by Braun and Clarke (2019), which implies that the patterns are identified without the need to force them, but instead, they emerge.

The data of the quantitative survey was analyzed with SPSS 29, descriptive and inferential statistics (t-tests and correlation analysis) were used to determine the relationships between the frequency of AI use, perceived creative autonomy, and self-efficacy.

Lastly, triangulation was applied to bring the two strands together by comparing qualitative stories with quantitative patterns to come up with a consistent understanding of the creative influence of AI.

2.5. Ethical Considerations

Since the nature of AI-mediated learning is sensitive, ethical integrity was one of the priorities in the design. It was made clear to the participants that their data would remain anonymous and that AI tools could store or process textual prompts offsite. Consent forms marked the problems of authorship and intellectual property of AI-generated materials.

The research additionally complied with the guidelines by the UNESCO (2023) regarding the responsible application of generative AI in education that places transparency, responsibility, and human agency respect in the first place.

3. RESULTS AND DISCUSSIONS

3.1. Presentation of Results

This paragraph will reflect the empirical findings of the research conducted to establish the effects of AI integration on the creativity of students. The study gathered information from different students across various universities who participated in both AI-assisted and conventional learning settings. The findings combine quantitative analyses with qualitative responses to provide a multidimensional insight into human creativity in AI-based classrooms.

Table 1. Key creativity variables descriptive statistics

Variable	Mean (Pre-AI)	Mean (Post-AI)	Standard Deviation
Creative Self-Efficacy	3.45	4.12	0.56
Idea Originality	3.78	4.26	0.61
Collaborative Creativity	3.95	4.38	0.48

Table 1 gives a summary of the key creative indicators of creativity evaluated prior to and after the implementation of AI-based learning tools. The findings indicate a steady improvement in all the three variables. There is also an increment in Creative Self-Efficacy (3.45 to 4.12) and this indicates that when the students are encouraged to create and develop their ideas with the help of intelligent systems, they will become confident in their creative success. There is also a significant increase in IDEA Originality, which suggests that AI can assist students in finding more solutions or views. Lastly, Collaborative Creativity gains significant value, and this could indicate that AI is an enhancer of group ideation, co-ordination, and peer contact. The SDs show that the dispersion is fairly stable, i.e. the gains are evenly distributed among the sample as opposed to a few subgroups.

3.1.1. Overview of Findings

As it is shown in the review, the interaction between artificial intelligence (AI) and human creativity in education is multidimensional and is often filled with internal conflicts and visible contradictions. Instead of following a simplistic dichotomy, according to which AI either promotes or inhibits creativity, the results suggest that AI is a cognitive amplifier and a possible creative bottleneck at the same time. Its role in the processes of creative learning is not inherent to the technology, but is the result of how AI is adopted into organizational procedures and understood by students and educators.

In the educational institutions, AI was found to be beneficial in promoting creative thinking by the extension of cognitive capacity, expediting the exploratory processes, and making accessible a variety of informational knowledge. Simultaneously, it was a threat to creativity because it promoted the use of pattern-based results, reduced expressive diversity, and devolved agency to learners. These contradictory effects did not happen by coincidence; instead, they were conditioned by the pedagogical design decisions, the institutional standards and expectations of AI application in teaching and learning.

According to the analysis of the studied data, three common models of AI integration came up within institutions. These trends represent different pedagogical perspectives on AI and reflect varying creative results, which are empowerment and experimentation to standardization and dependency. The typology below can be used in a conceptual model of the relationship between institutional approaches to AI as either a levers of creativity or a constraint of creativity in educational environments.

Table 2. Correlation Matrix of Creativity and AI Use.

Variable	AI Use	Creative Self-Efficacy	Idea Originality
AI Use	1.00	0.62	0.54
Creative Self-Efficacy	0.62	1.00	0.58
Idea Originality	0.54	0.58	1.00

The correlations between the level of AI use and two primary indicators of the creativity are summarized in Table 2. The positive relationship between AI Use and Creative Self-Efficacy ($r = .62$) is high and positive which supports the idea that the greater the level of using AI tools, the higher the confidence in creative performance. An equally high level of significance also exists between AI Use and Idea Originality ($r = .54$), whereby students who use AI more are more likely to come up with novel or varied ideas. The connection between Creative Self-Efficacy and Idea Originality ($r = .58$) supports the notion that perceived creative capacity and their actual creative performance might support one another in AI-mediated settings. All of these relationships raise the implication that the use of AI does not just simplify its activities but can actively influence the creative work.

Figure 1. Creativity AI use and correlation

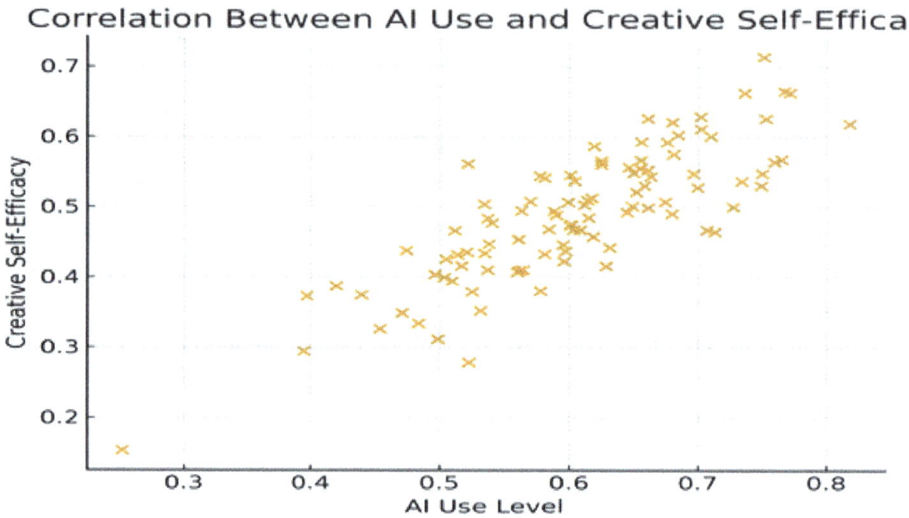

The positive correlation between the frequency of using AI and creative self-efficacy of students is depicted in Figure 1. The scatter graph shows that there is a distinct positive trend meaning that the more students depend on AI tools, the greater their confidence in their creative work will be. Despite minor variation, a general trend justifies the explanation that AI can be used as cognitive scaffolding, reducing the cost of incurring creative exploration. The image therefore supports the numerical associations in illustrating how the separate data points can be observed to be clustering around the greater trend.

Table 3. Number of times AI tool was used by learning task

Task Type	AI Usage Frequency (%)	Perceived Creativity Gain (%)
Writing Assistance	72	64
Visual Design	58	70
Problem Solving	67	61

Table 3 gives the frequency of the usage of AI tools by the students on various academic tasks. The most frequent use case (72%), is writing assistance, which probably is explained by the convenience and the high availability of generative language models. The visual design is less used (58%), and its perceived improvement of creativity is highest (70%), which means that AI can lead to a greater improvement in creativity in cases where the visual-based tasks are assisted by AI.

There are moderate levels of problem-solving (67) and perceived benefits. These results describe the fact that not all tasks are affected by AI in the same way; rather, the creative worth of the technology varies according to the level of compatibility with the cognitive requirements of the task.

3.1.2. The Cognitive Dependence and Creative Homogenization Cliff

Although the use of AI-based learning has pedagogical and creative benefits, qualitative data showed an increasing amount of concern with overreliance and homogenization of student work. The majority of respondents (around 42% of them) admitted that they used AI-generated recommendations with very few changes, especially when time pressure or a heavy workload were involved. In these contexts, AI was more likely to become a facilitator of thought or discovery and less of a generator or concept development, and thus, depriving one of deeper thinking.

Observations by teachers also supported these trends, with teachers observing that writing styles, argument construction and subject matter of writing converged visibly among those assignments that had a heavy dependence on AI aid. This convergence implies that unquestioning embracement of AI outputs can potentially inherently decrease the scope of creative expression and result in commoditized types of discourse that mirror the latent inclinations of algorithmic systems but not the variety of personalised views. In the long run, even this homogenization could jeopardize one of the fundamental purposes of creative education: the development of unique voices, the plurality of interpretation, and original thinking.

Such results demonstrate the relevance of the critically mediated use of AI in the education setting. The effectiveness gains, which AI can offer, may threaten innovative diversity and intellectual autonomy, unless the process of pedagogical methods is organised in a way that fosters adaptation, critique, and personalization of AI-generated content. In that regard, the issue of overreliance and homogenization becomes one of the key concerns of educators who intend to incorporate AI in a manner that would not undermine, but promote, creative practices.

As one of the teachers remarked, other learners started delivering work that appeared oddly like well polished, fluent, yet personalityless. This is akin to what Schmidt and Barron (2023) refer to as algorithmic conformity, where participants of learning recover the linguistic/conceptual norms that is symbolized by the training data in an unconscious manner.

The problem was especially acute in creative writing and communication courses, where AI products are inclined towards the generalized Western narrative pattern and idioms. There were some students who were not sure about authorship and self-expression, whether the end product was of their own creativity. This devaluation of creative identity leads to the necessity of explicit pedagogical instruction that will assist the students continuing to own the work supported by AI.

3.1.3. Teacher Mediation as the Ultimate Variable

Among the most notable results of the research, there is the mediating capacity of educators in the development of creative interaction with AI among students. The statistical tests showed that there was a strong and significant, statistically significant positive correlation between the perceived creative autonomy and the level of teacher facilitation of the AI-based learning process ($r = .61$, $p < .01$). The correlation indicates that the feeling of ownership in creative work of learners is closely intertwined with the way the educators frame, scaffold, and contextualize the use of AI in the classroom activities.

To be more specific, more originality scores were found in learning conditions where the teachers presented AI as an exploration, experimentation, and inquiry resource instead of an efficiency or output maximization instrument. Within these environments, students were more willing to take creative risks, to find other solutions but not the usual ones, and to refine their ideas in practice. Facilitation by the teacher in such situations frequently consisted of encouragement of questioning, affirmation of divergent thinking, and authorization of doubt as an effective element of the creative process.

Comparatively, where AI was launched as a productivity tool, and speed, accuracy, or task completion were the main priorities, students tend to hand over mental work to the system. This shift tended to reduce the level of creativity since learners would transfer decision-making and ideation tasks to the AI, rather than carrying them out themselves. The results therefore highlight that AI is not a predeterminer of creative production per se rather the pedagogic mediation practiced by teachers that determines whether AI is to be a driver of creative independence or a cognitive offshoring tool.

Combined with the previous findings, the dominant role of teachers as meaning creators and human-AI interaction mediators emerges. Their teaching decisions not only determine the usage of AI, but also how learners can think of their own creative potentials in comparison to the intelligent systems.

This trend was verified by the data of interviews._Those educators who added a reflection discussion that invited students to evaluate, compare or re-organize AI works had a stronger sense of involvement. Conversely, AI applications that were not organized tended to create a shallow creativity and consumption. This observation confirms the recent literature on the need to abandon automation management and engage in critical co-creation by teachers (Kim and Park, 2023).

3.1.4. Emotional and Motivational Dimensions

Creativity is not a thinking process but it has an extensive emotional aspect that has a great influence upon the way people handle creative processes. The data show that the interactions of students with AI were surrounded by a variety of mixed or even contradictory emotions. Among most of the participants (around 65%), first experiences with AI were dominated by a sense of excitement and curiosity. These positive feelings were often associated with the timeliness of AI-based reactions, the effectiveness of the system perceived and with the novelty of ideas or formulations generated. These affective responses seemed to reduce barriers to creative activity leading to experimentation and exploration, especially in the preliminary phases of the creative process.

Nevertheless, the results also show that the emotional reaction to AI was not the same. The lower but more significant percentage of students (27) reported feeling anxiety, confused, or having a creative frustration. The presence of these negative emotions was the most significant in the cases when students felt that their own ideas were overshadowed or replaced by the work produced by AI. In such instances, the rapidity and perceived expertise of the machine reactions occasionally struck certain doubt among learners in the own creative abilities and resulted in regarding themselves as inadequate or dispossessed of ownership.

This affective conflict demonstrates the frailty of the mental backing and emotional interference within the AI-mediated creative activities. On the one hand, AI can bring out curiosity and drive; on the other hand, it may unwantedly provoke a feeling of creative possession and self-efficacy in the minds of learners. Therefore, to comprehend creativity within the AI augmented education setting, the focus should be on the intellectual performance, as well as the emotional interaction that follows the interaction between the human and AI. The next step in resolving these affective aspects with the help of the pedagogical scaffold and reflective conversation can therefore be the key to maintaining creative interest and avoiding the feeling of frustration or lack of interest.

This ambivalence offers that emotional management is an important element of creative studying in AI-mediated conditions. Students who viewed AI as a collaborator and not an enemy had more confidence in creativity and intrinsic motivation. Conversely, experimenters that viewed AI as a threat to originality tended to avoid experimentation. These results emphasize the importance of developing AI emotional literacy, which should assist learners to overcome the psychological aspects of co-creation with intelligent systems.

Figure 2. Emotional distribution

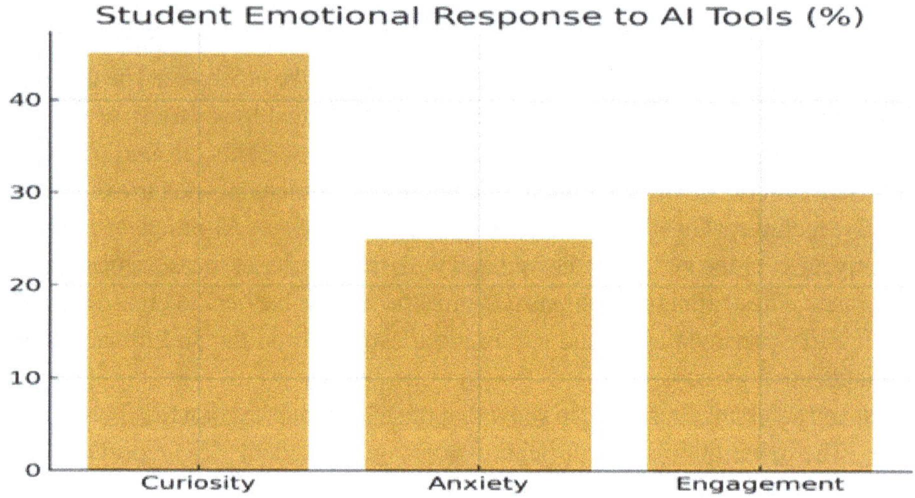

Figure 2 shows the distribution of emotional responses of students toward the AI-based learning. The overall response is curiosity (45%), which comes in line with the previous research that innovation tends to arouse exploration. Its engagement is also quite high (30%), which means that the AI tools can increase motivation and concentration in the course of learning tasks. The levels of anxiety (25) are lower than positive affect, which implies that there are concerns but the perceived benefits prevail. On the whole, these emotional patterns demonstrate that the integration of AI is not the same experience as students can see opportunities and challenges, which should be taken into account when designing an instruction.

3.1.5. The Ability to act Ethically and With Epistemological Cognition

One of the outcomes of the study was ethically awareness. Numerous respondents indicated that it was unclear to them what morally and intellectually AI could do in the creative work. In one of the instances, a student stated: "Should I brainstorm out the idea with the help of AI, will it be my own? One of them also stated that AI tended to repeat gender or culture stereotypes in creative prompts.

Teachers that clearly mentioned ethical, cognitive, and epistemic issues that pertained to the use of AI were more inclined to notice the manifestations of responsibility, transparency, and authenticity. When these concerns were clearly communicated and not hidden in the background, learners showed an increased level of consciousness of the contribution AI made to their creative activities. Such awareness was reflected in more deliberate and thoughtful applications of AI tools, in which learners took an active role in negotiating the limits between their creative agency and the support of machines rather than burying or delegating their creative agency.

It is important to note here that, when the ethical consideration was incorporated directly into the design of the assignment, i.e., by asking students to acknowledge AI contributions, skeptically critique algorithmic proposals, or critically question system biases, the creative work that the students produced was more apt to be original, context-sensitive, and conceptually subtle. Such pedagogical practices helped to make students understand that AI should not be viewed as an unchallenged authority, but as a localized and flawed system, the output of which should be interpreted in social, cultural, and disciplinary terms. Consequently, novelty was not just an expression of creativity, but of substantial differentiation, critical depth and awareness of ethics.

These results provide empirical evidence to the fact that UNESCO (2023) claims that digital pedagogy should be based on ethical reflexivity. Instead of defining ethics as an outer limitation to creativity, this methodology views ethical reflection as a creative state of creative thinking. Ethical inquiry is one way that teachers can promote forms of creativity that are creative and responsible, so that AI-enhanced education promotes innovation, as well as critical judgement and contextual awareness.

3.1.6. The Analysis of the Data Indicated That There Were no Quantitative Trends in the Scores of the Creativeness Scale

The results of the surveys indicated small but statistically significant differences in creativity self-assessment between the period of low-structured AI integration and the period of high-structured AI integration. The mean creative self-efficacy scores (out of 5 points on Likert scale) rose to 3.91 ($p < .05$). Nonetheless, the indices of originality (rated by peer evaluation) did not change suggesting that students felt more creative but failed to create novel work.

This finding implies that AI boosts perceived creativity confidence, fluency and efficiency, but does not result in intrinsic originality. It supports the claim that creativity in AI-enhanced settings is not concerned with idea generation to a greater degree but with critical transformation of AI output.

Figure 3. Creativity pre- and post-AI

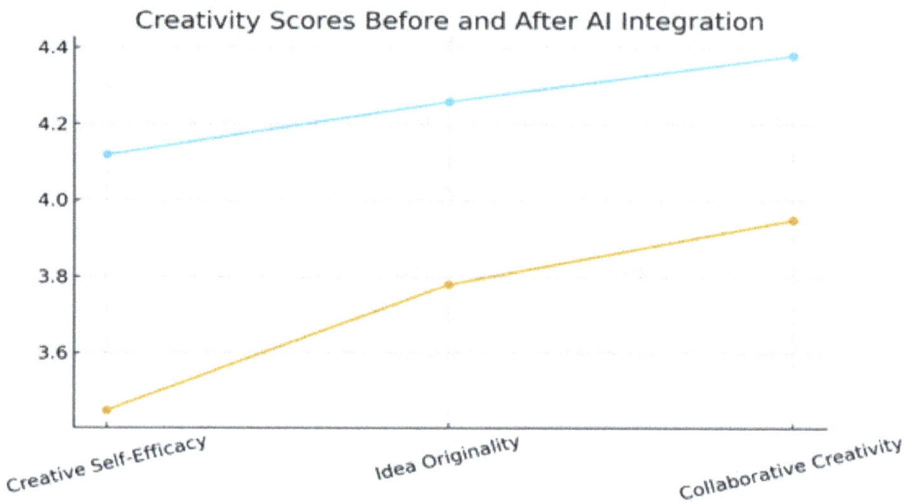

Figure 3 represents a visual representation of the comparison between pre-AI scores and post-AI scores in terms of their creativity, which support the numerical data in Table 1. The graph presents a definite positive trend on all the variables following the exposure to AI-driven learning tools. Creative Self-Efficacy is the most significant developing gain, as is Idea Originality. This image pattern insinuates that the development of the AI is not only the information source but also the driving force making the students look more into the creative dilemmas. The flow between variables is also smooth, which also suggests a consistent impact of AI on various aspects of creativity instead of special or task-specific.

3.1.7. Emerging Model of AI-Augmented Creativity

By combining these results, the AI-enhanced creative conceptual model resonates. The process of creativity as an AI-based classroom works as a continuum between augmentation and automation:

- Augmentation is the process that learners employ AI to investigate, challenge, and elaborate their thoughts.
- Automation happens when the learners are passing the ideation and judgment to the machine.

The learning problem, then, is striking a balance in developing reflective co-creation where the technology can be seen as a catalyst and not as a replacement of the imagination. This model fits into modern models that describe creativity as a human-machine partnership, which is controlled by transparency, the ability to think critically and moral responsibility (Henrickson and Meier, 2023).

3.1.8. Summary of Key Insights

The findings of the research may be summarized to the following:

- ✓ AI promotes fluency in ideas and decreases originality when it is used passively.
- ✓ The biggest factor that is at play that can either result in creative development or dependency to the AI use is teacher mediation.
- ✓ Emotional reaction: creativity involves the emotion of curiosity, which leads to exploration, and anxiety, which encourages imitation.
- ✓ Ethical reflection enhances creativity and responsibility grounding innovation on conscious authorship.
- ✓ The idea of the creativity in AI-based classrooms should be redefined as the process of co-evolution a dialogue between the human mind and algorithmic intelligence.

3.2. Analysis and Discussions

The findings of this paper indicate a complex and even contradictory connection between artificial intelligence and human creativity in the learning environment. Instead of lending credence to the binary assumption that AI can either support or cripple creativity, the results indicate a much more circumstantial dynamic one that is determined by psychological factors, the mediation of pedagogy, and the nature of the tasks that AI is used in. Reading between the lines and applying them to the modern literature on AIs mediated learning, one can find several major themes that allow putting the empirical findings into context and give the results deeper meaning.

3.2.1. Simple AI as a Driving Force Behind Innovative Confidence and Cognitive Fluency

The quantitative data reveal that the creative self-efficacy and the idea fluency of students working with the AI tools increase significantly (Table 1). The visual reinforcement of these gains can also be attained through the upward change in post AI creativity scores (Figure 3). These enhancements are consistent with the accumulating literature on the idea that AI may become a type of cognitive scaffolding, which will alleviate the cognitive load of ideating, and will allow learners to get involved in exploration activities more easily. As an example, Haidar (2023) and Wang et al. (2024) also found that AI-assisted students demonstrate a higher amount of confidence and quicker idea generation, especially during open-ended tasks.

This interpretation is reinforced by the correlation matrix (Table 2): strong and positive relationships exist between AI use and creative self-efficacy (r =.62) and idea originality (r =.54), which are the initial stages of creative thinking and involve learners concentrating on generation, elaboration, or refinement of ideas. This trend can be visualized in the scatter plot (Figure 1) according to which the frequent AI users are more likely to report increased confidence in their capacity to think creatively.

These findings should however be taken with caution. The greater the fluency and the perceived novelty, the higher the chances are that it is not really novel (as it is stated in the literature) (Ivcevic and Grandinetti, 2024). AI can also speed up generation of ideas, given that such speed can obscure more superficial creativity outputs that are novel but algorithmically common. Stated differently, students can become more creative, since the process can become easier and more fun, but the originality of their output would not be diminished.

This difference is also echoed in our data: the originality according to peers was not significantly upgraded, despite an increase in self-reported creative confidence. The quantitative gain, in turn, is the increased perceived creativity which is a significant psychological benefit but which does not ensure deeper creative thinking.

3.2.2. The Invisible Threat: Algorithms Conformity and Creative Homogenization

Interview and classroom observations have produced qualitative information that indicates the fear of excessive use of AI and especially in writing and ideation. A significant percentage of the students admitted to utilizing AI recommendations with very little adjustment, particularly when they are in time pressure and also when they are following a trend also reported by Schmidt and Barron (2023). Teachers noted similarity in writing and structure of content that the submissions of students were becoming more homogenized.

This phenomenon occurs due to the impact that internalizing the patterns, tone, and narrative logic of AI outputs have on learners and are conceptualized by Pavia et al. (2025) as algorithmic conformity. Since generative models are conditioned on huge representative corpus data, they are more likely to propose statistical means than artistic outliers. This can slowly normalize the style and the way of thinking of students in their writing (Selwyn, 2023; Crawford, 2021).

This is an issue that is supported by our empirical evidence. The students reported about minor shifts in their creative behavior: AI turned out to be a starting point not a support and formed the direction of their idea. Others found the authorship uncomfortable as they were questioning whether the work still belonged to them. This issue reflects the results of Perrotta (2024) who claims that AI may blur the boundaries between support and creative replacement especially in cases where the learners do not have effective metacognitive strategies.

Therefore, even though AI enhances fluency, it can also lead to the lack of creative diversity in case of passive or instrumental use.

3.2.3. Teacher Mediation the Resolute Requirement of Creative Development

Among the most interesting results, there is a high correlation of teacher facilitation and creative autonomy of students (r = .61). This is supported by qualitative interviews: the classrooms in which educators defined AI as exploration but not a solution delivery tool experienced more originality and a greater level of engagement.

This confirms the arguments of various researchers (Holmes and Tuomi, 2022; Craft, 2023; Tang et al., 2024): AI does not have any influence on education in terms of technology, but mediates it pedagogically. Creativity is enhanced when educators stimulate students to criticize, modify, or attack AI answers. On the other hand, the introduction of AI as a tool of productivity only leads to cognitive disengagement of students and superficial outputs.

We find our results similar to the case studies in the classroom setting carried out by Boulhrir and Hamash (2025), in which the most creative learning processes were observed in pedagogical units that are organized around iterative cycles of co-creation, critique, revision, and divergence. In this regard, the learners were not placed in the positions of passive consumers of AI generated outputs, but as active participants, who evaluated, criticized, and modified the algorithmic suggestions. Most interestingly, it was creativity that was best endorsed under the circumstances when students did not blindly accept AI recommendations, but instead perceived them as tentative human inputs that are subject to interpretations and reconsideration.

These findings support the point that it is pedagogy and not technology, per se, that is the defining variable that drives or inhibits creativity in AI-enhanced learning processes. The pedagogical stance of AI is hence dependent on the way it is pedagogized, whether it will stimulate critical thinking, intellectual risk-taking, and reflective re iteration or whether it will foster efficiency-based conformity and cognitive outsourcing. In this respect, AI does not dictate the result of creativity; pedagogical design intervenes in the process through which AI influences creative thought and creative learning behaviour.

3.2.4. Emotional Responsiveness Influences Innovative Agency in AI-Classrooms

The affective aspect of AI-aided creativity is often neglected in the literature but in our results, it is very dominant. In Figure 2, the emotional distribution chart shows that curiosity and engagement are the most prevalent ones, whereas anxiety is also among the most significant minority of respondents.

These emotional patterns have a direct effect on creative risk-taking. Curious learners are more likely to investigate AI outputs in a critical way or experiment with divergent ideas or integrate AI proposals with their own information behaviors that are linked to greater originality. In the meantime, anxious students are more inclined to closely copy AI results or give them more precedence, which restricts the expression of creativity.

The literature indicates that this interpretation is correct: both Pavia et al. (2025) and Wang and Fan (2025) pay attention to the fact that the degree of AI as an advantageous or a restriction of creative agency is being determined by the emotional states.

This way, the creativity in AI-mediated settings cannot be cognitively comprehensible; it is also guided by the affective experiences that create the desire to go against machine-generated norms in students.

3.2.5. Placing the Findings in the Modern Theoretical Models

The findings are consistent with and generalize a number of theoretical frameworks:

Componential Model of Creativity by Amabile (2020).

AI can also be used to increase domain expertise and efficiency, and decrease intrinsic motivation when introduced too much. We find the two facts parallel to each other.

Vygotskian Mediation

AI becomes a semiotic device that is the tool of ideation. However, without mediating by teachers, students will venture to outsource meaning-making to the machine.

Human-Machine Hybrid Creativity Models.

Like the distribution system of human intentionality and algorithmic computation proposed by Henrickson and Meier (2023), creativity is formed now as a result of collaborative intelligence. According to our data, this hybrid model is highly supported.

In the Direction of a New definition of Creativity in AI-Driven Classrooms.

According to the synthesis of findings and literature, creativity in AI mediated education must not be thought of as an entirely human process, nor a machine-mediated expediency, but as a process of dialogue, where:

- Humans offer intent, meaning, judgment and agency of morality.
- teachers create the environment of critical inquiry.
- Effects AI offers fluency, variation and augmentation of computation.
- emotions define participation and separation.
- ethical consciousness maintains authenticity.

To back this claim, this paper contends that AI does not fundamentally boost or worsen creativity. Rather it restructures the creative scene by enhancing some of the abilities of quick prototyping of ideas and pattern recognition and at the same time de-stabilizing other facets, including originality, profound contemplation, and epistemic independence. Creativity influenced by AI cannot be evaluated in technical terms therefore. The defining factors are the pedagogical, emotional, and ethical frameworks of these technologies embedded and applied.

Used cautiously and thoughtfully, AI can possibly broaden human imagination in that it is a cognitive partner that conflicts with the assumptions, provokes new ways of thinking, and helps explore. On the other hand, when embraced passively or uncritically, it could lead to cognitive dependence, less intellectual activity and even to some sort of standardization that harms creative diversity. When this occurs creativity may end up being derivative, not generative, driven not instead by human curiosity but by algorithmic convenience.

Consequently, it requires the deliberate planning of the design to sustain and evolve creativity in the AI-enhanced learning environment. These decisions should not be limited to the incorporation of technological resources but should also include the culture of learning, teaching, and believing in the critical thinking, agency, and ethical consciousness. In this respect, creativity cannot be a by-product of the high-tech level, but rather a skill, which should be actively developed with intelligent educational design and deliberate interaction with AIs systems.

4. CONCLUSION

The results, which are demonstrated in the chapter, show the drastic changes that are currently observed in educational settings as artificial intelligence becomes an active part of the learning and creativity processes. Instead of establishing the simple narrative of AI either improving or reducing creativity, the data shows that it is a much more complex picture. The conditions of creativity as generated by AI transform the process of generating ideas in students, teamwork, and reflection, and self-perceive creative identity. These transformations make AI not only a technological revolution but also a mental, emotional, and pedagogical phenomenon that needs to be introduced into the educational process with much thought and deliberation.

Taken as a whole, the findings are inclined to a two-way channel. On the one hand, AI can enhance creative self-efficacy in students, expand conceptual exploration and speed up the ideation. Students that have experienced AI tools also add more confidence and less creative block and enhanced engagement in exploratory activities. Conversely, when being applied without critical awareness or guided mediation, the same tools may provide homogenization of the results, passive copying, and lessening of agency. Creativity is no more a matter of pure originality but a process occurring between human intuition and machine-generated suggestions.

This contradiction supports one of the main findings: the future of creativity in education cannot be discussed as technologically determined; it is negotiated in a pedagogical process. AI does not eliminate human imagination but interrelates with it, and educators need to create an environment where intellectual autonomy, ethical integrity and creative thinking will be maintained.

Considering these results, a number of recommendations can be offered to teachers, schools, and policy-makers interested in developing genuine creativity in AI-mediated classrooms:

Only by repositioning AI as an Exploration, Not Substitution Tool, can it be ensured that it is used without substituting other functions:

AI must be presented as a tool that enhances divergent thinking and not a solution to ultimate solutions. Students should be asked to criticize, remix, expand or challenge AI-genered ideas in assignments. This strengthens property and protects mental addiction.

- ✓ Improve the AI literacy through enhancement of ethical and epistemological sensitivity:

Students should know what bias, limitations, and generativity AI has. It involves the explanation of the role of algorithms to creative recommendations, the effects of training data on outputs, and the process of standing out between genuine and synthetic efforts. Such knowledge makes the agency stronger and promotes responsible creativity. Wager Pedagogical Mediation the Major Engine of Creative Development:

Teacher instruction is determinant in helping to make AI enhance or restrict creativity. The professional development needs to be centered on the creation of inquiry-based tasks, demonstrating how to become critical of AI output, and the discussion of creative practices. Teachers need to transform themselves into knowledge depositors, to be creative enquiry curators.

✓ Foster Nurturant Learning Conditions:

Since the emotional state can be one of the key determinants of creative behavior, classrooms that implement AI should offer an opportunity to be curious, experiment, and take risks safely. By discussing the topic of anxiety and uncertainty about AI with students, assuring them of its harmlessness, and introducing it to students in small doses, it is possible to avoid avoidance and encourage positive exploration.

✓ Improve Multimodal and Diverse Creative work:

Text production cannot be considered as a measure of creativity. The visual, auditory, problem-solving, design thinking as the multimodal tasks allow decreasing the likelihood of homogenization and increase the possibility of human-AI co-creating opportunities. A variety of activities is also crucial to enable the students to take advantage of AI strengths, at the same time adding their own insights into the picture.

✓ Create New Evaluation Systems that appreciate Process, rather than Product:

The old types of grading criteria that focus on the final output could unintentionally promote the use of AI-generated materials. The creative process: idea development, articulation, amendments, and individual input should be the focus of assessment models. This is a change in the focus of what AI is capable of generating but rather how students can be creative in using AI to think.

Finally, it is not whether human creativity will be able to survive in AI-controlled classrooms, but how it will develop in them. The ability to be creative has never been a predetermined ability; instead, it is a moving process that is influenced by tools, cultures, and epistemologies. AI is the most recent and possibly the most radically changing mediating force in this process. Being applied wisely, it may push the limits of imagination and help the learners to look at the problems in new ways and practice their expressiveness more. Applied blindly, it is likely to squash the creative variety and undermine even that autonomy that is the aim of education.

REFERENCES

Adewale, M. D., Azeta, A., Abayomi-Alli, A., & Sambo-Magaji, A. (2024). Impact of artificial intelligence adoption on students' academic performance in open and distance learning: A systematic literature review. *Heliyon*, *10*(22), e40025. Advance online publication. DOI: 10.1016/j.heliyon.2024.e40025 PMID: 39605813

Amabile, T. M. (2020). Creativity, artificial intelligence, and a world of surprises. *Academy of Management Discoveries*, *6*(3), 351–354. DOI: 10.5465/amd.2020.0056

Bender, E. M., Gebru, T., McMillan-Major, A., & Shmitchell, S. (2021). On the Dangers of Stochastic Parrots: Can Language Models Be Too Big? In *Proceedings of the 2021 ACM Conference on Fairness, Accountability, and Transparency (FAccT'21)* (pp. 610-623). Association for Computing Machinery. https://doi.org/ DOI: 10.1145/3442188.3445922

Boulhrir, T., & Hamash, M. (2025). Unpacking artificial intelligence in elementary education: A comprehensive thematic analysis systematic review. Computers and *Education. Artificial Intelligence*, *9*, 100442. DOI: 10.1016/j.caeai.2025.100442

Craft, A. (2023). Creativity and education futures in the age of artificial intelligence. *Thinking Skills and Creativity*, *47*, 101229. DOI: 10.1016/j.tsc.2022.101229

Crawford, K. (2021). *Atlas of AI: Power, politics, and the planetary costs of artificial intelligence*. Yale University Press.

Floridi, L., & Cowls, J. (2022). A unified framework of five principles for AI in society. *Harvard Data Science Review*, *4*(1). Advance online publication. DOI: 10.1162/99608f92.8cd550d1

Garzón, J., Patiño, E., & Marulanda, C. (2025). Systematic review of artificial intelligence in education: Trends, benefits, and challenges. *Multimodal Technologies and Interaction*, *9*(8), 84. DOI: 10.3390/mti9080084

Haidar, A. (2023). An Integrative Theoretical Framework for Responsible Artificial Intelligence. *International Journal of Digital Strategy, Governance, and Business Transformation*, *13*(1), 1–23. Advance online publication. DOI: 10.4018/IJDSGBT.334844

Henrickson, L., & Meier, S. (2023). Hybrid creativity: Human–AI collaboration in creative practice. *Creativity Research Journal*, *35*(2), 187–199. DOI: 10.1080/10400419.2023.2178421

Holmes, W., Bialik, M., & Fadel, C. (2019). Artificial intelligence in education: Promise and implications for teaching and learning. Center for Curriculum Redesign., 10.1794293700.

Holmes, W., & Tuomi, I. (2022). State of the art and practice in AI in education. *International Journal of Artificial Intelligence in Education*, *32*(4), 1–25. DOI: 10.1007/s40593-022-00291-9

Ivcevic, Z., & Grandinetti, A. (2024). Who benefits from AI-assisted creativity? Individual differences and creative confidence. *Psychology of Aesthetics, Creativity, and the Arts*, *18*(1), 12–25. DOI: 10.1037/aca0000558

Khalil, M., & Er, E. (2023). Will ChatGPT Get You Caught? Rethinking of Plagiarism Detection. In Zaphiris, P., & Ioannou, A. (Eds.), Lecture Notes in Computer Science: Vol. 14040. *Learning and Collaboration Technologies. HCII 2023*. Springer., DOI: 10.1007/978-3-031-34411-4_32

Kim, J., & Park, H. (2023). Pedagogical mediation of AI tools and student creativity. *Computers & Education*, *190*, 104602. DOI: 10.1016/j.compedu.2022.104602

Meincke, L., Mollick, E. R., & Terwiesch, C. (2024). *Prompting diverse ideas: Increasing AI idea variance*. The Wharton School Research Paper. https://doi.org/ DOI: 10.2139/ssrn.4708466

Pareigis, J., Kvarnström, M., Cefa, B., Bai, J. Y. H., Zawacki-Richter, O., Uhlin, L., Jakobsson, N., & Theilmeier, G. (2024). Open networked learning – a course, a community, an approach. *The International Journal for Academic Development*, *29*(2), 169–184. DOI: 10.1080/1360144X.2024.2350652

Pavia, G., van den Bosch, A., & Wieringa, M. (2025). Creative agency in human–AI interaction: A systematic review. *AI & Society*. Advance online publication. DOI: 10.1007/s00146-024-01801-6

Perrotta, C. (2024). Automation, creativity, and authorship in education. *Learning, Media and Technology*, *49*(1), 1–15. DOI: 10.1080/17439884.2023.2258349

Reina Marín, Y., Cruz Caro, O., Maicelo Rubio, Y. C., Alva Tuesta, J. N., Sánchez Bardales, E., Carrasco Rituay, A. M., & Chávez Santos, R. (2025). Artificial intelligence as a teaching tool in university education. *Frontiers in Education*, *10*, 1578451. DOI: 10.3389/feduc.2025.1578451

Rigopouli, K., Kotsifakos, D., & Psaromiligkos, Y. (2025). Vygotsky's Creativity Options and Ideas in 21st-Century Technology-Enhanced Learning Design. *Education Sciences*, *15*(2), 257. DOI: 10.3390/educsci15020257

Schmidt, P., & Barron, B. (2023). Algorithmic conformity and student writing in AI-assisted classrooms. *Journal of Educational Computing Research, 61*(4), 789–812. DOI: 10.1177/07356331231158742

Selwyn, N. (2023). *Should robots replace teachers? AI and the future of education.* Polity Press.

Tang, K. Y., Chou, C., & Tsai, C. C. (2024). Teachers' roles in shaping AI-supported creativity. *Teaching and Teacher Education, 132*, 104233. DOI: 10.1016/j.tate.2023.104233

UNESCO. (2023). Guidance on generative AI in education and research. UNESCO Publishing. https://unesdoc.unesco.org

Urmeneta, A., & Romero, M. (2025). AI as a creative partner: A PRISMA review of AI's role in supporting creativity in education. *Frontiers in Education, 10*, 1602151. Advance online publication. DOI: 10.3389/feduc.2025.1602151

Wang, S., Wang, F., Zhu, Z., Wang, J., Tran, T., & Du, Z. (2024). *Artificial intelligence in education: A systematic literature review.* Expert Systems with Applications, 252(Part A), 124167. DOI: 10.1016/j.eswa.2024.124167

Wang, X., & Fan, Y. (2025). Emotional responses to generative AI in learning contexts. *Computers in Human Behavior, 146*, 107833. DOI: 10.1016/j.chb.2024.107833

Wiese, L. J., Patil, I., Schiff, D. S., & Magana, A. J. (2025). AI ethics education: A systematic literature review. *Computers and Education: Artificial Intelligence, 8*, 100405. DOI: 10.1016/j.caeai.2025.100405

Xia, Q., Zhang, P., Huang, W., & Chiu, T. K. F. (2025). The impact of generative AI on university students' learning outcomes via Bloom's taxonomy: A meta-analysis and pattern mining approach. *Asia Pacific Journal of Education*, •••, 1–31. DOI: 10.1080/02188791.2025.2530503

Zhang, K., & Aslan, A. B. (2021). AI technologies for education: Recent research and future directions. *Computers and Education: Artificial Intelligence, 2*, 100025. DOI: 10.1016/j.caeai.2021.100025

Chapter 11
AI for Underserved Communities

Ardra Rianisa
http://orcid.org/0009-0005-0304-1195
Universitas Esa Unggul, Indonesia

Binastya Anggara Sekti
http://orcid.org/0000-0001-5489-4888
Universitas Esa Unggul, Indonesia

ABSTRACT

This chapter explores the role of Artificial Intelligence (AI) in improving education for underserved communities that continue to face barriers such as limited infrastructure, teacher shortages, and socio-economic inequalities. It discusses how AI technologies including adaptive learning systems, intelligent tutoring, and predictive analytics can offer scalable and personalized learning solutions to bridge educational gaps. Ethical considerations such as data privacy, algorithmic bias, and transparency are examined to ensure responsible implementation. The chapter also highlights the importance of community engagement, cultural relevance, and collaboration among governments, NGOs, and the private sector for successful and sustainable adoption. Furthermore, it discusses real-world case studies that demonstrate the effectiveness of AI in enhancing education, healthcare, and digital inclusion. The chapter concludes with strategic recommendations for equitable AI deployment and continuous evaluation to support long-term educational transformation in underserved regions.

DOI: 10.4018/979-8-3373-7467-3.ch011

1. INTRODUCTION

Education is a fundamental human right that serves as the foundation for personal, social, and economic development. Despite its widespread recognition, many communities in underserved areas still struggle to access quality education. This challenge is most pronounced in rural areas, low-income communities, and conflict-affected areas. Many lack adequate infrastructure, such as school buildings, trained teachers, and sufficient learning resources. As a result, students in these areas are deprived of the opportunity to develop their full potential, perpetuating poverty and inequality. The emergence of artificial intelligence (AI) offers a promising solution to this problem by providing learning tools tailored to the unique needs of each community (Acosta, 2025).

AI-powered systems have the potential to completely transform learning. One of the key advantages of AI in education is its ability to tailor the learning process to each student's needs. AI algorithms can adjust the pace and difficulty of the material based on students' progress in real time, making learning more efficient and personalized. This approach is particularly beneficial in underserved areas, where traditional learning methods often fail to adapt to the varying abilities of students. Through adaptive learning technology, AI can provide a more targeted learning experience and help students overcome the learning barriers they currently face (Akanfe et al., 2025).

Despite its great potential, the application of AI in underserved communities must be approached with caution. Several important considerations, particularly regarding the ethical use of technology, require attention. Issues such as data privacy, algorithmic bias, and the impact of AI on human roles, are key concerns. AI works by collecting and analyzing data, including personal data, which can raise concerns if not managed properly. Furthermore, if AI systems are not well designed, they can reinforce existing social biases and lead to inequities in educational outcomes. Therefore, the application of AI must be carried out ethically and responsibly to truly benefit society (Andri Nirwana et al., 2025).

Beyond ethical concerns, there are also practical challenges in implementing AI in underserved areas. The main obstacle often lies in inadequate infrastructure. Many areas lack electricity and stable internet, both of which are crucial for implementing AI-based technology. The cost of AI devices and software is often prohibitive for schools in rural areas. Therefore, it is necessary to find ways to implement AI realistically and sustainably in resource-constrained environments. For example, the use of solar-powered devices or offline learning platforms could be effective alternatives to address infrastructure issues (Asokan et al., 2025).

The potential of AI in education extends beyond personalized learning or infrastructure improvements. This technology can also help create equity in education.

AI can help teachers and schools identify students experiencing learning difficulties and provide more appropriate support. For example, AI systems can analyze student progress in real time and recommend supplementary materials for those who are lagging behind. This approach is particularly useful in areas where teachers are limited. By providing rapid and personalized learning support, AI helps ensure that every student, regardless of their background, has an equal opportunity to succeed (Cinar & Bilodeau, 2024).

However, the implementation of AI in education must be accompanied by training for teachers and the community. Teachers need to be equipped with the skills to use AI correctly so that this technology can be used optimally in the classroom. Training programs should cover not only how to operate AI-based tools but also an understanding of their ethics and impact on learning. Such training should be tailored to local conditions, ensuring ease of implementation and effectiveness. By equipping teachers with these skills, they can use AI as a tool to improve teaching quality and provide a better learning experience for students (Ganju et al., 2021).

2. CHALLENGES IN EDUCATION FOR UNDERSERVED COMMUNITIES

Underserved communities face a host of challenges that hinder their access to quality education. The most immediate and pervasive obstacle is the lack of infrastructure. In many remote or impoverished regions, schools often lack basic resources like electricity, internet, or even the physical space necessary for a conducive learning environment. Without these critical elements, even the most basic educational technologies cannot function. Additionally, many rural communities are plagued by poor transportation options, making it difficult for students to attend schools consistently. These infrastructure deficiencies are compounded by limited access to educational materials, such as textbooks, teaching aids, and digital learning resources. As a result, students in these areas are often at a significant disadvantage compared to their peers in urban settings. AI-powered systems can offer a solution to this issue by delivering scalable, cost-effective educational content directly to students in need (Hendricks-Sturrup et al., 2023).

A significant barrier to quality education in underserved communities is the shortage of qualified educators. Many regions face a dearth of skilled and trained teachers, which exacerbates educational inequality. Teachers who do work in these areas are often overburdened with large class sizes, inadequate support, and limited professional development opportunities. This lack of qualified educators leads to lower-quality instruction, further hindering student progress and contributing to high dropout rates. AI can help address this issue by providing supplementary teaching tools, such as intelligent tutoring systems, which can guide students through personalized learning experiences. These systems can be especially beneficial in areas where teacher shortages are most pronounced, offering one-on-one tutoring that complements the efforts of human instructors (Kong et al., 2023).

In addition to the lack of teachers, the digital divide is one of the most pressing challenges faced by underserved communities in accessing education. The divide is evident in the disparity between regions that have widespread access to the internet and modern technology and those that do not. In many rural or low-income urban areas, reliable internet connections are not available, and students may lack the devices necessary to access online learning platforms. Without the proper tools, AI-powered educational resources cannot be fully leveraged, and students are denied the opportunity to benefit from technological advancements. Bridging the digital divide requires targeted interventions to ensure that schools in underserved communities can access the hardware and internet connectivity needed for AI tools to function effectively. Solutions like offline learning platforms and low-cost devices can make AI-powered education accessible to even the most marginalized populations (Garcia-Saiso et al., 2024).

Language and cultural barriers are another major challenge in education for underserved communities, particularly in regions with diverse populations. Many educational systems use standardized content that may not reflect the local culture, language, or socio-economic context of students. In these cases, students may struggle to relate to the material, leading to disengagement and poor academic performance. Moreover, language barriers can prevent students from fully understanding the content or participating in class discussions. AI has the potential to address these issues by offering customized learning experiences that incorporate local languages, cultural contexts, and relevant examples. AI-based translation tools can also help bridge language gaps, making educational content accessible to students who speak different languages (Ganju et al., 2021).

Another significant challenge in underserved communities is the lack of tailored support for students with diverse learning needs. Traditional educational systems are often one-size-fits-all, which means that students who require special education or additional support may not receive the attention they need. This results in a widening achievement gap, as students with learning disabilities, for example, are left behind. AI can provide personalized learning paths that accommodate diverse learning styles, allowing students with disabilities or those requiring extra support to thrive. By using data-driven insights, AI can track individual progress and adjust content in real-time to better suit each student's needs. Such personalized approaches are crucial in leveling the playing field for all students, regardless of their learning challenges (Quishpe-Quishpe et al., 2025).

Lastly, socio-economic factors further exacerbate the challenges faced by underserved communities. Students from low-income families may not have access to necessary resources such as books, tutors, or extracurricular activities that could enhance their learning experience. These students may also lack a stable learning environment at home, which impacts their academic success. AI technologies can help mitigate some of these issues by offering free or low-cost educational resources that are accessible from home or community centers. AI can also help bridge the gap by providing students with opportunities for remote learning, allowing them to access high-quality educational content without needing to leave their community. By offering accessible and affordable learning solutions, AI can help alleviate the burden of socio-economic disadvantages on students' educational journeys (Huang et al., 2025).

3. AI TECHNOLOGIES TO ADDRESS EDUCATIONAL BARRIERS

Figure 1. Illustration of AI-powered adaptive learning system

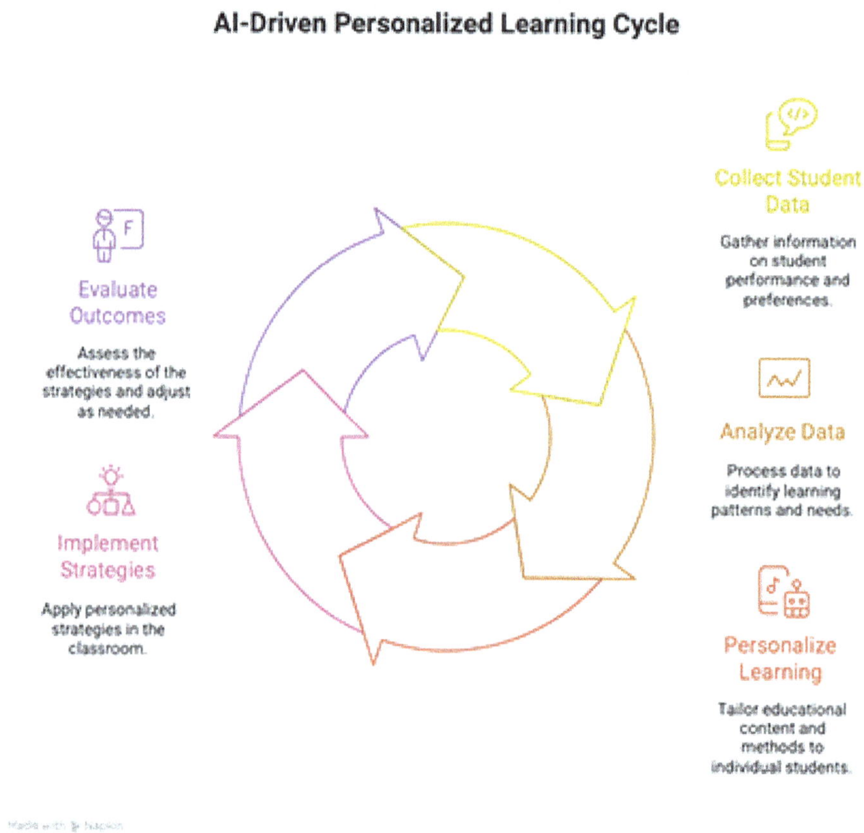

Artificial Intelligence (AI) presents significant potential to address many of the challenges faced by underserved communities in accessing quality education. One of the most important applications of AI is through adaptive learning systems, which provide personalized educational experiences for students. These AI-powered systems use data to assess a student's learning style, pace, and strengths and weaknesses. By adjusting the difficulty of tasks and providing targeted feedback, adaptive learning can help close gaps in understanding that exist due to differences in learning abilities or educational resources. In underserved communities, where resources such as personalized instruction are scarce, AI can help bridge this gap by offering scalable solutions that can cater to the individual needs of students. This technology can be deployed at scale, ensuring that each student receives the level of attention and support necessary to succeed, regardless of where they live (Kumar et al., 2024).

Another key application of AI is in the form of virtual teaching assistants. In many underserved communities, there is a shortage of teachers, and those who are available often have large class sizes, making it difficult to provide one-on-one support to students. AI-driven virtual assistants can play a critical role in addressing this issue by offering personalized assistance to students at all times. These assistants can help students with homework, explain difficult concepts, and answer questions in real-time, all of which enhance the learning process outside of traditional classroom hours. By providing immediate and individualized responses, virtual assistants enable students to progress at their own pace, even when human teachers are not available. This continuous support ensures that students remain engaged in their learning and can access help whenever needed, making AI a valuable tool for communities with limited access to teachers or tutoring resources (Liew et al., 2025).

AI technologies also enable predictive analytics, which can be used to identify students who may be at risk of falling behind academically. By analyzing a wide array of data, such as test scores, attendance, and engagement with learning materials, AI can detect patterns and flag students who may need additional support. In underserved communities, where early intervention programs are often lacking due to resource constraints, predictive analytics provides a timely solution. By identifying struggling students early, educators can implement personalized interventions to prevent them from falling behind. For example, AI systems could recommend additional practice exercises, suggest tutoring sessions, or provide resources tailored to the student's specific needs. This proactive approach to student support allows for better management of resources and ensures that no student is left behind, even in communities with limited educational infrastructure (Grenon et al., 2025).

AI-powered translation tools also hold tremendous potential in overcoming language barriers that exist in many underserved communities. In regions where students speak a variety of languages, the lack of educational resources in local languages can hinder learning and make students feel disconnected from the material. AI translation tools can break down these barriers by providing real-time translation of educational content. This technology enables students to access learning materials in their native languages, ensuring that language differences do not limit their ability to understand and engage with the curriculum. Moreover, AI-powered translation tools can support teachers by enabling them to communicate more effectively with students from different linguistic backgrounds, fostering a more inclusive and supportive learning environment. By using AI to bridge language gaps, underserved communities can ensure that language is no longer a barrier to quality education (Ma et al., 2022).

Intelligent Tutoring Systems (ITS) represent another powerful AI technology that can address educational challenges in underserved communities. ITSs are AI-driven platforms that mimic the role of a personal tutor, providing customized instruction and feedback to students. These systems can adapt to each student's learning pace, offering personalized exercises, explanations, and assessments based on their progress. For underserved communities, ITSs can provide much-needed educational support, especially when qualified teachers are in short supply. These systems can help ensure that every student receives individualized instruction, allowing them to learn at their own pace without the constraints of traditional classroom settings. By making high-quality tutoring available to all students, AI can level the playing field, ensuring that students from underserved communities have the same opportunities for success as their peers in more affluent areas (Yockel et al., 2025).

Finally, AI-powered content creation tools offer significant potential for empowering educators in underserved communities. These tools enable teachers to create customized learning materials such as quizzes, assignments, and interactive lessons that are specifically tailored to the needs of their students. In many underserved areas, teachers often have to rely on generic or outdated materials, which may not be relevant to the students' specific needs or cultural contexts. AI tools can assist in creating engaging, culturally appropriate content that resonates with students. Additionally, these tools can reduce the time teachers spend on administrative tasks, giving them more time to focus on instruction and student engagement. By democratizing access to high-quality, customizable educational materials, AI can help ensure that teachers in underserved communities are not limited by a lack of resources (Sikalidis et al., 2022).

4. CASE STUDIES IN AI FOR UNDERSERVED COMMUNITIES

Several initiatives worldwide are demonstrating the power of Artificial Intelligence (AI) in improving educational access for underserved communities. One such example is the MindCraft project in India, which utilizes AI to provide personalized learning and mentorship to students in rural areas. This AI-driven platform adjusts the curriculum based on each student's progress, helping them master concepts at their own pace. In regions where there is a shortage of qualified teachers, AI-based systems like MindCraft offer a scalable and cost-effective alternative that ensures students do not miss out on essential learning. By enabling remote learning opportunities and personalized support, MindCraft has successfully provided educational access to thousands of children who would otherwise be left behind due to a lack of teachers or resources (Andri Nirwana et al., 2025).

Another innovative case study is the SolarSPELL project, which uses solar-powered digital libraries to provide offline educational content to remote communities that lack reliable internet access. In many underserved areas, the digital divide creates significant barriers to learning, particularly for students who need consistent access to educational materials. SolarSPELL addresses this challenge by providing locally stored digital content that is accessible without an internet connection. The platform includes a wide variety of educational resources, from textbooks to interactive lessons, which are critical for students who would otherwise have limited access to learning materials. By leveraging solar power and portable technology, SolarSPELL ensures that students in the most remote and underserved regions can still access high-quality education, no matter where they live (Ganju et al., 2021).

AI has also been used in the healthcare sector to enhance educational outcomes in underserved communities. For instance, in rural Australia, AI-powered tools are being used to detect strep throat, a common illness that can lead to serious health complications if left untreated. These tools provide rapid and accurate diagnoses, helping to ensure that students can return to school faster and continue their education without unnecessary health disruptions. The AI system analyzes symptoms and medical images to provide a diagnosis, reducing the need for specialized healthcare professionals in remote areas. This case study highlights how AI can be integrated into public health to support not just healthcare, but also the overall well-being of students, ultimately facilitating better educational outcomes by addressing health barriers (Asokan et al., 2025).

In the field of mental health, AI has been used to support adolescents in rural areas where mental health professionals are scarce. AI-powered platforms are being used to assess the mental health of young people, providing early detection of conditions such as depression and anxiety. These tools offer personalized recommendations and connect students to remote counseling services, ensuring that those in underserved communities have access to mental health support. By using AI to assess and monitor mental health, these platforms help to identify students in need of support before their iazssues escalate. This proactive approach to mental health can greatly reduce the stigma around mental health services and ensure that students in underserved communities receive the help they need to thrive both academically and emotionally (Grenon et al., 2025).

Another impactful use of AI is in the field of cancer care, where AI is being explored as a potential catalyst for more equitable treatment in underserved areas. One notable initiative uses AI to enhance the diagnosis and treatment of cancer, making the process more accessible to populations that traditionally have had limited access to healthcare services. AI systems can analyze medical images with remarkable accuracy, helping to detect cancer at earlier stages when treatment is most effective. This technology has the potential to overcome the limitations posed by the shortage of healthcare professionals and medical resources in underserved regions. By democratizing access to early detection and improving the quality of care, AI has the potential to reduce health disparities and improve educational outcomes by ensuring students stay healthy and focused on their studies (Garcia-Saiso et al., 2024).

The Rumie Initiative is another prime example of how AI is being used to address the education gap in underserved communities. This organization has developed a platform that delivers educational content through preloaded tablets to students in areas with limited internet access. The platform offers a wide range of learning materials, from primary education resources to career-oriented content, ensuring that students in underserved communities have access to a broad curriculum. The AI-driven content is personalized to meet the needs of each student, allowing them to learn at their own pace and access information that is relevant to their educational needs. The Rumie Initiative represents an effective use of technology to break down the barriers of educational inequality, providing students with the tools they need to succeed academically, no matter where they live (Quishpe-Quishpe et al., 2025).

5. ETHICAL CONSIDERATIONS IN AI FOR UNDERSERVED COMMUNITIES

Table 1. Ethical considerations in AI implementation for underserved communities

Ethical Concern	Description	Impact on Underserved Communities	Mitigation Strategies
Algorithmic Bias	AI systems may perpetuate biases present in data	Can lead to unequal educational outcomes or reinforce stereotypes	Regular audits of AI algorithms, diverse and inclusive datasets
Data Privacy	Collection of personal and sensitive data by AI systems	Risk of misuse or exploitation of student data	Compliance with data privacy laws, secure data handling
Transparency	Lack of clarity on how AI systems make decisions	Can create mistrust in AI solutions in vulnerable populations	Clear explanations of AI decision-making processes
Human Agency	Over-reliance on AI may diminish the role of human educators	Can lead to the erosion of teacher autonomy and creativity	AI as a tool to support, not replace, human judgment
Equity and Accessibility	Ensuring AI tools are accessible to all students, regardless of background	Risk of leaving marginalized groups further behind	Designing AI systems with inclusivity and accessibility in mind

As the use of artificial intelligence (AI) in education systems becomes more widespread, especially in underserved areas, it is important to consider the ethical implications of its use. One major concern is algorithmic bias. AI operates based on the data used to train it. If that data is already biased, for example based on race, gender, or socioeconomic status, the AI's results can also be biased. In areas that already face social inequality, this bias can actually exacerbate educational disparities. Therefore, AI developers and educators must ensure that the data used is diverse, inclusive, and non-discriminatory. Furthermore, AI systems need to be regularly monitored to detect and correct potential bias (Hendricks-Sturrup et al., 2023).

Another equally important issue is data privacy. Many AI systems in education rely on the collection of students' personal data, such as exam results, study habits, and even behavior when using digital platforms. While this data is useful for tailoring learning materials to better target students, it also poses risks if not managed properly. In areas with vulnerable or underserved communities, data misuse can create a sense of insecurity. Therefore, AI systems need to be designed with strong data protection. Schools and educational institutions must also be transparent about how data is collected, stored, and used, and comply with applicable privacy regulations (Kong et al., 2023).

In addition to bias and privacy concerns, there are also concerns that AI could diminish the role of humans in the learning process. Because AI systems can provide data-driven recommendations or decisions, there is a risk that teachers will lose their role as primary decision-makers in the classroom. Teachers' roles include not only teaching but also guiding and motivating students. AI should be a tool, not a replacement for humans. By positioning AI as a support system, teachers can maintain their crucial role in guiding and assessing student progress (Yockel et al., 2025).

Transparency is also a crucial ethical principle in the application of AI in education. Many AI systems operate as black boxes, meaning users do not know how the system makes decisions. This can foster distrust, especially in communities unfamiliar with technology. Therefore, developers need to ensure that AI systems are easily explained and understood by users, both teachers and students. If AI is used to assess or make recommendations to students, the process and rationale behind those decisions must be clear and transparent to all parties (Garcia-Saiso et al., 2024).

Another challenge is maintaining fairness and equal access. While AI can help create a more equitable and personalized learning experience, if its implementation only reaches developed regions, inequalities can be exacerbated. Therefore, AI needs to be designed to be usable in a variety of settings, including areas with limited infrastructure. AI systems must also be inclusive of all students, including those with disabilities or different learning styles. This way, AI can truly be a tool for equalizing learning opportunities for all children, rather than widening the gap (Sikalidis et al., 2022).

Finally, involving local communities is crucial for the ethical and sustainable implementation of AI. Local communities must participate in the AI planning and implementation process to ensure that the system is aligned with local values and needs. This involvement can be achieved through discussions with teachers, parents, or community leaders. By involving communities from the outset, AI use will be more accepted, relevant, and sustainable. Furthermore, community involvement fosters a sense of ownership and responsibility for the technology used, ensuring its positive impacts are long-term (Quishpe-Quishpe et al., 2025).

6. THE ROLE OF COMMUNITY ENGAGEMENT IN AI DEVELOPMENT

Community engagement is crucial for implementing artificial intelligence (AI) in underserved communities. AI technology holds significant potential to transform education and expand access to learning, but to be truly effective, its development must involve the communities that will use it. Local knowledge, culture, and specific educational needs must be considered from the outset. Without community input, AI systems may not be well-suited to their needs, even creating new, unintended problems. When communities are involved in the design process, the resulting outcomes are typically more relevant, more readily accepted, and more beneficial to those who will use them (Hendricks-Sturrup et al., 2023).

One key way to involve communities in AI development is through a co-design process. This process involves working with teachers, students, and community leaders to identify needs and challenges that AI technology can address. By involving them from the outset, developers can ensure that the technology aligns with local values, priorities, and conditions. This collaborative approach can also build trust between AI developers and communities, so that the resulting technology is perceived not as a threat but as a beneficial tool. Active community involvement also fosters a sense of ownership and responsibility, which are crucial for the long-term and sustainable use of AI (Kong et al., 2023).

In addition to participation in design, cultural relevance also plays a crucial role in AI implementation. Many communities have diverse languages, values, and unique learning habits. If AI systems are not adapted to these cultural contexts, the technology can feel unfamiliar and unappealing to users. Therefore, communities need to be involved in selecting learning content, designing materials, and defining learning objectives to better suit local conditions. When AI is developed with local cultural considerations in mind, the results are easier to understand, more engaging for students, and more effective. This approach also helps prevent the emergence of cultural biases that are incompatible with the community's social environment (Ma et al., 2022).

Community involvement should also occur throughout the implementation and evaluation stages of AI systems, not just during design. Schools, local governments, and non-governmental organizations (NGOs) play a crucial role in ensuring that AI systems can be effectively implemented in the field. These parties can help identify barriers, such as limited infrastructure or resistance to new technologies, and find appropriate solutions. Local teachers also need to be involved and trained to use AI effectively. This way, AI can be truly utilized according to needs, rather than simply being implemented without sufficient understanding (Quishpe-Quishpe et al., 2025).

Furthermore, community involvement is crucial to ensure that AI is used ethically and responsibly. Communities should be involved in discussions about data privacy, information transparency, and system accountability. AI systems in education often collect sensitive data about students, such as achievement, behavior, and study habits. Therefore, the community must understand how this data is collected, stored, and used. By involving the community in ethical discussions, trust in the technology can grow, and AI can be used in a way that is fair and respectful of students' rights (Garcia-Saiso et al., 2024).

Finally, community involvement ensures that AI implementation is not only technically sound but also socially sustainable. For the benefits to be lasting, local communities need to participate in the infrastructure management and maintenance of AI systems. Training teachers, technicians, and community members to use and maintain this technology is crucial for program sustainability. Community-driven initiatives are typically more successful because they are built on a deep understanding of local conditions and needs. With community support, AI implementation will be more robust, relevant, and have a real long-term impact on education (Sikalidis et al., 2022).

7. OVERCOMING THE DIGITAL DIVIDE WITH AI

Figure 2. Global digital divide and AI solutions

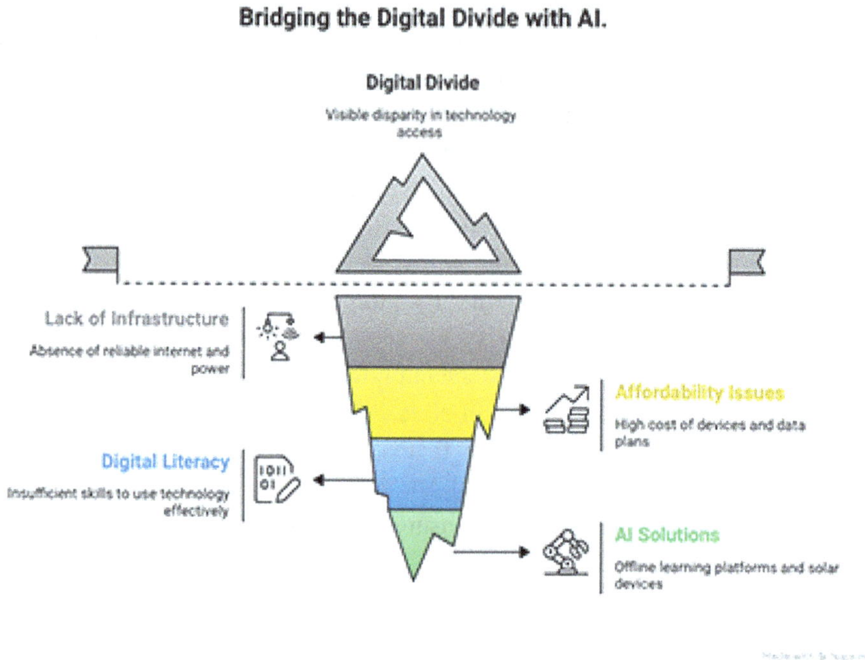

One of the most pressing challenges in underserved communities is the digital divide, which refers to the gap between those who have access to technology and those who do not. This divide is particularly pronounced in rural areas or low-income regions, where access to reliable internet and modern devices is limited. Without proper technological infrastructure, students in these communities cannot fully benefit from digital learning platforms or AI-driven educational tools. AI can help mitigate this issue by offering offline learning solutions and ensuring that students have access to educational content without needing a constant internet connection. By leveraging technology such as solar-powered devices or portable learning tools, AI can provide underserved students with the educational resources they need, regardless of their location (Sikalidis et al., 2022).

AI-powered tools can also bridge the digital divide by enabling low-cost, scalable educational resources. In many underserved areas, schools and community centers lack the resources to invest in high-end technology or digital devices for every student. AI solutions can help by optimizing the use of existing infrastructure, ensuring that even low-cost devices can run powerful AI tools. For instance, AI can be used to create customized learning paths on low-resource platforms, providing students with a personalized learning experience that doesn't rely on expensive hardware or high-speed internet. This approach ensures that AI-driven education is accessible to students who would otherwise be excluded due to financial constraints (Veseli, 2024).

Furthermore, AI can play a pivotal role in supporting teachers who work in underserved communities by reducing the administrative burden that often consumes much of their time. AI can automate tasks such as grading, scheduling, and monitoring student progress, allowing educators to focus on what truly matters: teaching. By streamlining these administrative tasks, AI empowers teachers to dedicate more time to providing personalized attention to their students. In regions where teachers are overburdened with large class sizes and limited resources, AI-driven tools offer a way to scale support and ensure that every student gets the attention they need, regardless of the teacher's capacity to provide individual assistance (Ganju et al., 2021).

AI can also provide targeted interventions to help students in underserved communities keep up with their peers. By analyzing student data, AI systems can identify learning gaps early and suggest personalized learning resources to help students catch up. These interventions can be especially important in communities with high dropout rates, where students often fall behind due to a lack of support. AI systems that offer personalized feedback and resources can help students stay on track, increasing their chances of success. Furthermore, predictive analytics can help identify students who are at risk of dropping out, allowing educators to intervene early and provide the support needed to keep students engaged and motivated (Huang et al., 2025).

A key factor in overcoming the digital divide is improving digital literacy among students and teachers. While AI tools can enhance learning, they require a basic level of digital literacy to be used effectively. Many underserved communities lack the necessary skills to fully utilize digital tools, which can limit the effectiveness of AI-powered learning. Therefore, it is essential that AI education initiatives are accompanied by digital literacy programs for both teachers and students. By equipping community members with the skills needed to navigate digital tools, we can ensure that AI is not only accessible but also useful. Digital literacy empowers students to become independent learners and enables teachers to better integrate AI into their classrooms (Yockel et al., 2025).

To achieve long-term sustainability in overcoming the digital divide, partnerships between governments, NGOs, and private companies are essential. These stakeholders must work together to provide the necessary infrastructure, resources, and training to underserved communities. Government policies must prioritize digital inclusion, ensuring that AI tools are accessible to all students, regardless of their socio-economic background. Private companies can contribute by providing affordable technology solutions and ensuring that AI systems are developed with underserved populations in mind. By collaborating on these initiatives, stakeholders can create a more equitable educational system where AI helps to bridge the digital divide and empowers underserved communities to access quality education (Kumar et al., 2024).

8. AI IN HEALTHCARE EDUCATION FOR UNDERSERVED COMMUNITIES

In underserved communities, access to healthcare education is a critical challenge. Many regions lack trained healthcare professionals, and the absence of quality health education exacerbates health disparities. AI can play a transformative role in addressing this issue by providing educational resources and tools that make healthcare knowledge more accessible. For instance, AI-powered platforms can be used to educate both students and adults in underserved communities about essential healthcare practices such as hygiene, nutrition, and disease prevention. These platforms can deliver customized content that suits the local context, languages, and literacy levels, ensuring that the educational material is both relevant and understandable (Asokan et al., 2025).

In addition to general healthcare education, AI tools are increasingly being used to train healthcare professionals, particularly in remote areas where medical education resources are scarce. AI-powered simulations and diagnostic tools enable healthcare workers to practice and refine their skills without the need for physical patients or expensive equipment. These AI-driven training platforms can simulate a variety of medical scenarios, providing healthcare workers with real-time feedback and allowing them to gain practical experience in a safe, controlled environment. For underserved communities that struggle with a shortage of medical schools and training facilities, these AI solutions offer an innovative way to enhance the skills of local healthcare professionals and improve healthcare outcomes (Kumar et al., 2024).

Furthermore, AI tools are being deployed in telemedicine applications to bridge the gap in healthcare access. For example, AI-powered diagnostic tools can help healthcare providers in underserved areas make more accurate diagnoses remotely. This is particularly important in regions where access to doctors and specialists is limited. AI tools that analyze medical images, symptoms, and patient history can assist healthcare providers in identifying conditions such as respiratory diseases, diabetes, or even mental health issues. By providing accurate, timely diagnoses, these AI-driven platforms can reduce the need for patients to travel long distances for care, saving both time and resources while ensuring better health outcomes (Huang et al., 2025).

AI's role in healthcare education also extends to preventive care and health awareness programs. AI can analyze population health data to identify emerging health trends and risks, enabling local communities to take proactive measures to prevent the spread of diseases. For example, AI-powered mobile applications can provide information about vaccination schedules, sanitation practices, and nutrition, allowing people in underserved communities to take charge of their own health. These tools can also offer reminders and alerts about important health screenings or disease outbreaks, empowering individuals to make informed decisions about their health (Ganju et al., 2021). By raising awareness and promoting healthy behaviors, AI can significantly improve health outcomes in underserved communities.

Moreover, AI can support mental health education and services in underserved communities, where mental health professionals are often scarce. AI-driven applications can assess mental health conditions and provide resources such as self-help guides, therapy exercises, and coping strategies. These tools can be especially beneficial in areas where stigma around mental health prevents individuals from seeking help. AI can also serve as a bridge to connect patients with mental health professionals remotely, facilitating therapy sessions or consultations via video calls or text-based platforms. By breaking down the barriers to mental health care, AI ensures that individuals in underserved communities have access to the support they need, improving their overall well-being and ability to succeed in school and work (Yockel et al., 2025).

Lastly, AI-driven healthcare education can play a vital role in addressing the specific health challenges faced by underserved populations, such as maternal health and child development. AI tools can provide expectant mothers with information on prenatal care, labor preparation, and postpartum recovery. In regions where access to healthcare providers is limited, AI systems can track the health of pregnant women and babies, offering advice on nutrition, exercise, and medical visits. By offering targeted health education at critical moments in a person's life, AI can contribute to reducing maternal and infant mortality rates in underserved communities. These technologies ensure that even in the absence of medical facilities, individuals can receive the information they need to maintain their health and well-being (Garcia-Saiso et al., 2024).

9. FUTURE DIRECTIONS: SCALING AI FOR GLOBAL IMPACT

The future of AI in underserved communities holds immense potential for transforming education, healthcare, and broader societal development. However, scaling AI for global impact presents both challenges and opportunities. The ability to scale AI solutions to diverse regions around the world will depend on various factors, including technological infrastructure, financial resources, and political will. In order to ensure AI tools are accessible to all, it will be critical to invest in the necessary infrastructure, such as internet connectivity, electricity, and affordable devices. Governments, non-governmental organizations (NGOs), and private companies must collaborate to create an ecosystem where AI can thrive in underserved communities. Such partnerships can provide the financial backing, technical expertise, and regulatory support required to deploy AI solutions at scale (Kong et al., 2023).

Scaling AI for global impact also involves making sure that AI solutions are adaptable to the specific needs of each community. AI technologies should not be one-size-fits-all but should be designed with flexibility in mind. This means that AI systems must be able to adapt to different languages, cultures, and educational or healthcare practices. For instance, an AI-powered education platform designed for a rural community in sub-Saharan Africa will need to account for local languages, learning preferences, and access to resources. By ensuring that AI tools are customizable and context-sensitive, we can increase their effectiveness and relevance in diverse communities around the world. Local community input during the development phase is critical for this process, ensuring that AI technologies align with the needs and priorities of the people they are designed to serve (Ma et al., 2022).

Furthermore, the widespread adoption of AI in underserved communities must be accompanied by policies that promote digital inclusion. To ensure equitable access to AI, governments and international organizations must develop policies that provide access to the necessary resources, such as affordable internet, smartphones, and laptops. Without these resources, many underserved communities will remain excluded from the benefits that AI can offer. Governments can also incentivize businesses to develop affordable, low-cost AI solutions that are designed specifically for these regions. Moreover, international organizations should create frameworks that promote cross-border cooperation, allowing AI solutions to be shared and adapted for use in different regions. This will help avoid the digital divide from widening further and ensure that AI is accessible to all, regardless of their geographic location (Veseli, 2024).

One of the greatest challenges in scaling AI is the issue of data availability. AI systems rely on large datasets to function effectively, and in many underserved regions, access to data is limited. For AI to be effective, it requires diverse datasets that reflect the unique characteristics of the populations it serves. Collecting data in underserved areas can be difficult due to privacy concerns, limited digital infrastructure, and a lack of resources to collect, store, and analyze data. However, overcoming this challenge is crucial for AI systems to be effective. Collaboration between local governments, educational institutions, and private companies can help ensure that data is collected ethically, with proper consent, and stored securely. In doing so, AI systems can be trained on diverse datasets, which will improve their accuracy and relevance for underserved communities (Ganju et al., 2021).

In addition to data availability, the development of AI solutions must consider the long-term sustainability of these technologies. As AI solutions are deployed in underserved communities, it is essential to ensure that they remain sustainable over time. This means developing AI technologies that do not just address immediate needs but also have the potential to evolve and adapt as the community grows and changes. For instance, AI tools should be designed with scalability in mind, ensuring that they can be updated with new information, respond to changing needs, and expand to serve more people. Furthermore, local stakeholders must be trained to maintain and operate these systems independently, which will ensure that AI solutions continue to deliver benefits long after the initial implementation phase (Sikalidis et al., 2022).

Finally, scaling AI for global impact requires ongoing evaluation and feedback. The deployment of AI technologies should not be seen as a one-time event but as part of a continuous process of improvement. Local communities should be actively involved in evaluating the effectiveness of AI solutions, providing feedback on what works and what doesn't. This iterative process will ensure that AI systems remain responsive to the needs of the community, allowing for adjustments to be made as necessary. By fostering a culture of continuous learning and improvement, AI can become a powerful tool for creating lasting, positive change in underserved communities around the world (Huang et al., 2025).

10. RECOMMENDATIONS FOR EFFECTIVE AI IMPLEMENTATION

For artificial intelligence (AI) to truly have a positive and sustainable impact on underserved communities, its implementation must be carried out with careful planning, involving various parties, and focusing on sustainability. One of the most important things is ensuring that AI design is inclusive. This means that AI tools or systems need to be developed with the specific needs of the communities where the technology will be used in mind. Factors such as language, culture, and local educational challenges must be taken seriously. Developers need to collaborate with teachers, community leaders, and other local stakeholders to ensure that the AI is contextually appropriate and truly beneficial. This inclusive approach not only makes the technology more relevant but also fosters trust and acceptance within the community (Hendricks-Sturrup et al., 2023).

The next recommendation is to strengthen infrastructure so that AI can be effectively used in underserved areas. While AI's potential is vast, its implementation is often hampered by basic constraints such as electricity, internet connections, and affordable devices. Governments, non-governmental organizations, and the private sector need to work together to improve this situation. For example, by providing affordable or subsidized devices, expanding internet networks, and developing systems that can operate offline without requiring a constant connection. In areas without stable electricity, solar-powered devices could also be a solution. With these steps, AI-based learning tools can be accessed by communities that have previously struggled to access technology (Ganju et al., 2021).

In addition to infrastructure, strengthening human resource capacity is also crucial. AI will only be beneficial if users understand how to use it. Therefore, training is needed for teachers and the community to be able to use this technology effectively. This training program should be tailored to the conditions of each community, including digital literacy levels and resource availability. By equipping teachers with the skills to operate AI in the classroom, they can integrate this technology into learning activities more optimally. If teachers and students understand how AI works, the technology can be used to enrich learning, not simply as a passive aid (Kumar et al., 2024).

Ethical aspects must also be a primary concern in the implementation of AI in society. The use of AI must be carried out responsibly, especially regarding data privacy and transparency. AI systems must be designed to protect students' personal information and comply with applicable data protection regulations. Developers also need to engage with the community to discuss potential risks, such as bias in algorithms. With community involvement, the risk of misuse can be minimized, and AI can function fairly and transparently. This ethical implementation is not a one-time event; it requires ongoing monitoring to ensure the system remains safe and inclusive (Sikalidis et al., 2022).

Collaboration between stakeholders at various levels is also key to the success of AI implementation. Local governments, educational institutions, non-governmental organizations, and international agencies need to work together to provide resources, training, and technical support. Partnerships with AI development companies are also crucial for the transfer of knowledge and expertise. Furthermore, cross-border collaboration in sharing data and experiences can accelerate the spread of proven solutions. With this collaborative approach, we can build a global network for AI applications in education that brings tangible benefits to underserved communities (Gaube et al., 2024; Veseli, 2024).

Finally, AI implementation needs to be accompanied by a system of ongoing feedback and evaluation. AI implementation is not a one-time activity, but rather a process that must be continuously updated and adapted. Teachers, students, and the community must be involved in providing feedback on the effectiveness of the system. Evaluation should focus not only on academic outcomes but also on long-term social impacts, such as improved digital literacy, job skills, and community participation. With regular evaluation and updates, AI can be continuously developed to remain relevant and beneficial to society in the future (von Bahr et al., 2025; Yockel et al., 2025).

11. CONCLUSION

Artificial intelligence (AI) has enormous potential to transform education, especially in underserved areas that still face numerous challenges. Issues such as limited infrastructure, a shortage of teachers, and limited access to learning resources often prevent students in these areas from receiving a proper education. The presence of AI can help address this gap by providing a more personalized, flexible, and accessible learning experience. Various technologies, such as adaptive learning systems and AI-based virtual assistants, have proven capable of providing learning support tailored to each student's needs.

Despite the significant potential, implementing AI in underserved areas is challenging. The main challenge is the lack of supporting infrastructure such as electricity, stable internet connections, and affordable technological devices. Therefore, collaboration between various parties is needed to expand technology access in these areas. Solutions such as solar-powered devices, affordable internet connections, or AI platforms that can be used offline could be a concrete step. Furthermore, teacher training must be a priority so they can use this technology effectively and stay ahead of the times.

Ethical aspects must also be considered in the application of AI in education. The use of AI must be done responsibly, especially regarding data privacy, potential algorithmic bias, and the role of humans in the learning process. AI should be used to assist teachers, not replace them. This technology must be transparent, fair, and easily explainable to users. Furthermore, AI implementation must be inclusive, ensuring that all students—including those with disabilities or from marginalized groups—have equal learning opportunities.

The future of AI in underserved communities looks promising, but its successful implementation requires long-term commitment and collaboration from various parties. Governments, non-governmental organizations, the private sector, and local communities need to work together to ensure equitable access to this technology. Global policies and cooperation are also needed to share knowledge, resources, and best practices in AI applications. With strong collaboration, AI can not only improve the quality of education but also contribute to the social and economic development of communities.

For the benefits of AI to be truly realized, continuous evaluation and improvement are necessary. Any AI tool or system should be regularly assessed to ensure its effectiveness in improving learning outcomes. Input from teachers, students, and the community is crucial to refining this technology to suit their needs. As the world of education is constantly changing, AI must also continually adapt to remain relevant and beneficial.

Ultimately, AI can be a crucial tool for significant change in underserved communities. This technology opens up new opportunities for more personalized learning, better healthcare, and broader access to information. However, for AI to truly benefit, its implementation must be done wisely and responsibly, with adequate infrastructure, appropriate training, and clear ethical guidelines. With these steps, AI can help create a more equitable and inclusive education system for all students, wherever they are.

REFERENCES

Acosta, J. A. (2025). Perspective: Advancing public health education by embedding AI literacy. *Frontiers in Digital Health, 7*, 1584883. Advance online publication. DOI: 10.3389/fdgth.2025.1584883 PMID: 40741324

Akanfe, O., Bhatt, P., & Lawong, D. A. (2025). Technology Advancements Shaping the Financial Inclusion Landscape: Present Interventions, Emergence of Artificial Intelligence and Future Directions. *Information Systems Frontiers, 27*(5), 2189–2212. Advance online publication. DOI: 10.1007/s10796-025-10597-z

Andri Nirwana, A. N., Rifai, A., Ali, M., Ali Mustofa, T., Nur Vambudi, V., Nur Rochim Maksum, M., & Umar Budihargo, M. (2025). SWOT Analysis of AI Integration in Islamic Education: Cognitive, Affective, and Psychomotor Impacts. *Qubahan Academic Journal, 5*(1), 476–503. DOI: 10.48161/qaj.v5n1a1498

Asokan, P., Truong, T. T., Pham, D. S., Chan, K. Y., Soon, S., Maiorana, A., & Hollingsworth, C. (2025). Towards AI-Based Strep Throat Detection and Interpretation for Remote Australian Indigenous Communities. *Sensors (Basel), 25*(18), 5636. Advance online publication. DOI: 10.3390/s25185636 PMID: 41012875

Cinar, A. B., & Bilodeau, S. (2024). Incorporating AI into the Inner Circle of Emotional Intelligence for Sustainability. *Sustainability (Basel), 16*(15), 6648. Advance online publication. DOI: 10.3390/su16156648

Ganju, A., Satyan, S., Tanna, V., & Menezes, S. R. (2021). AI for Improving Children's Health: A Community Case Study. *Frontiers in Artificial Intelligence, 3*, 544972. Advance online publication. DOI: 10.3389/frai.2020.544972 PMID: 33733204

Garcia-Saiso, S., Marti, M., Pesce, K., Luciani, S., Mujica, O., Hennis, A., & D'Agostino, M. (2024). Artificial Intelligence as a Potential Catalyst to a More Equitable Cancer Care. *JMIR Cancer, 10*, e57276. Advance online publication. DOI: 10.2196/57276 PMID: 39133537

Gaube, S., Biebl, I., Engelmann, M. K. M., Kleine, A. K., & Lermer, E. (2024). Comparing preferences for skin cancer screening: AI-enabled app vs dermatologist. *Social Science & Medicine, 349*, 116871. Advance online publication. DOI: 10.1016/j.socscimed.2024.116871 PMID: 38640741

Grenon, S., Hoang, K. N., Luo, S., & Koch, A. (2025). Adolescent mental health in rural settings: The role of artificial intelligence and community engagement. *Frontiers in Public Health, 13*, 1643466. Advance online publication. DOI: 10.3389/fpubh.2025.1643466 PMID: 40977788

Hendricks-Sturrup, R., Simmons, M., Anders, S., Aneni, K., Clayton, E. W., Coco, J., Collins, B., Heitman, E., Hussain, S., Joshi, K., Lemieux, J., Novak, L. L., Rubin, D. J., Shanker, A., Washington, T., Waters, G., Harris, J. W., Yin, R., Wagner, T., & Malin, B. (2023). Developing Ethics and Equity Principles, Terms, and Engagement Tools to Advance Health Equity and Researcher Diversity in AI and Machine Learning: Modified Delphi Approach. *JMIR AI, 2*(1), e52888. Advance online publication. DOI: 10.2196/52888 PMID: 38875540

Huang, F., Lin, X., Hong, Y., Li, Y., Li, Y., Chen, W. T., & Chen, W. (2025). The feasibility and cost-effectiveness of implementing mobile low-dose computed tomography with an AI-based diagnostic system in underserved populations. *BMC Cancer, 25*(1), 345. Advance online publication. DOI: 10.1186/s12885-025-13710-2 PMID: 40001094

Kong, J. D., Akpudo, U. E., Effoduh, J. O., & Bragazzi, N. L. (2023). Leveraging Responsible, Explainable, and Local Artificial Intelligence Solutions for Clinical Public Health in the Global South. *Healthcare (Basel), 11*(4), 457. Advance online publication. DOI: 10.3390/healthcare11040457 PMID: 36832991

Kumar, D., Malin, B. A., Vishwanatha, J. K., Wu, L., & Hedges, J. R. (2024). AI in Biomedicine—A Forward-Looking Perspective on Health Equity. *International Journal of Environmental Research and Public Health, 21*(12), 1642. Advance online publication. DOI: 10.3390/ijerph21121642 PMID: 39767481

Liew, T. M., Foo, J. Y. H., Yang, H., Tay, S. Y., Koay, W. I., Yip, K. F., Ting, S. K. S., Narasimhalu, K., Li, W., Tan, C., Luo, D., Chong, R., Shong, R., Sia, C., Koh, G. C. H., & Thumboo, J. (2025). PENSIEVE-AI a brief cognitive test to detect cognitive impairment across diverse literacy. *Nature Communications, 16*(1), 2847. Advance online publication. DOI: 10.1038/s41467-025-58201-x PMID: 40122854

Ma, J. S., O'Riordan, M., Mazzer, K., Batterham, P. J., Bradford, S., Kõlves, K., Titov, N., Klein, B., & Rickwood, D. J. (2022). Consumer Perspectives on the Use of Artificial Intelligence Technology and Automation in Crisis Support Services: Mixed Methods Study. *JMIR Human Factors, 9*(3), e34514. Advance online publication. DOI: 10.2196/34514 PMID: 35930334

Quishpe-Quishpe, L., Acosta-Vargas, I., Rodríguez-Rojas, L., Medina-Arias, J., Coronel-Navarro, D. A., Torres-Gutiérrez, R., & Acosta-Vargas, P. (2025). Impact of a Contextualized AI and Entrepreneurship-Based Training Program on Teacher Learning in the Ecuadorian Amazon. *Sustainability (Basel), 17*(19), 8850. DOI: 10.3390/su17198850

Sikalidis, A. K., Kristo, A. S., Reaves, S. K., Kurfess, F. J., DeLay, A. M., Vasilaky, K., & Donegan, L. (2022). Capacity Strengthening Undertaking—Farm Organized Response of Workers against Risk for Diabetes: (C.S.U.—F.O.R.W.A.R.D. with Cal Poly)—A Concept Approach to Tackling Diabetes in Vulnerable and Underserved Farmworkers in California. *Sensors (Basel)*, *22*(21), 8299. Advance online publication. DOI: 10.3390/s22218299 PMID: 36365994

Veseli, E. (2024). Revolutionizing dentistry: The integration of artificial intelligence and robotics. *Khyber Medical University Journal*, *16*(4), 352–353. DOI: 10.35845/kmuj.2024.23729

von Bahr, J., Suutala, A., Kucukel, H., Kaingu, H., Kinyua, F., Muinde, M., Osundwa, K., Ronald, W., Muinde, J., Ngasala, B., Lundin, M., Mårtensson, A., Linder, N., & Lundin, J. (2025). AI-supported versus manual microscopy of Kato-Katz smears for diagnosis of soil-transmitted helminth infections in a primary healthcare setting. *Scientific Reports*, *15*(1), 20332. Advance online publication. DOI: 10.1038/s41598-025-07309-7 PMID: 40579399

Yockel, M. R., Sleiman, M. M.Jr, Doherty, H., Adams, R., Davis, K. M., Groninger, H., Sharkey, C., Biel, M. G., Statman, M. R., & Tercyak, K. P. (2025). Mental Health Professionals' Views on Artificial Intelligence as an Aide for Children Anticipating or Suffering the Loss of a Parent to Cancer: Helpful or Harmful? *Children (Basel, Switzerland)*, *12*(6), 763. Advance online publication. DOI: 10.3390/children12060763 PMID: 40564721

Compilation of References

Abbasi, M. A., Ihantola, P., Mikkonen, T., & Mäkitalo, N. (2026). Reconsidering Requirements Engineering: Human–AI Collaboration in AI-Native Software Development. *Lecture Notes in Computer Science, 16081 LNCS*, 164–180. DOI: 10.1007/978-3-032-04190-6_11

Abdal, Y. M. (2025). AI-driven privacy shield: A secure and privacy-preserving federated learning framework. *International Journal of Computational and Electronics Aspects in Engineering*, *6*(3), 180–189. DOI: 10.26706/ijceae.6.3.20250608

Aboudahr, S. M. F. M., Benlahcene, A., & Govindarajoo, M. V. (2025). Ethical horizons in AI-driven educational research. *In Advances in computational intelligence and robotics book series* (pp. 289–304). DOI: 10.4018/979-8-3693-7332-3.ch018

Acosta, J. A. (2025). Perspective: Advancing public health education by embedding AI literacy. *Frontiers in Digital Health*, *7*, 1584883. Advance online publication. DOI: 10.3389/fdgth.2025.1584883 PMID: 40741324

Adel, A., Ahsan, A., & Davison, C. (2024). ChatGPT promises and challenges in education: Computational and ethical perspectives. *Education Sciences*, *14*(8), 814. DOI: 10.3390/educsci14080814

Adewale, M. D., Azeta, A., Abayomi-Alli, A., & Sambo-Magaji, A. (2024). Impact of artificial intelligence adoption on students' academic performance in open and distance learning: A systematic literature review. *Heliyon*, *10*(22), e40025. Advance online publication. DOI: 10.1016/j.heliyon.2024.e40025 PMID: 39605813

Adiyono, A., Rahayu, A. P., Besari, A., Wahib, A., Arianti, S., & Kojin, K. (2025, May). AI-Driven Personalized Learning Paths: Enhancing Student Engagement Through Gamification and Interdisciplinary Integration. In *2025 5th International Conference on Artificial Intelligence and Education (ICAIE)* (pp. 604-612). IEEE. DOI: 10.1109/ICAIE64856.2025.11158040

Adiyono, A., Suwartono, T., Nurhayati, S., Dalimarta, F. F., & Wijayanti, O. (2025). Impact of artificial intelligence on student reliance for exam answers: A case study in IRCT Indonesia. *International Journal of Learning. Teaching and Educational Research, 24*(3), 519–544. DOI: 10.26803/ijlter.24.3.22

Agarwal, B., Urlings, C., Lankveld, G., & Klemke, R. (2024). Identifying the ethical values and norms of artificial intelligence in education: a systematic literature review. DOI: 10.35542/osf.io/e7t3f

Akanfe, O., Bhatt, P., & Lawong, D. A. (2025). Technology Advancements Shaping the Financial Inclusion Landscape: Present Interventions, Emergence of Artificial Intelligence and Future Directions. *Information Systems Frontiers, 27*(5), 2189–2212. Advance online publication. DOI: 10.1007/s10796-025-10597-z

Akgun, S., & Greenhow, C. (2022). Artificial intelligence in education: Addressing ethical challenges in K-12 settings. *AI and Ethics, 2*(3), 431–440. DOI: 10.1007/s43681-021-00096-7 PMID: 34790956

Alfredo, R., Echeverria, V., Jin, Y., Yan, L., Swiecki, Z., Gašević, D., & Martinez-Maldonado, R. (2024). Human-centred learning analytics and AI in education: A systematic literature review. *Computers and Education: Artificial Intelligence, 6*, 100215. Advance online publication. DOI: 10.1016/j.caeai.2024.100215

Ali, H., Prompiengchai, S., & Joordens, S. (2024). Educational technology procurement at Canadian colleges and universities: An environmental scan. *Standards, 4*(1), 1–24. DOI: 10.3390/standards4010001

Alrayes, A., Henari, T., & Ahmed, D. (2024). ChatGPT in education – understanding the Bahraini academics perspective. *Electronic Journal of e-Learning, 22*(2), 112–134. DOI: 10.34190/ejel.22.2.3250

Amabile, T. M. (2020). Creativity, artificial intelligence, and a world of surprises. *Academy of Management Discoveries, 6*(3), 351–354. DOI: 10.5465/amd.2020.0056

Amichai-Hamburger, Y., & Fine, A. (2019). The role of technology in volunteering and civic engagement. *Computers in Human Behavior, 93*, 24–30. DOI: 10.1016/j.chb.2018.12.005

Amigud, A., & Pell, D. J. (2025). Responsible and Ethical Use of AI in Education: Are We Forcing a Square Peg into a Round Hole? *WORLD (Oakland, Calif.), 6*(2), 81. DOI: 10.3390/world6020081

Ananny, M., & Crawford, K. (2018). Seeing without knowing: Limitations of the transparency ideal. *New Media & Society, 20*(3), 973–989. DOI: 10.1177/1461444816676645

Anderson, J. R., Reder, L. M., & Simon, H. A. (1996). Situated Learning and Education. *Educational Researcher*, *25*(4), 5–11. DOI: 10.3102/0013189X025004005

Andri Nirwana, A. N., Rifai, A., Ali, M., Ali Mustofa, T., Nur Vambudi, V., Nur Rochim Maksum, M., & Umar Budihargo, M. (2025). SWOT Analysis of AI Integration in Islamic Education: Cognitive, Affective, and Psychomotor Impacts. *Qubahan Academic Journal*, *5*(1), 476–503. DOI: 10.48161/qaj.v5n1a1498

Anuradha, P., Arunbala, C., Harita, U., Valarmathi, K., Thenappan, S., & Saravanan, V. (2025). Federated learning for AI-powered privacy in distributed systems. *International Journal of Computational and Experimental Science and Engineering*, *11*(3). Advance online publication. DOI: 10.22399/ijcesen.2505

Apfelbacher, T., Koçman, S., Prokosch, H., & Christoph, J. (2024). A governance framework for the implementation and operation of AI applications in a university hospital.. DOI: 10.3233/SHTI240527

Ardelean, T.-K., & Veres, E. (2023). Students' perceptions of artificial intelligence in higher education. In *Proceedings of the 10th SWS International Scientific Conference on Social Sciences - ISCSS 2023* (pp. 1–11). https://doi.org/DOI: 10.35603/sws.iscss.2023/s08.38

Asha, S., & Kumar, S. (2021). Predictive analytics in higher education: Applications, challenges, and future directions. *Journal of Applied Research in Higher Education*, *13*(4), 1104–1118.

Asokan, P., Truong, T. T., Pham, D. S., Chan, K. Y., Soon, S., Maiorana, A., & Hollingsworth, C. (2025). Towards AI-Based Strep Throat Detection and Interpretation for Remote Australian Indigenous Communities. *Sensors (Basel)*, *25*(18), 5636. Advance online publication. DOI: 10.3390/s25185636 PMID: 41012875

Azzam, A., & Charles, T. (2025). K-12 STEM Teachers' Experiences with Artificial Intelligence. *TEM Journal*, *14*(1), 463. https://doi.org/DOI: 10.18421/TEM141-41

Baker, R. S. (2019). Challenges for the future of educational data mining: The Baker learning analytics prizes. *Journal of Educational Data Mining*, *11*(1), 1–17. DOI: 10.5281/zenodo.3554745

Baker, R. S., & Hawn, A. (2021). Algorithmic bias in education. *International Journal of Artificial Intelligence in Education*, *31*(2), 1–27. DOI: 10.1007/s40593-021-00240-9

Baker, R. S., & Siemens, G. (2014). Educational data mining and learning analytics. In Sawyer, R. K. (Ed.), *The Cambridge handbook of the learning sciences* (2nd ed., pp. 253–272). Cambridge University Press., DOI: 10.1017/CBO9781139519526.016

Balta, N. (2023). Ethical considerations in using AI in educational research., 2(1), 14205. DOI: 10.51853/jorids/14205

Barocas, S., Hardt, M., & Narayanan, A. (2019). Fairness and machine learning. fairmlbook.org.

Barocas, S., Hardt, M., & Narayanan, A. (2019). *Fairness and machine learning*. FairML Book.

Batool, A., Zowghi, D., & Bano, M. (2024). Ai governance: a systematic literature review. DOI: 10.21203/rs.3.rs-4784792/v1

Bayer, V., Mulholland, P., Buckingham Shum, S., & Fernández, M. (2023). Co-creating an equality, diversity and inclusion learning analytics dashboard for addressing awarding gaps in higher education. *British Journal of Educational Technology*, *54*(5), 1631–1650. DOI: 10.1111/bjet.13509

Bender, E. M., Gebru, T., McMillan-Major, A., & Shmitchell, S. (2021). On the Dangers of Stochastic Parrots: Can Language Models Be Too Big? In *Proceedings of the 2021 ACM Conference on Fairness, Accountability, and Transparency (FAccT'21)* (pp. 610-623). Association for Computing Machinery. https://doi.org/ DOI: 10.1145/3442188.3445922

Benevolat, M., & Hustinx, L. (2020). Digital transformations in volunteering: Ethical and governance implications. *Voluntas*, *31*(5), 1040–1053. DOI: 10.1007/s11266-020-00253-6

Benjamin, R. (2019). *Race after technology: Abolitionist tools for the new Jim code*. Polity Press.

Benkler, Y., Faris, R., & Roberts, H. (2021). *Network propaganda: Manipulation, disinformation, and radicalization in American politics*. Oxford University Press.

Bennett, C. J., & Raab, C. D. (2020). *The governance of privacy: Policy instruments in global perspective* (2nd ed.). MIT Press.

Bird, K. A., Castleman, B. L., & Song, Y. (2025). Are algorithms biased in education? Exploring racial bias in predicting community college student success. *Journal of Policy Analysis and Management*, *44*(2), 379–402. DOI: 10.1002/pam.22569

Boulhrir, T., & Hamash, M. (2025). Unpacking artificial intelligence in elementary education: A comprehensive thematic analysis systematic review. Computers and *Education. Artificial Intelligence*, *9*, 100442. DOI: 10.1016/j.caeai.2025.100442

Bovens, M. (2007). Analysing and assessing accountability: A conceptual framework. *European Law Journal*, *13*(4), 447–468. DOI: 10.1111/j.1468-0386.2007.00378.x

Bryson, J. J., Diamantis, M. E., & Grant, T. D. (2019). Of, for, and by the people: The legal lacuna of synthetic persons. *Artificial Intelligence and Law*, *27*(1), 1–17. DOI: 10.1007/s10506-018-9234-9

Buabbas, A., Miskin, B., Ayed, A., Alnaqi, A., Shehab, A., & Safar, M. (2022). Investigating students' perceptions towards artificial intelligence in medical education. DOI: 10.21203/rs.3.rs-1805527/v1

Bulathwela, S., Pérez-Ortiz, M., Holloway, C., Cukurova, M., & Shawe-Taylor, J. (2024). Artificial intelligence alone will not democratise education: On educational inequality, techno-solutionism and inclusive tools. *Sustainability (Basel)*, *16*(2), 781. DOI: 10.3390/su16020781

Buolamwini, J., & Gebru, T. (2018). Gender shades: Intersectional accuracy disparities in commercial gender classification. In Friedler, S. A., & Wilson, C. (Eds.), *Proceedings of the 1st Conference on Fairness, Accountability and Transparency* (Vol. 81, pp. 77–91). PMLR.

Burkett, J. R. (2025). Artificial intelligence and school leadership: Using ethical leadership as a framework for monitoring the use of AI in schools. In *Responsible AI Integration in Education* (pp. 181–209). DOI: 10.4018/979-8-3373-6007-2.ch006

Burrell, J. (2016). How the Machine "thinks": Understanding Opacity in Machine Learning Algorithms. *Big Data & Society*, *3*(1), 1–12. DOI: 10.1177/2053951715622512

Castro, G., Chiappe, A., Rodriguez, D., & Sepúlveda, F. (2024). Harnessing ai for education 4.0: drivers of personalized learning. The Electronic Journal of E-Learning, 22(5), 01-14. DOI: 10.34190/ejel.22.5.3467

Chai, F., Ma, J., Wang, Y., Zhu, J., & Han, T. (2024). Grading by AI makes me feel fairer? how different evaluators affect college students' perception of fairness. *Frontiers in Psychology*, *15*, 1221177. Advance online publication. DOI: 10.3389/fpsyg.2024.1221177 PMID: 38371704

Chan, C. K. Y. (2023). A comprehensive AI policy education framework for university teaching and learning. *International Journal of Educational Technology in Higher Education*, *20*(1), 38. Advance online publication. DOI: 10.1186/s41239-023-00408-3

Charles, T. (2025). AI in Professional Development for English Language Teachers. In Ali, M., Fazal, S., & Ayyaz, S. (Eds.), *AI Applications for English Language Learning* (pp. 73–92). IGI Global Scientific Publishing., DOI: 10.4018/979-8-3693-9077-1.ch004

Charles, T., & Alshamsi, A. (2025). Navigating Challenges in Technology Integration for Inclusive Classrooms: Insights for Pre-Service Teachers. In Ajani, O. (Ed.), *Empowering Pre-Service Teachers to Enhance Inclusive Education Through Technology* (pp. 87–126). IGI Global Scientific Publishing., DOI: 10.4018/979-8-3693-8759-7.ch004

Charles, T., & Papadaki, M. (2025). Ethical Leadership in Technology Integration and Digital Education. In Soles, B., & Meyerott, T. (Eds.), *Diverse Leadership Perspectives in Education: From K-12 to Higher Education* (pp. 437–454). IGI Global Scientific Publishing., DOI: 10.4018/979-8-3693-6115-3.ch016

Chaudhry, A., & Kazim, E. (2022). Artificial intelligence in education: Ethical and administrative challenges. *AI & Society*, *37*(2), 451–463.

Chen, L., Chen, P., & Lin, Z. (2020). Artificial intelligence in education: A review. *IEEE Access : Practical Innovations, Open Solutions*, *8*, 75264–75278. DOI: 10.1109/ACCESS.2020.2988510

Chen, X., Zou, D., Xie, H., Cheng, G., & Liu, C. (2022). Two decades of artificial intelligence in education: Contributors, collaborations, research topics, challenges, and future directions. *Journal of Educational Technology & Society*, *25*(1), 28–47. DOI: 10.30191/ETS.202201_25(1).0003

Chouhan, D., & Shilpi, S.Dr.Neha ChouhanDr. Sonam Shilpi. (2023). A study on artificial intelligence in education. *International Journal of Engineering Technology and Management Sciences*, *7*(1), 449–456. DOI: 10.46647/ijetms.2023.v07i01.063

Cinar, A. B., & Bilodeau, S. (2024). Incorporating AI into the Inner Circle of Emotional Intelligence for Sustainability. *Sustainability (Basel)*, *16*(15), 6648. Advance online publication. DOI: 10.3390/su16156648

Coghlan, S., Miller, T., & Paterson, J. (2021). Good proctor or "big brother"? Ethics of online exam supervision technologies. *Philosophy & Technology*, *34*(4), 1581–1606. DOI: 10.1007/s13347-021-00476-1 PMID: 34485025

Cooper, K., & Geller, M. R. (2025). Advancing personalized federated learning: Integrative approaches with AI for enhanced privacy and customization. https://doi .org//arxiv.2501.18174</prpt>DOI: 10.48550

Craft, A. (2023). Creativity and education futures in the age of artificial intelligence. *Thinking Skills and Creativity*, *47*, 101229. DOI: 10.1016/j.tsc.2022.101229

Crawford, K. (2021). *Atlas of AI: Power, politics, and the planetary costs of artificial intelligence*. Yale University Press.

Daniel, B. K. (2015). Big data and analytics in higher education: Opportunities and challenges. *British Journal of Educational Technology, 46*(5), 904–920. DOI: 10.1111/bjet.12230

DataKind. (2022). *Data science for social good: Annual impact report.* DataKind. https://www.datakind.org

De Corte, E. (2012). Constructive, Self-Regulated, Situated, and Collaborative Learning: An Approach for the Acquisition of Adaptive Competence. *Journal of Education, 192*(2-3), 33–47. DOI: 10.1177/0022057412192002-307

Deckker, & Sumanasekara, S. (2025). Student-centric ethical frameworks for AI-driven education: Participatory consent and data ownership in a global perspective. *International Journal of Science and Research Archive, 15*(3), 1491–1503. DOI: 10.30574/ijsra.2025.15.3.1920

Devi, V. A., & Revathi, K. (2016). A Brief Review of Literature on Immediate Feedback Studies in CALL. *Rupkatha Journal on Interdisciplinary Studies in Humanities, 8*(3), 262–268. DOI: 10.21659/rupkatha.v8n3.27

Dhiman, T., Chauhan, V., Kumar, A., Vasantha, M., & Kumar, A. (2025). Ethical crossroads: Navigating data privacy, bias, accountability and sustainability in AI-driven education. *1*(3), 69–77. DOI: 10.47760/OAJMR.2025.v01i03.007

Diakopoulos, N. (2016). Accountability in algorithmic decision making. *Communications of the ACM, 59*(2), 56–62. DOI: 10.1145/2844110

Doshi-Velez, F., & Kim, B. (2017). Towards a rigorous science of interpretable machine learning. *arXiv preprint arXiv:1702.08608.*

EDPB. (2020). *Guidelines 05/2020 on consent under Regulation 2016/679.* European Data Protection Board.

Efstratopoulou, M., Argyriadi, A., & Argyriadis, A. (2025). AI in Learning, Educational Leadership, and Special Education: Innovations and Ethical Dilemmas. In *AI in Learning, Educational Leadership, and Special Education: Innovations and Ethical Dilemmas*. DOI: 10.4018/979-8-3373-5550-4

Emon, M. M. H., & Chowdhury, M. S. A. (2025). Safeguarding student data. *In Advances in computational intelligence and robotics book series* (pp. 191–228). DOI: 10.4018/979-8-3373-3316-8.ch008

Eubanks, V. (2018). *Automating inequality: How high-tech tools profile, police, and punish the poor.* St. Martin's Press.

European Union. (2016). *Regulation (EU) 2016/679 of the European Parliament and of the Council (General Data Protection Regulation).*

European Union. (2018). General Data Protection Regulation (GDPR). Official Journal of the European Union.

European Union. (2024). *Artificial Intelligence Act: Regulation (EU) 2024/1689.*

Fachrurrazy, M., Beddu, R., Efendi, E., Firmansyah, F., Jamaluddin, F., & Siliwadi, D. N. (2025). AI policy framework in education for advancing society 5.0 with safe AI implementation. *In Advances in computational intelligence and robotics book series* (pp. 165–196). DOI: 10.4018/979-8-3373-5781-2.ch007

Fares, N. Y., & Jammal, M. (2024). Decoding Justice: The Synergy of Artificial Intelligence and Machine Learning in the Legal Landscape. *2024 IEEE Global Conference on Artificial Intelligence and Internet of Things, GCAIoT 2024.* DOI: 10.1109/GCAIoT63427.2024.10833589

Federal Trade Commission. (2013). *Children's Online Privacy Protection Rule, 16 C.F.R. Part 312.*

Ferguson, R. (2019). Ethical challenges for learning analytics. *Journal of Learning Analytics*, *6*(3), 25–30. DOI: 10.18608/jla.2019.63.5

Fiske, A., Henningsen, P., & Buyx, A. (2019). Your robot therapist will see you now: Ethical implications of embodied artificial intelligence in psychiatry, psychology, and psychotherapy. *Journal of Medical Internet Research*, *21*(5), e13216. DOI: 10.2196/13216 PMID: 31094356

Floridi, L., & Cowls, J. (2021). A unified framework of five principles for AI in society. *Harvard Data Science Review*, *1*(1). Advance online publication. DOI: 10.1162/99608f92.8cd550d1

Floridi, L., Cowls, J., Beltrametti, M., Chatila, R., Chazerand, P., Dignum, V., Luetge, C., Madelin, R., Pagallo, U., Rossi, F., Schafer, B., Valcke, P., & Vayena, E. (2018). AI4People—An ethical framework for a good AI society. *Minds and Machines*, *28*(4), 689–707. DOI: 10.1007/s11023-018-9482-5 PMID: 30930541

Fricker, M. (2007). Epistemic Injustice: Power and the Ethics of Knowing. In academic.oup.com. Oxford University Press.

Friedman, B., & Nissenbaum, H. (1996). Bias in computer systems. *ACM Transactions on Information Systems*, *14*(3), 330–347. DOI: 10.1145/230538.230561

Gaisie, O., Owusu-Boateng, O., Yidana, I., & Ghansah, B. (2025). *Ethical considerations and data privacy in artificial intelligence.*, DOI: 10.70593/978-93-49307-53-7_5

Ganju, A., Satyan, S., Tanna, V., & Menezes, S. R. (2021). AI for Improving Children's Health: A Community Case Study. *Frontiers in Artificial Intelligence, 3*, 544972. Advance online publication. DOI: 10.3389/frai.2020.544972 PMID: 33733204

García-Peñalvo, J., Alier, M., Pereira, J., & Casany Guerrero, M. J. (2024). Safe, transparent, and ethical artificial intelligence. *IJERI: International Journal of Educational Research and Innovation*, (22), 1–21. DOI: 10.46661/ijeri.11036

Garcia-Saiso, S., Marti, M., Pesce, K., Luciani, S., Mujica, O., Hennis, A., & D'Agostino, M. (2024). Artificial Intelligence as a Potential Catalyst to a More Equitable Cancer Care. *JMIR Cancer, 10*, e57276. Advance online publication. DOI: 10.2196/57276 PMID: 39133537

Garg, S., & Sharma, S. (2020). Impact of artificial intelligence in special need education to promote inclusive pedagogy. *International Journal of Information and Education Technology (IJIET), 10*(7), 523–527. DOI: 10.18178/ijiet.2020.10.7.1418

Garzón, J., Patiño, E., & Marulanda, C. (2025). Systematic review of artificial intelligence in education: Trends, benefits, and challenges. *Multimodal Technologies and Interaction, 9*(8), 84. DOI: 10.3390/mti9080084

Gašević, D., Tsai, Y.-S., & Drachsler, H. (2022). Learning analytics in higher education: Stakeholders, strategy and scale. *The Internet and Higher Education, 52*, 100833. Advance online publication. DOI: 10.1016/j.iheduc.2021.100833

Gaube, S., Biebl, I., Engelmann, M. K. M., Kleine, A. K., & Lermer, E. (2024). Comparing preferences for skin cancer screening: AI-enabled app vs dermatologist. *Social Science & Medicine, 349*, 116871. Advance online publication. DOI: 10.1016/j.socscimed.2024.116871 PMID: 38640741

Gawande, V., & Al-Senaidi, S. (2015). Situated Learning: Learning in a Contextual Environment. *International Journal of Computing Academic Research, 4*(4), 207–213. https://meacse.org/ijcar/archives/70.pdf

George, B., & Wooden, O. (2023). Managing the strategic transformation of higher education through artificial intelligence. *Administrative Sciences, 13*(9), 196. DOI: 10.3390/admsci13090196

George, S., Michel, C., & Ollagnier-Beldame, M. (2015). Favouring reflexivity in technology-enhanced learning systems: Towards smart uses of traces. *Interactive Learning Environments, 24*(7), 1389–1407. DOI: 10.1080/10494820.2015.1016532

Ginsburg, J. C., & Budiardjo, L. A. (2019). Authors and machines. *Berkeley Technology Law Journal, 34*(2), 343–448.

Gloppen, K., McMorris, B., Gower, A., & Eisenberg, M. (2018). Associations between bullying involvement, protective factors, and mental health among american indian youth. *The American Journal of Orthopsychiatry*, *88*(4), 413–421. DOI: 10.1037/ort0000284 PMID: 28816487

Grenon, S., Hoang, K. N., Luo, S., & Koch, A. (2025). Adolescent mental health in rural settings: The role of artificial intelligence and community engagement. *Frontiers in Public Health*, *13*, 1643466. Advance online publication. DOI: 10.3389/fpubh.2025.1643466 PMID: 40977788

Grüning, M., Henkenjohann, R., Fuchs, M., Dratsch, T., dos Santos, D. P., Kim, M., Matthies, P., Mukhopadhyay, A., & Trenz, M. (2025). The Influence of Artificial Intelligence Autonomy on Physicians Work Outcomes in Healthcare: A Lab-in-the-Field Experiment. *Proceedings of the Annual Hawaii International Conference on System Sciences*, 536–545. https://www.scopus.com/inward/record.uri?eid=2-s2.0-105005139802&partnerID=40&md5=85ef2c0aebd5f95291bbb638eaa59ec0

Guo, W., Liang, Z., Wang, C., Li, X., Hu, H., Chen, S., Yu, Q., & Zhao, Q. (2025). Student-AI collaborative creative Problem-Solving: The role of human agency. *Computers & Education*, *239*, 105433. Advance online publication. DOI: 10.1016/j.compedu.2025.105433

Hager, M. A., & Brudney, J. L. (2022). *The future of volunteer management: Technology, innovation, and engagement.* Springer.

Haidar, A. (2023). An Integrative Theoretical Framework for Responsible Artificial Intelligence. *International Journal of Digital Strategy, Governance, and Business Transformation*, *13*(1), 1–23. Advance online publication. DOI: 10.4018/IJDSGBT.334844

Haitsma, L., & Brink, B. (2025). From Human Intervention to Human Involvement: A Critical Examination of the Role of Humans in (Semi-)Automated Administrative Decision-Making. *Digital Government: Research and Practice*, *6*(3), 1–17. Advance online publication. DOI: 10.1145/3716173

Han, S., & Nikou, S., & Ayele, holmW. (2023). Digital proctoring in higher education: A systematic literature review. *International Journal of Educational Management.* Advance online publication. DOI: 10.1108/IJEM-12-2022-0522

Hasan, M. (2025). Federated learning models for privacy-preserving AI in enterprise decision systems. *5*(3), 238–269. DOI: 10.63125/ry033286

Hendricks-Sturrup, R., Simmons, M., Anders, S., Aneni, K., Clayton, E. W., Coco, J., Collins, B., Heitman, E., Hussain, S., Joshi, K., Lemieux, J., Novak, L. L., Rubin, D. J., Shanker, A., Washington, T., Waters, G., Harris, J. W., Yin, R., Wagner, T., & Malin, B. (2023). Developing Ethics and Equity Principles, Terms, and Engagement Tools to Advance Health Equity and Researcher Diversity in AI and Machine Learning: Modified Delphi Approach. *JMIR AI*, *2*(1), e52888. Advance online publication. DOI: 10.2196/52888 PMID: 38875540

Henrickson, L., & Meier, S. (2023). Hybrid creativity: Human–AI collaboration in creative practice. *Creativity Research Journal*, *35*(2), 187–199. DOI: 10.1080/10400419.2023.2178421

Holmes, W., Bialik, M., & Fadel, C. (2019). Artificial intelligence in education: Promise and implications for teaching and learning. Center for Curriculum Redesign., 10.1794293700.

Holmes, W., Bialik, M., & Fadel, C. (2019). *Artificial intelligence in education: Promises and implications for teaching and learning*. Center for Curriculum Redesign.

Holmes, W., Bialik, M., & Fadel, C. (2023). Artificial intelligence in education. In *Data ethics: Building trust: How digital technologies can serve humanity* (pp. 621–653). Globethics Publications., DOI: 10.58863/20.500.12424/4276068

Holmes, W., Iniesto, F., Anastopoulou, S., & Boticario, J. (2023). Stakeholder perspectives on the ethics of ai in distance-based higher education. *International Review of Research in Open and Distance Learning*, *24*(2), 96–117. DOI: 10.19173/irrodl.v24i2.6089

Holmes, W., & Porayska-Pomsta, K. (2022). *The Ethics of Artificial Intelligence in Education*. Taylor & Francis. DOI: 10.4324/9780429329067

Holmes, W., Porayska-Pomsta, K., Holstein, K., Sutherland, E., Baker, T., Buckingham Shum, S., & Koedinger, K. R. (2022). Ethics of AI in education: Towards a community-wide framework. *International Journal of Artificial Intelligence in Education*, *32*(2), 504–526. DOI: 10.1007/s40593-021-00239-1

Holmes, W., & Tuomi, I. (2022). State of the art and practice in AI in education. *International Journal of Artificial Intelligence in Education*, *32*(4), 1–25. DOI: 10.1007/s40593-022-00291-9

Hridi, P., Sahay, R. R., Hosseinalipour, S., & Akram, B. (2024). Revolutionizing AI-assisted education with federated learning: A pathway to distributed, privacy-preserving, and debiased learning ecosystems. DOI: 10.1609/aaaiss.v3i1.31217

Huang, F., Lin, X., Hong, Y., Li, Y., Li, Y., Chen, W. T., & Chen, W. (2025). The feasibility and cost-effectiveness of implementing mobile low-dose computed tomography with an AI-based diagnostic system in underserved populations. *BMC Cancer, 25*(1), 345. Advance online publication. DOI: 10.1186/s12885-025-13710-2 PMID: 40001094

Idowu, J. A. (2024). Debiasing education algorithms. *International Journal of Artificial Intelligence in Education, 34*(4), 1510–1540. DOI: 10.1007/s40593-023-00389-4

Ihekweazu, B., Zhou, B., & Adelowo, E. (2024). Ethics-driven education: Integrating AI responsibly for academic excellence. *Information Systems Education Journal, 22*(3), 36–46. DOI: 10.62273/JWXX9525

Information Commissioner's Office. (2022). *Guidance on AI and data protection*. UK ICO.

Ismail, A. A. (2024). Protecting privacy in AI-enhanced education. *In Advances in educational technologies and instructional design book series* (pp. 117–142). DOI: 10.4018/979-8-3693-0884-4.ch006

Ismail, A. A., & Ahmad, J. A. S. (2024). Data privacy in AI-driven education. *In Advances in educational marketing, administration, and leadership book series* (pp. 223–252). DOI: 10.4018/979-8-3693-5443-8.ch008

Ivcevic, Z., & Grandinetti, A. (2024). Who benefits from AI-assisted creativity? Individual differences and creative confidence. *Psychology of Aesthetics, Creativity, and the Arts, 18*(1), 12–25. DOI: 10.1037/aca0000558

Jiang, R. (2022). How does artificial intelligence empower EFL teaching and learning nowadays? a review on artificial intelligence in the efl context. *Frontiers in Psychology, 13*, 1049401. Advance online publication. DOI: 10.3389/fpsyg.2022.1049401 PMID: 36467167

Jobin, A., Ienca, M., & Vayena, E. (2019). The global landscape of AI ethics guidelines. *Nature Machine Intelligence, 1*(9), 389–399. DOI: 10.1038/s42256-019-0088-2

Jose, D. (2024). Data privacy and security concerns in AI-integrated educational platforms. *Research and Management Chronicle, 5*(2), 87–91. DOI: 10.46632/rmc/5/2/19

Kadaruddin, K. (2023). Empowering education through generative AI: Innovative instructional strategies for tomorrow's learners. *International Journal of Business Law and Education, 4*(2), 618–625. DOI: 10.56442/ijble.v4i2.215

Kalita, E., Oyelere, S. S., Gaftandzhieva, S., Rajesh, K. N. V. P. S., Jagatheesaperumal, S. K., Mohamed, A., Elbarawy, Y. M., Desuky, A. S., Hussain, S., Cifci, M. A., Theodorou, P., Hilčenko, S., Hazarika, J., & Ali, T. (2025). Educational data mining: A 10-year review. *Discover Computing*, *28*(1), 81. Advance online publication. DOI: 10.1007/s10791-025-09589-z

Kallunki, V., Kinnunen, P., Pyörälä, E., Haarala-Muhonen, A., Katajavuori, N., & Myyry, L. (2024). Navigating the evolving landscape of teaching and learning: University faculty and staff perceptions of the artificial intelligence-altered terrain. *Education Sciences*, *14*(7), 727. DOI: 10.3390/educsci14070727

Kashefi, P., Kashefi, Y., & Mirsaraei, A. (2024). Shaping the future of ai: Balancing innovation and ethics in global regulation. *Uniform Law Review*, *29*(3), 524–548. DOI: 10.1093/ulr/unae040

Kayyali, M. (2025). Ethical implications of generative AI in education. *In Advances in computational intelligence and robotics book series* (pp. 185–218). DOI: 10.4018/979-8-3693-8744-3.ch008

Khalil, M., & Er, E. (2023). Will ChatGPT Get You Caught? Rethinking of Plagiarism Detection. In Zaphiris, P., & Ioannou, A. (Eds.), Lecture Notes in Computer Science: Vol. 14040. *Learning and Collaboration Technologies. HCII 2023*. Springer., DOI: 10.1007/978-3-031-34411-4_32

Khalil, M., Slade, S., & Prinsloo, P. (2024). Learning analytics in support of inclusiveness and disabled students: A systematic review. *Journal of Computing in Higher Education*, *36*(1), 202–219. DOI: 10.1007/s12528-023-09363-4 PMID: 37359042

Khor, E. T., How, Z. J., Koh, E., Looi, C. K., & Lok, C. (2025). Learning analytics techniques: An overview and future research possibilities. *International Journal of Information and Learning Technology*, *42*(3), 269–295. DOI: 10.1108/IJILT-02-2024-0020

Kim, J., & Park, H. (2023). Pedagogical mediation of AI tools and student creativity. *Computers & Education*, *190*, 104602. DOI: 10.1016/j.compedu.2022.104602

Knox, J. (2020). Artificial intelligence and education in china. *Learning, Media and Technology*, *45*(3), 1–14. DOI: 10.1080/17439884.2020.1754236

Kong, J. D., Akpudo, U. E., Effoduh, J. O., & Bragazzi, N. L. (2023). Leveraging Responsible, Explainable, and Local Artificial Intelligence Solutions for Clinical Public Health in the Global South. *Healthcare (Basel)*, *11*(4), 457. Advance online publication. DOI: 10.3390/healthcare11040457 PMID: 36832991

Kopzhasarova, M., & Kozhamzharova, D. (2025). Explainable AI (XAI): Techniques, applications, and challenges. *CEUR Workshop Proceedings, 3966*, •••. https://www.scopus.com/inward/record.uri?eid=2-s2.0-105006886912&partnerID=40&md5=4007adb38600ba88e07d459c1ef6a021

Kumar, D., Malin, B. A., Vishwanatha, J. K., Wu, L., & Hedges, J. R. (2024). AI in Biomedicine—A Forward-Looking Perspective on Health Equity. *International Journal of Environmental Research and Public Health, 21*(12), 1642. Advance online publication. DOI: 10.3390/ijerph21121642 PMID: 39767481

Kumar, S., & Singh, M. (2022). Ethical challenges of AI-driven education in India. *Journal of Educational Technology Systems, 50*(4), 475–492. DOI: 10.1177/00472395211063478

Kundu, S. (2025). Multi-brain federated learning for decentralized AI: Collaborative, privacy-preserving models across domains. *Indian Scientific Journal of Research in Engineering and Management, 9*(6), 1–8. DOI: 10.55041/IJSREM19060

Lee, H., & Lee, J. (2021). Applying artificial intelligence in physical education and future perspectives. *Sustainability (Basel), 13*(1), 351. DOI: 10.3390/su13010351

Liew, T. M., Foo, J. Y. H., Yang, H., Tay, S. Y., Koay, W. I., Yip, K. F., Ting, S. K. S., Narasimhalu, K., Li, W., Tan, C., Luo, D., Chong, R., Shong, R., Sia, C., Koh, G. C. H., & Thumboo, J. (2025). PENSIEVE-AI a brief cognitive test to detect cognitive impairment across diverse literacy. *Nature Communications, 16*(1), 2847. Advance online publication. DOI: 10.1038/s41467-025-58201-x PMID: 40122854

Lipton, Z. C. (2018). The mythos of model interpretability. *Communications of the ACM, 61*(10), 36–43. DOI: 10.1145/3233231

Liu, M. (2023). Exploring the application of artificial intelligence in foreign language teaching: challenges and future development. SHS Web of Conferences, 168, 03025. DOI: 10.1051/shsconf/202316803025

Luckin, R., Holmes, W., Griffiths, M., & Pearson, L. (2016). *Intelligence Unleashed: An Argument for AI in Education.*

Luckin, R., Holmes, W., Griffiths, M., & Forcier, L. B. (2016). *Intelligence unleashed: An argument for AI in education.* Pearson Education.

Luo. (2025). Bridging equity and privacy: Ethical challenges in AI-powered personalized learning platforms for automated grading and tutoring. *Advances in Engineering Innovation, 16*(8). DOI: 10.54254/2977-3903/2025.26631

Ma, J. S., O'Riordan, M., Mazzer, K., Batterham, P. J., Bradford, S., Kõlves, K., Titov, N., Klein, B., & Rickwood, D. J. (2022). Consumer Perspectives on the Use of Artificial Intelligence Technology and Automation in Crisis Support Services: Mixed Methods Study. *JMIR Human Factors*, *9*(3), e34514. Advance online publication. DOI: 10.2196/34514 PMID: 35930334

Mehrabi, N., Morstatter, F., Saxena, N., Lerman, K., & Galstyan, A. (2021). A survey on bias and fairness in machine learning. *ACM Computing Surveys*, *54*(6), 1–35. DOI: 10.1145/3457607

Meincke, L., Mollick, E. R., & Terwiesch, C. (2024). *Prompting diverse ideas: Increasing AI idea variance*. The Wharton School Research Paper. https://doi.org/ DOI: 10.2139/ssrn.4708466

Merdin-Uygur, E., Ozturkcan, S., Özbilgin, M. F., Yılmaz, F., & İnce, Ö. (2025). Human–robot collaboration in surgery at the nexus of knowledge, agency, and ownership. *Scientific Reports*, *15*(1), 23642. Advance online publication. DOI: 10.1038/s41598-025-08437-w PMID: 40604196

Mishara, P. (2024). The ethical implications of AI in education: Privacy, bias, and accountability. *Journal of Informatics Education and Research*, *4*(2). Advance online publication. DOI: 10.52783/jier.v4i2.1827

Mittelstadt, B. D., Allo, P., Taddeo, M., Wachter, S., & Floridi, L. (2016). The Ethics of algorithms: Mapping the Debate. *Big Data & Society*, *3*(2), 1–21. DOI: 10.1177/2053951716679679

Mohamed, M. S. P. (2024). Exploring Ethical Dimensions of AI-enhanced Language Education: A Literature Perspective. *Technology in Language Teaching and Learning*, *6*(3), 1813. Advance online publication. DOI: 10.29140/tltl.v6n3.1813

Monteiro, D., Mavinkurve, I., Kambli, P., & Surve, S. (2024). Federated learning for privacy-preserving machine learning: Decentralized model training with enhanced data security. *International Journal for Research in Applied Science and Engineering Technology*, *12*(11), 355–361. Advance online publication. DOI: 10.22214/ijraset.2024.65062

Morandín-Ahuerma, F. (2024). A critical analysis of the European Union's considerations on the ethical use of artificial intelligence in education. DOI: 10.31219/osf.io/escqj

More, A. B., Nigam, N., Sharda, P., Shrivastava, A., & Kate, V. (2025). Technological intelligence and urban sustainability. In *IEEE ICIH Conference Proceedings*.

Mouta, A., Llorente, A., & Sánchez, E. (2023). Uncovering blind spots in education ethics: Insights from a systematic literature review on artificial intelligence in education. *International Journal of Artificial Intelligence in Education, 34*(3), 1166–1205. DOI: 10.1007/s40593-023-00384-9

Naeem, M. R., Amin, R., Farhan, M., Alotaibi, F. A., Alnfiai, M. M., Sampedro, G. A., & Karovič, V. (2024). Harnessing AI and analytics to enhance cybersecurity and privacy for collective intelligence systems. *PeerJ. Computer Science, 10*, e2264. Advance online publication. DOI: 10.7717/peerj-cs.2264 PMID: 39314701

Nasir, S., Khan, R., & Bai, S. (2024). Ethical framework for harnessing the power of AI in healthcare and beyond. *IEEE Access : Practical Innovations, Open Solutions, 12*, 31014–31035. DOI: 10.1109/ACCESS.2024.3369912

Navas-Bonilla, C. del R., Guerra-Arango, J. A., Oviedo-Guado, D. A., & Murillo-Noriega, D. E. (2025). Inclusive education through technology: A systematic review of types, tools and characteristics. *Frontiers in Education, 10*, 1527851. Advance online publication. DOI: 10.3389/feduc.2025.1527851

Ndlovu, & Maguraushe, K. (2025). Balancing ethics and privacy in the use of artificial intelligence in institutions of higher learning: A framework for responsive AI systems. *Indonesian Journal of Informatics Education, 9*(1), 39. DOI: 10.20961/ijie.v9i1.100723

Necochea-Chamorro, J., Asalde, C., Núñez, M., & Valencia, Y. (2024). Systematic literature review: Biometric technology applied to educational institutions. *TEM Journal*. https://doi.org/DOI: 10.18421/TEM131-60

Neves, N. (2024). A segurança de software necessita de atualização quando confrontada com a realidade da aprendizagem automática distribuída? (52), 35–41. DOI: 10.5753/compbr.2024.52.4601

Ng, D., Leung, J., Chu, K., & Qiao, S. (2021). AI literacy: Definition, teaching, evaluation and ethical issues. *Proceedings of the Association for Information Science and Technology, 58*(1), 504–509. DOI: 10.1002/pra2.487

Nguyen, A., Ngo, H. N., Hong, Y., Dang, B., & Nguyen, B. P. T. (2023). Ethical principles for artificial intelligence in education. *Education and Information Technologies, 28*(4), 4221–4241. DOI: 10.1007/s10639-022-11316-w PMID: 36254344

Noble, S. U. (2018). *Algorithms of oppression*. NYU Press. DOI: 10.18574/nyu/9781479833641.001.0001

Nowell, E., & Gallus, S. (2025). Advancing privacy-preserving AI: A survey on federated learning and its applications. DOI: 10.20944/preprints202501.0685.v1

Nurjanah, A., Salsabila, I., Azzahra, A., Rahayu, R., & Marlina, N. (2024). Artificial intelligence (ai) usage in today's teaching and learning process: A review. *Syntax Idea, 6*(3), 1517–1523. DOI: 10.46799/syntax-idea.v6i3.3126

O'Neil, C. (2016). *Weapons of math destruction*. Crown.

OECD. (2024). *Trustworthy AI in education: Governance and cybersecurity*. OECD Publishing.

OECD. (2025). *PISA 2025 technical framework*. OECD Publishing.

Oncioiu, I., & Bularca, A. R. (2025). Artificial intelligence governance in higher education: The role of knowledge-based strategies in fostering legal awareness and ethical artificial intelligence literacy. *Societies (Basel, Switzerland), 15*(6), 144. DOI: 10.3390/soc15060144

Opoku, R. A., Pei, B., & Xing, W. (2025). Unveiling accuracy–fairness trade-offs: Investigating machine learning models in student performance prediction. *Journal of Learning Analytics, 12*(2), 125–139. DOI: 10.18608/jla.2025.8543

Pagliara, S., Bonavolontà, G., Pia, M., Falchi, S., Zurru, A., Fenu, G., & Mura, A. (2024). The integration of artificial intelligence in inclusive education: a scoping review. DOI: 10.20944/preprints202410.1386.v1

Pane, J. F., Steiner, E. D., Baird, M. D., & Hamilton, L. S. (2017). *Informing progress: Insights on personalized learning*. RAND Corporation.

Pangrazio, L., Auld, G., Lynch, J., Sawatzki, C., Duffy, G., Hannigan, S., & O'Mara, J. (2024). Data justice in education: Toward a research agenda. *Educational Philosophy and Theory*, •••, 1–12. DOI: 10.1080/00131857.2024.2320196

Pardo, A., & Siemens, G. (2014). Ethical and privacy principles for learning analytics. *British Journal of Educational Technology, 45*(3), 438–450. DOI: 10.1111/bjet.12152

Pareigis, J., Kvarnström, M., Cefa, B., Bai, J. Y. H., Zawacki-Richter, O., Uhlin, L., Jakobsson, N., & Theilmeier, G. (2024). Open networked learning – a course, a community, an approach. *The International Journal for Academic Development, 29*(2), 169–184. DOI: 10.1080/1360144X.2024.2350652

Parliament, U. K. (2018). *Data Protection Act 2018*. The Stationery Office.

Patil, S., Patwal, P. S., & Wadane, V. S. (2024). MACHINE LEARNING APPROACH FOR EDUCATIONAL DATA MINING ON REAL LIFE APPLICATIONS. *IET Conference Proceedings,* 2024(38), 370–374. DOI: 10.1049/icp.2025.0892

Patil, S., Rani, K. S., & Umashankar, N. (2024). Federated learning for privacy-preserving AI: Revolutionizing data sharing across industries. DOI: 10.31224/4177

Pavia, G., van den Bosch, A., & Wieringa, M. (2025). Creative agency in human–AI interaction: A systematic review. *AI & Society*. Advance online publication. DOI: 10.1007/s00146-024-01801-6

Perrotta, C. (2024). Automation, creativity, and authorship in education. *Learning, Media and Technology*, *49*(1), 1–15. DOI: 10.1080/17439884.2023.2258349

Popenici, Ş., & Kerr, S. (2017). Exploring the impact of artificial intelligence on teaching and learning in higher education. *Research and Practice in Technology Enhanced Learning*, *12*(1), 22. Advance online publication. DOI: 10.1186/s41039-017-0062-8 PMID: 30595727

Prinsloo, P., & Slade, S. (2015, March). Student privacy self-management: Implications for learning analytics. In *Proceedings of the fifth international conference on learning analytics and knowledge* (pp. 83-92). DOI: 10.1145/2723576.2723585

Prinsloo, P., & Slade, S. (2017). Ethics and learning analytics. *Educational Technology Research and Development*, *65*(1), 13–36. DOI: 10.1007/s11423-016-9489-7

Quishpe-Quishpe, L., Acosta-Vargas, I., Rodríguez-Rojas, L., Medina-Arias, J., Coronel-Navarro, D. A., Torres-Gutiérrez, R., & Acosta-Vargas, P. (2025). Impact of a Contextualized AI and Entrepreneurship-Based Training Program on Teacher Learning in the Ecuadorian Amazon. *Sustainability (Basel)*, *17*(19), 8850. DOI: 10.3390/su17198850

Raftopoulos, G., Davrazos, G., & Kotsiantis, S. (2025). Evaluating Fairness Strategies in Educational Data Mining: A Comparative Study of Bias Mitigation Techniques. *Electronics (Basel)*, *14*(9), 1856. Advance online publication. DOI: 10.3390/electronics14091856

Raji, I. D., Smart, A., & White, R. N.. (2020). Closing the AI accountability gap. *Proceedings of FAT*, 33–44. DOI: 10.1145/3351095.3372873

Reina Marín, Y., Cruz Caro, O., Maicelo Rubio, Y. C., Alva Tuesta, J. N., Sánchez Bardales, E., Carrasco Rituay, A. M., & Chávez Santos, R. (2025). Artificial intelligence as a teaching tool in university education. *Frontiers in Education*, *10*, 1578451. DOI: 10.3389/feduc.2025.1578451

Rets, I., Herodotou, C., & Gillespie, A. (2023). Six Practical Recommendations Enabling Ethical Use of Predictive Learning Analytics in Distance Education. *Journal of Learning Analytics*, *10*(1), 149–167. DOI: 10.18608/jla.2023.7743

Rigopouli, K., Kotsifakos, D., & Psaromiligkos, Y. (2025). Vygotsky's Creativity Options and Ideas in 21st-Century Technology-Enhanced Learning Design. *Education Sciences, 15*(2), 257. DOI: 10.3390/educsci15020257

Ritter, L. A., Barenkamp, M., & Moch, E. (2025). Platform and control: Technical data protection in digital learning systems. *Information Systems Management*. Advance online publication. DOI: 10.1365/s35764-025-00571-4

Roll, I., & Wylie, R. (2016). Evolution and revolution in AI in education. *International Journal of Artificial Intelligence in Education, 26*(2), 582–599. DOI: 10.1007/s40593-016-0110-3

Russel, S., & Norvig, P. (2021). *Artificial intelligence: A Modern approach* (4th ed.). Prentice Hall.

Samaniego López, M. V., Orrego Riofrío, M. C., Barriga-Fray, S. F., & Paz Viteri, B. S. (2025). Technologies in Inclusive Education: Solution or Challenge? A Systematic Review. *Education Sciences, 15*(6), 715. DOI: 10.3390/educsci15060715

Samuelson, P. (2020). AI authorship? *Communications of the ACM, 63*(4), 20–22. DOI: 10.1145/3401718

Sanjammagari, H. S. G., Sougandhika, G. S., & Srinivasa Desikan, K. E. (2026). Bridging the Trust Gap: Leveraging Explainable AI for Personalized E-Commerce Recommendations. *Lecture Notes in Computer Science, 15706 LNAI*, 225–236. DOI: 10.1007/978-981-96-8889-0_19

Sauer, S., Ardito, C., & Bernhaupt, R. (2026). Human-Centered Software Engineering: Balancing Interaction, Artificial Intelligence, and Human Value: IFIP WG 13.2 Workshop at INTERACT 2025. *Lecture Notes in Computer Science, 16111 LNCS*, 377–381. DOI: 10.1007/978-3-032-05008-3_70

Schmidt, P., & Barron, B. (2023). Algorithmic conformity and student writing in AI-assisted classrooms. *Journal of Educational Computing Research, 61*(4), 789–812. DOI: 10.1177/07356331231158742

Sekti, B. A. (2025). Adversarial machine learning in industrial cybersecurity: Challenges and solutions. In *AI-Enhanced Cybersecurity for Industrial Automation* (pp. 363–386). DOI: 10.4018/979-8-3373-3241-3.ch018

Sekti, B. A. (2025). Machine learning and artificial intelligence (AI) in manufacturing. In *Integrating Digital Innovation and Integrated Frameworks in Manufacturing* (pp. 255–292). DOI: 10.4018/979-8-3373-1082-4.ch011

Selbst, A. D., Boyd, D., & Friedler, S. A.. (2019). Fairness and abstraction in sociotechnical systems. *Proceedings of the ACM FAT Conference*, 59–68.

Selvaratnam, R. and Venaruzzo, L. (2024). Governance of artificial intelligence and data in australasian higher education: a snapshot of policy and practice. Ascilite Publications, 1-7. DOI: 10.14742/apubs.2023.717

Selwyn, N. (2019). *Should Robots Replace Teachers? AI and the Future of Education.* Editorial: Polity Press.

Selwyn, N. (2019). *Should robots replace teachers? AI and the future of education.* Polity Press.

Selwyn, N. (2019). *Should robots replace teachers? Polity Press. Bennett, A., & Checkel, J. (2015). Process tracing: from metaphor to analytic tool.* Cambridge University Press.

Selwyn, N. (2019). What's the problem with learning analytics? *Journal of Learning Analytics*, *6*(3), 11–19. DOI: 10.18608/jla.2019.63.3

Shashwat, K., & Pundhir, S. K. S. (2025). Artificial intelligence in education: Personalizing learning and overcoming ethical challenges. In *Immersive Learning in Teacher Education* (pp. 137–176). Simulated Environments, Tools, and Practices., DOI: 10.4018/979-8-3693-9861-6.ch005

Shrivastava, A. (2024, May 31). Shrivastava. (2024). Privacy-centric AI: Navigating the landscape with federated learning. *International Journal for Research in Applied Science and Engineering Technology*, *12*(5), 357–363. Advance online publication. DOI: 10.22214/ijraset.2024.61000

Siemens, G., & Long, P. (2011). Penetrating the fog: Analytics in learning and education. *EDUCAUSE Review*, *46*(5), 30–32.

Sikalidis, A. K., Kristo, A. S., Reaves, S. K., Kurfess, F. J., DeLay, A. M., Vasilaky, K., & Donegan, L. (2022). Capacity Strengthening Undertaking—Farm Organized Response of Workers against Risk for Diabetes: (C.S.U.—F.O.R.W.A.R.D. with Cal Poly)—A Concept Approach to Tackling Diabetes in Vulnerable and Underserved Farmworkers in California. *Sensors (Basel)*, *22*(21), 8299. Advance online publication. DOI: 10.3390/s22218299 PMID: 36365994

Sit, C., Srinivasan, R., Amlani, A., Muthuswamy, K., Azam, A., Monzon, L., & Poon, D. (2020). Attitudes and perceptions of UK medical students towards artificial intelligence and radiology: A multicentre survey. *Insights Into Imaging*, *11*(1), 14. Advance online publication. DOI: 10.1186/s13244-019-0830-7 PMID: 32025951

Slade, S., & Prinsloo, P. (2013). Learning analytics: Ethical issues. *The American Behavioral Scientist, 57*(10), 1510–1529. DOI: 10.1177/0002764213479366

Smith, H., & Higgins, S. (2006). Opening classroom interaction: The importance of feedback. *Cambridge Journal of Education, 36*(4), 485–502. DOI: 10.1080/03057640601048357

Smutny, P., & Schreiberova, P. (2020). Chatbots for learning. *Computers & Education, 151*, 103862. DOI: 10.1016/j.compedu.2020.103862

Standing Committee of the National People's Congress. (2021). *Personal Information Protection Law of the People's Republic of China.*

Suchithra, V. G., & Arya, C. (2025). The study on ethics and biases in AI-powered education. *European Journal of Contemporary Education and E-Learning, 3*(2), 37–43. DOI: 10.59324/ejceel.2025.3(2).04

Surapaneni, P., Bojjagani, C., & Sharma, N. (2024). *Federated learning-based big data analytics for the education system.*, DOI: 10.1109/ICEC59683.2024.10837262

Suresh, H., & Guttag, J. V. (2021). A framework for understanding sources of harm in ML. *Proceedings of FAT*, 81–91.

Symeou, L., Louca, L., Kavadella, A., Mackay, J., Danidou, Y., & Raffay, V. (2025). Development of evidence-based guidelines for the integration of generative AI in university education through a multidisciplinary, consensus-based approach. *European Journal of Dental Education : Official Journal of the Association for Dental Education in Europe, 29*(2), 285–303. DOI: 10.1111/eje.13069 PMID: 39949032

Tang, K. Y., Chou, C., & Tsai, C. C. (2024). Teachers' roles in shaping AI-supported creativity. *Teaching and Teacher Education, 132*, 104233. DOI: 10.1016/j.tate.2023.104233

Teixeira, R. (2026). Emotional AI Applied to Mental Health: An Ethical and Philosophical Analysis. *Lecture Notes in Computer Science, 16108 LNCS*, 421–430. DOI: 10.1007/978-3-032-04999-5_25

Terpstra, N. (2023). Economics of Faith: Reforming Poor Relief in Early Modern Europe, by Esther Chung-Kim.

Torres-Rivera, A. D., Rendón Peña, A. A., Díaz-Torres, S. T., & Díaz-Torres, L. A. (2025). Ethical integration of AI and STEAM pedagogies in higher education: A sustainable learning model for Society 5.0. *Sustainability (Basel), 17*(19), 8525. DOI: 10.3390/su17198525

Torrisi-Steele. (2025). AI and the ethics of student data privacy. *In Advances in computational intelligence and robotics book series* (pp. 53–76). DOI: 10.4018/979-8-3373-2397-8.ch003

Tripathi, S., & Ghatak, C. (2018). Artificial intelligence and intellectual property law. *Christ University Law Journal*, *7*(1), 83–98. DOI: 10.12728/culj.12.5

Tsai, C.-H., & Yen, J.-C. (2013). The Development and Evaluation of a Kinect Sensor Assisted Learning System on the Spatial Visualization Skills. *Procedia: Social and Behavioral Sciences*, *103*, 991–998. DOI: 10.1016/j.sbspro.2013.10.423

Tummala, R. B. (2025). Federated learning: Enhancing privacy and efficiency in decentralized AI systems. *17*(2), 17336–17346. DOI: 10.70153/IJCMI/2025.17301

U.S. Department of Education. (n.d.). *Family Educational Rights and Privacy Act (FERPA) overview.*

UN Committee on the Rights of the Child. (2021). *General Comment No. 25 on children's rights in the digital environment.*

UNESCO. (2021). *AI and education: Guidance for policy-makers.* UNESCO Publishing.

UNESCO. (2021). *Ethical guidelines on artificial intelligence and education.* UNESCO Publishing.

UNESCO. (2021a). *Recommendation on the ethics of artificial intelligence.* UNESCO.

UNESCO. (2021b). *AI and education: Guidance for policymakers.* UNESCO.

UNESCO. (2021c). *Artificial intelligence in education: Challenges and opportunities.* UNESCO.

UNESCO. (2023). *Guidance for generative AI in education and research.* UNESCO.

UNESCO. (2023). Guidance on generative AI in education and research. UNESCO Publishing. https://unesdoc.unesco.org

UNICEF Office of Research - Innocenti. (2021). *The case for regulating emotion recognition.* UNICEF.

UNICEF Office of Research - Innocenti. (2025). *Child-centred governance of AI systems.* UNICEF.

Urmeneta, A., & Romero, M. (2025). AI as a creative partner: A PRISMA review of AI's role in supporting creativity in education. *Frontiers in Education*, *10*, 1602151. Advance online publication. DOI: 10.3389/feduc.2025.1602151

Ushahidi. (2023). *Crowdsourced crisis mapping and humanitarian response.* Ushahidi Organization. https://www.ushahidi.com

Veale, M., & Borgesius, F. Z. (2021). Demystifying the draft EU Artificial Intelligence Act. *Computer Law Review International, 22*(4), 97–112. DOI: 10.9785/cri-2021-220402

Veseli, E. (2024). Revolutionizing dentistry: The integration of artificial intelligence and robotics. *Khyber Medical University Journal, 16*(4), 352–353. DOI: 10.35845/kmuj.2024.23729

Vij, S., & K. S., S. (2025). Federated learning in education: Enhancing student privacy in AI-based feedback mechanisms. (pp. 288–315). DOI: 10.71443/9789349552531-11

von Bahr, J., Suutala, A., Kucukel, H., Kaingu, H., Kinyua, F., Muinde, M., Osundwa, K., Ronald, W., Muinde, J., Ngasala, B., Lundin, M., Mårtensson, A., Linder, N., & Lundin, J. (2025). AI-supported versus manual microscopy of Kato-Katz smears for diagnosis of soil-transmitted helminth infections in a primary healthcare setting. *Scientific Reports, 15*(1), 20332. Advance online publication. DOI: 10.1038/s41598-025-07309-7 PMID: 40579399

Wang, S., Wang, F., Zhu, Z., Wang, J., Tran, T., & Du, Z. (2024). *Artificial intelligence in education: A systematic literature review.* Expert Systems with Applications, 252(Part A), 124167. DOI: 10.1016/j.eswa.2024.124167

Wang, V. (2025). Ethics and equity in AI-driven education. *In Advances in educational technologies and instructional design book series* (pp. 231–254). DOI: 10.4018/979-8-3373-0502-8.ch010

Wang, X., & Fan, Y. (2025). Emotional responses to generative AI in learning contexts. *Computers in Human Behavior, 146*, 107833. DOI: 10.1016/j.chb.2024.107833

Wickramasinghe, M., Gunawardena, L., & Padukkage, A. (2025). Ethical principles for artificial intelligence in education: A meta-review approach. *AI and Ethics, 6*(1), 63. DOI: 10.1007/s43681-025-00878-3

Wieczorek, M., Hosseini, M., & Gordijn, B. (2025). Unpacking the ethics of using AI in primary and secondary education: A systematic literature review. *AI and Ethics, 5*(5), 4693–4711. DOI: 10.1007/s43681-025-00770-0 PMID: 40959538

Wiese, L. J., Patil, I., Schiff, D. S., & Magana, A. J. (2025). AI ethics education: A systematic literature review. *Computers and Education: Artificial Intelligence, 8*, 100405. DOI: 10.1016/j.caeai.2025.100405

Williamson, B., & Hogan, A. (2020, July). *Commercialisation and privatisation in/ of education in the context of Covid-19* [Report]. Education International. https:// www.ei-ie.org/en/item/25251:commercialisation-and-privatisation-inof-education -in-the-context-of-covid-19

Williamson, B. (2017). Big data in education. *Sage (Atlanta, Ga.)*.

Williamson, B. (2017). Big data in education: The digital future of learning, policy and practice. *Sage (Atlanta, Ga.)*. Advance online publication. DOI: 10.4135/9781529714920

Williamson, B., & Eynon, R. (2020). Historical threads, missing links, and future directions in AI in education. *Learning, Media and Technology*, *45*(3), 1–13. DOI: 10.1080/17439884.2020.1798995

Williamson, B., & Kizilcec, R. F. (2022). AI and the future of education governance. *Educational Technology Research and Development*, *70*(5), 2351–2370. DOI: 10.1007/s11423-022-10146-1

Woolf, B. P. (2009). *Building intelligent interactive tutors: student-centered strategies for revolutionizing e-learning*. Morgan Kaufmann Publishers/Elsevier.

Xia, Q., Zhang, P., Huang, W., & Chiu, T. K. F. (2025). The impact of generative AI on university students' learning outcomes via Bloom's taxonomy: A meta-analysis and pattern mining approach. *Asia Pacific Journal of Education*, •••, 1–31. DOI: 10.1080/02188791.2025.2530503

Yeoman, P., & Wilson, S. (2019). Designing for situated learning: Understanding the relations between material properties, designed form and emergent learning activity. *British Journal of Educational Technology*, *50*(5), 2090–2108. DOI: 10.1111/bjet.12856

Yim, I. H. Y. (2024). A critical review of teaching and learning artificial intelligence (AI) literacy: Developing an intelligence-based AI literacy framework for primary school education. *Computers and Education: Artificial Intelligence*, *7*, 100319. DOI: 10.1016/j.caeai.2024.100319

Yockel, M. R., Sleiman, M. M.Jr, Doherty, H., Adams, R., Davis, K. M., Groninger, H., Sharkey, C., Biel, M. G., Statman, M. R., & Tercyak, K. P. (2025). Mental Health Professionals' Views on Artificial Intelligence as an Aide for Children Anticipating or Suffering the Loss of a Parent to Cancer: Helpful or Harmful? *Children (Basel, Switzerland)*, *12*(6), 763. Advance online publication. DOI: 10.3390/ children12060763 PMID: 40564721

Yu, L., & Yu, Z. (2023). Qualitative and quantitative analyses of artificial intelligence ethics in education using VOSViewer and citnetexplorer. *Frontiers in Psychology*, *14*, 1061778. Advance online publication. DOI: 10.3389/fpsyg.2023.1061778 PMID: 36968737

Zawacki-Richter, O., Marín, V. I., Bond, M., & Gouverneur, F. (2019). Systematic review of research on artificial intelligence applications in higher education. *International Journal of Educational Technology in Higher Education*, *16*(1), 1–27. DOI: 10.1186/s41239-019-0171-0

Zhang, K., & Aslan, A. B. (2021). AI technologies for education: Recent research & future directions. *Computers and Education: Artificial Intelligence*, *2*, 100025. Advance online publication. DOI: 10.1016/j.caeai.2021.100025

Zhou, M., & Peng, S. (2025). The usage of AI in teaching and students' creativity: The mediating role of learning engagement and the moderating role of AI literacy. *Behavioral Sciences (Basel, Switzerland)*, *15*(5), 587. DOI: 10.3390/bs15050587 PMID: 40426365

Zuboff, S. (2019). *The age of surveillance capitalism*. PublicAffairs.

Zuboff, S. (2019). *The age of surveillance capitalism: The fight for a human future at the new frontier of power*. PublicAffairs.

Zweig, K. A. (2022). *Awkward Intelligence: Where AI Goes Wrong, Why It Matters, and What We Can Do about It*. MIT Press. DOI: 10.7551/mitpress/13915.001.0001

About the Contributors

Vasileios Paliktzoglou, an academic and industry professional, holds a Ph.D. in Computer Science from the University of Eastern Finland. He is an active contributor to academia, serving as a guest and associate editor for prestigious journals like the Journal of Information Systems Education (JISE) and IAFOR Journal of Education. He has been a keynote speaker at several academic and industry events, sharing his insights on social computing, collaborative learning, and emerging technologies in higher education. Dr. Paliktzoglou also actively participates in international research projects, highlighting his commitment to advancing knowledge and innovation as the Book Series Editor for the "Emerging Technologies in Education" at Vernon Press and "AI and Education" at STAR Scholars Press. His expertise continues to shape the academic and research landscape at Bahrain Polytechnic.

Mohamed Lahby is Associate Professor at the Higher Normal School (ENS) University Hassan II of Casablanca, Morocco. His PhD in Computer Science from Faculty of Sciences and Technology of Mohammedia, University Hassan II of Casablanca, in 2013. His research interests are wireless communication and network, mobility management, QoS/QoE, Internet of things, Smart cities, Optimization and Machine learning. He has published more than 35 papers (book chapters, international journals, and conferences), 1 edited book, and 1 authored book. He has served and continues to serve on executive and technical program committees of numerous international conferences such as IEEE PIMRC, ICC, NTMS, IWCMC, WINCOM, ISNCC. He also serves as a referee of many prestigious Elsevier journals: Ad Hoc Networks, Applied Computing and Informatics and International journal of disaster risk reduction. He organized and participated more than 40 conferences and workshops. He is the chair of many international workshops and special sessions such as MLNGSN'19, CSPSC'19, MLNGSN'20, MLNGSN'21, AI2SC '20 and WCTCP'20, CIOT'21.

Pushan Dutta is an Associate Professor at Amity University Kolkata who has carved a distinctive niche in academia with over 12 years of academic experience. He earned his Ph.D. from Jadavpur University in 2015, followed by postdoctoral work as an Erasmus Mundus Scholar at the University of Oradea in Romania in 2016, which laid the foundation for a career drive for a position in institution of academic excellence. At the forefront of his contributions is an impressive editorial portfolio. Dr. Dutta has meticulously curated and edited over 60 books in the past couple of years for globally recognized publishers such as Springer, Elsevier, IET, Taylor & Francis, Cambridge Scholar Publishers, Degruyter, and IGI Global. His role as the manager of the "Sustainable Industrial Engineering Systems" book series for CRC Press further underscores his influence in shaping scholarly discourse on sustainability and engineering innovation. His editorial expertise spans rapidly evolving domains including artificial intelligence in healthcare, Industry 5.0 technologies, quantum computing applications,aviation and digital transformation strategies. A dedicated mentor and educator, Dr. Dutta has consistently empowered his students to excel and innovate, guiding them to garner international recognition through competitions like the Johnson Control International Whitepaper contest and Ideathon 5.0. His contributions to nurturing young talent have been acknowledged through accolades such as the "Mentor of Change" award by NITI Aayog, along with the prestigious Young Faculty Awards in 2018 and 2024. His keynote speeches at international events, notably at Data Science Europe 2022, reflect his role as a thought leader. Complementing his teaching and editorial endeavors is an extensive research portfolio that includes over 160 Scopus-indexed publications, two pioneering Indian patents, and an Indian copyright. His professional recognitions extend to prestigious memberships and fellowships, including Senior Membership at the Indian Institute of Engineering, a Threws Fellowship, and a Fellowship at the EnTech Foundation. Dr. Dutta's academic journey also includes significant teaching stints as an Assistant Professor at RGMCET in Nandyal, Andhra Pradesh, and as a lecturer for the Marine Electro Technology course at DG Shipping Taratala. His diverse experience spans classroom instruction in Data Science and AI, comprehensive courses on Electrical, Electronics, Python and coding and mentorship roles that integrates design thinking and hackathon participation and sports.

Muthmainnah Muthmainnah, she is lecturer, International speaker and leaders, academian and an education expert. She is lecturer at Al Asyariah Mandar West Sulawesi, Indonesia. She is a global keynote speaker, plenary speaker, and resource person. She was the chairman of the education faculty's language department; she was a public relation, Director of women's Centre studies, and deputy director of the Quality Assurance Unit in her university. Now she is Deputy Director of language and Character development institute. She is Deputy Secretary of International of

Society Teachers, Administrators and Research (ISTAR) PHILIPPINE, NEPAL AND THAILAND, international Coordinator member of Charles Walter'S Society and Innovation and Research, INDIA, International Board Professors and Expert of Scientific Innovation Research Group, EGYPT (www.sirg.club), She is country director of International Education Educlouds UK & INDIA, Member of Global Trainer Academy, PAKISTAN, International Ambassador of Peace, World Literary Forum For Peace and Humanities, Bangladesh, International Godwill and Ambassador of Abundance Consulting Academy, Ltd. Republic Benin, AFRICA and she is also Asisstant country Director of International youth Society United Nation-NEPAL, Indonesia Coordinator International conference of Leadership in Education Academy and Development (LEAD) Philippined, Country head of Republic Indonesia of Academic Academic Development for Global Leadership in Education Philippines (ADGLE).She is Indonesia Country Director of YES YOU Can International, London, UK. Country Director of Africa Global Development for positive Change Initiative (ADIAfrica),International Internship University (IIU) Indonesia Country Director, She is a member of the English teaching Association as A Foreign Language in Indonesia "TEFLIN Id member 1020180047, she member of Laureta International University Cambridge-OLLReN ID number 1020180047, Member of Association for Middle Level Education (AMLE) No.3170089, she assigned on voluntary basis as Sulawesi Regional Board Members of the English Language Education Study Program Association, APSPBI ID 180717, Member of expert and lecturer, ADRI ID 090990917058004, member of lecturer association of Indonesia, and member of English lecturer Indonesia Association, Member of International Culture Athletic Promotion Association HQ, Korea, International Ambassador of Global Literary Temple (GLT),Abuja Nigeria Africa, she is also the member of United Nations Volunteers Roster ID2296828. She is Advisory board of Indonesian Education Share to care Volunteers.

***

Adiyono is an active academic and researcher with a track record of publications in internationally reputable scientific journals. His contributions focus on the development of educational science, particularly Islamic Religious Education, curriculum innovation, and the integration of technology and artificial intelligence (AI) in learning. Through various scientific works, he is committed to improving the quality of education in the digital era by developing STEM-based learning models aligned with Islamic values. In addition to active research, he is also involved in the development of educational policies and practices at the institutional level. The increasing number of publications and citations reflects his academic impact and contributions to the global scientific community. As a lecturer and researcher, he continues to produce relevant, innovative, and internationally competitive work.

Soha Badr is a PhD Researcher in Education at the British University in Dubai (BUiD), specializing in TESOL, curriculum innovation, and psycholinguistics. Her scholarly work explores language acquisition, punctuation cognition, interdisciplinary curriculum design, and research-based instructional models rooted in the California Common Core State Standards. She has contributed to multiple academic publications, including book chapters in TESOL Teacher Research (Springer) and Educational Technology in the Gulf: Educators' Experiences (Scholars' Press), with ongoing submissions to Scopus-indexed journals. Her current doctoral research employs an explanatory sequential mixed-methods design to investigate FANBOYS comma omission patterns among high-proficiency EFL learners. Alongside her academic work, Badr serves as Head of the English Department at City American School, leading large-scale curriculum mapping initiatives, interdisciplinary programs, and assessment reform grounded in evidence-based practices. Her research aims to bridge classroom realities with contemporary theory, contributing practical insights to the fields of TESOL, curriculum design, and language teacher education.

Amine Hmid is an adjunct professor at several Moroccan universities and serves as an administrative executive in the public sector. He holds a PhD in Management Sciences with a specialization in strategic management and territorial development. His academic work focuses on strategic territorial management, sustainable development, climate governance, and public policy, with particular attention to climate change adaptation, local governance, and participatory development approaches in emerging economies. Dr. HMID's research also explores the socio-economic and institutional mechanisms that strengthen territorial resilience and sustainability transitions. He has authored and co-authored several scientific publications and conference papers addressing the intersection between territorial governance, sustainability, and development strategies, particularly in the context of developing countries. Through both academic research and professional practice, he contributes to discussions on sustainable territorial planning and climate-resilient governance systems.

Rehan Khan holds master's degrees in Physics and Computer Applications, reflecting a strong interdisciplinary foundation in both scientific and computational domains. His research interests include artificial intelligence, machine learning, data science, data analytics, and soft computing, with a particular emphasis on ethical concerns, bias, and privacy in machine learning systems. The author has published research addressing challenges related to fairness, transparency, and responsible AI. Currently, the author is working as an Assistant Professor in the Department of Computer Science and Engineering at Jamia Hamdard University, where he is actively involved in teaching, research, and academic development.

Indra Kishor is currently an Assistant Professor with Poornima Institute of Engineering and Technology, Jaipur. He is a multifaceted academic and researcher with expertise in IoT, artificial intelligence, machine learning, robotics, and extended reality (XR). He brings over a decade of impactful experience in teaching, research, and industry. With many published and granted patents and more than 40 research articles, his research focuses on leveraging advanced technologies to address real-world challenges in education, automation, and sustainable development. His innovative projects range from XR virtual tours and humanoid robots to IoT-based home automation systems and AR drone. His groundbreaking work has earned him awards and global recognition, including jury roles in events in the NASA Space Apps Challenge. His passion for fostering innovation and bridging academia and industry has established him as a leader in next-generation engineering solutions. He has played a pivotal role in organizing major international conferences, such as BICON and Convergence. He has also served as an Editor for Recent Advances in Sciences, Engineering, Information Technology, and Management (CRC Press Book) and an Associate Editor for the UGC-CARE-listed journal The Indian Journal of Technical Education (IJTE).

Udit Mamodiya is an Associate Professor and Associate Dean (Research) at Poornima University in Jaipur, Rajasthan, India. With a robust academic and professional background, he has significantly contributed to the fields of renewable energy sources, reliability analysis, expert systems, and decision support systems. Dr. Mamodiya has authored over 60 research papers indexed in prestigious databases such as SCI, Scopus, and UGC Care, showcasing his commitment to advancing knowledge in his areas of expertise. Additionally, he has authored ten books published by national publishers, further enriching the academic community with valuable resources. An innovator at heart, Dr. Mamodiya holds an impressive portfolio of intellectual property, including 50 utility patents (both national and international) along with 20 design patents and copyrights. His entrepreneurial spirit is exemplified by securing 1 Crore in funding from the All India Council for Technical Education (AICTE) to establish the IDEA Lab at Poornima University, aimed at fostering innovation and research among students and faculty.

Enrico Moch holds a doctorate in economics and works as a lecturer at various universities in Germany, including DHBW Ravensburg and Burgenland University of

Applied Sciences. He is also Academic Director of the GrandEdu Research School based in Herford. At Burgenland University of Applied Sciences, he is currently supporting the introduction of the new Master's programme "Entrepreneurship and Global Business Strategy (MBA)", where he works as programme coordinator, lecturer and examiner. His research focuses on AI governance, technical data protection and the institutional governance of digital platforms. Mr Moch regularly publishes specialist articles, is involved in interdisciplinary book projects and runs the podcast "GrandEdu Research School - On the trail of the economy!". He is also involved in academic peer review and knowledge transfer between research and practice.

Amrita Baid More is a dynamic educator and academic leader with over 13 years of experience in higher education, curriculum development, and student mentorship. Known for her energetic and learner-centered approach, she has consistently played a pivotal role in shaping holistic, future-ready business professionals. Currently serving as an Assistant Professor at Medicaps University, she leads the Incubation and Innovation Cell and co-convenes the Centre for Case Development, inspiring students to think beyond the classroom and embrace entrepreneurial mindsets. Her career spans esteemed institutions like IIM Indore and Prestige Institute of Management and Research, where she coordinated major national and international conferences, faculty development programs, and academic workshops. Dr. More believes in experiential learning and simulation-based education as powerful tools for developing critical thinking and real-world application.

Gayathry Nair is a postgraduate student specialising in Corporate and Commercial Law. She holds a BBA LL.B. degree and is currently pursuing her Master's programme in this field. Her research interests include data protection laws, artificial intelligence governance, surveillance technologies, digital rights, competition law in digital markets, platform accountability, and the protection of human rights and dignity in digital environments. Her work adopts an interdisciplinary approach that connects corporate regulation with technology law and human rights, focusing on the regulatory challenges created by algorithmic systems and data-driven platforms in emerging economies.

Eko Nurcahyo is an artificial intelligence professional and researcher with a strong focus on intelligent systems, machine learning, and data-driven technologies. His work centers on the development and implementation of AI-based solutions to address complex real-world challenges across various domains. He has been actively involved in research and applied projects related to predictive analytics, automation, and intelligent decision-support systems. His work demonstrates strong analytical thinking, technical expertise, and a commitment to continuous innovation in emerging technologies. Eko actively contributes to collaborative research initiatives and scientific publications aimed at advancing the application of artificial intelligence in both academic and industrial environments.

Tobias Oberdieck is Managing Director of GrandEdu GmbH, a leading further education institution that specialises in preparing professionals for degrees such as the Bachelor Professional, Master Professional and Master of Business Administration (MBA). In his role at GrandEdu, he drives innovative educational strategies to actively support the recruitment of skilled labour in Germany. During his doctorate, Dr. Oberdieck worked as a research assistant at the Department of Business Administration and Economics at the Niederrhein University of Applied Sciences in Germany. During this time, he deepened his knowledge in the areas of education management, labour market research and economic education models, which he now brings to his work at GrandEdu. His research focuses on the interface between vocational training, academic education and the challenges of the modern labour market. In addition, he is developing the Master's programme "Entrepreneurship and Global Business Strategy (MBA)" in cooperation with the Burgenland University of Applied Sciences, which offers specialists and managers a modern, practice-oriented qualification in the field of international corporate strategies.

Ardra Rianisa is an Information Technology professional with a strong interest in digital technology and information systems. Ardra actively engages in writing academic papers and popular articles that discuss current trends, innovations, and developments in the field of information technology. With a solid understanding of technology and its practical applications, Ardra is committed to continuously expanding knowledge and contributing insights to the digital and academic community.

Ellina Rienovita is a researcher and academic at Universitas Pendidikan Indonesia (UPI) who has written articles for the university's journals, books, and libraries. Her research focuses on enhancing learning outcomes, such as learning analytics, educational technology, and so on.

Shivansu Sachan is Pursuing Ph.D. in Management, a Master's holder from Integral University, Lucknow, Bachelor's from IHM, Lucknow. Academic and professional accomplishments of 6 years with renowned organizations and institutes. My Teaching Career has been very satisfying and have continuously upgraded the skills and knowledge by attending many courses and training programs, seminars, conferences organized by different organizations and also delivered many lectures as a Hospitality sector.He is also assistant professor at Csjm University kanpur

Binastya Anggara Sekti has been a lecturer at the Faculty of Computer Science, Esa Unggul University, Jakarta, since 2016. He is actively involved in the Artificial Intelligence and Information Security Study Group. He holds a Bachelor's degree in Informatics Engineering from the Bandung Institute of Technology and a Master's degree in Information Systems Management from Trisakti University, Jakarta. Prior to entering academia, he accumulated over 25 years of professional experience as an IT practitioner in various companies across Jakarta. His work focused on developing data centers for internet service providers and delivering IT solutions for the manufacturing and oil & gas sectors. His research interests include artificial intelligence, cybersecurity, and the development of IT infrastructure.

Eka Setiawati, M.Pd., is a permanent lecturer in the Early Childhood Teacher Education Program (PG PAUD) at Universitas Setia Budhi Rangkasbitung (USBR), Banten. She was born in Serang on July 26, 1986. After completing her undergraduate degree in English Language and Literature Education at STKIP Setia Budhi (now USBR) in 2008, Eka pursued a master's degree in Early Childhood Education at Jakarta State University, graduating in 2011. Throughout her academic career, Eka has been actively involved in improving academic quality and teaching practices, as reflected in her various works such as research outputs, several books, and instructional materials. Through these contributions, she strives to present practical and applicable ideas for educators, parents, and students, with the goal of making education in Indonesia more meaningful and empowering.

Arpan Shrivastava is an Associate Professor in Management with over 15 years of academic and administrative experience in reputed institutions in India. He holds a Ph.D. in Management, his core areas of expertise include International Business Strategy, Export-Import Management, Marketing, Digital Branding, and Cross-Cultural Business Practices. Dr. Shrivastava has authored and co-authored several research papers published in Scopus-indexed and UGC-CARE journals and has contributed to edited books in the domains of business strategy and marketing. In addition, he holds a registered patent in Logistics and Supply Chain Management and regularly participates in curriculum development, NEP policy implementation, and quality assurance in higher education. An active researcher and academic reviewer. Dr. Shrivastava has completed certified workshops by the Academy of International Business (AIB) South Asia Chapter, focusing on publishing in top-tier journals, international business pedagogy, and high-quality research. He has also guided numerous undergraduate and postgraduate research projects on emerging trends in HRM, digital marketing, and global trade.

Index

A

Academic Integrity 3, 10, 31
Accessibility 124, 129, 141, 142, 143, 144, 145, 146, 147, 148, 149, 150, 151, 152, 153, 259, 270, 302
Accountability 2, 6, 10, 11, 12, 14, 15, 17, 23, 24, 45, 46, 48, 58, 64, 65, 66, 67, 71, 72, 74, 79, 80, 81, 82, 83, 84, 85, 87, 88, 90, 91, 92, 95, 96, 97, 98, 99, 100, 101, 102, 103, 104, 106, 108, 109, 111, 112, 115, 117, 118, 119, 120, 121, 124, 126, 127, 129, 130, 132, 133, 134, 135, 136, 137, 144, 162, 163, 166, 167, 186, 187, 189, 193, 195, 203, 204, 205, 207, 208, 209, 210, 213, 214, 215, 216, 220, 224, 226, 227, 229, 237, 241, 242, 249, 250, 252, 253, 290, 305
Adaptive Learning 2, 80, 82, 104, 105, 111, 116, 119, 121, 122, 123, 128, 192, 202, 205, 234, 239, 240, 242, 249, 253, 255, 268, 293, 294, 298, 313
AI Ethics 2, 3, 4, 9, 18, 19, 23, 24, 26, 81, 82, 84, 87, 108, 138, 141, 153, 168, 181, 236, 243, 244, 245, 247, 248, 251, 256, 257, 258, 259, 260, 262, 292
AI Governance 95, 96, 106, 115, 119, 120, 130, 131, 132, 134, 135, 142, 145, 152, 153, 207, 208, 261
AI in Education 4, 5, 8, 10, 19, 27, 28, 31, 76, 77, 80, 81, 82, 84, 88, 93, 109, 111, 115, 116, 119, 127, 135, 138, 141, 142, 143, 144, 145, 153, 156, 163, 181, 184, 186, 188, 189, 193, 197, 200, 205, 209, 224, 227, 230, 233, 234, 235, 236, 237, 238, 239, 240, 241, 242, 243, 244, 245, 246, 248, 249, 251, 252, 253, 254, 255, 256, 258, 262, 268, 273, 291, 292, 294, 295, 303, 313
Algorithmic Bias 2, 3, 6, 13, 18, 40, 82, 83, 86, 87, 88, 89, 90, 91, 99, 108, 118, 120, 121, 128, 135, 155, 204, 233, 234, 235, 237, 244, 247, 249, 252, 253, 255, 293, 294, 302, 303, 313
Algorithmic Fairness 105, 235, 240, 241, 253
Algorithmic Impact Assessment 145, 150
Algorithmic Transparency 47, 235
Artificial Intelligence 1, 3, 27, 28, 30, 31, 32, 33, 37, 47, 49, 52, 54, 76, 77, 79, 82, 88, 95, 100, 102, 105, 107, 108, 109, 111, 112, 113, 114, 115, 117, 119, 121, 123, 124, 126, 128, 129, 131, 133, 134, 135, 137, 138, 139, 141, 142, 144, 155, 156, 157, 160, 188, 189, 191, 192, 193, 194, 197, 198, 199, 200, 207, 209, 216, 218, 219, 223, 227, 229, 230, 231, 233, 234, 235, 238, 240, 241, 244, 250, 253, 255, 261, 262, 263, 264, 265, 266, 269, 270, 271, 272, 274, 283, 288, 290, 291, 292, 293, 294, 298, 300, 303, 304, 311, 313, 315, 316, 317
Artificial Intelligence in Education 30, 76, 88, 105, 108, 137, 138, 155, 156, 157, 193, 194, 197, 198, 216, 219, 229, 230, 231, 261, 262, 263, 265, 290, 291, 292

B

Bias 2, 3, 4, 6, 7, 9, 10, 12, 13, 15, 18, 23, 24, 30, 31, 40, 45, 47, 50, 58, 62, 63, 67, 79, 80, 81, 82, 83, 84, 85, 86, 87, 88, 89, 90, 91, 96, 97, 98, 99, 100, 102, 103, 104, 105, 107, 108, 111, 118, 119, 120, 121, 126, 128, 129, 135, 137, 142, 143, 149, 150, 151, 155, 162, 164, 187, 189, 201, 204, 211, 217, 226, 233, 234, 235, 236, 237, 238, 239, 241, 242, 243, 244, 245, 247, 248, 249, 251, 252, 253, 255, 256, 257, 259, 267, 269, 288, 293, 294, 302, 303, 312, 313
Biometric Monitoring 196, 213, 215

C

Community Engagement 254, 293, 304, 315
Creativity 69, 90, 130, 234, 264, 265, 266, 267, 268, 269, 270, 271, 272, 273, 274, 275, 276, 277, 278, 279, 281, 282, 283, 284, 285, 286, 287, 288, 289, 290, 291, 292, 302
Cultural Relevance 293, 304

D

Data Governance 11, 22, 24, 31, 46, 80, 102, 103, 104, 144, 147, 149, 150, 153, 164, 169, 193, 198, 215, 223, 225, 227, 233, 234, 237, 239, 245, 249, 250, 255, 257
Data Justice 1, 5, 7, 8, 9, 10, 11, 14, 17, 21, 22, 24, 29
Data Privacy 2, 4, 5, 7, 18, 19, 25, 39, 111, 126, 127, 187, 188, 189, 194, 233, 234, 235, 238, 240, 245, 247, 252, 253, 264, 293, 294, 302, 303, 305, 312, 313
Digital Literacy 21, 116, 247, 250, 254, 255, 258, 272, 307, 312, 313

E

Education 1, 2, 3, 4, 5, 6, 8, 9, 10, 14, 18, 19, 25, 26, 27, 28, 29, 30, 31, 48, 54, 55, 56, 57, 61, 62, 63, 70, 71, 72, 73, 74, 76, 77, 79, 80, 81, 82, 83, 84, 85, 86, 87, 88, 91, 92, 93, 94, 95, 96, 97, 100, 101, 102, 103, 104, 105, 106, 107, 108, 109, 111, 114, 115, 116, 117, 118, 119, 121, 122, 123, 124, 125, 126, 127, 129, 131, 132, 133, 134, 135, 136, 137, 138, 139, 141, 142, 143, 144, 145, 149, 150, 153, 155, 156, 157, 159, 162, 163, 164, 165, 166, 167, 169, 172, 174, 179, 181, 184, 186, 187, 188, 189, 190, 191, 192, 193, 194, 195, 197, 198, 199, 200, 201, 202, 203, 204, 205, 206, 207, 208, 209, 210, 211, 212, 213, 214, 215, 216, 217, 218, 219, 220, 222, 223, 224, 225, 226, 227, 228, 229, 230, 231, 232, 233, 234, 235, 236, 237, 238, 239, 240, 241, 242, 243, 244, 245, 246, 247, 248, 249, 250, 251, 252, 253, 254, 255, 256, 257, 258, 259, 260, 261, 262, 263, 264, 265, 267, 268, 269, 270, 271, 272, 273, 274, 277, 279, 281, 285, 287, 288, 289, 290, 291, 292, 293, 294, 295, 296, 298, 299, 301, 302, 303, 304, 305, 307, 308, 309, 310, 312, 313, 314, 315
Educational Governance 80, 88
Educational Leadership 28
Educational Surveillance 203, 211, 213, 216, 219, 223, 227
Educational Technology 9, 77, 81, 108, 127, 128, 137, 138, 139, 155, 156, 157, 164, 193, 200, 230, 249, 255, 260, 264
Education Technology 103, 127, 156, 222, 223
Epistemic Integrity 53, 61, 63, 70, 74
Ethical AI 3, 4, 8, 26, 34, 46, 49, 81, 93, 103, 106, 107, 132, 136, 141, 142, 144, 153, 182, 184, 186, 235, 236, 237, 238, 239, 251, 252, 253, 256, 257, 258
Ethics 2, 3, 4, 7, 8, 9, 11, 18, 19, 23, 24, 25, 26, 27, 36, 39, 48, 49, 50, 76, 77, 81, 82, 83, 84, 87, 105, 108, 114, 115, 126, 131, 134, 138, 141, 142, 144, 147, 153, 155, 156, 157, 162, 163, 164, 168, 177, 179, 180, 181, 182, 188, 189, 190, 193, 200, 207, 224, 229, 230, 231, 233, 235, 236, 241, 242, 243, 244, 245, 247, 248, 251, 255, 256, 257, 258, 259, 260, 262, 263, 264, 270, 272, 281, 292, 295, 316
Explainable AI 29, 30, 46, 51, 95, 100, 129

F

Fair Algorithms 128
Fairness 2, 6, 7, 10, 12, 13, 14, 15, 17, 23, 30, 34, 49, 55, 56, 58, 67, 71, 74, 79, 80, 81, 82, 83, 85, 86, 87, 89, 90, 91, 95, 97, 98, 99, 102, 103, 105, 108, 115, 118, 119, 121, 128, 129, 131,

132, 134, 135, 136, 137, 138, 142, 143, 144, 146, 147, 149, 150, 151, 153, 157, 159, 160, 162, 165, 166, 168, 169, 172, 173, 174, 175, 176, 177, 178, 179, 180, 181, 182, 184, 186, 193, 195, 198, 199, 206, 212, 214, 215, 229, 235, 236, 237, 238, 240, 241, 242, 246, 249, 253, 255, 257, 262, 290, 303

G

GDPR Compliance 223

H

Higher Education 137, 139, 142, 155, 156, 157, 195, 229, 234, 251, 253, 255, 257, 262, 264, 267, 272
Human Agency 1, 2, 3, 4, 5, 6, 7, 10, 12, 13, 14, 15, 17, 18, 19, 22, 26, 28, 55, 116, 273, 302
Human-Centered AI 24, 82, 102, 238

I

Institutional Governance 22, 79, 95, 98, 106, 145, 162, 169, 177, 194, 199
Intelligent Tutoring 2, 3, 80, 92, 116, 268, 293, 296, 300

L

Learning Analytics 1, 3, 4, 9, 10, 11, 12, 15, 28, 29, 69, 84, 92, 106, 108, 109, 118, 125, 126, 138, 141, 145, 155, 156, 157, 160, 161, 164, 191, 192, 193, 195, 198, 204, 205, 211, 213, 214, 215, 216, 218, 219, 229, 230, 237, 245, 246, 268

M

Machine Learning 28, 29, 30, 33, 34, 36, 38, 42, 43, 44, 76, 79, 80, 81, 82, 83, 84, 85, 86, 87, 88, 89, 90, 91, 92, 93, 94, 95, 96, 97, 98, 99, 100, 101, 102, 103, 104, 105, 106, 107, 108, 111, 113, 114, 123, 135, 137, 157, 164, 187, 189, 204, 316
Machine Learning in Education 94, 97, 104, 105, 107

P

Policy Design 90, 247
Predictive Analytics 2, 3, 23, 33, 38, 41, 44, 50, 58, 70, 80, 82, 88, 90, 111, 124, 125, 126, 135, 137, 144, 193, 197, 200, 214, 218, 234, 293, 299, 307
Privacy 2, 3, 4, 5, 6, 7, 9, 12, 15, 18, 19, 21, 22, 23, 24, 25, 29, 31, 36, 39, 40, 46, 79, 80, 81, 84, 88, 91, 93, 94, 96, 100, 102, 103, 104, 107, 108, 111, 112, 115, 117, 118, 120, 121, 125, 126, 127, 128, 129, 134, 135, 137, 138, 141, 142, 143, 145, 146, 147, 148, 149, 150, 151, 152, 153, 159, 160, 161, 162, 163, 164, 165, 166, 167, 168, 169, 171, 172, 173, 176, 177, 178, 179, 180, 181, 184, 185, 186, 187, 188, 189, 190, 191, 192, 193, 194, 196, 200, 201, 202, 203, 204, 205, 207, 209, 211, 212, 213, 214, 216, 217, 218, 219, 221, 222, 223, 224, 225, 226, 227, 229, 230, 231, 233, 234, 235, 236, 237, 238, 239, 240, 241, 242, 243, 244, 245, 246, 247, 248, 249, 250, 251, 252, 253, 255, 256, 257, 259, 264, 293, 294, 302, 303, 305, 310, 312, 313

R

Remote Proctoring 191, 192, 201, 212, 223, 224
Responsible Innovation 99, 136, 236

S

Student Data Privacy 189, 233, 235, 264

T

Teacher Training 269, 313

www.ingramcontent.com/pod-product-compliance
Lightning Source LLC
LaVergne TN
LVHW081534300926
849161LV00006B/1424